DANCE FILM AND VIDEO GUIDE

Dance Films Association, Inc.

Compiled by Deirdre Towers

A Dance Horizons Book
Dance Horizons/
Princeton Book Company, Publishers
Princeton, NJ

Prepared in part with a grant from Capezio-Ballet Makers Dance Foundaton, Inc. Portions of this book are based on *Modern Dance and Ballet on Film and Video: A Catalog*, previously published by Dance Films Association. Copyright © 1986.

A Dance Horizons Book
Princeton Book Company, Publishers
P.O. Box 57
Pennington, NJ 08534

Cover design by Janet Hautau
Interior design and typesetting by Falco & Falco Inc.

Library of Congress Cataloging-in-Publication Data

The Dance film and video guide / Dance Films Association ; compiled
  by Deirde Towers.
      p.   cm.
  Includes indexes.
  ISBN 0-87127-171-0
  1. Dancing—Film catalogs. 2. Dancing—Video catalogs.
I. Towers. Deirde. II. Dance Films Association.
GV1595.D32 1991
792.8′ 0216—dc20   91-25015

CONTENTS

INTRODUCTION

The *Dance Film and Video Guide* provides a resource tool for members of the dance profession, educators, librarians, curators, producers, and anyone interested in dance on film and video. Over 2,000 films and videos produced over the last century are listed as available for either rent or sale.

Ever since April 4, 1896, when Thomas Edison first allowed the public to see dancing girls on the big white screen of his invention, the Kinetoscope, artists have committed their works to media. Whether for historical preservation, anthropological research, or aesthetical experimentation, people have been exploring space, time, and the intellectual and visceral possibilities of movement as captured by the camera.

The prime purpose of the Guide is to consolidate nonjudgmental information on all the dance on film and video in distribution for either sale or rental. We have made no attempt to disclaim or endorse the quality of the material. To be listed, films and videotapes simply had to have distributors for noncommercial use in the United States. No sale or rental prices have been given, since these differ from source to source, and are changed without notice.

Form of entries

The titles are presented in alphabetical order and cover the full range of dance around the world. Each entry includes title, distributor, date of production, length, format, and whether black-and-white (abbreviated b&w) or color. Whenever possible, credits are given for producer, director, choreographer, principal dancers, dance company, composer, editor, and set designer. A brief description following the credits indicates the content and names of the excerpts or full-length dances shown.

Indexes

Whether the reader is in search of performance records, documentaries, instructional programs, or dances conceived for the camera, the *Dance Film and Video Guide* should be of service.

The Guide is indexed according to the screen credits and style of dance (ballet, ballroom, folk, modern, Middle Eastern, jazz, Spanish, tap); purpose (anthropological, documentary, experimental, instructional, teacher education, theatrical); and geographical location (African, Asian, European, Indian, Oceanian, Russian, South American). Under the category of "excerpts," you can look up specific dances. For example, there is no film entitled GREEN TABLE, but the Kurt Jooss ballet of that name can be found within the documentary called THE DANCE.

Legal obligations

When arrangements are made for film or videotape rentals (or purchase), the borrower accepts the following obligations:

Films and videotapes are for nontheatrical, nonprofit purposes only.

Films and videotapes may be not used on television.

No duplications of any film or videotape or sections of film or videotape may be made.

Dance Films Association (DFA)

Dance Films Association, Inc. is a nonprofit, membership service organization, founded in 1956 by Susan Braun, Executive Director. The *Dance Film and Video Guide* is the fourth such publication by DFA, the first to be published and marketed by Princeton Book Company, Publishers. DFA publishes for its members a bimonthly newsletter announcing new releases, interviews, resources, competitions, festivals, and funding sources. Members also have telephone access to the continually updated database, and may rent and purchase a number of films and videos available solely through DFA. As part of its service, DFA sponsors the oldest, annual competitive dance film and video festival DANCE ON CAMERA in New York City. Additional activities and services include members' use of a tri-standard monitor, research on lost titles, curatorial assistance, and marketing/distribution suggestions.

Disclaimer

To the best of our knowledge and ability, the information contained in the *Dance Film and Video Guide* was true at the time of publication. Please be aware that distributors frequently change their addresses and their holdings. The editor and Dance Films Association do not assume and hereby disclaim any liability for any errors, or omissions, whether resulting from inaccurate information, negligence, or any other cause.

Acknowledgments

Dance Films Association wishes to acknowledge with gratitude the help of the following in the publication: Susan Braun (Founder), data programmer Fred Rowley, proofreader Mark Stevens, readers and board members Virginia Brooks, William Claiborne, Emily Jones, Susan Macaluso, Louise Spain (President), Judith Riccio, Pauline Tisch, and Penny Ward.

DANCE FILM AND VIDEO GUIDE

A BAILAR! THE JOURNEY OF A LATIN DANCE COMPANY

    1988, 29:37 min., color, video, film
Distributor: The Cinema Guild
Producer/Director: Catherine Calderon
Choreographer/Dancer: Eddie Torres
Composer: Tito Puente
Dance on Camera Festival, 1991 Honorable Mention

The salseros, Hispanic club and street dancers, in New York City, prepare for their first public performance at the Apollo Theatre in Harlem.

ABORIGINAL DANCE

    1966–1978, 16 min., color, video
Distributor: Film Australia
Producers: Tom Manefield, John Martin-Jones
Directors: David Roberts, Ian Dunlop

An aborigine named Gulpilil performs two solos, THE EMU and THE KANGAROO, and a group dance, THE FISH, with children from Bamyili in the northern territory of Australia. Five native dances from Cape York were also filmed: ATHA and PANTIJI, in which three men die and change into a crow, dove, and gecko lizard; MAIPAKA, on the death punishment for adultery; NINGKUSHUN and ORPUL, in which a spirit girl creates a freshwater shark; PIKUWA and KENA, on the art of fighting crocodiles, and PIPAPEPE on the courting and mating of curlews.

ACCUMULATION WITH TALKING PLUS WATER MOTOR

    Series: Alive from Off Center
1986, 30 min., color, video
Distributor/Producer: KTCA-TV
Director: Jonathan Demme
Choreographer/Dancer: Trisha Brown

Modern dancer Trisha Brown simultaneously tells three stories and performs two solos.

ACROBATIC DANCE OF THE SNAKE MAIDENS

    1968, 33 min., color, film
Distributor: Pennstate #EO1579
Producer/Director: H. Himmelheber for Wissen

Three small girls from the villages of Dan and Guere along the western Ivory Coast in Africa perform acrobatic feats to the accompaniment of drums and an iron clinking instrument. Then, they are whirled into the air by their trainer and wound around his body like snakes.

ACROBATS OF GOD

    Series: Three by Martha Graham
1968, 22 min., color, film, video
Distributor: Pyramid
Producers: John Houseman, H. Poindexter for Martha Graham Center
Director: Dave Wilson
Choreographer: Martha Graham
Principal Dancers: Martha Graham, Bertram Ross, Robert Cohan, Mary Hinkson, Helen McGehee, Takako Asakawa, Clive Thompson
Dance Company: Martha Graham Dance Company
Composer: Carlos Surinach
Set Designer: Isamu Noguchi

Adapted for television by John Butler, this modern dance celebrates the trials, denials, and glories of being a dancer.

THE ADDICTS

    1989, 7:50 min., color, video
Distributor/Producer/Choreographer: Melanie Stewart
Director: Robert Palumbo
Principal Dancers: Renee Gomila, Christopher Hawks, Kyle Sheldon
Composer: Zoltan Kodaly

Conceived for the camera, the dance tells the story of an obsessive love triangle among two men and a woman.

ADOLESCENCE

    1966, 22 min., b&w, film
Distributor: Films Inc.
Director: Vladimir Forgency
Principal Dancer: Sonia Petrovna
Dance Teacher: Madame Egorova
Cinematographer: Roger Bimpage
Composers: Frederic Chopin, Franz Schubert, Niccolo Paganini

Sonia Petrovna, a young French girl, studies ballet with eighty-four-year-old Madame Egorova, a former star of Serge Diaghilev's Ballet Russe. Despite her diligence, she fails her first audition. French dialogue with English subtitles.

ADRIENNE CHERIE INTERPRETS DANCES OF INDIA

    1988, 35 min., color, video
Distributor: ACA Enterprises
Producer/Choreographer/Dancer: Adrienne Cherie

Choreographer: Sujata
Composer: Jay Scott Hacklemann
Music: TARA

Performances of ALARIPPU (invocational dance), DEVADA-SI (temple dance), PARVATHI (dance of a goddess), WATER MAIDEN (Kathak dance), FISH STORY, and TARA (hand ballet), plus exercises for the hands.

AEROS

1990, 33 min., color, video
Distributor: Electronic Arts Intermix
Producer/Director: Burt Barr
Choreographer: Trisha Brown
Dance Company: Trisha Brown Company

Impressions of the modern dance company on tour in Russia and the relationship between choreographer/performer Trisha Brown and designer Robert Rauschenberg. The dancers, clad in silver unitards, move by the blinding lights of the set.

AFGHANISTAN – MEN'S DANCE WITH PANTOMIMIC INTERLUDES

1963, 10 min., color, film
Distributor: Pennstate #E00766
Producer: Wissen
Director: Herman Schlenker
Editor: G. Wolf

In a valley surrounded by mountains, seven men dance to a drum and wood instrument, with horse and a herd of cows mooing in the distance. The film closes in on the men's bodies draped in robes. The wind whistles, as the men clap and move their line dance around an open circle.

AFGHANISTAN DANCES (3 films)

1963, 10 – 14 min, color, b&w, film
Distributor: Pennstate #EOO766, EOO718, EOO717
Producer: Wissen

Three silent films of folk dances performed by men in Pashtun and Tadzhik in Badakhshan, and Pashtun in Wardak, Afghanistan.

AFRICA DANCES

Series: International Zone Series
1967, 27 min., color, film
Distributor: University of Michigan
Producer: United Nations
Dance Company: Les Ballets Africains

Les Ballets Africains, founded shortly after Guinea achieved its independence, performs at the United Nations General Assembly for the anniversary of the Universal Declaration of Human Rights. Introduced by H. E. M. Achkar Marot, UN Ambassador and permanent representative of Guinea, and translated by Alistair Cooke.

AFRICAN CARVING: A DOGON KANAGA MASK

1974, 19 min., color, film
Distributor: Phoenix Films
Producer: Film Study Center of Harvard University
Director: Eliot Elisofon

The Dogons of Mali, West Africa, perform a masked dance to release a dead man's spirit. Prior to the ritual, a man carves a mask from a Tagoda tree in a secluded cave. His carving gestures are repeated later by the masked dancers.

AFTERNOON OF A FAUN

1973, 11 min., color, film
Distributor: Dance Film Archive
Producer/Director/Editor: John Mueller
Choreographer/Dancer: Vaslav Nijinsky
Composer: Claude Debussy
Set Designer: Leon Bakst

An approximate reconstruction of the ballet choreographed and performed by Vaslav Nijinsky in 1912 using still photographs and drawings of Nijinsky. Explanatory subtitles.

AILEY DANCES

1982, 85 min., color, video
Distributor: Kultur #1152
Producer: James Lipton for ABC Video Enterprises & National Video Corp.
Director: Tim Kiley
Choreographer: Alvin Ailey
Composers: Duke Ellington, Ralph Vaughan Williams, Alice Coltrane, Laura Nyro, Voices of East Harlem
Principal Dancers: Judith Jamison, Donna Wood, Maxine Sherman, Roman Brooks, Deborah Manning, Ronald Brown
Dance Company: Alvin Ailey

The black modern dance company, recorded live at New York's City Center, performs NIGHT CREATURE, the woman's solo CRY, THE LARK ASCENDING, and the famous spiritual REVELATIONS.

AIR FOR THE G STRING

1934, 6 min., b&w, film, video
Distributor: Dance Films Association (for members only)
Choreographer/Dancer: Doris Humphrey
Principal Dancers: Ernestine H. Stodelle, Cleo Atheneos, Dorothy Lathrop, Hyla Rubin
Composer: Johann Sebastian Bach

Five women in floor-length robes, framed by two pillars, perform the adagio from Bach's "Air For the G String" choreographed by the modern dance pioneer.

AIRBORNE: MEISTER ECKHART

1987, 50 min., color, video
Distributor: Viacom Cablevision
Producer/Director: John Giamberso
Choreographer/Dancer: Robert Davidson
Principal Dancers: Kris Wheeler, Patricia Van Hemeryck
Composers: James Knapp, David Cooper
Dance on Camera Festival, 1987 Honorable Mention

Selections from a two-hour ballet inspired by the writings of the thirteenth-century Christian mystic Eckhart. Dancers soar on trapezes, seemingly free of limitations and perplexities.

AIRDANCE, LANDINGS
> Series: Alive from Off Center
> 1987, 30 min., color, video
> Distributor: Character Generators
> Producer: KTCA-TV
> Director/Editor: Michael Schwartz
> Choreographer/Dancer: Elizabeth Streb

Michael Schwartz and Elizabeth Streb collaborated on two short pieces, AIRDANCE, during which Streb never touches the ground, and LANDINGS, the series of touchdowns on specially designed pads. Both exemplify how an editor can shape the environment and rhythm of movement in a video dance.

AIRWAVES
> 1974, 5 min., color, film
> Distributor: Filmmaker's Coop
> Director: Dave Gearey
> Choreographer/Dancer: Dana Reitz

Modern dance solo.

AL GILBERT PRESENTS (60 videos)
> 1955-1990, 60-90 min. each, color, video
> Distributor/Producer: Stepping Tones
> Principal Dancers/Teachers: Al Gilbert, Ron Demarco, Janice Barringer, Nil Toledo, Robert Regger, Nancy Hays Highland, Julane Stites, Dorothy Vose, Darryl Retter

One of the first to produce teaching tapes, California-based tap teacher Al Gilbert has a line of graded technique and routine videos for tap, jazz, ballet, Hawaiian, and pointe. The voice-over instructions are geared for both children and adults.

ALBANIAN COUNTRY FOLK DANCES (3 films)
> 1971, 7-12 min. each, color, b&w, film
> Distributor: Pennstate #EO1976, EO1975, EO1973
> Producers: H. Kaleshi, Sh. Pilana and H. J. Kibling for Wissen

From the country bordered by Yugoslavia and Greece, folk dances of Metohija (7 min.); men's dances from Zur (12 min.); women's dances from Zur (7 min.).

ALICIA
> 1976, 75 min., color, film, video
> Distributors: Video Arts International, New Yorker (film)
> Producer: Cuban Film Institute
> Director: Victor Casaus
> Choreographers: Marius Petipa, Alberto Alonso, Jean Coralli, Anton Dolin
> Principal Dancers: Alicia Alonso, Azari Plisetzki
> Dance Company: National Ballet of Cuba
> Composers: Leon Minkus, Cesare Pugni, Peter Ilyich Tchaikovsky, Georges Bizet, Adolphe Adam

This portrait of Cuban ballerina Alicia Alonso includes interviews with her and excerpts of her performances in GISELLE (Act 1), DON QUIXOTE, GRAND PAS DE QUATRE, the Black Swan from SWAN LAKE, and 30 minutes of Alberto Alonso's CARMEN. Both Spanish and English narration available.

ALL THAT BACH: A CELEBRATION
> 1980s, 50 min., color, video
> Distributor: University of Illinois
> Choreographer/Dancer: Robert Desrosiers
> Dance Companies: National Tap Dance Company, Cambridge Buskers
> Composer: Johann Sebastian Bach

A music and dance tribute to the composer, with short pieces by a wide range of artists.

ALL THAT JAZZ
> 1979, 120 min., color, video
> Distributors: CBS Fox, Swank
> Producer/Writer: Robert Alan Arthur for Columbia Pictures and Twentieth Century Fox
> Director/Choreographer: Bob Fosse
> Principal Dancers: Ann Reinking, Leland Palmer, Erzsebet Foldi, Ben Vereen
> Composers: Barry Mann, Peter Allen, Cynthia Weil, Jerry Leiber, Mike Stoller, Henry Creamer
> Cinematographer: Giuseppe Rotunno

Feature film, based on the life of Bob Fosse, who reveals his obsessions, his creative drive, his loves, and phobias as he struggles with his weakening heart. Dancers appear in rehearsal, in his dreams, and in his home, when his daughter and his latest girlfriend treat him to a specially choreographed gift.

ALL THE BEST FROM RUSSIA
> 1977, 60 min., color, video
> Distributor: Master Vision
> Producer: Nielsen Aerns for Canadian Broadcasting Co. in association with Standard Brands
> Dance Companies: Bolshoi Ballet, Don Cossack Dancers, Armenian Folk Ensemble
> Editor: Donald Ginsberg

Snatches of Russian cultural entertainment, from the robust and rough to the polished, interspersed with informal interviews, landscapes scenes, and shots inside the Hermitage Museum. The documentary conveys the feeling of the culture, the energy of the artists, yet with no specific dance excerpts to be noted.

ALMIRA 38
> 1978, 19:30 min., b&w, film
> Distributor: Film-maker's Coop
> Director: Nancy Larue Kendall
> Choreographer/Dancer: Gay Delanghe

A dance poem in tribute to a woman in search of freedom.

ALVIN AILEY: MEMORIES AND VISIONS
> Series: Soul
> 1975, 54 min., color, film, video
> Distributor: Phoenix Films #21079
> Producers: Ellis Haizlip and Alonzo Brown for WNET/13
> Director: Stan Latham

Choreographer: Alvin Ailey
Principal Dancers: Judith Jamison, Sara Yarborough, Ulysses Dove, Clive Thompson, Dudley Williams, Tina Yuan
Dance Company: Alvin Ailey
Composers: Ralph Vaughan Williams, Patricia Sciortini, Mary Lou Williams, traditional gospel arranged by Howard Roberts and Leon Russell

A performance documentary, introduced by the late choreographer, with excerpts from BLUES SUITE, THE LARK ASCENDING, MARY LOU'S MASS, HIDDEN RITES, CRY, A SONG FOR YOU, REVELATIONS, HOUSE OF THE RISING SUN, THE LORD SAVES, ACT OF CONTRITION.

ALWAYS FOR PLEASURE

1978, 58 min., color, film, video
Distributor/Producer/Director: Les Blank for Flower Films

Documentary on the Black Indian dances and parades as part of the celebrations in Mardi Gras in New Orleans, with stops at a jazz funeral and St. Patrick's festivities.

AMERICAN BALLET THEATRE: A CLOSE-UP IN TIME

1973, 90 min., color, film
Distributor: Arthur Cantor
Director: Jerome Schur
Choreographers: Antony Tudor, Agnes de Mille, Alvin Ailey, Michel Fokine, Marius Petipa, Harald Lander, Lev Ivanov
Principal Dancers: Cynthia Gregory, Ivan Nagy, Sallie Wilson, Christine Sarry, Eleanor D'Arturo, Ted Kivitt
Dance Company: American Ballet Theatre
Composers: Arnold Schoenberg, Peter Ilyich Tchaikovsky, Aaron Copland, Karl Czerny, Duke Ellington
Commentators: Agnes De Mille, Lucia Chase, and Antony Tudor

The choreographers and company founder Lucia Chase discuss ABT's history and repertoire. Selections from PILLAR OF FIRE (Tudor/Schonberg), Black Swan Pas de Deux from SWAN LAKE (Ivanov-Petipa/Tchaikovsky), LES SYLPHIDES (Fokine/Chopin), RODEO (deMille/Copland), ETUDES (Lander/Czerny) and THE RIVER (Ailey/Ellington).

AMERICAN BALLET THEATRE AT THE MET

1984, 100 min., color, video
Distributors: HBO #3555, Pioneer (Laserdisk)
Producer: Robin Scott for National Video Corp.
Director: Brian Large
Choreographers: Marius Petipa, Michel Fokine, George Balanchine, Kenneth MacMillan
Principal Dancers: Mikhail Baryshnikov, Cynthia Gregory, Cynthia Harvey, Fernando Bujones, Amanda McKerrow, Patrick Bissell, Martine Van Hamel
Dance Company: American Ballet Theatre

Composers: Sergei Prokofiev, Leon Minkus, Leo Delibes, Frederic Chopin

Four ballets filmed at the Metropolitan Opera House: the pas de deux from PAQUITA (Makarova after Petipa/Minkus), LES SYLPHIDES (Fokine/Chopin), pas de deux from SYLVIA (Balanchine/Delibes), and TRIAD (MacMillan/Prokofiev).

AMERICAN BALLET THEATRE IN SAN FRANCISCO

1985, 105 min., color, video
Distributors: Home Vision #AME01, Pioneer, Dance Horizons Video
Producer: Robin Scott for National Video Corp.
Director: Brian Large
Choreographers: Paul Taylor, Antony Tudor, Kenneth MacMillan, Marius Petipa, Lynn Taylor-Corbett
Principal Dancers: Natalia Makarova, Fernando Bujones, Cynthia Gregory, Kevin MacKenzie
Dance Company: American Ballet Theatre
Composers: George Frideric Handel, Ernest Chausson, Peter Ilyich Tchaikovsky, Sergei Prokofiev, Louis Gottschalk
Dance on Camera Festival, 1987 Silver Award

Among the selections are: JARDIN AUX LILAS (Tudor/Chausson), the Black Swan pas de deux from SWAN LAKE (Petipa/Tchaikovsky), ROMEO AND JULIET (MacMillan/Prokofiev), AIRS (Taylor/Handel), and GREAT GALLOPING GOTTSCHALK.

AMERICAN BALLROOM DANCING (6 videos)

1979–87, 60–102 min. each, color, video
Distributor/Producer/Dancer: Jim Forest
Choreographer/Dancer: Bobbi McDonald

A comprehensive training course in American ballroom: foxtrot, waltz, swing, hustle, polka, Peabody, soft shoe, and Latin: cha cha, tango, rumba, mambo, samba, merengue, bossa nova, bolero, and paso doble. The late Jim Forest, an itinerant teacher/performer, demonstrates, with Bobbi McDonald, 1974 Grand Nationals Professional American Latin Champion and compiler of the American Standard of Ballroom Dancing.

AMERICAN INDIAN DANCE THEATRE:
FINDING THE CIRCLE

Series: Dance in America
1989, 58 min., color, video
Distributor: Intermedia Arts
Distributor/Producer: WNET with Catherine Tatge/Lasseur Prod.
Director: Merrill Brockway
Choreographers: Hanay Geiogamah, Raoul Trujillo

Documentary on America's first internationally touring American Indian company, founded in 1988, with a repertory drawn from more than a dozen tribes. The company members share their feelings about their art and its role in Indian life, with segments taped at an intertribal powwow in Oklahoma and at the Zuni pueblo in New Mexico.

American Indian Dance Theatre: Finding the Circle
Eddie Swimmer performing the virtuosic Hoop dance. Photo by Don Perdue.

AMERICAN INDIAN SOCIAL DANCING

1980, 28 min., color, film
Distributor/Producer/Director: Nick Manning for Green
Mountain Cine

Social dances performed and described by Iroquois Indians
living in the northeast of the United States.

AMICI DANCE

29 min., color, video
Distributor: Franciscan #F7390
Producer: CTVCA

Group improvisation by mentally handicapped people, filmed
in California.

EL AMOR BRUJO

1986, 100 min., film, video
Distributor: Cinematheque
Director: Carlos Saura
Choreographer: Antonio Gades
Principal Dancers: Antonio Gades, Cristina Hoyos
Composer: Manuel de Falla

The last of a trilogy, involving a famous flamenco troupe
and one of Spain's most perceptive directors, in which
a young Spanish widow, obsessed with visions of her
husband, dances nightly with his ghost.

AMPHIBIAN

1985, 9 min., color, video
Distributor: Electronic Arts Intermix
Distributor/Producer/Director: Mary Lucier
Choreographer/Dancer: Elizabeth Streb
Editor: Gregg Featherman

Abstraction of a body in natural environments of water,
land and air, a collaboration between modern dancer
Elizabeth Streb and Mary Lucier, known for her video in-
stallations and poetic approach to landscapes.

ANASTENARIA

1969, 17 min., b&w, film
Distributor: University of California Extension Media Center
Producer/Director: Peter Haramis

Documentary of the firedancing and sacrificial ceremony
held in Serres in Northern Greece. The villagers sacrifice an
animal and divide it among themselves. The initiates dance
in a trance on embers, unmarked by the flames.

ANATOMY AS A MASTER IMAGE IN
TRAINING DANCERS

1989, 59 min., color, video
Distributor/Producer/Teacher: Ruth Solomon for
University of California at Santa Cruz
Director: Gus Solomons
Dance on Camera Festival, 1989 Gold Award

Fundamental movement principles presented in a warm-up
class geared for dancers at the University of Santa Cruz.

THE ANATOMY LESSON

1968, 25 min., color, film, video
Distributor: Netherlands Consulate General
(free loan)
Producer: Margaret Dale
Producer/Director: Stewart Lippe
Choreographer: Glen Tetley
Principal Dancers: Jaap Flier, Willy de la Bye, Alexandra
Radius, Ger Thoma
Dance Company: Netherlands Dance Theater
Composer: Marcel Landowski
Set/Costume Designer: Nicholas Wijenberg

A ballet inspired by Rembrandt's 1632 group portrait entitled
THE ANATOMY LESSON OF DR. TULP. In a series of flashbacks, one sees the tormented past of a man on the dissecting
table.

THE ANCIENT ART OF BELLY DANCING

1977, 30 min., color, film, video
Distributor: Phoenix Films
Producer/Director: Stewart Lippe
Principal Dancers: Little Egypt, Janis Lippe,
Theodora Leavens
Dance Companies: Juliana and Bal Anat Dancers,

Babaganous Dancers
Writer/Narrator: Anne Lippe

History of this 5000-year-old art supported by stills of sculpture, painting, and locations inspired by and associated with the dance, along with performances by today's dancers in clubs, studios, and outdoor events. Includes rare footage of Little Egypt at the 1893 Chicago World's Fair.

AND STILL WE DANCE

1989, 60 min., color, film, video
Distributor: Searchlight Films
Director: Ashley James
Dance on Camera Festival, 1989 Gold Award

This documentary records the tenth anniversary of an annual international folk dance festival in San Francisco, with performance and shots of the participating companies based in the Bay area performing dances from the Philippines, Eastern Europe, Asia, Africa, Spain, and the Americas.

ANIMA

1988, 15 min., color, video
Distributor/Producer/Director/Choreographer: Jan Marce Locketz
Principal Dancers: Earne Stevenson, Barbara Ziegler, Zonni Bauer, Barbara Canner, Nina D'Abbracci, Rob O'Neil
Composer: Uakti

Abstract study in slow motion, with sensual close-ups of dancers jumping, turning, and colliding.

ANIMAL DANCES: PHYE-MA-LEB AND SAN-GE

1968, 4 min., color, film
Distributor: Pennstate #EO1609
Producer: A.M. Dauer for Wissen

A folk dance from Tibet inspired by the flight of a butterfly, accompanied by flute and solo voice, and another folk dance in honor of snow lions accompanied by drums, cymbals, and a flute.

ANIMALS IN MOTION

1968, 7 min., color, film
Distributor: Biograph Entertainment
Producer/Director: John Straiton

Silent, experimental documentary on the components of movement with stills by Edward Muybridge (1830-1904) of women, men, and children dancing, boxing, exercising.

ANNA KARENINA

1974, 120 min, color, film, video
Distributors: Corinth, Kultur #1203 (81 min. video)
Producers: B. Boguslavsky & B. Geller for Mosfilm Studios
Choreographer/Dancer: Maya Plisetskaya
Principal Dancers: Alexander Godunov (Vronsky), Vladimir Tihonov (Karenin), Yuri Vladimirov (Station Master)
Dance Company: Bolshoi Ballet
Composer: Rodion Shchedrin
Screenwriter: Bavov-Arbhin

The first work by Russian prima ballerina Maya Plisetskaya based on Tolstoy's novel of a woman who abandons her husband and child for a man who subsequently abandons her. Set to music composed by Plisetskaya's husband, Rodion Shchedrin.

ANNA SOKOLOW, CHOREOGRAPHER

1978, 20 min., color, film
Distributor: Dance Horizons Video
Producer/Directors: Lucille Rhodes, Margaret Murphey
Choreographer: Anna Sokolow
Composers: Kenyon Hopkins, Johann Sebastian Bach, Karl von Webern
Chicago International Film Festival, 1978 Gold Plaque

Portrait of modern choreographer Anna Sokolow, who began her career in the 1930s studying with Martha Graham and Louis Horst. Illustrated with moments of her teaching class, and directing excerpts from ROOMS (a series of solos and ensemble pieces suggesting urban alienation) and DREAMS (a memorial to victims of the Holocaust).

Anna Sokolow, Choreographer
Anna Sokolow today. Photo by David Fullard.

ANNUNCIATION

1977, 16 min., color, film, video
Distributor: Phoenix Films
Director: Marcelo Epstein
Choreographer/Dancer: Sandra Adominas
Cinematographer: Stephen Posey
Composer: Joellen Lapidus
Dance on Camera Festival, 1977 Gold Award

Moments from a woman's past, present, and future traversed to reveal her many levels of consciousness.

ANTIGONE/RITES FOR THE DEAD

1989, 85 min., color, film, video
Distributor: Eclipse Productions
Producer/Director/Dancer/Editor: Amy Greenfield
Cinematographer: Hilary Harris, Judy Irola
Principal Dancers: Bertram Ross (Oedipus), Janet Eilber
Composers: Glenn Branca, David Van Tieghem, Elliot Sharp, Paul Lemos, Diamanda Galas

This dance film of the 400 B.C. Greek drama of the woman who defied the state to bury her murdered brother was filmed in woods, caves, deserts, and in Albany, New York.

ANYUTA

1982, 68 min., color, video
Distributor: Kultur #1116
Director: Alexander Belinsky
Choreographer/Dancer: Vladimir Vasiliev (Ofets Anioti)
Principal Dancer: Ekaterina Maximova (Anyuta)
Dance Companies: Bolshoi Ballet, Kirov Ballet, and Maly
Composer: Valery Gavrilin

A narrative ballet inspired by Anton Chekhov's ANNA ROUND THE NECK depicting a young woman, forced to marry a rich but indifferent husband, who eventually finds admirers crowding at her feet.

APPALACHIAN SPRING (2 videos)

1958, 1976, 31 min. each, b&w, color, film
Distributors: Phoenix Films, Dance Film Archive
Producer: Nathan Kroll for WQED-TV, Pittsburgh
Director: Peter Glushanok
Choreographer: Martha Graham
Principal Dancers: Martha Graham, Linda Hodes, Stuart Hodes, Yuriko Kimura, Bertram Ross, Helen McGehee, Ethel Winter, Miriam Cole, Matt Turney
Dance Company: Martha Graham
Composer: Aaron Copland
Set Designer/Consultant: Isamu Noguchi
Venice Film Festival Award, Edinburgh Film Festival Award

Martha Graham performs in the 1958 filming of her stark classic, which premiered in 1944, of a pioneer wedding in the Appalachian Mountain wilderness. Dance Film Archive also carries the 1976 version starring Yuriko Kimura and Janet Eilber.

ARAB DANCES FROM CENTRAL SUDAN (11 films)

1964-1965, 4-10 min. each, color, film
Distributor: Pennstate #EOO951, EO1015, EO1016, EO1014, EOO365, EO1363, EO1365, EO1364, EO1350, EO1351,

EO1441
Producer: Wissen

A couple dance, DJERSISS, as performed by the Omar and Haddad Arabs in Chad, Africa, with clapping and leaping to the rhythms of women singing songs in praise of the rich and famous. An excerpt of the AL BEHER dance performed by couples and the AM HARABA, originally a war dance; the KIFET dance, in which women and girls sing and sway in a semicircle until the men advance, choose partners, dance in couples, and then withdraw to pick new partners. Finally, the ZINUGI, a circle dance, and NUGARAFOLK, a line dance.

ARABIAN DANCE FEVER

1988, 55 min., color, video
Distributor: Sphinx Records
Producer/Director: Dr. Sammy Farag
Principal Dancers: Nagwa Fouad, Suhaila Salimpour

Features the Sophia Loren of the Middle East in a show-biz special with belly dancing from Egypt.

ARABIAN DANCES

1960, 3 min., b&w, film
Distributor: Pennstate #EOO429
Producer: Wissen

A social dance common among the camel herdsmen of southern Arabia, performed by both men and women after they have led their animals to drink at a spring.

ARABIAN MELODIES

1988, 50 min., color, video
Distributor: Sphinx Records
Producer/Director: Dr. Sammy Farag
Choreographer/Dancer: Suhaila Salimpour

A performance of an American Middle-Eastern dancer backed by a blend of western and Middle-Eastern music.

ART AND MOTION

1952, 16 min., color, film
Distributor: Encyclopaedia Britannica Educational Corp.
Producer: University of California Extension Media Center

This teacher's guide explains motion as an integral element in the visual arts, demonstrated by a dancer and a skater. Reviews contemporary trends and ways in which artists use motion in painting, mobiles, and camera techniques.

ART AND TECHNIQUE OF THE BALLET

1967, 11 min., b&w, film
Distributor: The Cinema Guild
Producer: Richard Scheinflug for Lehrfilm Institut
Choreographers: Lev Ivanov, Marius Petipa
Principal Dancers: Helmut Ketels, Christa Kempf, Uta Graf
Composer: Peter Ilyich Tchaikovsky

Depicts the formal vocabulary of ballet and examines the pas de quatre from SWAN LAKE, in rehearsal and performance.

THE ART OF BODY MOVEMENT (11 videos)
  1970, 12-63 min., b&w, film, video
  Distributor/Producer: Mettler Studios
  Producer: Will Carbo
  Director/Teacher: Barbara Mettler

Improvisations by amateurs of all ages before an audience at the Tucson Creative Dance Center. Created by Barbara Mettler, whose films and videos on improvisation include: MOVI-MIENTO CREATIVO EN COSTA RICA, 31 min. in Spanish, 1989; BABY DANCE, 12 min., 1989, four young mothers dancing with their babies; THE LANGUAGE OF MOVEMENT, 24 min., 1985; PURE DANCE, 58 min., 1980; CREATIVE DANCE FOR CHILDREN, 63 min.(four films), 1966-1977; GROUP DANCE IMPROVISATION, 34 min., 1978; A NEW DIRECTION IN DANCE, 58 min., 1978, group improvisation.

THE ART OF DANCING: AN INTRODUCTION TO BAROQUE DANCE
  1979, 21 min., b&w, video
  Distributor/Producer/Directors: Celia Ipiotis and Jeff Bush for ARC Video
  Producer/Choreographer/Director/Dancer: Catherine Turocy
  Choreographers: Kellom Tomlinson, Louis Pecour
  Principal Dancers: Ann Jacoby, Roger Tolle

A lesson on the minuet based on Kellom Tomlinson's dance manual THE ART OF DANCING, published in London in 1720, with a demonstration of notation symbols, comments on execution and style, followed by a short sequence of MINUET D'OMPHALLE by Louis Pecour, 1704, a stage version of the ballroom minuet.

ART OF MEMORY
  1987, 36 min., color, video
  Distributor: Electronic Arts Intermix
  Producer/Director: Woody Vasulka
  Principal Dancer: Daniel Nagrin

Modern dancer Daniel Nagrin appears briefly in this multidimensional, anti-war protest structured in seven acts. Black-and-white footage of Nagrin's WATERGATE SKETCHES, shot in the early 1970s, is inset as a symbol of civic opposition.

ART OF SILENCE SERIES (9 videos)
  1975, 7-11 min. each, color, film
  Distributor: University of California Extension Media Center
  Producer/Director: John Barnes
  Mimes: Marcel Marceau, Pierre Verry
  Cinematographer: Adam Giffard

Nine short sketches, available individually, by the French master of pantomime. PANTOMIME: THE LANGUAGE OF THE HEART, the technique and philosophy of the art with illustrative clips; CAGE, a man struggles to escape invisible walls; CREATION OF THE WORLD, Adam and Eve's story; DREAM; HANDS, struggle between good and evil; MASK-MAKER, the vulnerable craftsman; PAINTER, making others see the invisible; SIDESHOW, the tightrope walker; YOUTH, MATURITY, OLD AGE, DEATH, the cycle of life.

ARTISTS OF THE DANCE
  1977, 55:45 min., color, video
  Distributor/Producer/Director: Louise Tiranoff
  Choreographers/Teachers: Doris Jones, Claire Haywood
  Principal Dancer: Sandra Fortune

Two black choreographers and teachers direct and choreograph a production in their school in Washington, D.C. One of their students, Sandra Fortune, the first black dancer to win the international ballet competition in Varna, performs a solo, THE BLACK SWAN.

ARUANA MASKED DANCES
  1959, 20 min., color, film
  Distributor: Pennstate #E00443
  Producer: Wissen
  Director: H. Schultz

A silent film of the ritual in Jatoba in the Araguaia region of Brazil, during which men in masks run to the village, dance with the women, and return home.

AS SEEN ON TV
  Series: Alive from Off Center
  1987, 30 min., color, video
  Distributors: Electronic Arts Intermix, WGBH-TV
  Producer: Susan Dowling for KTCA, WGBH, and Channel 4, London
  Director: Charles Atlas
  Principal Dancers: Bill Irwin, Beatriz Rodriguez

Bill Irwin plays a job-hunting hoofer who goes to a television audition only to be drawn inside the monitor. Trapped in the world of TV, he stumbles through electronic adventures, cavorts with the soap opera stars and attempts to partner a ballerina.

ASHANTI DANCE ADJEMLE AT KOUADJIKRO
  1968, 12 min., color, film
  Distributor: Pennstate #E01572
  Producer/Director: H. Himmelheber for Wissen

In Baule, Ivory Coast, Africa, young men perform an acrobatic dance to the accompaniment of three drums, an iron bell, rattle calabash, and rub-rattle. In 1967, a three-minute record was also made of the GBAGBA dance of Baule, for which the performers wear masks parodying sheep, women, and a cowherd.

ASHES, MIST AND WIND-BLOWN DUST
  1987, 30 min., color, video
  Distributor: Billie Mahoney for Dance On Video
  Producer: Norwegian Broadcasting Corp.
  Director: Jannike Falk
  Choreographer: Kjersti Alveberg
  Principal Dancer: Claude Paul Henry
  Composer: Antonio Bibalo
  Grand Prix winner for best director of a contemporary work and best music commissioned for a dance video, 1988

A surreal, modern dance video from Norway divided into sections introduced by quotes from Henrik Ibsen's PEER GYNT.

ASIA SOCIETY COLLECTION (21 videos)

1960–1990, 30 min. each, color, video
Distributor/Producer: Beate Gordon for Asia Society
Principal Dancers: Surasena (Sri Lanka), Yamini Krishnamurti, Hu Hung-yen, Sun Ock Lee, Sitara, Birju Maharaj, Bando Yaenosuke, Osaka Garyokai

Performance records of Asian artists invited to perform at the Asia Society in New York by impresario Beate Gordon:

HEEN BABA AND HIS DANCE AND DRUM, Vannamas dances in praise of the butterfly, the elephant, and as part of the sacred ritual of Sri Lanka, Ves;
YAMINI KRISHNAMURTI: SOUTH INDIAN DANCE, NINE CLASSICAL SENTIMENTS in the Bharata Natyam style, and THE FROG WHO BECAME A QUEEN (Kuchipudi);
AAK: KOREAN COURT MUSIC AND DANCE, 1000-year-old tradition performed in long silk gowns;
POGSAM MASKED DANCE DRAMA FROM KOREA, three of seven episodes of a festive comedy;
MASKED DANCE-DRAMA OF BHUTAN, pantomime from a small Himalayan kingdom called Pholay Molay;
FUIJAN HAND PUPPETS FROM THE PEOPLE'S REPUBLIC OF CHINA, 500-year-old tradition with acrobatics, song, and dance;
KATHAKALI: SOUTH INDIAN DANCE-DRAMA FROM THE KERALA KALAMANDALAM, sixteenth-century technique stemming from martial arts combined with music, sung text, mime, and dance;
CHHAU: THE MASKED DANCE OF BENGAL, ancient Indian war dances that incorporate stories from the Ramayana;
HU HUNG-YEN: ASPECTS OF PEKING OPERA, demonstrates makeup and a scene from THE BUTTERFLY DREAM and THE SCARF DANCE;
SUN OAK LEE: KOREAN DANCER, SAL POO RI, originating from shamanistic rituals, SHINJANG NORI and SEUNG MOO, originally performed by monks as part of a meditation;
DANCERS AND MUSICIANS OF THE BURMESE NATIONAL THEATRE, exercises and dances;
NAT VOTARESS, an appeal to the spirits, and from the Ramayana, a contest between kings for the hand of Sita;
MARTIAL ARTS OF KABUKI FROM THE NATIONAL THEATER INSTITUTE OF JAPAN, demonstrates stage fighting and two excerpts from HAMA MATSUKAZE and KUJIRA NO DANMARI;
THOVIL: RITUAL CHANTING, DANCE AND DRUMMING OF EXORCISM, demon-masked dancers eat fire, twirl torches, and perform four other dances;
BUGAKU: THE TRADITIONAL COURT, TEMPLE AND SHRINE DANCES FROM JAPAN;
YAKSHAGANA: RITUAL DANCE THEATER FROM SOUTH KANARA, INDIA;
SITARA, an invocation to the elephant god Ganesha, the Toru Tukra, Mayur Nritya (peacock), and Tatkar, all in the Indian Kathak style;

PENCA AND TOPENG BABAKAN FROM SUNDA, INDONESIA, dances based on martial arts and animal movements with masks;
KATHAK: NORTH INDIAN DANCE, Vandana, a prayer dance, and Geetopadesh, the gambling scene from the *Mahabharata;*
FORGOTTEN DANCES, three folk dances;
MUSIC AND DANCE OF THE SIBERIAN ASIANS, music, Shaman dances, storytelling, and songs by the Nani, Ulchi, and Koryak tribes.

ASIA SOCIETY COLLECTION (5 videos)

1960–1990, 30 min. each, b&w, video
Distributor/Producer: Asia Society

Performance videos of artists invited to the New York center:

P'ANSORI, Korea's leading singer and mime with three musicians who play the kayageum, kuhmoongo, and the p'iri;
THE TOPENG DANCE THEATER OF BALI, Djimat performs a scene from "The End of King Bungkut" with gamelan accompaniment;
TRADITIONAL JAPANESE DANCE, Koisaburo Nishikawa and Company perform FUJI MUSUME, KOTKOBUKI SAMBASO, and SAGI MUSUME;
CHINESE SHADOW PLAYS, lecture-demonstration;
SAEKO ICHINOHE AND COMPANY, modern dance inspired by Japanese tradition with poems recited by Joan Baez.

ASLI ABADI SERIES

1977, 10 min., color, film
Distributor: Embassy of Malaysia
Dance Companies: Badan Budaya, Kememterian Kesenian, Belia Dan Sokan (Ministry of Culture, Youth and Sports)

A series of traditional Malaysian dances.

ASPECTS OF SYMMETRY

1970, 18 min., color, film
Distributor: International Film Bureau
Producer: Polytechnic Institute of Brooklyn

Mathematicians, scientists, artists, and dancers explore the presence and application of symmetry in their respective fields.

ASTAIRE, FRED (29 videos)

1933–1957, features, color, film, video
Distributors/Producers: MGM, Paramount, Turner Home Entertainment, RCA/Columbia Pictures
Directors: Vincente Minnelli, Stanley Donen, Mark Sandrich, Gordon Stevens, Charles Walters, Leo McCarey, Stuart Heisler, Sidney Lanfield, Rouben Mamoulian, Thornton Freeland, William Seiter
Choreographers: Fred Astaire, Hermes Pan, Michael Kidd
Principal Partners: Ginger Rogers, Ann Miller, Audrey Hepburn, Rita Hayworth, Cyd Charisse, Eleanor Powell
Composers: Harry Warren, George & Ira Gershwin, Jimmy McHugh, Burton Lane, Cole Porter, Irving Berlin

Fred Astaire
Ginger Rogers and Fred Astaire in Swing Time. *Courtesy Turner Entertainment Co.*

Of the 31 musical films with the famous dancer born in 1899 in Omaha, Nebraska, twenty-nine had been released on video at press time. The above credits represent his collaborators on the titles below. For a complete rundown on this influential dancer, see John Mueller's book *Astaire Dancing.*

Two titles from Columbia Pictures:
YOU'LL NEVER GET RICH (1941, with Rita Hayworth)
YOU WERE NEVER LOVELIER (1942, with Rita Hayworth)

Thirteen titles from MGM:
BAND WAGON (1953, with Cyd Charisse)
BARKLEYS OF BROADWAY (1949, with Ginger Rogers)
BROADWAY MELODY OF 1940 (with Eleanor Powell)
BELLE OF NEW YORK (1952, with Vera-Ellen)
DANCING LADY (1933, with Joan Crawford and Clark Gable)
EASTER PARADE (1948, with Ann Miller)
FLYING DOWN TO RIO (1933, with Rita Hayworth)
ROBERTA (1935, with Ginger Rogers)
ROYAL WEDDING (1951, with Jane Powell)
SILK STOCKINGS (1957, with Cyd Charisse)
THREE LITTLE WORDS (1950, with Debbie Reynolds)
YOLANDA AND THE THIEF (1945)
ZIEGFIELD FOLLIES (1946, with Lucille Ball and Gene Kelly)

Two titles from Paramount:
FUNNY FACE (1957, with Audrey Hepburn)
LET'S DANCE (1950, with Betty Hutton)

Eleven titles from RKO, distributed by Turner:
CAREFREE (1938, with Ginger Rogers)
CARIOCA (1933)
DAMSEL IN DISTRESS (1937, with Joan Fontaine)
FOLLOW THE FLEET (1936, with Ginger Rogers)
GAY DIVORCEE (1934, with Ginger Rogers)
ONCE UPON A HONEYMOON (1942, with Ginger Rogers)
SKY'S THE LIMIT (1942, with Ginger Rogers)
STORY OF VERNON & IRENE CASTLE (1939, with Ginger Rogers)
SWING TIME (1936, with Ginger Rogers)
TOP HAT (1935, with Ginger Rogers)
TWO TICKETS TO BROADWAY (1951, with Ann Miller)

One from Swank:
BLUE SKIES (1946, with Joan Caulfield and Bing Crosby)

ATOLL LIFE IN KIRIBATI

Series: Human Face of the Pacific
1983, 28 min., color, video
Distributor: University of Illinois #86291

Presents the song and dance of the Micronesian people who preserve their traditional culture.

ATTITUDES IN DANCE

1964, 28 min., b&w, film
Distributor: Dance Film Archive
Director: Merrill Brockway
Choreographers: Gerald Arpino, Norman Walker
Principal Dancers: Lisa Bradley, Lawrence Rhodes, Paul Sutherland, Norman Walker, Cora Cahan
Dance Companies: Robert Joffrey Ballet, Norman Walker
Composers: Maurice Ravel, Alan Hovhaness, Antonio Vivaldi, Vittorio Rieti

Four works by Gerald Arpino, current director of the Joffrey Ballet, and Norman Walker, head of the dance department at Adelphi University, including: BALLET FOR FOUR (Arpino/Rieti), SEA SHADOW (Arpino/Ravel), COURTLY DUET (Walker/Vivaldi), DANCE FINALE (Walker/Hovhaness).

L' AURORA

1989, 8 min., color, video
Distributor: Antenna
Producer: Agent Orange/Twin Cities Public Television
Director: Bernar Heber
Choreographer/Composer: Jelon Vieira
Dance Company: Dance Brazil
Composers: Gaetan Gravel, Bill Vorn

Adaptation of three short pieces in Afro-Brazilian style, with the martial art *capoeira*, a purification ritual, and a dance in honor of Oxala, the most important Afro-Brazilian God.

AVIARY

1988, 30 min., color, video
Distributor/Director/Composer: Ellen Sebring
Choreographer/Dancer: Sarah Skaggs
Broadcast on WGBH/WNET New Television

Modern dance set among exotic birds, tropical plants, and an elaborate bird cage.

AWA ODORI

1971, 15 min., color, film
Distributors: Iowa State University, Japan Foundation
Producer: Broadcast Programming Center of Japan

A documentary on a 400-year-old tradition honoring All Souls Day of Buddhism observed by the Japanese, every August 15th in Tokushima City. Forty groups of dancers rehearse and perform from dawn to midnight.

THE AWAJI PUPPET THEATER OF JAPAN

1970s, 20 min., color, film
Distributor/Producer: Asia Society
Dance Company: Awaji Puppet Theatre

Filmed at the Asia Society in New York, the performance short shows scenes from classic Japanese tales: KAISEI AND NARUTO, THE MIRACLE OF THE TSIBOSA TEMPLE, and EBISU-MAI. Demonstration as to how to manipulate the puppets.

BACKSTAGE AT THE KIROV

1983, 79 min., color, film, video
Distributors: New Yorker Films, Direct Cinema
Producers: Kenneth Locker, Gregory Saunders
for Armand Hammer
Produced in association with Channel 4
Director/Writer: Derek Hart
Choreographer: Marius Petipa
Cinematographer: Ivan Strasburg
Principal Dancers: Alytynai Assylmouratova, Oleg Vinogradov, Olga Moiseyeva, Galina Mezentseva, Konstantin Zaklinsky
Dance Company: Kirov Ballet
Composer: Peter Ilyich Tchaikovsky

This inside look at the Kirov Ballet of Leningrad focuses on a young girl about to make her debut as the Swan Queen, followed by excerpts from SWAN LAKE.

LE BAL

1980, 112 min., color, film, video
Distributor: Direct Cinema
Producer: Giorgio Silvagni for Almi/Warner Brothers
Director: Ettore Scola
Principal Dancers: Etienne Guichard, Francesca de Rosa
Best Foreign Film of 1983

Shot in a Paris dance hall, the Italian-directed film suggests a political and historical perspective of France, from the 1930s to the 1980s, by using a silent cast of individuals who come alone and leave alone, yet communicate to each other through body language and the social dance typical of each decade.

BAL-ANAT

1975, 20 min., color, film

Distributor: Canyon Cinema
Producer/Director: John Carney

Traces the development of a troupe of belly dancers in the San Francisco Bay area, from studio training to a live performance at The Renaissance Pleasure Fair.

BALANCES

1980, 9:30 min., color, film, video
Distributor: Coe Films Associates
Producer/Director: Whitney Green for Cine Light Prod.
Choreographer/Dancer: Tom Ruud
Principal Dancers: Allyson Deane, Nancy Dickson
Composer: Aram Khachaturian
Dance Company: San Francisco Ballet

Three dancers rehearse with choreographer Tom Ruud and then perform MOBILE, a trio set to the adagio from Khachaturian's GAYNE.

BALI: ISLE OF TEMPLES

1978, 27 min., color, film
Distributor: Syracuse University
Producer: Bay Street Pictures Corporation

Barong and Ketjack dances amidst the bustle of the marketplace, the weaving, painting, rice harvesting, Hindu shadow plays, festivals, and religious ceremonies. Also, Pennsylvania State University carries a 5-minute, black-and-white film of the men's Ketjak dances, along with the exorcistic Sanghyang danced by two girls, both to ward off evil through the dance.

BALI: THE MASK OF RANGDA

1974, 30 min., color, film, video
Distributor/Producer/Director: Elda Hartley

Seeking the link between man and God, conscious and unconscious, in Bali, by dancing in village squares the BARONG-RANGDA and KETJAK, both trance dances to ward off evil spirits. Also made by and available from Hartley is SACRED TRANCES IN BALI AND JAVA, a 30-minute film made in 1976 about altered states of consciousness, animistic, Hindu, and Muslim rites.

BALI TODAY

1967, 18 min., color, film
Distributor/Producer: Hartley Productions
Director: Elda Hartley

Dr. Margaret Mead, anthropologist, talks about modern life relative to the slow-to-change island of Bali, its people, culture, and religion. Balinese painting, music and native dances shown as part of two ceremonies, a wedding and cremation of the dead.

BALKAN DANCING

1968, 16 min., color, film
Distributor: University of Illinois
Producer: Mario Casetta

Folk dances from Albania, Greece, Bulgaria, Turkey, Yugoslavia, and Romania. Explains their origins and chief characteristics.

BALLADE

1978, 28 min., color, video
Distributor: French American Cultural Services
Producer: Espace et Mouvement

A collection of folk songs and dances from France.

IL BALLARINO: THE ART OF RENAISSANCE DANCE

1990, 33 min., color, video
Distributor: Dance Horizons Video
Producer/Narrator: Julia Sutton
Directors: Julia Sutton, Johannes Holub
Principal Dancers: Patricia Rader, Charles Perrier

Renaissance court dances, for couples and groups, are demonstrated and described, then analyzed and taught. Accompanied by period musical instruments, dancers perform finished pieces in full costume. An instructional video of 16th-century dances.

A · DANCE · HORIZONS · VIDEO

IL BALLARINO
THE ART OF
RENAISSANCE
DANCE
Narrated
by *Julia Sutton*

Il Ballarino: The Art of Renaissance Dance
Cover art courtesy Dance Horizons Video.

BALLERINA

1963, 28 min., b&w, film
Distributor/Producer: National Film Board of Canada
Producer: Nicholas Balla
Director/Choreographer: George Kaczender
Choreographers: Ludmilla Chiriaeff, George Kaczender
Principal Dancer: Margaret Mercier
Dance Company: Les Grands Ballets Canadiens
Composer: Sergei Prokofiev

Margaret Mercier, Prima Ballerina of Les Grands Ballets

Canadiens, a graduate of Sadler's Wells Ballet (now Royal Ballet) School, rehearses a scene from CINDERELLA.

BALLERINA LYDIA KUPENINA

1972, 10 min., b&w, film
Distributor: National Council for American Soviet Friendship
Principal Dancer: Lydia Kupenina

Interview with the Russian ballerina.

BALLERINA: LYNN SEYMOUR

1979, 60 min., color, video
Distributor: Master Vision
Producer: Pat Ferns for Nielsen-Ferns International Productions
Director: Karin Altmann
Choreographers: Frederick Ashton, Lar Lubovitch, Kenneth MacMillan, Lynn Seymour
Principal Dancers: Lynn Seymour, Rudolph Nureyev, Galina Samsova, Stephen Jefferies, Christopher Gable, Werner Dittrich, David Wall
Narrator: John Sterland
Composers: Alexander Scriabin, Kurt Weill, Andre Messager, Leos Janacek, Sergei Prokofiev

Portrait of the English ballerina and character actress with rehearsals, interviews, and performance excerpts of TWO PIGEONS, ROMEO AND JULIET, INTIMATE LETTERS.

THE BALLERINAS

1987, 108 min., color, film, video
Distributor: Kultur #1166
Producer: Joseph Wishy with Polivideo-TVE
Choreographers: Michel Fokine, Marius Petipa, Anna Pavlova, Jean Coralli, Lev Ivanov, Jules Perrot, Leonide Massine
Composers: Adolphe Adam, Peter Ilyich Tchaikovsky, Frederic Chopin, Leo Delibes, Cesare Pugni
Principal Dancers: Carla Fracci, Peter Schaufuss, Vladimir Vasiliev, Richard Cragun
Editors: Peppe Menegatti, Tazio Tami
Writer: Domenico De Martini

Italian prima ballerina Carla Fracci portrays the romantic ballerinas of the nineteenth century: Maria Taglioni, Carlotta Grisi, Anna Pavlova, Fanny Elssler, Tamara Karsavina, and others, while Peter Ustinov serves as Theophile Gautier, the ballet critic/poet, and then as Sergei Diaghilev, the impresario. Excerpts from LA SYLPHIDE, LE PAPILLON, GISELLE, LA CACHUCHA, COPPELIA, SLEEPING BEAUTY, ESMERALDA, LES SYLPHIDES, LA FARRUCA.

BALLET ADAGIO

1971, 10 min., color, film, video
Distributors: Dance Film Archive, Pyramid
Producer: National Film Board of Canada
Director: Norman McLaren
Cinematographers: Jaques Fogel, Douglas Kiefer
Choreographers: Asaf Messerer, David Holmes
Dancers: David Holmes, Anna Marie Holmes
Composer: Tommaso Albinoni

A classic ballet duet, SPRING WATER.

BALLET BASICS

> 1986, 40 min., color, video
> Distributor: Ballet Basics
> Producer/Director/Dancers: Mildred Blanchard,
> Grace Maduell

Grace Maduell, a former principal with the San Francisco Ballet Company, presents a beginner's ballet class.

BALLET BY DEGAS

> 1951, 11 min., color, film
> Distributor: University of Illinois
> Producer/Director: J.H. Lenauer
> Cinematographer: George Jacobson
> Composers: Frederic Chopin, Irma Jurist

A kinetic presentation of the paintings of dancers by Edward Degas: THE BALLET CLASS, CORYPHEE RESTING, BALLERINA and LADY WITH FAN, from the Philadelphia Museum, and ON STAGE, DANCERS PRACTICING AT THE BAR, and PINK AND GREEN from the Metropolitan Museum of Art in New York City.

BALLET CLASS (3 videos)

> 1986-88, 40-60 min. each, color, video
> Distributor: Kultur #1133, 1134, 1136
> Producers: Seymour Klempner, Marc Chase Weinstein,
> Gary Jacinto for AVHL
> Directors: Lee Kraft, Gary Donatelli
> Teacher: David Howard
> Principal Dancers: Cynthia Harvey, Peter Fonseca,
> Allison Potter
> Composers: Whit Kellog, Doug Corbin, Lynn Stanford

A ballet class for beginners (40 min.), for the intermediate-advanced (55 min.), and SHAPE-UP (58 min.), a third tape, an exercise program designed for dancers and nondancers. Taught by David Howard, the New York–based teacher and coach, former–soloist with the Royal Ballet and National Ballet of Canada.

BALLET CLASSES: A CELEBRATION

> 1987, 60 min., color, video
> Distributor/Producer/Director: Jack Churchill
> Teacher: Jacqueline Cronsberg
> Dance on Camera Festival, 1987 Silver Award

Follows over an eight-year period the students in the Ballet Workshop of Sudbury, Massachusetts.

BALLET COMES TO BRITAIN

> Series: Ballet for All, # 6
> 1972, 25 min., b&w, film
> Distributor: University of Illinois
> Director: Nicholas Ferguson
> Choreographers: Vaslav Nijinsky, Leonide Massine, Bronislava Nijinska, Ninette de Valois
> Principal Dancers: Christopher Bruce, David Wall,
> Marilyn Williams, Brenda Last, Johaar Mosaval
> Dance Companies: Royal Ballet, Ballet Rambert
> Composers: Claude Debussy, Gioacchino Rossini, Francis Poulenc, Gavin Gordon

> Narrator: David Blair

Most of these excerpts are from English versions of Diaghilev ballets: the Ballet Rambert version of Nijinsky's AFTERNOON OF A FAUN, the cancan duet from Massine's BOUTIQUE FANTASQUE (1919), the hostess' solo from Nijinska's LES BICHES, (1924). Also excerpts from Ninette de Valois' THE RAKE'S PROGRESS.

BALLET ENTERS THE WORLD STAGE

> Series: Ballet for All, # 2
> 1972, 28 min., b&w, film
> Distributor: University of Illinois
> Director: Nicholas Ferguson
> Choreographers: August Bournonville, Jean Coralli
> Principal Dancers: Margaret Barbieri, Nicholas Johnson,
> Marion Tate, Bridget Taylor
> Dance Company: Ballet for All
> Composers: Adolphe Adam, Herman Lovenskjold

During a version of GISELLE for 4 dancers, piano, and viola, narrator David Blair touches on the innovations of dancing on toe, dancing with less cumbersome costumes, and communicating through mime, all of which were introduced at the time of GISELLE's premiere. The sylph's opening dance in August Bournonville's LA SYLPHIDE is also shown.

BALLET ETOILES

> 1989, 20 min., color, video
> Distributor: French American Cultural Services (cas 157)
> Principal Dancers: Sylvie Guillem, Patrick Dupond

Rehearsal and discussion between two French ballet dancers.

BALLET FAVORITES

> 1982-85, 59 min., color, video
> Distributors: HBO, Pioneer (laserdisk)
> Producers: Gerald Sinstadt, Robin Scott, Svetlana
> Konnonchuk for National Video Corporation
> Directors: John Vernon, Peter Wright, Preben Montell, Colin
> Nears, Brian Large, Elena Macheret
> Choreographers: Konstantin Sergeyev, Alexander Gorski,
> Marius Petipa, Lev Ivanov, Jean Coralli, Kenneth
> MacMillan, Mikhail Baryshnikov, Frederick Ashton
> Principal Dancers: Alessandra Ferri, Wayne Eagling,
> Mikhail Baryshnikov, Cynthia Harvey, Natalia Makarova,
> Lesley Collier, Anthony Dowell, Galina Mezentseva,
> Konstantin Zaklinsky
> Dance Companies: American Ballet Theatre, Kirov Ballet,
> Royal Ballet
> Composers: Adolphe Adam, Peter Ilyich Tchaikovsky, Sergei
> Prokofiev, Leon Minkus
> Set/Costume Designers: Santa Loquasto, Simon Virsaladze
> Nicholas Georgiadis, Leslie Hurry, Julia Trevelyan Oman

Excerpts of films taken of three ballet companies with a compilation of classical solos, pas de deux and ensembles from DON QUIXOTE, SWAN LAKE, THE NUTCRACKER, ROMEO & JULIET, SLEEPING BEAUTY, and GISELLE.

BALLET FOLKLORICO NACIONAL DE MEXICO

> 1988, 110 min., color, video

Distributor/Producer: Gessler Productions
Choreographer: Silvia Lozano

Performance by Mexico City's globe-trotting troupe of eighty dancers, presenting the traditional music and dance of Mexico. The selections include BODA TARASCA, JARABE MIXTECO, EL NORTE, LOS QUETZALES, ALEGRIA JALISCIENCE, and LA HUASTECA. Worksheets created by Thomas Alsop are also supplied.

BALLET IN JAZZ

1962, 11 min., b&w, film
Distributor: The Cinema Guild
Producer: Roto-film, Hamburg
Choreographer/Dancer: Heinz Schmieder
Director: Hans Reinhard
Principal Dancers: Maria Litto, F. Friedman, R. Owens
Composer: Siegfried Franz

A German ballet influenced by American jazz dance.

BALLET MECHANIQUE

1924, 15 min., b&w, film
Distributors: Canyon, Museum of Modern Art
Director: Fernand Leger
Cinematographer: Dudley Murphy

Images of wire whisks and funnels, copper pots and lids, and baking pans, combined with those of a woman climbing again and again a steep flight of stairs with a heavy sack on her back. The only film made by the French painter Fernand Leger, an artist of the Cubist school, BALLET MECHANIQUE plays with the theme of the mechanization of humans and the humanization of objects.

BALLET MECHANIQUE FOR SIX MECHANICAL SWEEPERS

1983, 30 min., color, video
Distributor: Feldman Gallery
Producer: Sanitation Department of New York City
Choreographer/Director: Mierle Ukeles

A ballet for sanitation trucks mounted with mirrors conceived by an artist known for her art made from garbage. Commissioned by the Sanitation Department of New York City, the ballet was shot in rehearsal with the truck drivers obediently tracing the road patterns on Randall's Island, as well as in performance as the finale in a New York City art parade.

BALLET ROBOTIQUE

1983, 8 min., color, film, video
Distributor: Pyramid
Producer/Director: Bob Rogers
Cinematographer: Reed Smoot
Composers: Georges Bizet, Peter Ilyich Tchaikovsky
Arranger: David Spear

In this winner of 18 awards, pirouetting robots at the General Motors assembly line drill holes in auto shells, spray paint on chassis, and shoot welding sparks in time with the cannon fire of the 1812 Overture.

BALLET RUSE

Series: State of the Art
1988, 35 min., color, video
Distributor: Proscenium Entertainment
Producer: Eric S. Luskin for New Jersey Network
Director: Eric Vuolle
Choreographer: Peter Anastos
Dance Company: Garden State Ballet
Composers: Frederic Chopin, Peter Ilyich Tchaikovsky

This farce by the choreographer known for his work with Ballet Trockadero and American Ballet Theatre includes two ballets: YES VIRGINIA, ANOTHER PIANO BALLET in which Anastos pokes fun at the genre of ballets set to Chopin's piano music and FORGOTTEN MEMORIES, which mocks adulterous triangles.

BALLET STUDY FILMS (6 films)

1950s, 5-16 min. each, b&w, film
Distributor: Dance Film Archive
Choreographers: Michel Fokine, Marius Petipa, Lev Ivanov, Enrico Cecchetti
Principal Dancers: Lois Smith, David Adams, Nina Novak, Michael Maule, Melissa Hayden
Composers: Peter Ilyich Tchaikovsky, Frederic Chopin, Leo Delibes

Classical pas de deux and excerpts from: COPPELIA, SLEEPING BEAUTY, SWAN LAKE, and LES SYLPHIDES.

BALLET WITH EDWARD VILLELLA

1970, 27 min., color, film, video
Distributor: Coronet/MTI #LEH502
Producer: Robert Saudek for I. Q. Films
Choreographers: George Balanchine, Marius Petipa, Jean Coralli
Principal Dancers: Edward Villella, Patricia McBride
Dance Company: New York City Ballet
Composers: Igor Stravinsky, Adolphe Adam

Edward Villella illustrates the muscular power and control necessary to partner a ballerina. A pas de deux and segment of GISELLE (Coralli/Adam, 1841) demonstrate the qualities of classical ballet. A segment of APOLLO (Balanchine/Stravinsky, 1928) and RUBIES, from the three-act ballet JEWELS (Balanchine/Stravinsky, 1967) represent the neoclassical style.

BALLET'S GOLDEN AGE (1830-1846)

1966, 8 min., color, b&w, film
Distributor: Kent State
Producer: Walter P. Lewisohn

Prints of the romantic ballerinas Maria Taglioni (1804-1884), Fanny Elssler (1810-1884), Carlotta Grisi (1821-1899), and Lucile Grahn (1821-1907) with quotations from letters and reviews to convey a sense of the period.

LES BALLETS TROCKADERO DE MONTE CARLO IN PARIS

>1980s, 60 min, color, video
>Distributor: Coe Films Associates
>Producer: Telemusic Corp.
>Choreographers: Marius Petipa, Peter Anastos
>Dance Company: Ballet Trockadero
>Composer: Peter Ilyich Tchaikovsky

This "all-male" troupe from America performs a new SWAN LAKE.

BALLROOM DANCING FOR BEGINNERS

>1987, 57 min., color, video
>Distributor: Kultur #1206
>Producer: Michael Major for Promenade Productions
>Director: Rick Allen Lippert
>Principal Dancers: Teresa Mason, Susan Major
>Composer: Richard Bugg

Basic course in the foxtrot, tango, waltz, rumba, cha cha, and swing.

BANGUZA TIMBILA

>1982, 30 min., color, video
>Distributor: Facets #SO8248
>Producer/Director: Ron Hallis

10 players of hand-made timbilas, similar to marimbas, accompany 15 dancers performing in Banguza, Mozambique.

BARBARA IS A VISION OF LOVELINESS

>1978, 6 min., b&w, film
>Distributor: Lightworks
>Producer/Director: Bruce Elder

An experimental film abstraction of a dancing figure.

BARBARA MORGAN

>Series: Photoprofiles
>1983, 30 min., color, video
>Distributor/Producer: Images
>Producer: Thomas R. Schiff
>Directors: John and Rebecca Morgan, Paul R. Schranz, Margaretta Mitchell

Profiles photographer Barbara Morgan, known to the dance world for the photos she took of Martha Graham in the 1930s and 40s. The artist discusses her photographs and her early work as a painter.

BARBARA MORGAN – EVERYTHING IS DANCING

>1983, 18 min., color, video
>Distributor: American Federation of the Arts
>Producer: Edgar B. Howard for Checkerboard Productions
>Principal Dancer: Martha Graham

The photographer recounts her first encounters with Native American rituals in the Southwest and explains how movement and dance became important subjects for her.

BAROQUE DANCE 1675–1725

>1978, 22 min., color, film, video
>Distributor: University of California Extension Media Center

>Producer/Director: Allegra Fuller Snyder
>Reconstructionist: Shirley Wynne
>Principal Dancers: Sue Wanven, Ron Taylor
>Dance on Camera Festival, Certificate of Merit

Introduces the social and theatrical dancing of the baroque period in context with the architecture, landscape gardening, music, design, and costume of that time. Includes SUITE FOR THEATRE (Rondeau, Minuet, Hornpipe, and Slow Air) and SUITE FOR DIANA AND MARS. Demonstrates the minuet's hand and finger movements and ways to interpret baroque notation. Accompanied with a 104-page book.

BART COOK – CHOREOGRAPHER

>1986, 30 min., color, video
>Distributor: American Federation of the Arts
>Producers: Patricia Tarr, Edgar Howard for Checkerboard Fdtn.
>Director/Editor: Kit Fitzgerald
>Choreographer: Bart Cook
>Composer: Gioacchino Rossini

Shows Bart Cook of the New York City Ballet working with students from the School of the American Ballet, closing with a performance of his choreography.

BARYSHNIKOV DANCES SINATRA AND MORE WITH ABT

>1988, 60 min., color, video
>Distributor: Kultur #1167
>Producer/Director: Don Mischer
>Choreographer: Twyla Tharp
>Principal Dancers: Mikhail Baryshnikov, Deirdre Carberry, Elaine Kudo
>Dance Company: American Ballet Theatre
>Composers: Alexander Glazunov, Franz Joseph Haydn, Joseph Lamb

Mikhail Baryshnikov plays an impossible, irresistible lover in SINATRA SUITE, a virtuoso clown in PUSH COMES TO SHOVE, the pun-filled satire set to rags by Joseph Lamb and symphonies of Joseph Haydn, and a sweet-tempered partner in THE LITTLE BALLET.

BARYSHNIKOV: THE DANCER AND THE DANCE

>1983, 82 min., color, video
>Distributor: Kultur #1137
>Producer: Harriet & Victor Millrose with Melvyn Bragg and London Weekend Television
>Director: Tony Cash
>Choreographers: Choo San Goh, Marius Petipa
>Principal Dancers: Mikhail Baryshnikov, Marianna Tcherkassky
>Dance Company: American Ballet Theatre
>Narrator: Shirley MacLaine
>Composers: Samuel Barber, Adolphe Adam

Mikhail Baryshnikov rehearses, coaches, and performs his commissioned ballet CONFIGURATIONS, choreographed by the late Choo San Goh. In the course of his reflection on his career and early training in Russia, Baryshnikov, in footage as a young man, performs the role of the pirate in CORSAIRE.

BASIC TAP, JACK STANLY

> 1950s, 15 min. each, color, film (5 reels), video
> Distributor/Producer: See-Do Productions
> Principal Dancer/Teacher: Jack Stanly

A visual dictionary with notes.

THE BAUHAUS DANCES OF OSKAR SCHLEMMER–
A RECONSTRUCTION

> 1986, 31:15 min., color, video
> Distributor: Kitchen
> Producers: Mary Salter, Debra McCall
> Directors: Robert Leacock, Debra McCall
> Composer: Craig Gordon

A reconstruction of the abstract dances made in Germany as a spinoff of the energy and philosophy emanating from the Bauhaus, the influential German school of art and architecture founded in 1919.

LA BAYADERE

> 1977, 126 min., color, video
> Distributor: Kultur #1113
> Producer: Gostelradio
> Director: Elena Macharet
> Choreographers: Vakhtang Chabukiani, Vladimir Ponomarev after Marius Petipa
> Principal Dancers: Gabriella Komleva (Nikia, The Doomed Temple Dancer), Tatiana Terekhova, (Gamzatti, The Rajah's Daugher), Rejen Abdyev (Solor)
> Dance Company: Kirov Ballet
> Composer: Leon Minkus
> Set Designers: Orest Allegri, Konstantin Ivanov, Adolf Kvapp

The 1877, three-act ballet based on the Indian classic, KALISDASA: SAKUNTALA and THE CART OF CLAY, filmed live at the Kirov Theatre. Murdered by a jealous lover, Nikia, the Bayadere, continues to haunt a young warrior, Solor, the object of her affection, as she dances in the Kingdom of the Shades.

BAYADERKA BALLET (La Bayadere)

> 1943, 10 min., b&w, film
> Distributor: Corinth
> Choreographer: Marius Petipa
> Principal Dancers: Natalia Dudinskaya, Vakhtang Chabukiani
> Dance Company: Leningrad State Academy Theatre of Opera & Ballet
> Composer: Leon Minkus

An excerpt from the 1877 ballet. (See plot described above.)

BAYANIHAN

> 1962, 60 min., color, film
> Distributor: Masterworks Video Enterprises
> Producer: Robert Snyder
> Director/Writer/Editor: Allegra Fuller Snyder
> Choreographer: Lucrecia Reyes Urtula
> Cinematographer: Theodore Pale
> Dance Company: Bayanihan Philippine Dance Company

> Cine Golden Eagle

The rituals, customs and traditions of the Philippines as reflected in dance. Based upon research in the Bayanihan Folk Arts Center of Manila with examples of the mountain dances for the occasions of combat and victory: SA-GAYAN SA KULONG; funeral: BANBIBANB, ASIK (Slave dance), ITICK ITICK (duck dance), IFUGAO; dances of Spanish heritage: POLKABAL, MAZURKA BOHOLANA; HABANERA BOTOLENA; and JOTA MONCADENA; dances of Moslem Philippines, and dances of the rural Philippines, and others.

BEAUTY AND THE BEAST

> 1966, 50 min., color, film
> Distributor: Films Inc.
> Producer: Gordon Waldear for ABC Film Release
> Choreographer: Lew Christensen
> Dance Company: San Francisco Ballet Company
> Principal Dancers: Robert Gladstein, Lynda Meyer, David Anderson
> Composer: Peter Ilyich Tchaikovsky
> Narrator: Hayley Mills

A fairy tale about a girl who saves her father's life by agreeing to live with a beast who magically transforms himself into a prince.

BECAUSE WE MUST

> 1989, 50 min., color, video
> Distributors: Electronic Arts Intermix, Kitchen
> Producer: Jolyon Winhurst of Best Endeavors Productions for Channel 4 in association with La Sept
> Director/Editor: Charles Atlas
> Choreographer/Dancer: Michael Clark
> Costume Designers: Body Map, Leigh Bowery
> Dance Company: Michael Clark Company
> Composers: Frederic Chopin, T Rex, Graham Lewis, Velvet Underground, Dome
> Editor: Hugh Chaloner

A satiric romp in which trained male ballet dancers from London prance about in drag and sing around the grand piano. Punctuated by the repeated regurgitations from the lead and a solo by a nude woman who dances with a roaring chain saw.

BEEHIVE

> 1985, 15 min., color, film, video
> Distributor: Frank Moore
> Producer/Director/Set and Costume Designer: Frank Moore
> Choreographer/Dancer: Jim Self
> Principal Dancer: Teri Weksler
> Composer: Man Parrish
> BESSIE Award, 1985; Dance on Camera, 1987 Honorable Mention

A bumbling bee unwittingly causes a worker bee to be transformed into a queen. A related ballet by the same title was commissioned by the Boston Ballet and premiered in 1987. The cast includes thirty-six bees and eight flowers.

Beehive
Jim Self as Drone. Photo by Frank Moore.

BEFORE HOLLYWOOD: TURN-OF-THE-CENTURY FILM
FROM AMERICAN ARCHIVES

> 1895–1915, six-program series, 68–108 min. each, b&w,
> film
> Distributor/Producer: American Federation of the Arts
> Directors: Maya Deren, Shirley Clarke, Willard Maas,
> Stan Brakhage

This series includes in Program I dance shorts made in
1895-96: ANNABELLE BUTTERFLY DANCE, ANNABELLE
SERPENTINE DANCE, and SERPENTINE DANCE in the
period when the film cameras and projectors were just being developed in small production companies in New York,
New Jersey, Philadelphia, Chicago and other sites. Selected
by the late Jay Leyda, renowned historian of early cinema
and American literature, and Charles Musser, film scholar
and filmmaker. Also available from AFA is A HISTORY OF
THE AMERICAN AVANT-GARDE CINEMA with seven programs showing thirty-six films produced by twenty-eight
artists between 1943 and 1972 with Maya Deren's works
among them.

BEGINNING BELLYDANCING WITH BEDIA (8 videos)

> 1988, 90 min., color, video
> Distributor/Producer/Director/Dancer: Bedia

Alignment and posture, isolations, and hip movements,
with zill instruction in volume two. Also available from Be-
dia: BELEDI CHOREOGRAPHY, BODY CONDITIONING,
INTRODUCTION TO BHARATA NATYAM FOR MIDDLE
EASTERN DANCERS WITH STEWART CARRERA (80 min.),
INTRODUCTION TO SPANISH DANCE WITH JOANA DEL
RIO, ELLI WORKSHOPS: GHAWAZEWE, TUNISIAN,
OULED NAIL, and YOUSRY SHARIF SEMINAR SHOW (90
min.).

BEGINNING MODERN DANCE FOR HIGH SCHOOL GIRLS

> 1958, 20 min., b&w, film
> Distributor: University of Iowa
> Producers: Stanley E. Nelson, Dr. L. Porter
> Choreographer: Lolita F. Dinoso

Explores methods of problem solving in dance composition.

BEGINNINGS

> 1976, 30 min., color, film
> Distributor: Arthur Cantor
> Producer/Directors: Maren and Reed Erskine
> Choreographer: Arthur Saint-Leon
> Teachers: Suki Shorer, Alexandra Danilova
> Dance Company: New York City Ballet
> Composer: Leo Delibes
> Dance on Camera Festival, 1977 Honorable Mention

This study of the School of American Ballet, founded in 1934
by Lincoln Kirstein and George Balanchine, shows the aims
and attitudes of the students and faculty, who demonstrate the
ballet vocabulary, and concludes with scenes from a performance of COPPELIA.

THE BEGINNINGS OF TODAY

> Series: Ballet for All, #5
> 1972, 27 min., b&w, film
> Distributor: University of Illinois
> Director: Nicholas Ferguson
> Choreographers: Michel Fokine, Marius Petipa
> Principal Dancers: Anna Pavlova, Shirley Grahame,
> Graham Usher
> Composers: Frederic Chopin, Peter Ilyich Tchaikovsky, Igor
> Stravinsky

Celebrates the poetic expression of the romantic period with
excerpts from LES SYLPHIDES, SWAN LAKE, SLEEPING
BEAUTY, and PETROUCHKA. Anna Pavlova performs two solos, LA NUIT and DYING SWAN.

BEING ME

> 1969, 13 min., b&w, film
> Distributor: University of California Extension
> Media Center
> Producer/Teacher: Hilda Mullin
> Director: Joe Carmichael

Nine girls, eight to thirteen years old, improvise in a dance
class shot in the Pasadena Art Museum in California.

BELL DANCE FOR THE CONJURATION OF THE
SACRED BUSH COW

> 1954, 3:30 min., b&w, film
> Distributor: Pennstate #E00590
> Producer/Director: E. Leuzinger for Wissen

In this silent film, dancers of Afo, Nigeria, swing large iron
bells and civet cat pelts as symbols of their sacred bush cow,
their protective power, to drive evil spirits away.

BELLY DANCE! MAGICAL MOTION

> 1985, 60 min., color, video
> Distributor/Producer: Magical Motion Enterprises
> Producer/Choreographer/Dancer: Cheryl Simon, known as Atea
> Director: Mitch Merbach
> Composer: Ramal Lamarr

Introduction to belly dance technique with historical background, exercises for finger cymbals and veil work, with a chapter on costuming and examples of the baladi and Saudi-style garments, as well as cabaret costumes.

BELLY DANCING: IMAGES FROM VANCOUVER

> 1979, 30 min., color, video
> Distributor: Melkim Productions
> Producer: Elvira Lount
> Principal Dancers: Badawia, Farideh

Twenty solos and group performances in honor of the Moon Goddess Artemis, plus Egyptian sword, Bedouin fan, Guedra, and candle dances.

BERIMBAU

> 1974, 12 min., color, film
> Distributor: New Yorker Films
> Producer/Director: Tony Talbot

In this ethnomusicology film, Nana, a black musician, uses a berimbau, a one-stringed musical bow, to play traditional melodies to accompany the capoeira, a dance based on the Brazilian martial art form. Presents the history and harmonies of the berimbau, one of the oldest musical instruments.

BERKELEY, BUSBY (9 videos)

> 1933–1962, feature length, color, film, video
> Distributor/Producer: (retail outlets) MGM, Warner Bros., 20th Century Fox
> Director/Choreographer: Busby Berkeley
> Directors: Ray Enright, Lloyd Bacon, Vincente Minnelli, Norman Taurog
> Principal Dancers: Ruby Keeler, Dick Powell, James Cagney, Fred Astaire, Gene Kelly, Esther Williams
> Composers: Nacio Herb Brown-Arthur Freed, Richard Rodgers, Lorenz Hart, Eubie Blake, Noble Sissle, Harold Arlen, E.Y. Harburg, Gus Arnheim, Burton Lane, Vernon Duke, Harry Warren, George Gershwin

Busby Berkeley (1895–1976) directed 21 dance musicals on Broadway before he went to Hollywood in 1930 at the invitation of Samuel Goldwyn. In the 1930s, he choreographed 35 extravaganzas, and directed 21 others known for their inventive camera work and kaleidoscopic visions. The following of his musicals, made with the collaboration of the above talents, are available on video:

> BABES IN ARMS (1939, with Mickey Rooney, Judy Garland)
> 42nd STREET (1933, with Ruby Keeler, Ginger Rogers)
> FOOTLIGHT PARADE (1933, with Ruby Keeler)
> GIRL CRAZY (1943)
> GOLD DIGGERS OF 1933 (with Ruby Keeler, Ginger Rogers)
> GOLD DIGGERS OF 1935 (with Dick Powell)

> DAMES (1934, with Ruby Keeler)
> STRIKE UP THE BAND (1940)
> TAKE ME OUT TO THE BALLGAME (1949, with Esther Williams and Gene Kelly)

BESIDE HERSELF

> 1987, 7:45 min., b&w, film
> Distributor: Filmmaker's Coop
> Director: Power Boothe
> Choreographer/Director: Catlin Cobb
> Composer: A. Leroy

An experiment in which a woman in black on one side of the screen carries on a non-verbal dialogue with the same woman in white on the other.

BEST OF ALL A DANCER

> 1982, 11 min., color, film, video
> Distributor: Direct Cinema
> Producers: Richard Heus, Robert Marinaccio
> Director/Writer: Richard Heus
> Choreographer/Teacher: David Morgan
> Dancer/Choreographer: Rusty Hartman
> Composer: Warren R. McCommons

Rusty Hartman, a thirty-two-year-old man with Down's Syndrome, performs dances he choreographed over the last eight years with the help of a supportive teacher. The documentary shows how dance and music can ease communication and self-esteem.

BINO-DANCE

> 1963, 2 min., b&w, film
> Distributor: Pennstate #E00918
> Producer: G. Koch for Wissen

Filmed in the Pacific, men and women from Tabiteuea, Gilbert Islands, perform BINO, a traditional folk dance performed from a sitting position. Same year, same place, Wissen produced 2 other 3-minute films of the KAWAWA, the introductory song and dance of the Gilbert Islands, and the KAMEI, WA N TARAWA and the KABUAKAKA dances.

BIP AS A SOLDIER (3 films)

> 1975, 18 min. each, color, film
> Distributor: University of Illinois
> Producer/Director: John Barnes
> Cinematographer: Adam Giffard
> Mime: Marcel Marceau

A denunciation of war by the master mime Marcel Marceau. Also, two other films made by the same crew in the same year are available from University of Illinois: BIP AT A SOCIETY PARTY (13 min.), in which Marceau portrays various characters at a society party, and BIP HUNTS BUTTERFLIES (10 min.) in which Marceau expresses concern for a dying butterfly.

BIRDS OF A FEATHER

> 1990, 28 min., color, video
> Distributor: University of California Extension Media Center
> Producers: Birds of a Feather, Show Place Video Productions, Eugene, Oregon

A dance therapy film in which five members of a troupe dance, sing, act despite their individual disabilities. Signed for the hearing impaired.

BITTER MELONS

    1971, 28 min., color, film
    Distributors: Documentary Educational Resources, University of California Extension Media Center
    at Berkeley
    Producer: Center For Documentary Anthropology
    Director: John K. Marshall

Igwikhwe bushmen of the Kalahari Desert area in southwest Africa, perform animal songs about the tribe's dependence on the land for their livelihood, and their continual search for water. Shot in the mid 1950s as part of a Peabody Museum expedition.

BLACK AND WHITE

    1985, 7 min., color, film
    Distributor/Choreographer: Sally Gross
    Director: Joan Kurahara
    Composer: Gary Haase
    Editor: Joshua Blum

An experimental effort to superimpose the movements of dancers with slides painted by Joan Kurahara.

BLACK GIRL

    Series: Planning Ahead
    1982, 30 min., color, film, video
    Distributor: University of California Extension Media Center
    Producer: Barbara Wolfinger for Berkeley Productions
    Directors: Marilyn and Hal Weiner
    Writer: J. E. Franklin
    American Film Festival Award, National Council
    on Family Relations, National Educational Film Festival
    Award

A young black teenager drops out of school and secretly takes a job as a dancer and waitress at a local bar. She dreams of becoming a ballet dancer, but doesn't know how to pursue her goal in the face of violent opposition from her family.

BLACK TIGHTS

    1962, 120 min., color, film, video
    Distributors: Dance Film Archive, Video Arts International
    Producer: Joseph Kaufman for Les Grandes Projections
    Cinematographiques/Talma Doperfilms
    Director: Terence Young
    Choreographer/Dancer: Roland Petit
    Principal Dancers: Zizi Jeanmaire, Moira Shearer, Cyd
    Charisse, Hans Van Manen, Henning Kronstam
    Composers: Georges Bizet, Marius Constant, Jean
    Michel Damase
    Costume Designer: Yves Saint Laurent
    Set Designer: Georges Wakhevitch

Four-part feature film set in Paris: CARMEN, in which a cigarette girl seduces a young soldier and leaves him for a matador; CYRANO DE BERGERAC, based on the play by Edmond Rostand about a man's attempt to woo his love by proxy through a young soldier; DIAMOND CRUNCHER, a beautiful pickpocket who has a passion for eating stolen diamonds; and A MERRY MOURNING, (originally known as DEVIL IN TWENTY-FOUR HOURS), in which a woman purchases a black dress to dance with a suitor who murdered her husband.

BLOCKHAUS

    1987, 17 min., color, video
    Distributor: Videographe, Inc.
    Producer: Taxiderme
    Directors: Johanne Charlebois, Harold Vasselin
    Dance on Camera Festival, 1989 Honorable Mention

In this experimental venture filmed in Normandy in a place marked by the war, the wind, and the sea, dancers suggest the search for equilibrium.

BLOOD WEDDING

    1981, 71 min., color, film, video
    Distributor: Cinematheque
    Producer: Emiliano Piedra
    Choreographer: Antonio Gades
    Director: Carlos Saura
    Principal Dancers: Antonio Gades, Cristina Hoyos

This flamenco dance/theater is based on Federico Garcia Lorca's tragic play of a young bride who runs off with a previous lover. Subsequently, her lover and new husband kill each other.

THE BLUE ANGEL

    1988, 78 min., color, video
    Distributor: Kultur #1226
    Producers: Telemondis, La Sept, FR3, WK Productions
    Director: Dirk Sanders
    Choreographer: Roland Petit
    Principal Dancers: Dominique Khalfouni (Rosa),
    Roland Petit (Professor Unrat), Pierre Aviotte (Lohman)
    Dance Company: Ballet National de Marseille
    Composer: Lou Bruder

Story of Rosa Frohlich, the cabaret dancer Josef Von Sternberg made so famous with his 1930 classic starring Marlene Dietrich. The ballet flirts with the joys of toying with a man's obsessive lust.

BLUE SNAKE

    1986, 54 min., color, film, video
    Distributors: Rhombus International, Bullfrog Films
    Producers: Niv Fichman, Louise Clark for TV Ontario
    and Canada Council
    Director: Niv Fichman
    Choreographer: Robert Desrosiers
    Dance Company: National Ballet of Canada
    Composers: John Lang, Ahmed Hassan

Cannibalism, revenge, and transcendence, the unusual sequence for this surreal ballet of Robert Desrosiers, commissioned by the National Ballet of Canada, unfolds through rehearsals, costume fittings, and performance. This collaborative effort equally involves all the participating artists and producers.

BLUE STUDIO: FIVE SEGMENTS

>1976, 15 min., color, film, video
>Distributor/Producer: Cunningham Dance Foundation
>Director: Charles Atlas
>Choreographer/Dancer: Merce Cunningham

A silent solo performed in a 15' by 15' studio seemingly transformed through chromakey, a method whereby imagery can be superimposed on a blue backdrop, giving the choreographer the freedom to transport the dancers to any environment, real or surreal, or to dance with multiple clones of himself. Also see the variation on this video by Nam June Paik in MERCE BY MERCE BY PAIK.

THE BODY AS AN INSTRUMENT

>Series: Dance as an Art Form
>1973, 27 min., color, film, video
>Distributor: Pro Arts
>Producer: Jack Leib Productions
>Director/Choreographer/Narrator: Murray Louis
>Dance Company: Murray Louis Dance Company
>Principal Dancers: Murray Louis, Carolyn Carlson,
>Les Diston, Helen Kent
>Composer: Alwin Nikolais
>Costume Designer: Frank Garcia
>Cinematographer: Warren Leib

After examining various sizes, shapes, and temperaments represented by a group of actors, athletes, children, animals, and university dance students, modern dancer Murray Louis assures us that anyone can dance. Louis performs excerpts of his repertoire with his company.

BODY TALK: EIGHT MOVEMENT THERAPIES

>1975, 58 min., b&w, video
>Distributor/Producer/Director: Sybil Meyer
>Producer: American Dance Therapy Association
>(Northern California chapter)

Eight sessions at a dance therapy conference with an explanation of the therapy goals and a variety of approaches for self-expression and nonverbal communication.

BOLD STEPS

>1984, 81 min., color, video
>Distributor: Home Vision
>Producer: Pat Ferns for Primedia, Christopher Martin for BBC in association with Canadian Broadcasting Corporation
>Director: Cyril Frankel
>Choreographers: Harald Lander, Erik Bruhn, Marius Petipa, Constantin Patsalas, Glen Tetley
>Principal Dancers: Celia Franca, Lorna Geddes, Karen Kain, Erik Bruhn, Rudolf Nureyev, Mikhail Baryshnikov
>Dance Company: National Ballet of Canada
>Composers: Peter Ilyich Tchaikovsky, Karl Czerny, Morton Gould, Leon Minkus, Harry Freedman, Bohuslav Martinu
>Narrator: Robert Cushman

Traces the development of the Toronto-based National Ballet of Canada with statements by the founder/former artistic director Celia Franca, former dancer Lorna Geddes, supported by stills and footage. Rehearsals under Erik Bruhn's direction follow of ETUDES (Lander/Czerny), HERE WE COME (Bruhn/Gould), LA BAYADERE (Petipa/Minkus), DON QUIXOTE (Petipa/Minkus), OISEAUX EXOTIQUES (Patsalas/Freedman), SPHINX (Tetley/Martinu), SWAN LAKE (Petipa/Tchaikovsky), then performances at the company's gala.

BOLERO

>1961, 15 min., b&w, film
>Distributor: Dance Film Archive
>Producer/Director: Jean-Luc Landier
>Choreographer: Maurice Bejart
>Principal Dancer: Duska Sifinos
>Dance Company: Ballet of The Twentieth Century
>Composer: Maurice Ravel

A comically erotic ballet in which a soloist pulses above a circle of men sitting in chairs who gradually join forces with ritualistic ardor. One of the few works currently available by Maurice Bejart. For updated information as to the transfer of his films to video and availability, contact the Belgian Consulate.

BOLSHOI BALLET

>1964, 80 min., color, video
>Distributor: Kultur #1105
>Producer: Mosfilm
>Directors: Leonid Lavrovsky, Alexander Shelenkov
>Choreographer: Leonid Lavrovsky
>Principal Dancers: Raisa Struckhova, Nina Timofeeva, Alla Osipenko, Natalia Bessmertnova, Ekaterina Maximova
>Dance Company: Bolshoi Ballet
>Composers: Maurice Ravel, Sergei Prokofiev, Sergei Rachmaninov

Rehearsal and performance of PAGANINI, Lavrovsky's 1960 ballet set to music by Rachmaninov depicting the violin virtuoso being inspired by his muse; STONE FLOWER, choreographed in 1954 to music of Prokofiev about a sculptor's obsession with perfection; BOLERO, and WALTZ.

BOLSHOI BALLET IN THE PARK

>1986, 120 min., color, video
>Distributors: Home Vision, Pioneer (Laserdisk)
>Producer: Colin Nears for The Entertainment Corporation and BBC in association with National Video Corporation
>Choreographers: Marius Petipa, Yuri Grigorovich, Michel Fokine
>Director: John Vernon
>Principal Dancers: Irek Mukhamedov, Natalia Bessmertnova, Nina Ananiashvili
>Dance Company: Bolshoi Ballet
>Composers: Peter Ilyich Tchaikovsky, Aram Khatchaturian, Leon Minkus, Frederic Chopin

Divertissements filmed at the Battersea Pavilion in London with the following selections: LES SYLPHIDES, SPARTACUS (Act II), SLEEPING BEAUTY, LA BAYADERE, SWAN LAKE, GOLDEN AGE, SPRING WATERS, DON QUIXOTE.

THE BOLSHOI BALLET TOURS AMERICA

>1959, 45 min., b&w, film
>Distributor: National Council for American

Soviet Friendship
Choreographers: Michel Fokine, Lev Ivanov,
Marius Petipa, Leon Lavrovsky, Vasily Vainonen,
George Balanchine
Principal Dancers: Galina Ulanova, Maya Plisetskaya,
Ekaterina Maximova, Nikolai Fadeyechev
Dance Companies: Bolshoi Ballet, New York City Ballet
Composers: Peter Ilyich Tchaikovsky, Adolphe Adam,
Frederic Chopin, Sergei Prokofiev

Includes excerpts of ROMEO AND JULIET, A DYING
SWAN, GISELLE (Act II), SWAN LAKE, FLAMES OF PARIS,
STONE FLOWER and CHOPINIANA, and Balanchine's
AGON performed by the New York City Ballet.

BOLSHOI SOLOISTS CLASSIQUE

1987, 42 min., color, video
Distributor: V.I.E.W. Video
Producer: Soviet Film & TV
Choreographers: Michel Fokine, Nina Timofeyeva,
Leonide Lavrosky
Principal Dancers: Nina Timofeyeva, Leonide Lavrovsky
Dance Company: Bolshoi Ballet
Composers: Peter Ilyich Tchaikovsky, Adolphe Adam,
George Gershwin, Tommaso Albinoni

Program of solos and duets, performed by Nina Timofeyeva
and Leonide Lavrovsky, who both became members of the Bol-
shoi Ballet in 1961, includes THE DYING SWAN (Fokine/Saint-
Saens), PORGY AND BESS (Lavrosky/Gershwin), ADAGIO
(Timofeyeva/Albinoni), and PAS DE DEUX CLASSIQUE
(Timofeyeva/Adam).

BONE DREAM

1977, 7:30 min., b&w, video
Distributor: ARC Video
Producer/Directors: Jeff Bush and Celia Ipiotis
Choreographer/Dancers: Eiko & Koma

A meditation in the nude made in collaboration with the New
York–based Japanese couple Eiko and Koma, trained in the
Butoh school.

BONNIE BIRD DEMONSTRATES GRAHAM TECHNIQUE

1938-1939, 12 min., b&w, film
Distributor: Dance Film Archive
Dancer: Bonnie Bird

A member of Martha Graham's company, filmed at the Greek
Theatre at Mills College, in the course of doing the floor exercises developed by the modern dance pioneer.

BORN FOR HARD LUCK: PEG LEG SAM JACKSON

29 min., color, film
Distributor/Director: Tom Davenport Films

Portrait of one of the last of the medicine-show entertainers,
Arthur "Peg Leg Sam" Jackson, who played his blues
harmonica, sang and danced to attract a crowd in the rural
south for men pitching "snake oil" and other dubious cures.

BRANCHES

1975, 6:30 min., color, film

Distributor: Film-maker's Coop
Director: Dave Gearey
Principal Dancers: Carol Marcy, Dana Reitz, Nannette Sievert
Composer: Malcom Goldstein

An ode to the sensuality and mystery of light filtering through
bodies climbing among branches.

BREAK

1983, 27:48 min., color, video
Distributor: Intermedia Arts
Producer/Director: Mark Lowry and Kathryn Escher for
Twin Cities Public TV
Choreographer/Dancer: Bill T. Jones
Principal Dancers: Maria Cheng, Eric Barsness, Stephen
Rueff
Composer: Graham Lewis

Feelings of social unrest expressed by dancers in an open
landscape of dunes, cliffs, and gulleys.

BREAK DANCING

1986, 45 min., color, video
Distributor: Hoctor
Producer: Studio Music Corp.
Teachers: Luis and Alex Cataldi

An instructional video on techniques used in break dancing.

BREAKIN'

1984, 87 min., color, film, video
Distributor/Producer: MGM
Director: Joel Silberg
Principal Dancers: Adolfo Quinones,
Michael Chambers, Lucinda Dickey

Feature filmed in Los Angeles about a struggling jazz dancer
who teams up with two break dancers to win a competition.

BREAKING: STREET DANCING

1981, 23 min., color, video
Distributor: Gotham City Filmworks
Director: Ramsey Najm
Dance on Camera Festival, 1982 Gold Award in
Ethnic/Folk category

Displays the competitive street dance of Blacks and Hispan-
ics living in New York City's South Bronx, before the craze
spread across the country.

BRITISH BALLET TODAY

Series: Ballet for All, #7
1972, 26 min., b&w, film
Distributor: University of Illinois
Director: Nicholas Ferguson
Choreographers: Kenneth MacMillan, Frederick Ashton
Dance Company: Ballet for All
Principal Dancers: David Blair, Kerrison Cooke, Ronald
Emblem, Brenda Last, Patricia Ruenne
Composers: Dimitri Shostakovich, L.J.F. Herold
Narrator: Peter Brinson

Duet from MacMillan's CONCERTO, followed by portions of Ashton's 1960 character ballet LA FILLE MAL GARDEE, as part of a series on the history of dance.

BROADWAY TAP (2 videos)

> 1988–1989, 45 min. each, color, video
> Distributor: Hoctor Products
> Producer: Studio Music Corp.
> Choreographer/Dancer: Sonya Kerwin

Routines by one of the Rockettes, the dance team in residence at Radio City Music Hall in New York City.

BRUSH AND BARRE: THE LIFE AND WORK
OF TOULOUSE-LAUTREC

> 1979, 59 min., color, film, video
> Distributor: University of California Extension Media Center
> Choreographer: Linda Fowler

Documents the development and performance of TRECLAU, a master's thesis, performed by university students intercut with stills of Henri Toulouse-Lautrec's paintings and graphics with characters performing in costumes patterned after Lautrec.

BRYONY BRIND'S BALLET: THE FIRST STEPS

> 1988, 45 min., color, video
> Distributor: Kultur #1228
> Producer/Director: John Watkinson
> Choreographer: Joan Lawson
> Principal Dancer: Bryony Brind
> Composer: Paul Stobart

Bryony Brind, a principal with the Royal Ballet, explains the basic principles and movements of ballet.

BUCKDANCER

> 1966, 6 min., b&w, film, video
> Distributor: University of California Extension Media Center
> Producer: Bess Lomax Hawes
> Principal Dancer: Ed Young

Recorded on the Sea Islands of Georgia, black musicians dance on a front porch accompanied by singing and clapping, while a craftsman shows how he made his fife and how he plays it.

BUCKET DANCE VIDEO

> 1982, 110 min., color, video
> Distributor: Black Filmmaker Foundation
> Producer/Director: Warrington Hudlin
> Choreographer: Garth Fagan
> Dance Company: Bucket Dance Company
> Dance on Camera Festival, 1986 Honorable Mention

Performance by this Rochester-based modern dance company renowned for its mix of jazz, modern, and African dance.

BUFFALO SOLDIER

> 1981, 11 min, color, film
> Distributors: Sue Marx Films, American Federation of the Arts
> Producer: Urban Communications Group
> Choreographer: Carole Morisseau
> Principal Dancers: Carl Bailey, Warren Spears

> Dance Company: Detroit City Dance Company
> Composer: Quincy Jones
> CINE Golden Eagle, Emmy

Forerunner of feature film GLORY, this dance heralds the heroic deeds of the U.S. black cavalry soldiers of the 9th and 10th Regiments who fought in the Civil War.

BUILDING CHILDREN'S PERSONALITIES
WITH CREATIVE DANCING

> 1953, 30 min., color, film
> Distributor: University of Illinois
> Producers: Lawrence P. Frank, Jr., Gary Goldsmith
> Dance Teacher: Gertrude Copley Knight

Guiding children, aged five to ten, to gain confidence through the training and discipline of dance. The teacher suggests word pictures and praises the children's efforts to translate them in movement.

BULLFIGHT

> 1975, 9 min., color, film
> Distributor: Museum of Modern Art
> Producer: Halcyon Films
> Director: Shirley Clarke
> Choreographer/Dancer: Anna Sokolow
> Cinematographers: Bert Clarke, Peter Buckley
> Composer: Norman Lloyd

Modern solo suggesting the perspectives of both the bull and the matador, intercut with scenes of a bullfight. Anna Sokolow's arms curve with the grace and power of a Spanish dancer.

BUNRAKU PUPPET THEATRE OF JAPAN

> 1970s, 28 min., color, video
> Distributor/Producer: Asia Society
> Dance Company: Bunraku Puppet Theatre

Demonstration of the Japanese art of handling large dolls or stage and the craft of making the dolls, along with historical anecdotes on this ancient form of theater.

BUSTER COOPER WORKSHOP VIDEOS (28 videos)

> 1981–1987, 30 min. each, color, video
> Distributor/Producer/Teacher: Buster Cooper, Choreo Records
> Choreographer/Teachers: Terry Wolter, David Storey, W. M. Martin, Nathalie Krassovska, Eileen McKee

Popular tunes ranging from "Boogie Woogie Bugle Boy," "Material Girl," "The Way You Make Me Feel" to "Little Shop of Horrors." Graded ballet, jazz, and tap classes with routines and notes.

BUSTER COOPER'S HOW TO TAP (6 videos)

> 1986, 60 min. each, color, video
> Distributor/Teacher: Buster Cooper

Barre, center and travelling steps with a routine and notes for elementary grades. Also available, BUSTER COOPER'S TAP ROUTINES with two routines DARKNESS and GOLDEN SLIPPERS.

BUTOH

1990, 88 min., color, film, video
Distributor/Producer/Director: Michael Blackwood
Writer/Narrator: Bonnie Stein
Cinematographer: Christian Blackwood
Principal Dancers: Kazuo Ohno, Tatsumi Hijikata, Min Tanaka, Maijuku, Yoko Ashikawa Hakutobo, Akaji Maro, Isamu Ohsuka, Byakko-sha, Natsu Nakajima, Muteki-sha, Ushio Amagatsu
Dance Companies: Sankai Juku, Dai Rakuda Kan

Following a belief in perpetual change, these modern dancers of Japan try to express the beauty of the soul's dark side. The documentary covers the history of this revolutionary movement with interviews, rehearsals, archival footage, including that of the master Tatsumi Hijikata in his 1960 work, REVOLT OF THE FLESH.

CABARET

1972, 124 min., color, video
Distributors: CBS/Fox Video, Swank
Producer: Cy Feuer for Allied Artists and ABC Pictures
Choreographer/Director: Bob Fosse
Principal Dancers: Liza Minnelli, Joel Grey
Composer: John Kander
Writer: Jay Allen after the stories of Christopher Isherwood and the play of John Van Druten

This Academy Award–winning musical by Bob Fosse became almost as notorious as its subject, the Kit Kat Club, Berlin's hotbed of vice and anti-Semitism in pre–World War II Germany. A breakthrough film for the choreographer, CABARET shows the power of movement to manipulate emotions and the eye of the camera to clarify that intention.

THE CACHUCHA

1980, 14 min., color, film
Distributor: Dance Film Archive
Choreographer: Jean Coralli
Principal Dancer: Margaret Barbieri

The Spanish dance accompanied by castanets made popular in the middle of the nineteenth century by Fanny Elssler. Reconstructed in England from Zorn notation by Dr. Ann Hutchinson Guest.

THE CAGE

1975, 9 min., color, film
Distributor: Kent State
Producer/Director: John Barnes
Mime: Marcel Marceau
Cinematographer: Adam Giffard

The French soloist strives to escape from confinement, an enclosure of invisible walls, only to break through to find another invisible wall.

CALL OF THE DRUM – NAPOLEONIC DANCES

1972, 28 min., color, video
Distributor: Orion Enterprises
Producer: WTTW-TV, Chicago
Director: Richard J. Carter
Choreographer: Gus Giordano
Dance Company: Gus Giordano Dance Company

Set to French marches, the jazz dance plays around the theme of Napoleon's conflicting drives for love and glory.

THE CALL OF THE JITTERBUG

1989, 30 min., color, video
Distributor: Filmaker's Library
Producer/Directors: Tana Ross, Jasper Sorensen, Vibeke Winding
American Film & Video Festival, 1989 Blue Ribbon, CINE Golden Eagle, 1989

Interviews with musicians and dancers, plus vintage footage in this tribute to the dance craze that swept the nation in the 30s and crossed the color barrier.

CAMBODIAN DANCES

1979, 50 min., color, video
Distributor/Producer: Cornell Cooperative (Southeast Asia Collection)

Classical and folk dances performed at Cornell University with a program of APSARA, THE MAGIC SCARF, ELEPHANT HUNTING, SOVAN MACHA, CAMBODIAN MUSIC, KRAB, CHHAYAM, and DANCE OF GREETINGS AND BEST WISHES.

CANADIANS CAN DANCE

1966, 22 min., color, film, video
Distributor/Producer: National Film Board of Canada
Director: John Howe

Gathering of 1500 amateur folk dancers at the annual Canadian National Exhibition in Toronto.

CANON IN D

1977, 8 min., color, film
Distributor/Director: Virginia Brooks
Choreographer: Nolan T'sani
Composer: Johann Pachelbel

A single-camera record of a dance for four dancers filmed at the School of American Ballet.

CAPOEIRA OF BRAZIL

1980, 10 min., color, film, video
Distributor: WGBH-TV, Boston
Producer/Director: Warrington Hudlin
Cinematographer: Daniel Dawson

Performance of the Afro-Brazilian martial art in which men dance on their hands and fight with their feet.

CAPRICCIO ESPAGNOL

1941, 20 min., color, film
Distributor: Dance Films Association (for members only)
Producer: Warner Brothers Pictures
Director: Jean Negulesco
Dance Company: Ballet Russe de Monte Carlo
Choreographers: Leonide Massine, Argentinita
Principal Dancers: Tamara Toumanova, Alexandra Danilova, Frederic Franklin, Andre Eglevsky, Leonide Massine
Composer: Nicholas Rimsky-Korsakov

Set/Costume Designer: Mariano Andreu

The 1939 ballet of five divertissements, inspired by the regional rhythms and folk dance of Spain: ALBORADO, a dance of Galicia; VARIATION, a Seguidillas, from New Castile played with castanets; ALBORADO, a comic interlude; GYPSY SCENE AND DANCE; and FANDANGO ASTURIANA.

CARMEN

> 1984, 99 min., color, film, video
> Distributors: Swank, Cinematheque
> Producer: Orion, Emiliano Piedra
> Director: Carlos Saura
> Choreographer/Dancer: Antonio Gades
> Principal Dancers: Cristina Hoyos, Laura Del Sol
> Composers: Paco Da Lucia, Georges Bizet

This second in the flamenco trilogy made by the Spanish director Carlos Saura with Antonio Gades toys with the structure of a play-within-a-play. Carmen, the original femme fatale, exercises her erotic skills both on and off stage. For Hollywood's 1948 version of the story, see THE LOVES OF CARMEN starring Rita Hayworth and Glenn Ford.

CARMEN (Bolshoi Ballet)

> 1973, 73 min., color, film, video
> Distributor: Kultur #1200
> Producer: Corinth
> Choreographers: Alberto Alonso, Vladimir Vasiliev, Marius Petipa, Michel Fokine
> Director: Vadim Derbenev
> Principal Dancers: Maya Plisetskaya, Nikolai Fadeyechev
> Dance Company: Bolshoi Ballet
> Composers: Georges Bizet, Alexander Glazunov, J.S. Bach, Rodion Shchedrin, Camille Saint-Saens

The Russian ballerina Maya Plisetskaya stars in excerpts from her most famous roles with CARMEN, choreographed by a Cuban and a Russian, as the centerpiece. Also included are scenes from RAYMONDA, PRELUDE, and DYING SWAN.

CARNIVAL OF RHYTHM

> 1941, 20 min., b&w, film
> Distributor: Dance Films Association (for members only)
> Producer: Warner Brothers
> Director: Jean Negulesco
> Choreographer/Dancer: Katherine Dunham
> Principal Dancers: Katherine Dunham, Talley Beatty, Archie Savage, Lavinia Williams, Syvilla Fort

Features songs and dances from Brazil, a South American Indian courtship dance and a dance from Africa, as presented by the influential black dancer/researcher. Among the dances are CIUDADE MARAVILLOSA, LOS INDIOS, BATUCADA, and ADEUS TERRAS.

CAROLE MORISSEAU AND THE DETROIT
CITY DANCE COMPANY

> 1979, 14 min., color, film
> Distributor/Producer: Sue Marx
> Choreographer: Carole Morisseau
> Photographer/Editor: Robert Handley
> Dance Company: Detroit City Dance Company

EMMY Award, CINE Golden Eagle Award, 1980

Young company in rehearsal and in an opening night performance with the choreographer expressing her views about dance and her dreams for her company.

THE CAROLINA SHAG

> 1987, 90 min., color, video
> Distributor/Producer: Jim Forest
> Teachers: Charlie Womble, Jackie McGee

National professional champions of the shag, a popular social dance in the Southeast, break down all its steps with a final demonstration.

THE CATHERINE WHEEL

> 1982, 90 min., color, video
> Distributor: HBO #3397
> Producer: Alan Yentob for National Video Corporation
> Choreographer/Director: Twyla Tharp
> Dance Company: Twyla Tharp Dance Company
> Composer: David Byrne
> Editor: Rebecca Allen

Originally designed for Broadway, refashioned for television, using animation, computer-generated figures, shadow play, and reverse action, the production grew out of Twyla Tharp's fascination for Saint Catherine, the 4th-century martyr condemned to die on a spiked wheel.

CAUGHT

> 1987, 8 min., b&w, video
> Distributor/Producer/Director: Roberto Romano
> Choreographer/Dancer: David Parsons
> Composer: Robert Fripp

Solo shot in an urban ruin with the strobe-lit images of the former Paul Taylor dancer in leaping, hurtling flight.

CAVALCADE OF DANCE

> 1941, 10 min., b&w, film
> Distributor: Dance Films Association (for members only)
> Producer: Warner Brothers Pictures
> Director: Jean Negulesco
> Principal Dancers: Veloz and Yolanda

Presentation of social dances by a famous ballroom team in the 1940s: MAXIXE from Brazil, ONE STEP, TANGO from Argentina, CHARLESTON, BLACK BOTTOM, JITTERBUG, RUMBA, CHIAPENECAS (Mexican waltz). With narration.

CELEBRATION: A HISTORY OF THE ROYAL BALLET

> 1989, 50 min., color, video
> Distributor: Home Vision
> Producer: Jaras Entertainment/IFPA Ltd.
> Director: Jolyon Winhurst
> Choreographers: Frederick Ashton, Kenneth MacMillan, Robert Helpmann, Lynn Taylor Corbett
> Dance Company: Royal Ballet
> Composers: Francois Joseph Herold, Adolphe Adam, Edward Deldevez, Leon Minkus
> Narrator: James Mason
> Dance on Camera Festival, Silver Award, 1990

Documentary on Sadler's Wells Ballet and its brilliant, strong-willed founder, Dame Ninette de Valois, combines performances, rehearsals, interviews, and archival footage from company performances. Excerpts from POLONIA, GISELLE, LA FILLE MAL GARDEE, PAQUITA, THREE PICTURES, and ELITE SYNCOPATIONS.

CELEBRATION IN MONTE CARLO

  1990, 52 min., color, video
  Distributor: Wish Upon Productions
  Producer: Joe Wishy
  Director: Merrill Brockway
  Choreographers: Antony Tudor, George Balanchine, Boris Eifman, Michel Fokine, John Neumeier
  Dance Company: Ballet of Monte Carlo
  Composers: Jacques Offenbach, Gustav Mahler, Peter Ilyich Tchaikovsky, Anton Dvorak, Carl Maria von Weber

Performance excerpts from GAITE PARISIENNE, MAHLER'S TENTH SYMPHONY, SPECTRE DE LA ROSE, LEAVES ARE FADING, DVORAK, THEME AND VARIATIONS, and INTRIGUES OF LOVE, filmed in Monaco.

A CELEBRATION OF ROCK

  1971, 28 min., color, video
  Distributor: Orion Enterprises
  Producer/Director: Richard Carter for WTTW, Chicago
  Choreographer: Gus Giordano
  Dance Company: Gus Giordano Dance Company

Features THE MATRIARCH, a jazz ballet about a blind girl, her lover, and her overprotective mother, set to the music of IN A GADA DA VIDA performed by Chicago's Onstage Majority, and two short jazz pieces, SCORPIO and THE GETAWAY.

CERBERUS

  1978, 30 min., color, video
  Distributor: Solaris
  Producer/Choreographer/Dancer/Editor: Henry Smith
  Director/Editor: Skip Sweeney
  Principal Dancers: Sebastian Ellison, Kris Varjan, Harvey Konigsberg, Miguel Rivera
  Composer: Teiji Ito

In this fantasy shot near San Francisco, Henry Smith populates the woods and beaches of northern California with shamans, warriors, a sword-wielding Angel of Death, and the hero, Cerberus, the "clown warrior." Combining elements of Japanese theatre, dance and martial arts, Cerberus exposes his relationships: to himself, his enemies, and his gods.

LA CHAMBRE

  1988, 9:12 min., b&w, video
  Distributor: APA
  Producers: L'Esquisse, Ina, La Sept, Maison de la Culture du Havre
  Choreographers: Joelle Bouvier, Regis Obadia

In this French surreal short reminiscent of the films of the fifties, women sulk on chairs fixed on the wall of an empty room. They break from their passivity momentarily, only to return to an introspective collective.

CHANCE DANCE

  1976, 16 min., b&w, film, video
  Distributor: University of California Extension Media Center
  Producer/Writer: Trudi Ferguson
  Director: Jim Stodell
  Dance on Camera Festival, 1978 Merit Certificate

Three pairs of dancers demonstrate the notion of chance or randomness in dance.

CHANGING STEPS

  1989, 35 min., color/b&w, video
  Distributor: Cunningham Dance Foundation
  Producers: Cunningham Dance Foundation, La Sept
  Directors: Elliot Caplan, Merce Cunningham
  Dance Company: Merce Cunningham Dance Company
  Composer: John Cage
  Music: "Cartridge Music"
  Dance on Camera Festival, 1990 Gold Award

Choreographed in 1973, ten solos, adapted for television in 1988, are intercut with footage of a West German tour, and flashbacks of the original cast in rehearsal.

CHANNELS/INSERTS

  1982, 32 min., color, film, video
  Distributor/Producer: Cunningham Dance Foundation
  Director: Charles Atlas
  Choreographer: Merce Cunningham
  Dance Company: Merce Cunningham Dance Company
  Composer: David Tudor

The directors were interested in placing the cast and the scenes in such a way as to give the sense of dual events happening concurrently. They divided the studio into sixteen possible areas for dancing. Cunningham then applied the I Ching to determine the order in which the divisions were used. Atlas employed cross-cutting to indicate the simultaneity of events, as well as travelling mattes or wipes to allow for diversity in the continuity of the image.

CHARLES WEIDMAN: ON HIS OWN

  1990, 59 min., color, b&w, video
  Distributor: Dance Horizons Video
  Producer: Charles Weidman Dance Foundation
  Directors: Virginia Brooks, Janet Mendelsohn
  Choreographer: Charles Weidman
  Principal Dancers: Charles Weidman, Doris Humphrey
  Narrator: Alwin Nikolais
  Composers: Johannes Brahms, Johann Sebastian Bach, Roy Harris, Lionel Nowak
  Dance on Camera Festival, 1991 Silver Award; Dance Screen, 1990 Special Prize of the Jury

Charles Weidman: On His Own
Charles Weidman in A House Divided. *Photo by Gerda Peterich.*

Career of modern dance pioneer Charles Weidman is traced from his roots in Lincoln, Nebraska, to the last work he choreographed in 1974; through the period as performer with Denishawn and his renowned association with Doris Humphrey to the last thirty years on his own.

CHARLESTON
   1927, 20 min., b&w, film
   Distributor: Biograph
   Director: Jean Renoir
   Principal Dancers: Catherine Hessling, A. Cerf
One of the first efforts by the French director Jean Renoir. A silent, comic fantasy with gyrating semi-nude dancers.

CHARMAINE'S HAWAIIAN/TAHITIAN VIDEO PEARLS
   1990, 80 min., color, video
   Distributor/Producer/Dancer: Charmaine
Forty routines showing Tahitian aprimas and oteas, Hawaiian ancient, modern, and religious sit-down hulas with notes on history and costuming.

CHE CHE KULE: EXERCISES FOR KIDS
   1990, 59 min., color, video
   Distributor: Mica
   Producer: Bayne Williams Film Co.
   Choreographer/Dancer: Arthur Hall
   Editor: Bruce Williams

Children's class designed by Afro-American Arthur Hall and filmed in two Vermont elementary schools. Title refers to the Ghanaian dance evocative of the movements of rowing and boating.

CHIANG CHING: A DANCE JOURNEY
   1982, 30 min., color, film, video
   Distributor: University of California Extension Media Center
   Director/Producer: Lana Pih Jokel
   Choreographer/Dancer: Chiang Ching
   Dance Film Festival, Asian-American International Film Festival Honoree, Hong Kong Film Festival Honoree

A portrait of a talented Chinese-American dancer/choreographer, Chiang Ching. Traces her childhood in China, where she trained at the Peking Dance Academy and became a teenage movie star in Hong Kong. Several performances filmed in New York City and during a triumphant return visit to China reveal her style, which combines the rigor of the traditional Chinese dance with the free expression of the West.

Che Che Kule: Exercises for Kids
Arthur Hall dancing "Obatata" at Townsend, VI. Photo by Bruce B. Williams. Photo courtesy MICA.

CHILDREN DANCE

1970, 14 min., b&w, film
Distributor: University of California Extension
Media Center
Producer/Director/Dance Teacher:
Geraldine Diamondstein
Dance Teacher/Director: Naima Prevots

Children, ages five to nine, express their feelings, moods and ideas through rhythmic patterns and improvisations.

THE CHILDREN OF THEATRE STREET

1978, 92 min., color, film, video
Distributors: Kino, Kultur #1111
Producer/Directors: Earl Mack, Jean Dalyrmple for
Mack-Vaganova
Co-director: Robert Dornhelm
Artistic Director: Oleg Briansky
Principal Dancers: Galina Mezentseva,
Konstantin Zaklinsky
Narrator: Princess Grace
Cinematographer: Karl Kofler
Writer: Beth Gutcheon

Nominated for an Academy Award, this documentary on one of the world's finest ballet schools, the Vaganova Choreographic Institute (the Kirov School) in Leningrad, focuses on three students, at different stages of development, examining the intense competition for admission, and the eight years of subsequent training.

CHILDREN ON THE HILL

Series: Educational Performance Collection
1982, 20 min., color, video
Distributor/Producer: Dance Notation Bureau
Choreographer/Dancer: Moses Pendleton
Composers: Budd, Palmer/Beleu, Air, King Sunny Ade and
The African Beats, Mighty Diamonds, Material

Taped performance at City College starring The Grub, a lumpy being in a green padded costume and Mojo, a composite character choreographed by one of the founders of Pilobolus. Comes with an introductory article on Labanotation, intermediate/advanced level notated score by Terri Richards, critical text, and study/performance rights to the dance.

CHILDREN'S DANCE

1967–1968, 9 min., b&w, color, film
Distributor: Pennstate #EO1413, EO1608
Producer: A. M. Dauer for Wissen

Recorded in Tibet, performance of "bSilIDan-Gans-Ri," "sPugu' irtsed-than," and "rGyug-rtsed," children's folk dances with movements from games and pastimes accompanied by lute and flute.

CHILDREN'S DANCE

1982, 20 min., color, film
Distributor: National Council for American-Soviet
Friendship
Dance Company: Georgian Dance Company of the USSR

No description available.

CHILDREN'S DANCES

1965, 9 min., color, film
Distributor: Pennstate #EO1023
Producer: P. Fuchs for Wissen

Ten Dangaleat girls in Chad present seven dances of their own tribe and those of neighboring Arabs and Dadjo.

CHINESE FOLK ARTS

1976, 24 min., color, video
Distributor: Iowa State University
Producer: Free China Film Syndicate

Introduces dragon and lion dances along with the traditional folk arts of shadow puppetry, embroidery, paper cutting, kite flying, lanterns, and puppet shows.

CHINESE, KOREAN AND JAPANESE DANCE

1964, 30 min., color, film
Distributor: Asia Society
Producers: Bureau of Audio-Visual Instruction, New York
City Board of Education
Director: Clifford Ettinger
Cinematographer: Rosario Capotosto
Dancers: Dr. Wan-kyung Cho, Hu Hung-yen,
Hu Yung-fang, Suzushi Hanayagi
Narrator: Beate Gordon

Traditional steps and patterns explained by impresario Beate Gordon with performances of SORCERESS DANCE and the OLD MAN'S DANCE (Korea); WORD DANCE and the SCARF DANCE (Chinese); and Kabuki (Japan).

CHOICE CHANCE WOMAN DANCE

1971, 44 min., color, film
Distributors: Film-maker's Coop, Canyon
Director: Ed Emshwiller
Principal Dancers: Carolyn Carlson, Becky Arnold,
Susan Lazarus
Composers: Joan Friedman, David Borden, Steve Drews

A meditation, typical of its time, considering women in their various states of awareness while alone, with a child, and in a professional circumstance. A group improvisation inspired by the paradoxes and dilemmas confronting women today.

THE CHOPI TIMBILA DANCE

1980, 40 min., color, film, video
Distributor: Pennstate
Producer: Gei Zantzinger for Wissen
Writer/Director/Narrator: Andrew Tracey

African music specialist Andrew Tracey and Mozambican composer Venancio Mbande explain the elements of Chopi xylophone orchestral music and its relationship to mgodo, a suite of movements.

A CHOREOGRAPHER AT WORK: JOHN BUTLER

Series: A Time to Dance #4
1960, 29 min., b&w, film, video
Distributor: Indiana University
Producer: Jac Venza for WGBH-TV Boston

Principal Dancers: Glen Tetley, Carmen de Lavallade, James Moore, Bambi Linn
Choreographer: John Butler

Teacher/commentator Martha Myers and John Butler discuss how a choreographer works and demonstrates with members of his company the elements of rhythm, space, and theme with excerpts from his THREE PROMENADES WITH THE LORD.

CHOREOGRAPHY

1964, 11 min., b&w, film
Distributor: The Cinema Guild
Producers: J. Marks., LehrFilm-Institut
Director: Richard Scheinflug
Choreographer/Dancers: Heinz Claus, Christa Kempf
Composer: J. Sebastian Bach

A documentary on a ballet choreographer's creative process and vision, concluding with a performance.

CHRYSALIS

1973, 21:30 min., color, film
Distributors: Canyon, Museum at Large
Director/Sound-Score: Ed Emshwiller
Choreographer: Alwin Nikolais
Dance Company: Nikolais Dance Company

Improvisation altered in post-production by the late Californian filmmaker Ed Emshwiller, backed by a sound score made with the voices of the dancers.

CHUCK DAVIS: DANCING THROUGH WEST AFRICA

1987, 28 min., color, film, video
Distributor: Filmaker's Library
Choreographer: Chuck Davis
Director: Gorham Kindem
Dance Company: African American Dance Ensemble
Dance on Camera Festival, 1987 Honorable Mention, CINE Golden Eagle

Tour of Chuck Davis' African American Dance Ensemble through Senegal and Gambia, focusing on three tribes: Wolof, Mandinka, and Diola and their warmth and respect for dance. Concludes with a community performance celebrating peace and love.

CINDERELLA (Berlin Comic Opera)

1987, 75 min., color, video
Distributor: V.I.E.W.
Producers: Deutsche Fersefunk and Defa Studio Film
Choreographer: Tom Schilling
Principal Dancers: Hannelore Bey (Cinderella), Roland Gawlick
Dance Company: Berlin Comic Opera Ballet
Composer: Sergei Prokofiev

Performance documentary of this three-act classic ballet based on the fairy tale by the 17th-century poet Charles Perrault about a victim of child abuse who's pursued by a prince she happens to meet at the one ball she ever attends.

CINDERELLA (Bolshoi Ballet)

1961, 96 min., color, film, video
Distributors: Corinth Films, Kultur (81 min. video)
Producer: Gorky Film Studios
Directors: Alexander Row, Rostislav Zakharov
Choreographer: Rostislav Zakharov
Principal Dancers: Raisa Struchkova, Gennadi Lediakh, Ekaterina Maximova
Dance Company: Bolshoi Ballet
Composer: Sergei Prokofiev

The 1945 version of the fairy tale described above, filmed with multiple cameras with the orchestra of the State Academic Bolshoi Theatre.

CINDERELLA (Lyon Opera Ballet)

1990, 87 min., color, video
Distributors: Home Vision #CIN02, Pioneer (laserdisk)
Producer: Reiner Moritz
Director: Mans Reutersward
Choreographer: Maguy Marin
Dance Company: Lyon Opera Ballet
Composer: Sergei Prokofiev

This modern rendition of the classic fairy tale (described above) sets the ballet in a doll's house with all the masked characters only as mobile as their wooden bodies will allow. Swedish director Mans Reutersward heightens the vulnerability of this approach by following the tale largely with close-ups.

CINDERELLA (Paris Opera Ballet)

1989, 125 min. color, video
Distributor: Pioneer (laserdisk)
Producer: La Sept and SFP of Paris and National Video Corporation of London
Dance Company: Paris Opera Ballet
Producer/Director/Choreographer: Rudolf Nureyev
Director: Colin Nears
Principal Dancers: Sylvie Guillem, Charles Jude, Isabelle Guerin, Monique Loudieres
Composer: Sergei Prokofiev
Set Designer: Petrika Ionesco

Cinderella this time escapes her miserable existence at home to pursue the professional escapism of Hollywood. Set in the 1930's with giant pin-up girls and art deco facades, the ballet frolics around the dream of immediate and complete salvation from mediocrity. For other versions of Perrault's tale, look for the 1964 Hollywood feature film starring Ginger Rogers, and Walt Disney's animated film of 1950.

CIRCLE OF THE SUN

1960, 30 min., color, film
Distributor: University of California Extension Media Center
Producer: Tom Daly for National Film Board of Canada
Director: Colin Low

The Blood Indians of Alberta, Canada dance, pow wow, and confer on the power of circles. The SUN DANCE is captured on film for the first time.

CIRCLES-CYCLES KATHAK DANCE

1988, 28 min., color, film, video
Distributor: University of California Media Extension Center
Producer: Robert Gottlieb
Principal Dancers: Shawati Sen, Daksha Sheith, Jai Kishan
Narrator: Sakir Russain
Dance on Camera Festival, 1989 Honorable Mention

This documentary explores the traditions of kathak, the 1,000-year-old, classical dance of northern India with excerpts of the vast repertoire that reflects influences of both Hindu and Islamic cultures.

CIRLCES II

1972, 12 min., color, film, video
Distributors: Perspective Films, Doris Chase/Catalyst Films
Producers: Frank Olney, Robert Brown
Director: Doris Chase
Choreographer: Mary Staton
Dance Company: Mary Staton Ensemble of Seattle
Composer: William O. Smith
Avant Garde Festival, New York, 1972; CINE Golden Eagle, 1973; American Film Festival, NYC, 1973

Dancers move around giant fiberglass circles created by a director absorbed with color and spatial relationships. Also, see CIRCLES I distributed and directed by Doris Chase, who choreographed circles to revolve in, around, and through each other in time to the score by Morton Subotnik.

CIRCUMCISION

1965, 16 min., color, film
Distributor: Pennstate #EOO950
Producer: Wissen

As part of the public circumcision ceremony, women and girls of the Haddad tribe perform the *goshele* dance in front of the house where the boys are secluded for seven days. Filmed in Southern Wadai in Central Sudan, Africa.

CLASSICAL BALLET

Series: A Time to Dance #2
1960, 29 min., b&w, film, video
Distributor: Indiana University
Producer: Jac Venza for WNET/13
Choreographers: Marius Petipa, Lev Ivanov, Louis Merante
Principal Dancers: Maria Tallchief, Andre Eglevsky, Linda Yourth, George Li
Composers: Peter Ilyich Tchaikovsky, Leo Delibes

Martha Myers discusses the rules of classical ballet. Students of the Eglevsky school demonstrate the essential ballet steps and positions. Maria Tallchief and Andre Eglevsky perform a pas de deux from SWAN LAKE and Louis Merante's 1876 SYLVIA. Another pas de deux from Marius Petipa's SLEEPING BEAUTY is performed by Linda Yourth and George Li, who also performs the BLUE BIRD male variation.

CLINIC OF STUMBLE

1948, 13 min., color, film
Distributors: Film-maker's Coop, Museum of Modern Art
Producer/Directors: Sidney Peterson, Hy Hirsh
Choreographer: Marian Van Tuyl

Principal Dancers: Beth Osgood, Barbara Bennion, Edith Wiener
Set Designer: Arch Lauterer
Composer: Gregory Tucker
Dance on Camera Festival, 1978 Merit Award

An experiment in superimposition, with three women in long dresses and bonnets riding scooters, sitting, reading, dancing alone and together in a space dressed with exotic lamps.

CLOUD DANCE

1980, 13 min., color, film
Distributor: Filmmaker's Cooperative
Directors: Robyn Brentano, Andrew Horn
Choreographer/Dancer: Andrew De Groat
Poet: Christopher Knowles
Sculptor: Lenore Tawney
Composer: Michael Galasso

A minimalist romp in a translucent, sculptural maze of 13,000 threads installed in the New Jersey State Museum.

THE CLOWN WITHIN

1975, 30 min., color, video
Distributor: Ron Bozman
Producer/Directors: Bill Colville, Ron Bozman
Mime: Jacques LeCog
Dance Video and Film Festival, 1979 Merit Award

A documentary of the Paris-based mime, Jacques LeCoq, with footage of a teaching workshop, a lecture-performance and an interview.

COAST ZONE

1983, 27 min., color, film, video
Distributor/Producer: Cunningham Dance Foundation
Choreographer: Merce Cunningham
Director: Charles Atlas
Composer: Larry Austin and the Beachcombers
Dance Company: Merce Cunningham Dance Company
Finalist, American Film Festival

Merce Cunningham and Charles Atlas explore the layering possibilities of video by contrasting back- and foreground figures dancing in the vaulted Synod House of the Cathedral of St. John the Divine. The camera moves around the thirteen dancers, at one point circling the action in a single trajectory.

CODEX

1988, 26 min., color, video
Distributor: Actions et Prospectives Audiovisuelles
Producer: Gebeon with Canal and La Sept
Choreographer/Director/Dancer: Philippe Decoufle
Composer: Hugues de Courson
Principal Dancers: Christophe Salengro, Catherine Savy, Samuel Borne
Set Designer: Thierry de Brouckere

A graphic poem developed with a romanticism of the absurd by a French team. Awarded the prize for being the most original program by the lst Grand Prix International de Video Danse organized by UNESCO and the International Musik Zentrum (IMZ) of Vienna.

THE COLLABORATORS: CAGE, CUNNINGHAM, RAUSCHENBERG

1987, 55 min., color, video
Distributor: Cunningham Dance Foundation
Producer: KETC Public TV
Choreographer: Merce Cunningham
Dance Company: Merce Cunningham Dance Company
Composer: John Cage

A discussion among the choreographer and his longtime collaborators painter Robert Rauschenberg and composer John Cage is moderated by dance critic David Vaughan with archival footage of TRAVELOGUE, MINUTIAE, and ANTIC MEET intercut throughout. COAST ZONE, a piece choreographed in 1983, completes the program.

COLOR IN DANCE

1973, 5 min., color, film
Distributor: University of Iowa

A still camera catches the movements of dancers behind a screen, their shadows and effects from three colored spotlights.

COMMITMENT: TWO PORTRAITS

Series: Alive from Off Center
1989, 12 min., b&w and color, video
Distributor: Antenna
Producer: Alive from Off Center/KCET
Choreographer/Dancer: Blondell Cummings
Director: Bernar Herbert
Composers: Bill Vorn, Gaetan Gravel
Dance on Camera Festival, 1989 Honorable Mention

An introspective solo for modern dancer Blondell Cummings set in a kitchen, followed by a trio dressed in nuns' habits co-existing in a lunar landscape.

THE COMPANY

1984, 9:30 min., color, video
Distributor: Woodbury/Ririe Co.
Producer: KUTV-TV
Principal Dancers/Teachers: Joan Woodbury, Shirley Ririe
Dance on Camera Festival, 1985 Honorable Mention

Co-founders of a modern company based at the University of Utah work with their students.

COMPLETE FLAMENCO DANCE TECHNIQUE (8 videos)

1986, 90 min. each, color, video
Distributor/Producer/Choreographer/Dancer: Teo Morca
Emmy Award

Six videos describing a balanced approach to learning Spanish dance, its rhythmic structure, and style from an American teacher, known for his vast repertoire. Also available from Teo Morca: TEO MORCA IN SOLO CONCERT and ANTOLOGIA FLAMENCA.

THE CONCERT

1987, 12 min., color, video
Distributor: Coe Film
Producer: Pyramid Films
Principal Dancer: Julian Chagrin

Academy Award Nomination

Cavorting on the black and white pavement behind London's Royal Albert Hall, a pianist dances on his "keyboard" with a charm and whimsy reminiscent of Charlie Chaplin.

COPLAND PORTRAIT

1975, 29 min., color, film
Distributor/Producer: National Audio Visual Center
Producer: United States Information Agency
Choreographer: Eugene Loring
Dance Company: American Ballet Theatre
Blue Ribbon, American Film Festival

A documentary about the composer Aaron Copland, born in Brooklyn in 1900, with musical excerpts from his APPALACHIAN SPRING, RODEO, and a dance sequence from BILLY THE KID.

COPPELIA – ACT II

1967, 26 min., b&w, video
Distributor: Orion Enterprises
Producer: WTTW Chicago
Director: Richard Carter
Choreographers: Lev Ivanov, Enrico Cecchetti, adapted by Richard Ellis and Christine Duboulay
Composer: Leo Delibes
Dance Company: Illinois Ballet

The second act of the 1870 ballet, based on E.T.A. Hoffmann's fairy tale DER SANDMAN, about a mechanical doll in the mysterious workshop of Dr. Coppelius.

CORTEGE OF EAGLES

Series: Three by Martha Graham, #2
1969, 38 min., color, film, video
Distributor: Pyramid
Producers: John Houseman and H.R. Poindexter
Director: Dave Wilson
Choreographer/Dancer: Martha Graham
Principal Dancers: Martha Graham, Bertram Ross, Robert Cohan, Clive Thompson, Mary Hinkson, Takako Asakawa
Dance Company: Martha Graham Dance Company
Composer: Eugene Lester

Martha Graham as Queen Hecuba, the wife of King Priam, wrestles with the inevitable collapse of her kingdom, ancient Troy. Choked by a sense of doom, the queen is driven to violence.

COSTUMING – SKIRT AND ACCESSORIES (5 videos)

1988, 120 min., color, video
Distributor/Producer/Narrator: Chandra of Damascus

Lecture/demonstration covering costume construction techniques and ideas for Middle Eastern dance. The same distributor/producer carries other two-hour lecture/demonstrations: BEAD TECHNIQUES FOR COSTUMING, COSTUMING – DESIGN CONSIDERATIONS FOR ADVANCED COSTUMERS, BRA AND BELT CONSTRUCTION CLASS and a narrated video of items for sale, showing costumes on models in motion: CHANDRA'S DANCE EXTRAVAGANZA VIDEO CATALOG, 85 min.

THE COTTON CLUB

1984, 127 min., color, video
Distributor: Swank (retail outlets)
Producer: Robert Evans for Orion
Director/Writer: Francis Coppola
Choreographer/Dancers: Gregory and Maurice Hines,
Charles Honi Coles
Choreographers: Michael Smuin, Henry LeTang
Composers: Duke Ellington, Harry Akst-Grant Clarke,
Joseph Meyer, Roger Wolfe Kahan
Writers: William Kennedy, Mario Puzo

This 47-million-dollar feature, starring Richard Gere, Diane
Lane, Nicolas Cage, offers top-notch tap dancing and loving,
amidst dubious business associations carried on in one of
Harlem's most popular nightclubs of the late 1920s. Talent triumphs despite the climate of racism and crime.

COUNTRY CORNERS

1976, 27 min., color, film, video
Distributor: Phoenix Films
Producers: Robert Fiore, Richard Nevell with
White Mountain Films
Principal Dancer: Ed Larkin
1977 Dance Films Festival, first place in folk/ethnic category

Traces the history of contra dance back to the arrival of the
first settlers in New England, with Ed Larkin and his dancers
of East Bethel, Vermont, presenting the traditional and less
orthodox forms.

COURT DANCE: TAIHEIRAKU & ETENRAKU (2 films)

1972, 44 & 30 min., color, film
Distributor: Japan Foundation
Producer: EC Japan Archives

Taiheiraku, a dance of eternal peace, is performed by the music
department of the Imperial Household. Four dancers, armed
with Chinese-style helmets, swords, and spears, usher in the
age of peace. The second film features the court music of
Etenraku in which the winds and percussion gradually drop
out, leaving the Koto and Biwa strings in a solo role.

CREATION OF THE WORLD: A SAMBA OPERA

1978, 56 min., color, film, video
Distributor: The Cinema Guild
Director: Vera De Figueiredo
Venice People's Award, Venice International Film Festival

Photographed during the carnival in Rio de Janeiro, the Beija
Flor Samba School sets the story of genesis, according to Yoruba mythology, to dance, song, and drum.

CREOLE GISELLE (Dance Theatre of Harlem)

1986, 60 min., color, video
Distributor: Herman Krawitz
Producers: Danmarks Radio, WNET-TV 13
Director: Thomas Grimm
Choreographers: Jean Coralli, Jules Perrot,
Frederick Franklin
Principal Dancers: Virginia Johnson, Eddie Shellman,
Lowell Smith

Dance Company: Dance Theatre of Harlem
Composer: Adolphe Adam
Costume/Set Designer: Carl Michel

Transplants the classic story ballet, originally set in Europe,
to New Orleans and layers it with a suggestion of the class
war between blacks in the 1800s.

CRIME PAYS

1984, 5 min., color, video
Distributor/Choreographer: Claudia Murphey
Director: Michael Moser
Composers: Daryl Hall and John Oates
Dance on Camera Festival, 1985 Award

A modern dance inspired by the body language of prisoners.

Cross Body Ride
David Zambrano and Donald Fleming. Photo by Robert Flynt.

CROSS BODY RIDE

1988, 12 min., color, film
Distributor/Director/Choreographer: Jeff McMahon
Principal Dancers: David Zambrano, Donald Fleming
Composer: Charles Nieland

Sensual play of two men beside the Caribbean sea shifts in-
and outside with black-and-white footage intercut with
color and still photographs.

CULTIC DANCES IN A BUDDHIST PAGODA NEAR HUE

1963, 20 min., color, film
Distributor: Pennstate #EO2027
Producer: R. Kaufman for Wissen

Initiated by a Buddhist priest, this ceremony in Vietnam is
dominated by women dancing before an altar, who claim to
have been ordered to do so by ghosts.

CUNNINGHAM DANCE TECHNIQUE: ELEMENTARY LEVEL

1985, 35 min., color, video
Distributor/Producer: Cunningham Dance Foundation

Narrator/Choreographer: Merce Cunningham
Director: Elliot Caplan
Principal Dancers: Alison Cutri, Jill Diamond, Nancy Langsner, Kate Troughton
Teachers: Susan Alexander, Ruth Barnes, Merce Cunningham, June Finch, Susana Hayman-Chaffey, Chris Komar

Cunningham dancers and teachers demonstrate sequential exercises and simple combinations of movements, intercut with footage of classes. Merce Cunningham, whose no-nonsense technique has been evolving since 1959, offers a running commentary.

CUNNINGHAM DANCE TECHNIQUE: INTERMEDIATE LEVEL

1987, 55 min., color, video
Distributor/Producer: Cunningham Dance Foundation
Directors: Elliot Caplan and Merce Cunningham
Teachers: Merce Cunningham, Diane Frank, Catherine Kerr, Chris Komar, Robert Kovich, Rob Remley
Principal Dancers: Heidi Kreusch, David Kulick, Larissa McGoldrick, Dennis O'Connor, Yukie Okuyama, Carol Teitelbaum

The second in the educational series, this video offers a narrated technique class set in the Westbeth studio in New York.

CUP/SAUCER/TWO DANCERS/RADIO

1965/1983, 23 min., color, film
Distributor: Film-maker's Coop
Director: Jonas Mekas
Choreographer/Dancers: Kenneth King, Phoebe Neville

This performance, recorded in 1965 and later translated into a film, gives equal emphasis to all the elements listed in the title. Phoebe Neville, dressed in bra, girdle, curlers and toe shoes, marches across the floor on pointe with a radio clasped to her ear. King, dressed in an undershirt and shorts and a black tie, does calisthenics.

CURTAIN UP

1982, 27 min., color, film
Distributor: International Film Bureau
Producers: Royal Opera House, Charles Thompson
Director: Jolyon Winhurst
Choreographers: Frederick Ashton, Kenneth MacMillan, Marius Petipa, Enrico Cecchetti
Principal Dancers: David Ashmole, Desmond Kelly, Margaret Barbieri, Marion Tate, Susan Crow, David Bintley
Dance Company: Sadler's Wells Ballet
Composers: Leo Delibes, Scott Joplin, Andre Messager, Francois Joseph Herold

Discussions about touring, training, and the importance of professionalism. Excerpts from COPPELIA (Petipa and Cecchetti/Delibes), ELITE SYNCOPATIONS (MacMillan/Joplin), THE TWO PIGEONS (Ashton/Messager), LA FILLE MAL GARDEE (Ashton/Herold). Guide available with ballet synopsis and short histories of the Sadler's Wells Ballet and of ballet.

DAMBIO FESTIVAL DANCE FROM CENTRAL SUDAN

1965, 9 min., color, film
Distributor: Pennstate #EO1013

Producer: Wissen

Women performing at the annual feast of the *margai* for the Diongor clan in Chad, evidently tipsy from too much millet beer, attempt to keep the beat in this festival dance. Quarrels break out and the dance dissolves.

THE DANCE

1960, 74 min., b&w, film
Distributor: The Cinema Guild
Producers: Dr. Heinz Weris, J. Marks for Deutsche Wochenschau
Director: Heinrich Weidman
Choreographers: Katherine Dunham, Mary Wigman, Kurt Jooss, Harald Kreutzberg, Alan Carter, Dore Hoyer
Principal Dancers: Katherine Dunham, Ludmilla Tcherina, John Kriza, Melissa Hayden, Dore Hoyer, Harald Kreutzberg
Dance Company: Kurt Jooss
Composer: Frederick Cohen
Mime: Marcel Marceau
Dance Teacher: Lola Roget

This historical documentary includes the work of Katherine Dunham based on native dances of Africa, continues with folk dances from fifteen nations, social dances (waltz, fox-trot and mambo), and culminates with ballet and modern performances. Mary Wigman, the German choreographer, appears in a brief sequence teaching her students. Kurt Jooss' company performs the classic anti-war ballet THE GREEN TABLE.

THE DANCE

Series: Aujourd'Hui en France
1977, 26 min., color, film
Distributor: Society for French American Cultural Services (FACSEA)
Choreographer: Carolyn Carlson
Dance Teacher: Claude Bessy
Principal Dancers: Wilfrid Piollet, Jean Guizerox

An educational documentary with four episodes: THE DANCE, A FESTIVAL, on ballroom and popular dance; THE DANCE: AN EXPRESSION, about Carolyn Carlson, an American choreographer who directs the Theatrical Research Group of the Paris Opera; THE DANCE: AN ART, about the Paris Opera ballet school; DANCING IS LIVING, with a pas de deux performed by principals of the Paris Opera Ballet.

DANCE: A REFLECTION OF OUR TIMES

Series: USA Series
1960, 29 min., b&w, film, video
Distributor: Indiana University
Producer: Jac Venza for WNET/13
Principal Dancers: John Kriza, Ruth Ann Koesun, Lupe Serrano, Sallie Wilson, Scott Douglas, Enrique Martinez
Dance Company: American Ballet Theatre

Herbert Ross, dancer, choreographer, and the producer of such feature films as THE TURNING POINT and DANCERS, evaluates dance as a means of social commentary, in light of artists' efforts in other disciplines. Members of American Ballet Theatre perform excerpts from Ross' PAEON (1957), and CAPRICHOS (1949), based on Goya's etchings of man's weaknesses.

DANCE AND HUMAN HISTORY

Series: Movement Style and Culture Series
1974, 40 min., color, film
Distributor: University of California Extension Media Center
Producer/Directors: Alan Lomax, Forrestine Paulay

Analyzing dance from a geometric perspective, Alan Lomax explains his theory, polished over a ten-year, cross-cultural study. He grouped types of dance in terms of linear, curvilinear or spiral tendencies, and whether the dancer's torso is moved as a block or divided into units. Three variables, climate, method of food production, and sexual division of labor, appear to determine the shape of dance, as exemplified with footage taken around the world.

DANCE: ANNA SOKOLOW'S "ROOMS"

Series: USA Series
1967, 30 min., b&w, film
Distributors: Indiana University, Penn State
Producer: Jac Venza for WNET/13
Director: Dave Geisel
Choreographer: Anna Sokolow
Principal Dancers: Ze'eva Cohen, Jack Moore, Jeff Duncan
Composer: Kenyon Hopkins

A brief introduction to and performance of ROOMS, the four-part (Escape, Going, Desire, and Panic) classic choreographed in 1954 by the Polish-American choreographer. As she sets one or more dancers in a room, Sokolow expresses the sense of isolation, alienation, loneliness, and hunger of the soul.

DANCE BABY DANCE

1985, 30 min., color, video
Distributor/Producer: Hoctor Products
Teacher: Jimmie Ruth White

Jazz routines for teachers and students.

DANCE BLACK AMERICA

1983, 90 min., color, film, video
Distributor: Dance Horizons Video
Producers: State University of New York, Brooklyn Academy of Music, and Pennebaker Associates
Directors: Chris Hegedus, D.A. Pennebaker
Choreographers/Dancers: Alvin Ailey, Charles Moore, Garth Fagan, Al Perryman, Lenwood Sloan, Louis Johnson, Asadata Dafora, Katherine Dunham, Chuck Green
Dance Companies: Mama Lu Parks' Jazz Dancers, Alvin Ailey American Dance Theatre, Chuck Davis Dance Company, Jazzy Double Dutch Jumpers, Charles Moore Dance Theatre, Garth Fagan's Bucket Dance Theatre, Al Perryman as Earl "Snakehips" Tucker, Magnificent Force

An onstage/offstage documentary showing a cross section of the personalities and styles within the black American dance world. Dances performed include: FONTESSA AND FRIENDS (Alvin Ailey Co.), LINDY HOP (Mama Lu Parks' Jazz Dancers), FROM BEFORE (Garth Fagan), OSTRICH (Charles Moore Dance Theatre), LENJEN-GO MAN-DIANI (Chuck Davis), JUNKIE (Eleo Pomare), JUBA and CAKE-WALK (Leon Jackson and Halifu Osumare).

Dance Black America
Chuck Green tap dances in "Take the A Train." Photo by Kent Barker. Courtesy Pennebaker Associates and Dance Horizons Video.

DANCE CHROMATIC

1959, 7 min., color, film
Distributor: Film-maker's Coop
Director: Ed Emshwiller
Dancer: Nancy Fenster
Composer: Lou Harrison
Award of Exceptional Merit, Creative Film Foundation

"A fusion of dance, abstract painting, and a percussive score achieving a hypnotic and strongly rhythmic synthesis," says the late Ed Emshwiller, recognized for his experiments with video effects and his collaborations with artists of many mediums.

DANCE CLASS

1970s, 9 min., color, film
Distributor: Films Inc.
Producer: National Film Board of Canada
Director: Joan Henson
Choreographer: Peter Randazzo
Dance Company: Toronto Dance Theatre

Company members of The Toronto Dance Theatre rehearse A THREAD OF SAND, choreographed by a Martha Graham disciple.

DANCE CLASS WITH SERENA

1989, 97 min., color, video
Distributor/Producer/Dancer: Serena
Director: Alan Wilson
Editor: Tabco, Inc.

Comprehensive course on Middle Eastern dance, with tips on posture, isolations, hip articulations, hand and arm routines by the New York–based Serena, author of THE BELLY DANCE BOOK, published by McGraw Hill. Also available from Serena, VISIONS OF SALOME, a 1986 concert taped at Riverside Church, New York City.

DANCE DELILAH, DANCE

    1990, 30 min., color, video
    Distributor: Visionary Dance Productions
    Choreographer/Dancer: Delilah
    Composer: Steven Flynn
    Music: Tales of the Night Wind

Seven belly dance solos with Middle Eastern rhythms and modalities, excerpted from her three-volumed DELILAH'S BELLY-DANCE WORKSHOP. A short narrative introduces the artistry and discipline of this Seattle-based performer.

DANCE DESIGN: MOTION

    1975, 19 min., color, film, video
    Distributor: American Alliance of Health, Physical
    Education, Recreation and Dance (AAHPERD)
    Producer: The Athletic Institute
    Director: Robert Cooley
    Dancers: Lynda Davis, Susan Kennedy, Mary Ann Kellogg,
    Clay Taliaferro
    Composer: Larry Attaway

A teacher's guide with advice on how to build a kinetic vocabulary, develop a continuity of movement, and create design concepts.

DANCE DESIGN: SHAPING

    1975, 16 min., color, film
    Distributor: AAHPERD (see above)
    Producer: Athletic Institute
    Director: Robert Cooley
    Dancers: Clay Taliaferro, Mary Ann Kellogg, Susan Kennedy,
    Lynda Davis
    Art Director: Nik Krevitsky
    Composer: Larry Attaway

With the camera placed below a transparent floor, the viewer sees how dancers use the values of shape and time for accent, punctuation, and clarification.

DANCE DESIGN: SPACE

    1975, 19 min., color, film
    Distributor: AAHPERD (see above)
    Producer: Athletic Institute
    Director: Robert Cooley
    Principal Dancers: Lynda Davis, Susan Kennedy,
    Mary Ann Kellogg, Clay Taliaferro
    Composer: Larry Attaway
    Art Director: Nik Krevitsky

This teacher's aid shows how dancers relate to and move through space.

DANCE ELEVEN

    1975, 7:30 min., color, film
    Distributors: Catalyst Films, Film-makers Coop

    Producer/Director/Sculptor: Doris Chase
    Dancer: Cynthia Anderson
    Composer: Larry Spiegel

A woman dances a duet with her own image, multiplied, blurred, and dissolved through feedback techniques. The surrounding space, transformed into a viscous atmosphere of colored light, responds and bends to the dance.

THE DANCE EXPERIENCE (9 videos)

    1985–1990, 60–90 min. each, color, video
    Distributor/Producer: Tremaine Dance Conventions
    Teachers: Joe Tremaine and others from his faculty
    American Video Conference Award

Ten to twelve routines per tape, created by the hip, hot teachers from California who tour the country with their expanding circuit of conventions. Also available from Tremaine: JAZZ TECHNIQUE, PROGRESSIONS AND TURNS, and TAP TECHNIQUE.

A DANCE FANTASY

    1980s, 7:30 min., color, film
    Distributor: Coe Film Assoc.
    Producer/Director: Sue Gilbert

A little girl meets a life-size puppet in a costume warehouse. Sparks fly as they waltz, tango, soft-shoe, and clown around until her mother appears, breaking the spell.

DANCE FESTIVAL–MAKIRITARE (2 films)

    1955, 8 min.; 1969, 7 min., color, film
    Distributor: Pennstate #E00157, E01788
    Producer: M. Schuster for Wissen

The earlier silent film shows a dance festival held by the Makiritare of the Orinoco Head Water Region in Venezuela. Festival participants in the later film sport patterns painted on their bodies with red vegetable dye, and move in a line to suggest a herd of grunting, wild boars.

THE DANCE FILMS OF JAMAKE HIGHWATER

    1965, 31 min., color, b&w, film
    Distributor: The Cinema Guild
    Producer: San Francisco Contemporary Theatre
    Choreographer: Jamake Highwater

Three films choreographed by the writer and critic Jamake Highwater that reflect his interest in rituals: ORACLE OF THE BRANCH (12 min., color); KAMA SUTRAS (10 min., b&w); FIRE SERMON (9 min., b&w).

DANCE FIVE

    1976, 5 min., color, film
    Distributors: Film-maker's Coop, Catalyst Films
    Distributor/Producer/Director/Sculptor: Doris Chase
    Choreographer/Dancer: Kei Takei
    Composer: Timothy Thompson

A dancer's movements around a kinetic sculpture intertwined with optical patterns create a dynamic kaleidoscope.

DANCE FOUR

    1977, 6:30 min., color, film
    Distributor/Producer/Director: Doris Chase/Catalyst Films

Choreographer/Dancer: Kei Takei
Composers: George Kleinsinger, Eric Eigen, Mike Mahaffey

Another collaboration between the Asian choreographer Kei Takei and the filmmaker/sculptor Doris Chase.

DANCE: FOUR PIONEERS

Series: USA Series
1966, 30 min., b&w, film
Distributors: University of California Extension
Media Center, Pennstate
Producer: Jac Venza for National Educational Television
Director: Charles S. Dubin
Choreographer/Dancers: Martha Graham,
Doris Humphrey, Charles Weidman, Hanya Holm
Principal Dancers: Chester Wolenski, Lola Huth
Composer: Johann Sebastian Bach

Introduces four of the most influential American modern choreographers. Film clips from 1934 show the four working at Bennington College. The American Dance Theatre performs Doris Humphrey's PASSACAGLIA, shot at Lincoln Center.

DANCE FRAME

1978, 7 min., color, film, video
Distributors: Film-maker's Coop, Catalyst Films
Producer/Director: Doris Chase
Choreographer/Dancer: Sara Rudner
Composer: Joan Labarbara

An effort to create the third dimension in which the lines of a dancer are juxtaposed with a colored geometric form.

DANCE IN AMERICA (60 videos)

1976–1991, 60 min. each, color, video
Distributor: Lincoln Center Dance Collection
(to view only on the premises)
Producers: Merrill Brockway, Jac Venza, Emile Ardolino, Judy Kinberg for WNET/Channel 13 in association with a variety of European and domestic broadcasters
Dance Companies: The foremost dance companies in America

Four programs a year broadcast on national public television produced with the aim of preserving and sharing the best of American dance.

DANCE IN NEW DIMENSIONS

1970–1987, 40 min., color, video
Distributor: DanceMuseum
Producer: Mans Reutersward for Sveriges TV2
Director/Choreographer/Dancer: Birgit Cullberg
Principal Dancers: Gerd Andersson, Marianne Orlando, Willy Sandberg, Niklas Ek, Mona Elgh, Lenna Wennergren, Anne-Marie Lagerborg, Palina Panova
Composers: Igor Stravinsky, Ture Rangstrom, Gioacchino Rossini, Gunnar Sonstevold, Bela Bartok, Ludwig von Beethoven, Dag Wiren, Gosta Nystroem

Excerpts from the collaborations between Swedish choreographer Birgit Cullberg and Mans Reutersward over a twenty-year period with an accompanying text including interviews, articles, and credits for the individual ballets choreographed for the camera. RED WINE AND GREEN

GLASSES, MISS JULIE, REVOLT, and SCHOOL FOR WIVES demonstrate their pioneering use of chromakey and understanding of scale, depth, and illusion.

DANCE: IN SEARCH OF "LOVERS"

Series: USA Series
1966, 30 min., b&w, film
Distributor: Indiana University
Producers: Jac Venza, Virginia Kassel for National Educational Television
Choreographer: Glen Tetley
Principal Dancers: Carmen De Lavallade, Mary Hinkson, Scott Douglas
Set Designer: Willa Kim

With Tetley's ballet LOVERS as the centerpiece of this educational program, the choreographer reveals how he integrates his story line, choreography, costumes, sets, and music.

DANCE IN THE SUN

1953, 7 min., b&w, film
Distributor: Museum of Modern Art
Producer/Director: Shirley Clarke
Choreographer/Dancer: Daniel Nagrin

A solo by modern dance pioneer Daniel Nagrin, who begins in a studio and makes his final statement on a beach.

THE DANCE INSTRUMENT

1975, 27 min., color, film
Distributor: American Alliance of Health,
Physical Education, Recreation and Dance (AAHPERD)
Producer: Athletic Institute
Director: Robert Cooley
Principal Dancers: Lynda Davis, Susan Kennedy,
Mary Ann Kellogg, Clay Taliaferro
Art Director: Nik Krevitsky
Composer: Larry Attaway

This teacher's guide explores the range of creative possibilities within movement.

DANCE JOURNEYS

1981, 28 min., color, video
Distributor: WGBH
Producer: Fred Barzyk
Choreographer/Directors: Dawn Kramer,
Meredith Monk, Ruth Wheeler, and Sam Costa
Directors: Rick Hauser, Robin Doty, David Atwood
Principal Dancers: Susan Kinney, Martha Armstrong Gray, Harry Streep III, Hamish Blackman, Stephen Buck, Dawn S. Lane, Ellen Laviana, Terry Reeden, Janet Pomerantz, Stephen Goldbas, Gwyneth Jones, Molly T. McClure, Nancy Salmon, Larry Lee Vanhorne
Editor/Coordinator: Susan Dowling

Four modern dances choreographed for the camera: IMAGES DIFFUSED BY TIME (Wheeler/Hauser), taped on an island, evokes memories of ancient places; IMAGINARY CROSSING, a collaboration between Dawn Kramer and Robin Doty; INHABITANT OF ANOTHER PLACE, taped in the woods of Maine (Costa/Atwood); and an excerpt of Meredith Monk's ELLIS ISLAND.

DANCE LIKE A RIVER: OADAA! DRUMMING AND
DANCING IN THE U.S.

    1985, 45 min., color, film, video
    Distributor: Indiana University
    Producer/Directors: Barry Dornfeld, Tom Rankin for
    Oboade Institute of African Culture
    Director/Choreographer: Yacub Addy
    Dance Company: Ga
    Dance on Camera Festival, 1989 Silver Award

Documents the dance styles, purpose, and performances of Ga,
a nine-member dance company from Ghana, West Africa, living in Washington, D.C.

DANCE MASKS: THE WORLD OF MARGARET SEVERN

    1983, 33 min., color, film, video
    Distributor: University of California Media Extension Center
    Producer/Director/Cinematographer: Peter Lipskis
    Choreographer/Dancer: Margaret Severn
    Dance on Camera Festival, American Film Festival finalist,
    Choice Outstanding Nonprint Media Award

In the 1920s and 30s, Margaret Severn was acclaimed for her
short mask dances, each of which portrayed a character or
emotion. At age eighty, Severn performs briefly and comments
on the stills and film clips of her in her prime.

DANCE – NEW DIRECTIONS

    1980, 20 min., color, film, video
    Distributor: FACSEA #1203
    Producer: French Ministry of Foreign Affairs
    Choreographer: Douglas Dunn
    Teacher: Alwin Nikolais
    Principal Dancer: Michel Denard

A performance at Alwin Nikolais' school for choreographers
on the banks of the Loire River, in which Michel Denard, a
principal with the Paris Opera Ballet, performs a composition
by American modern dance choreographer Douglas Dunn.

DANCE: NEW YORK CITY BALLET

    Series: USA Series
    1966, 30 min., b&w, film
    Distributor: Pennstate, University of California Extension
    Media Center
    Producer: Jac Venza for National Educational Television
    Director: Charles S. Dubin
    Choreographer: George Balanchine
    Principal Dancers: Suzanne Farrell, Arthur Mitchell,
    Melissa Hayden, Jacques D'Amboise, Patricia McBride,
    Edward Villella
    Dance Company: New York City Ballet
    Composers: Igor Stravinsky, Louis Gottschalk, Peter Il-
    yich Tchaikovsky

Choreographer George Balanchine discusses his philosophy
of classical ballet, along with excerpts from AGON (Suzanne
Farrell and Arthur Mitchell), PAS DE DEUX (Melissa Hay-
den and Jacques d'Amboise), TARANTELLA (Patricia
McBride and Edward Villella), and MEDITATION (Suzanne
Farrell and Jacques d'Amboise).

DANCE NINE

    1975, 5 min., color, film, video
    Distributors: Doris Chase/Catalyst Films,
    Film-maker's Coop
    Producer/Director: Doris Chase
    Principal Dancer: Gus Solomons
    Composer: George Kleinsinger

Modern dancer seemingly partners kinetic patterns
generated by a Rutt/Etra Synthesizer. His image, multiplied
and colored, evolves into an abstract collage.

DANCE OF DARKNESS

    1989, 56 min., color, video
    Distributors: Electronic Arts Intermix, Pioneer (CD)
    Producer: La Sept, WGBH/WNET New Television
    Director: Edin Velez
    Principal Dancers: Kazuo Ohno, Tatsumi Hijikata
    Dance Companies: Dai Rakuda Kan, Byakko Sha,
    Hakutoboh

A personal statement as well as a historical perspective of
the Japanese dance *Butoh*, born in the 1960s in the middle
of the worldwide questioning of values. Edin Velez eliminated
the confines of the frame by alternately using footage of
rehearsals and performances shot outdoors, in studios and
then combining several kinetic images. During the running
narrative, Tatsumi Hijikata and Kazuo Ohno, *Butoh's* co-creators,
express their search to "break through the normal to individu-
alism, away from Japanese good manners, to personal freedom."

DANCE OF THE AGES/ON THE SHORE

    1913, 6 min., b&w, film
    Distributor: Dance Film Archive
    Director: Ted Shawn
    Principal Dancer: Ruth St. Denis

A "trick" film made by modern dance pioneer Ted Shawn with
theatrical posings by his partner Ruth St. Denis in 1906.

DANCE OF THE BUSHCLEARING SOCIETY "GUA"

    1968, 11 min., b&w, film
    Distributor: Pennstate #E01530
    Producer/Director: H. Himmelheber for Wissen

Men in Dan, Ivory Coast, dance for their employers, both before
and after clearing woodland for plantations. Every employee must
be equally gifted as a dancer and a laborer to hold his job.

DANCE ON VIDEO: AN INTRODUCTION TO
VIDEOTAPING DANCE

    1979, 30 min., b&w, video
    Distributor: ARC Video
    Producer/Director/Narrators: Jeff Bush and Celia Ipiotis
    Choreographer/Dancer: Celia Ipiotis

Ideas and experiences about the problems, benefits, and
techniques of videotaping dance. Best suited for closed circuit
viewing in a workshop, discussion, or research context. Includes
three versions of MOTHERLESS CHILD by Celia Ipiotis, the
producer/host for the talk show series EYE ON DANCE.

DANCE ON WITH BILLIE MAHONEY

    1979–1990, 30 min., color, video
    Distributor/Producer/Host: Billie Mahoney

A one-on-one cable talk show hosted by a dancer, dance notator, and teacher with guests representing the spectrum of the dance world.

DANCE OUTLINE

    1978, 4 min., color, film
    Distributor: Catalyst Films
    Distributor/Producer/Director: Doris Chase for WNYC-TV
    Choreographer/Dancer: Sara Rudner
    Composer: Joan Labarbara

A dance conceived for the camera by a modern dancer in collaboration with video pioneer Doris Chase.

DANCE PRELUDES (4 videos)

    1987, 60 min. each, color, video
    Distributor: Video D
    Producer: Philadelphia Dance Alliance
    Director: Dennis Diamond
    Choreographers: Senta Driver, Jose Limon, Richard Weiss
    Teachers: Finis Jhung, Daniel Lewis
    Dance Companies: Pennsylvania Ballet, Harry

Four documentary programs concerned with the creative process: PENNSYLVANIA BALLET IN REHEARSAL; Senta Driver talking about HARRY, her modern company, which performs segments of VIDEO 5000, MISSING PERSONS and REACHES; FINIS JHUNG'S BALLET FOR ADULT BEGINNERS by the popular New York–based teacher; and the JOSE LIMON TECHNIQUE, an hour class with Daniel Lewis in the basics of the modern style devised by the late Jose Limon.

DANCE: ROBERT JOFFREY BALLET

    Series: USA series
    1966, 30 min., b&w, film
    Distributor: University of California Extension Media Center
    Producer: Jac Venza for National Educational Television
    Director: Charles S. Dubin
    Choreographers: Robert Joffrey, Anna Sokolow, Gerald Arpino
    Principal Dancers: Lisa Bradley, Robert Blankshine, Luis Fuente
    Composers: Louis Harrison, T. Marcer, Antonio Vivaldi

Early film of Jac Venza's with rehearsal session and excerpts from PAS DE DEESES, based on a nineteenth-century French lithograph and GAMELAN (Robert Joffrey); OPUS 65 (Anna Sokolow); INCUBUS and VIVA VIVALDI (Gerald Arpino).

DANCE SEVEN

    1975, 7:15 min., color, film, video
    Distributor: Filmmaker's Coop, Catalyst Films
    Producer/Director: Doris Chase
    Dancer: Marnee Morris
    Composer: Teiji Ito

Through postproduction effects of feedback, de-beaming, and superimposition, a former New York City Ballet dancer appears as a moving painting, fragmented by color separations, her figure juxtaposed with close-ups of her face.

DANCE SPACE

    1980, 14 min., color, film
    Distributor: Films Inc.
    Producer: National Dance Institute
    Principal Dancers: Jacques D'Amboise, Mikhail Baryshnikov

Features Jacques d'Amboise, the former principal with New York City Ballet who founded the National Dance Institute. He supervises rehearsals of his students drawn from the public schools of the five boroughs of New York City and their annual performances with guest performers at Lincoln Center and Madison Square Garden. *See also* HE MAKES ME FEEL LIKE DANCIN'.

DANCE SQUARED

    1963, 4 min., color, film
    Distributor: University of Portland #01044
    Producer: National Film Board of Canada
    Director: Norman McLaren

The Scottish-born animator awakens a sense of how geometry underlines every movement by dividing, subdividing, and gyrating squares.

DANCE TEN

    1977, 8 min., color, film, video
    Distributors: Film-maker's Coop, Doris Chase/Catalyst Films
    Producer/Director/Sculptor: Doris Chase
    Choreographer: Johnathan Hollander
    Composer: William Bolcomb

Modern dance solo with a video-synthesized image of a kinetic sculpture, a "rocker" by director Doris Chase.

DANCE THEATRE OF HARLEM

    Series: Dance In America
    1976, 60 min., color, film, video
    Distributor: Indiana University #RC1005
    Producer: Emile Ardolino for PBS, RM, Gmbh and BBC
    Director: Merrill Brockway
    Choreographers: Lester Horton, Geoffrey Holder, Arthur Mitchell, George Balanchine
    Principal Dancers: Stephanie Dabney, Ronald Perry, Stanley Perryman, Eddie Shellman, Yvonne Hall
    Dance Company: Dance Theatre of Harlem
    Composers: Judith Hamilton, Edvard Grieg
    Costume and Set Designers: Zelda Wynn, Davis Hays
    Dance on Camera Festival, 1980 Gold Award

Members of the black ballet company appear informally, in rehearsal, and perform two movements from FORCES OF RHYTHM, set to "Do The Breakdown" and "He Ain't Heavy, He's My Brother"; BUGAKU, George Balanchine's erotic dance that premiered in 1963; THE BELOVED (Horton/Hamilton), restaged by James Truitte; THE HOLBERG SUITE, (Mitchell/Grieg); and DOUGLA, Hindu and African ritual choreographed by Geoffrey Holder.

DANCE THEATRE OF HARLEM

    1988, 117 min., color, video
    Distributor: Home Vision #DAN01
    Producer: WNET with RM Arts and Danmarks Radio
    Director: Thomas Grimm

Choreographers: Agnes de Mille, Robert North,
Lester Horton, Arthur Mitchell
Dance Company: Dance Theatre of Harlem
Composers: Morton Gould, Judith Hamilton, Bob Downes,
Milton Rosenstock

Four ballets by the New York–based company: de Mille's FALL RIVER LEGEND, inspired by the Lizzie Borden 1892 murder of her father and stepmother; North's TROY GAME, an acrobatic satire of the macho man; Horton's THE BELOVED, a duet in which a jealous man strangles his wife, whom he suspects of being unfaithful; Mitchell's JOHN HENRY, a tale of the steel drivin' man who challenged the steam drill, but died with a hammer in his hand.

DANCE THERAPY: THE POWER OF MOVEMENT

1983, 30 min., color, film, video
Distributor: University of California Extension Media Center
Producer: American Dance Therapy Association
Director: Norris Brock
Dance Therapists: Joan Chodorow, Jane Downes,
Susan Sandel, Barbara Estrin, Sharon Chaiklin
Narrator: Christopher Reeve
Dance Film Festival Award, National Coalition of Arts
Therapy Association honoree.

Five dance therapists work with their patients, ranging from an emotionally disturbed child in a psychiatric hospital to geriatrics in a nursing home, demonstrating that movement can communicate, even when words fail.

DANCE THREE

1977, 8:30 min., color, film
Distributors: Doris Chase/Catalyst Films,
Film-maker's Coop
Producer/Director: Doris Chase for WNYC/TV
Choreographer/Dancer: Kei Takei
Composer: George Kleinsinger

A dance based on a theme from Kei Takei's series called LIGHT.

DANCE TO THE MUSIC

Series: Jumpstreet
1980, 30 min., color, video
Distributor: University of Portland #40275
Principal Dancer: Honi Coles
Dance Company: Rod Rodgers Dance Troupe

Explores the black musical heritage from its African roots to its influence in modern American music.

DANCE TO THE MUSIC (4 videos)

1980s, 30 min. each, color, video
Distributor: Hoctor Products
Producer: Studio Music Corp.
Teachers: Dawn Carfton, Jimmi Ruth White,
Darryl Retter, Scott Benson, Kit Andree, Valene Tueller

Jazz routines demonstrated to drum and rhythm tracks.
Dance manuals for each video.

A DANCE TRIBUTE TO MICHAEL JORDAN

1989, 30 min., color video

Distributor: Orion Enterprises
Producer/Choreographer: Gus Giordano
Dance Company: Gus Giordano Company

A dance biography of the agile basketball player, from his dribbling youth to his superstar status today. Substantiated with newsclips of the athlete and interviews with the dancers.

DANCE VIDEOGRAPHY

1980s, 90 min., color, video
Distributor: G.A.B. Productions

Advice on camera choices and moves, lighting, make-up, and sets while videotaping dance.

Dance Works of Doris Humphrey, With My Red
Fires and New Dance
*Doris Humprey performing solo and in a group.
Cover art courtesy Dance Horizons Video.*

DANCE WORKS OF DORIS HUMPHREY, WITH MY RED FIRES AND NEW DANCE

1972, 60 min., color, video
Distributor: Dance Horizons Video
Choreographer/Performer: Doris Humphrey
Dance Company: American Dance Festival Company
Composer: Wallingford Rieger

Features three dances created in the 1930s by the modern dance pioneer that dramatize the conflicts between men and women and also between the individual and the group, and the power of love – maternal, romantic, and fraternal – and its capacity for passionate and destructive excesses. NEW DANCE, VARIATIONS AND CONCLUSION, WITH MY RED FIRES.

DANCEPROBE '78

> 1978, 28 min., color, video
> Distributor/Producer: S.W. Dance Association

A brief history of ballet; sacred deer dance of the Yaqui Indians, a performance by the Apache Mountain Spirit Dancers; and a circle dance by the audience.

DANCER FOR THE CORONATION

> 1988, 8 min., color, film
> Distributor: Film-maker's Coop
> Director: Caroline Avery

Caroline Avery, a painter who switched to film as her canvas in the early 1980s, plays with light and shadow to give the illusion of a dancer folding back on herself.

A DANCER MUST DANCE

> 25 min., color, video
> Distributor: Coe Films
> Producer: New Zealand National Film Unit
> Principal Dancer: Peter Gannett
> Dance Company: Royal New Zealand National Ballet

Shows the Royal New Zealand National Ballet in class and performance.

A DANCER'S GRAMMAR

> 1977, 18 min., color, film, video
> Distributor: Phoenix Films
> Producer/Director: Nina Feinberg
> Cinematographer: Peter Sova
> Principal Dancers: Lawrence Rhodes, Lois Bewley
> Dance on Camera Festival, 1977 Certificate of Honor

Barre and center work, and how each differs for the male and female bodies..

A DANCER'S WORLD

> 1957, 30 min., b&w, film, video
> Distributor: Phoenix Films
> Producer: Nathan Kroll for WGED-TV/Pittsburgh
> Director: Peter Glushanok
> Choreographer/Dancer: Martha Graham
> Principal Dancers: Yuriko, Helen McGehee, Gene McDonald, Ellen Siegel, David Wood, Miriam Cole, Lillian Biersteker, Robert Cohan, Ethel Winter, Bertram Ross, Mary Hinkson
> Dance Company: Martha Graham Dance Company
> Composer: Cameron McCosh

Choreographer/dancer Martha Graham shares her philosophy of life as a dancer. She talks about the dancer's world in her dressing room as she prepares for the role of Jocasta in her choreographic work NIGHT JOURNEY. Her company demonstrates their own technical and psychological preparation and then rehearses the dance.

DANCERS

> 1987, 97 min., color, film, video
> Distributor/Producer: Warner Home Video
> Director: Herbert Ross
> Choreographers: Marius Petipa, Mikhail Baryshnikov
> Principal Dancers: Mikhail Baryshnikov, Alessandra Ferri,

Julie Kent
> Dance Company: American Ballet Theatre
> Composer: Adolphe Adam

While on tour in Italy, an innocent corps member falls for the company playboy in this film-within-a-film feature. During a performance of GISELLE, she realizes that she is living the part of Giselle and flees from the theatre. Stronger of heart than the on-stage Giselle, she gets a tattoo and returns to her apologetic boyfriend.

DANCERS IN SCHOOL

> 1971, 45 min., color, film, video
> Distributor/Producer/Director: D.A. Pennebaker
> Principal Dancers: Bella Lewitsky, Virginia Tanner, Murray Louis

Three methods of teaching children demonstrated in the IMPACT program sponsored by the National Endowment's Artists in the Schools program and the Office of Education.

DANCERS OF THE THIRD AGE

> 1987, 26 min., color, video
> Distributor/Producer: Elizabeth Mackie
> Producer: Lesley Ann Patten
> Choreographer: Liz Lerman
> Dance on Camera Festival, 1987 Honorable Mention

Men and women in their 60s, 70s, and 80s join in with a choreographer eager to prove that dance is for everyone.

DANCES AND RITES AFTER THE DEATH OF A TRIBAL CHIEF

> 1962, 12 min., b&w, film
> Distributor: Pennstate #EO0590
> Producer: H. Jungraithmayr for Wissen

A peek into the sacrificial ceremonies that follow the death of a chief in Pankshin as practiced by the Angas tribe in Nigeria, West Africa.

DANCES FROM DJAYA (5 films)

> 1964-1965, 4-10 min. each, color, film
> Distributor: Pennstate #EO1444, EO1443, EO1022, EO1442, EO1000
> Producer: Wissen

Three circle dances from Central Sudan, Africa: the PARAMA; the NAPA with twenty boys dancing while girls sing songs of praise; the BARDJAT with three djele dances with the boys' long turban scarves waving in the air.

DANCES FROM THE CASBAH

> 1985, 48 min., color, video
> Producer/Distributor: Bastet Productions
> Dancer: Kathryn Ferguson

Collage of four solos by an Arizona-based performer who blends traditional Oriental dance with Western elements.

DANCES OF BUDDHIST PILGRIMS

> 1957, 4 min., color, film
> Distributor: Pennstate #E00260
> Producer: Rene von Nebesky-Wojkowitz for Wissen

Silent film of a man and a woman on a pilgrimage to a Buddhist monastery who earn food for their Tibetan journey by chanting and dancing.

DANCES OF INDIA

1959, 17 min., color, film
Distributor: University of Michigan
Producer: Serisawa Brothers Prod.

Four classical dances of India.

DANCES OF INDIA – KATHAKALI

1945, 10 min., b&w, film
Distributor: Portland State University

Explains the gesture language of India's dance drama, and shows three episodes from the MAHABARATA, which was filmed in its entirety in 1990 during the run of Peter Brook's production at Brooklyn Academy of Music in New York, NY.

DANCES OF MACEDONIA

1970, 10 min., color, film
Distributor: Dance Films Assoc. (for members only)
Producer: Julien Bryan for International Film Foundation
Director: Kenneth Richter

Men and women of Yugoslavia perform DANCE OF THE CZAROPOLE PEOPLE; women perform a dance of the HAREM WOMEN and men dance a work called THE AVENGING BRIGANDS.

DANCES OF MEXICO: ANIMAL ORIGINS

1981, 12 min., color, film
Distributor/Producer: Tempo Films
Directors: Mary Joyce, Annette Macdonald

This educational short expounds on the continuing importance of the deer, bird, snake, and horse in the dances of Mexico.

DANCES OF SOUTHERN AFRICA

1973, 55 min., color, film, video
Distributor: PennState #50482
Producer/Director: Gei Zantziger
Ethnochoreologist: Nadia Childovsky
Advisor: Andrew Tracey

The Xhosa shaking dance, high-kicking Ndlamu dance of the Zingili Zulo, and the tumbling dance of the Ndau tribes performed by mine workers of South Africa in the Tribal Trust lands.

DANCES OF THE SILK ROAD: AN INTRODUCTION TO UZBEK AND GEORGIAN DANCE (2 videos)

1988-1990, 60 min. each, color, video
Distributor/Producer: Uzbek Dance Society
Dance Company: Bakhor Ensemble

Solo and ensemble performances of the Turkic-speaking Sunni Muslim people with historical photos and stills of the art and elaborate costumes in the first video. The second video focuses on the traditional dance of Soviet Georgia, the ancient dances from the Caucasus Mountains, which run

between the Black and Caspian Seas. Also available: THE BAKHOR ENSEMBLE IN CONCERT, filmed in Tashkent.

DANCES OF THE WORLD (16 videos)

1987, 30-60 min. each, color, video
Distributors: American Alliance of Health, Physical Education, Recreation and Dance, Dance Horizons Video
Principal Dancers: Dr. John Ramsey and The Berea
Dance Companies: Kentucky College Country Dancers, Folklorico Gauteque Ballet, Compania Folklorica Las Mesas De Cayey, Ballet Folklorico De Colima and The Grupo Folklorico del Departamento de Bellas Artes, Guadalajara, Clan Na Gael, Rinnceoiri Idirnaisiunta, An Oige Na H'eireann Dance Groups, Monkseaton Dancers of Newcastle-upon-Tyne

Filmed at Folkmoot, Asheville, North Carolina, this series shows the colorful dances of Ireland, England, Korea, Appalachia, Mexico, Puerto Rico, Poland, and Russia.

DANCIN' USA (2 videos)

1980s, 30 min. each, color, video
Distributor: Hoctor Products
Producer: Studio Music Corp.
Dancers: Ben Bagby, Scott Benson, Joel Ruminier, Blair Farrington, Kit Andree, Casey Cole, Sandra Balestracci, Danny Hoctor, Dance Caravan Faculty Members

Seventy-three routines set to popular songs, including BOOGIE WOOGIE BUGLE BOY, A CHORUS LINE, LADY BE GOOD, SQUEEZING, MARY POPPINS, and TARANTELLA.

DANCING BOURNONVILLE

1980, 48 min., color, film
Distributor: Audience Planners, Inc.
Producers: Royal Danish Ministry for Foreign Affairs and The Danish Government Film Office
Choreographers: August Bournonville, Hans Beck
Dancers: Erik Bruhn, Kirsten Ralov, Hans Brenaa, Ib Anderson, Mette Honningen, Mette-Ida Kirk
Dance Company: Royal Danish Ballet

The traditions and training methods of the prolific Danish dancer/choreographer August Bournonville (1805-1879), as developed and codified by Hans Beck with excerpts from his ballets at different stages of preparation, from rehearsal to performance.

THE DANCING FOOL

1937, 7 min., b&w, film
Distributor: Ivy Films
Producer/Director/Animator: Max and Dave Fleischman
Principal Dancer: Betty Boop

The 1930s sex kitten goes to dancing school.

DANCING FOR MR. B. – SIX BALANCHINE BALLERINAS

1989, 90 min., color, film, video
Distributor: Seahorse
Producer/Director: Anne Belle

Principal Dancers: Mary Ellen Moylan, Maria Tallchief, Melissa Hayden, Allegra Kent, Merrill Ashley, Darci Kistler
Dance Company: New York City Ballet
Dance on Camera Festival, 1991 Silver Award

A documentary in homage to choreographer George Balanchine with six ballerinas, each representing a different era in Balanchine's career with the New York City Ballet, recounting how the artist influenced their lives. They reveal how they keep his ballets and inspiration alive.

DANCING HANDS

Series: Alive from Off Center
1988, 16 min., color, video
Distributors: Skip Blumberg, Electronic Arts Intermix
Producer: John Schott for KTCA-TV
Director: Skip Blumberg
Choreographers: Keith Terry, Ellen Fisher, Blondell Cummings, Sally Hess, Wendy Perron, Robert LaFosse
Composer: Frank Maya
Dance on Camera Festival, 1989 Honorable Mention

A series of short dances performed exclusively with hands, conceived for the camera by an assortment of modern, ballet, and funk dancers.

DANCING MAN

Series: Alive from Off Center
1985, 10 min., color, video
Distributor/Producer: KTCA/TV
Director: Mitchell Kriegman
Principal Performer: Bill Irwin

Bill Irwin's inspired clowning as a man unwittingly hooked on disco.

DANCING ON AIR

1989, 30 min., color, video
Distributor: Dancing On Air
Producer: Susan Winokur
Director: David Hahn
Choreographers: David Drummond, Michael Rahn
Principal Dancers: Nanette Glushak, Michael Rahn, Starr Danias
Composers: Anton Arensky, Swanstrom/Morgan/McCarron, Maurice Moszkowski
Editors: Stephanie Palewski, Michael Leura

Three romantic dance dramas BITTERSWEET, JAZZ BABY, and PALETTE with introductions to each by Paul Shenar.

DANCING ON THE EDGE

1980–1981, 28:49 min., color, video
Distributor: WGBH
Producers: Fred Barzyk with Nancy Mason Hauser
Director: Peter Campus
Choreographer/Dancer: Trisha Brown
Principal Dancers: Elizabeth Garren, Eva Karczag, Lisa Kraus, Stephen Petronio
Composer: Robert Ashley
Editor: Susan Dowling

Three video-dances choreographed by modern dancer Trisha

Brown: OPAL LOOP/802, WATERMOTOR FOR DANCER AND CAMERA, and LOCUS ALTERED.

DANCING PROPHET

1970s, 15 min., color, film, video
Distributor: Franciscan #F7125 and #F8105
Director: Bruce Baker
Choreographer/Dancer: Doug Crutchfield
Cine Golden Eagle

Pressured by his father to become a minister, Doug Crutchfield rebelled and found his own ministry in dance, as demonstrated by his interpretation of Christ's healing of the sick.

THE DANCING PROPHET

1970, 25 min., color, film, video
Distributor: Pyramid
Director: Edmund Penney
Dancer/Choreographer: Ruth St. Denis
Cinematographers: Swen Walnum, David Harrington

This documentary on the modern dance pioneer Ruth St. Denis traces her development and thought through still photographs, historical footage, graphics, recreated dance sequences, and solo dances by St. Denis. Dame Alicia Markova, Jack Cole, and Anton Dolin discuss her influence.

DANCING THROUGH THE MAGIC EYE: A PORTRAIT OF VIRGINIA TANNER

1979–1984, 35 min., color, video
Distributor/Producer: Virginia Tanner Creative Dance Program
Director: Claudia Sisemore
Principal Dancers: Mary Ann Lee, Linda Smith, Virginia Tanner

Interviews with the late Salt Lake City–based pioneer who developed a method of teaching children that awakened their creativity and belief in themselves.

DANCING THRU

1940s, 33 min., b&w, film
Distributor: Dance Film Archive
Choreographers: Marius Petipa, Jack Billings, Chris Gil
Principal Dancers: Galina Ulanova, Jack Billings, Diane Chase, Chris Gil
Composer: Peter Ilyich Tchaikovsky

Whimsical views of dance styles, with an excerpt of SWAN LAKE performed by the Russian prima ballerina Galina Ulanova, as well as two styles of tap: the ballroom mode with Jack Billings and Diane Chase and the acrobatic with Chris Gil.

DANCING'S ALL OF YOU

1982, 23 min., color, film, video
Distributors: Coe Film Assoc., De Nonno Pix
Producer/Director: Tony De Nonno
Principal Dancers: Alfredo Gustar, Carol Hess

Tales from a sixty-two-year-old hoofer who performed with Billie Holiday, Ella Fitzgerald, Dizzy Gillespie, and Duke Ellington as he coaches his students and performs THE TUNE OF THE HICKORY STICK and swirls around a young lady on a rooftop. Romance and reality merge as the two perform tap, soft shoe, and ballroom duets revealing private as well as public selves.

DANZAS REGIONALES ESPANOLAS
> Series: El Espanol por el Mundo
> 1966, 14 min., color, film
> Distributor: University of Syracuse
> Producer: Encyclopaedia Britannica

Dances of Spain performed on stage, in patios and courtyards with historical references and shots of the different regions where the dances originated. Narrated in Spanish.

DAPHNIS AND CHLOE
> 1988, 61 min., color, video
> Distributor: Films Inc.
> Producer: BBC
> Director: Derek Bailey
> Choreographer: Graeme Murphy
> Principal Dancers: Carl Morrow, Victoria Taylor, Paul Saliba, Kim Walter
> Dance Company: Sydney Dance Company
> Composer: Maurice Ravel
> Dance on Camera Festival, 1989 Gold Award

Not to be confused with the versions by Michel Fokine, John Cranko, or George Skibine, this story of love lost and regained is choreographed here by Australian Graeme Murphy in a pop vein with dancing nymphs on roller skates, Pan on a cloud, and Cupid swooping by on a skateboard.

DAS TRIADISCHE BALLETT
> 1970, 30 min., color, film
> Distributor: Modern Talking Picture Service #25110G
> Director/Dancer: Hannes Winkler
> Choreographer: Oskar Schlemmer
> Composer: Erich Ferstl

This reconstruction of Oskar Schlemmer's 1922 ballet, built around the number three as a mystical idea, demonstrates his Bauhaus philosophy of geometric forms, orders, and patterns.

DAVID GORDON
> Series: Alive from Off Center
> 1986, 20 min., color, video
> Distributor/Producer: KTCA
> Choreographer/Director/Dancer: David Gordon
> Dancer: Valda Setterfield

Highlights the work of choreographer David Gordon in two autobiographical duets. In DOROTHY AND EILEEN, two women dance while confiding stories about their mothers. In CLOSE-UP, David Gordon and his wife, Valda Setterfield, suggest the dynamics of relationships.

DAVIDSBUNTLERTANZE
> 1982, 43 min., color, video
> Distributors: Home Vision #DAV01, Pioneer (laserdisk)
> Producer: Catherine Tatge for National Video Corporation
> Director: Merrill Brockway
> Choreographer: George Balanchine
> Principal Dancers: Suzanne Farrell, Jacques D'Amboise, Peter Martins, Ib Anderson, Karin von Aroldingen, Adam Luders, Sara Leland, Heather Watts
> Dance Company: New York City Ballet

> Composer: Robert Schumann
> Set/Costume Designer: Rouben Ter-Arutunian

A ballet, set to Schumann's cycle of eighteen piano pieces, for four couples.

DAY ON EARTH
> 1972, 20 min., color, film
> Distributor: Dance Film Archive
> Director: Dwight Godwin
> Choreographer: Doris Humphrey
> Principal Dancers: Peter Sparling, Jane Eilber
> Composer: Aaron Copland

Choreographed in 1947, this work for a man, wife, child, and girl suggests the cycles of life and love. Reconstructed for two Juilliard students who both became members of Martha Graham's company and then developed solo careers.

DEAF LIKE ME
> 1981, 23:30 min., color, video
> Distributor: Franciscan #F7397
> Producer: Barr Films
> Director: Jim Callner

The story of Yollie, a shy deaf child who responds to a mime whom she later discovers is also deaf.

DEBBIE DEE TAP TECHNIQUE (4 videos)
> 1985-1986, 90-105 min. each, color, video
> Distributor: Taffy's
> Teacher/Dancer: Debbie Dee

Technique classes for different levels with turns, combinations, exercises, and progressions.

DEBONAIR DANCERS
> 1986, 27 min., color, film
> Distributor: Filmaker's Library
> Producer: Alison Nigh-Strelich
> Teacher: John Soiu
> Narrator: Jack Lemmon
> Dance on Camera Festival, 1987 Honorable Mention; 1987, CINE Golden Eagle

Mentally disabled young men and women improve through dancing under the supervision of John Soiu, a California ballroom instructor active among the disabled for forty years.

DELICOMMEDIA
> 1985, 18 min., color, film, video
> Distributor/Producer: Cunningham Dance Foundation
> Director: Elliot Caplan
> Choreographer/Director: Merce Cunningham
> Dance Company: Merce Cunningham Dance Company
> Costume Designer: Dove Bradshaw

Merce Cunningham's bow to vaudeville with hints of cakewalk, tango, lindy hop woven into his modern mode.

DELILAH'S BELLY DANCE WORKSHOP (3 videos)
> 1988, 80-90 min., color, video
> Distributor: Visionary Dance Productions

Choreographer/Dancer: Delilah
Composer: Steven Flynn

Exercises by the Seattle-based teacher/performer for the hips, torso, arms, hands, zills, and rhythms on video I; fast hips, Baladi, Masmoudi and Karshilama techniques for using a veil on video II; and undulations, belly rolls, coin tricks, floorwork and the Turkish drop with four demonstration pieces on video III.

THE DELPHI WAY

1964, 45 min., color, film, video
Distributor: New Yorker Films
Producer: Asia Society
Director: James Ivory

Documentary recording of classical Indian dancers by the maker of ROOM WITH A VIEW.

DERVISH 2

1972, 18 min., color, video
Distributor/Director/Choreographer/Performer:
Amy Greenfield

Superimpositions of a spinning figure wrapped in a white sheet.

THE DESPERATE HEART

1951, 11 min., b&w, film
Distributor: University of Minnesota
Director: Walter V. Strate
Choreographer/Dancer/Narrator: Valerie Bettis
Composer: Bernardo Segall

Solo performed to a poem by John Brinnin about a woman anguishing over a lost love.

THE DESPERATE HEART

1974, 21 min., color, film
Distributor/Dancer: Margaret Beals
Choreographer: Valerie Bettis
Narrator: Walter Terry
Composer: Bernardo Segall

Valerie Bettis' solo performed by Margaret Beals under Bettis' direction. The two artists and dance critic Walter Terry discuss the challenges of passing on a role.

DEVELOPING AESTHETIC CONCEPTS
THROUGH MOVEMENT

1966, 29 min., b&w, film
Distributor: Dance Films Association (for members only)
Producing Organizations: Teachers College,
Columbia University
Director: Paul Williams
Teacher: Betty Rowan

Third-grade children demonstrate aesthetic response through exploration, discussion, and interpretation of poetry and art under the guidance of their teacher. She describes concepts of rhythm, sound quality, and structural form as they relate to aesthetics and various modes of expression. Produced under a U.S. Office of Education grant.

DHANDYO

1961, 3 min., b&w, film
Distributor: Pennstate
Producer: Wissen

Stick dance of the Fakirani, a nomadic group of the Jat in the Indus delta of West Pakistan, performed at a celebration in honor of the ancestor Sanwelo.

DIALOGUE FOR CAMERAMAN AND DANCER

1972–1974, 25 min., color, video
Distributor: Film-maker's Coop
Producer/Director/Dancer: Amy Greenfield
Cinematographer: Wilson Barber

As a cameraman circles a nude woman, we hear the cameraman and the dancer share their feelings on the experience.

DIGITAL DANCE

1984, 5 min., color, video
Distributor/Producer/Choreographer: Claudia Murphey
Dance on Camera Festival, 1985 Honorable Mention

Experiment in digital effects to trumpet themes of equality, trust, and interdependence.

DIONYSUS

1963, 26 min., color, film
Distributor: Film-maker's Coop
Producer/Director: Charles Boultenhouse
Principal Dancers: Louis Falco (Dionysus), Anna Duncan (Agave), Nicholas Magallanes (Pentheus), Flower Hujer
Composer: Teiji Ito

The film conveys the psychological states implied in the Greek myth of Pentheus by circling hand-held cameras for intoxication, using slow-motion pans for hypnosis, single frame cutting for dismemberment, and multiple exposures for metamorphosis. A young Louis Falco opens the film with his leaps superimposed on double images of fists and flowers.

DIRTY DANCING

1987, 100 min., color, video
Distributor: Swank
Producer: Linda Gottlieb for Vestron
Director: Emile Ardolino
Choreographer: Kenny Ortega
Principal Dancers: Patrick Swayze, Jennifer Grey
Composers: Franke Previte, John DeNicola,
Donald Markowitz, Patrick Swayze, Merry Clayton
Writer: Eleanor Bergstein
Editor (dance sequences): Girish Bhargava

The 60-million-dollar feature about a young girl who learns to dance under pressure, as an emergency substitute for a professional club dancer, while vacationing with her family.

DISCOVERING AMERICAN INDIAN MUSIC

Series: Discovering Music
1971, 24 min., color, video
Distributor: University of Illinois #82261
Producer: Bernard Wilets
Composer: Louis Ballard

American Indian tribes from around the country gather to swap songs and dances, and share ritual ceremonies.

DISCOVERING RUSSIAN FOLK MUSIC

Series: Discovering Music
1975, 23 min., color, video
Distributor: University of Illinois #83591
Producer: Bernard Wilets

Plaintive songs, swirling dances, and explanations of the traditional and contemporary prevalence of music in villages, cities, and churches in Russia.

DISCOVERING THE MUSIC OF AFRICA

Series: Discovering Music
1967, 22 min., color, film
Distributors: Phoenix, Penn State
Producer: Bernard Wilets

Social and ceremonial dances of Africa with featured drummer Robert Ayitee of Ghana.

DISCOVERING THE MUSIC OF INDIA

Series: Discovering Music
1969, 22 min., color, video
Distributor: University of Illinois #52938
Producer: Bernard Wilets

Introduces the Carnatic music and instruments used in the south and the Hindustani music and instruments of the north of India. Concludes with a dance in which the artist implies the lyrics of a song through hand gestures and facial expressions.

DISCOVERING THE MUSIC OF LATIN AMERICA

Series: Discovering Music
1969, 20 min., color, video
Distributor: University of Illinois #52937
Producer: Bernard Wilets

Explores the evolution of the Latin American dance and music from Indian and Spanish traditions. Demonstrates the pre-Columbian instruments and the Latin American dance rhythms.

DISCOVERING THE MUSIC OF THE MIDDLE AGES

Series: Discovering Music
1968, 20 min., color, video
Distributor: University of Illinois #52939
Producer: Bernard Wilets

Performances of a peasant's dance, caccia, madrigal and court dance, troubadour's song, and explanations of the development of polyphony and medieval instruments.

DISCOVERING THE MUSIC OF THE MIDDLE EAST

Series: Discovering Music
1968, 20 min., color, film
Distributor: Portland State University #10434
Producer: Bernard Wilets

Explores the music dating back to the seventh-century movement of the Muslims conquering peoples through Middle East, Balkans, Africa, and Spain, illustrated by dancers and musicians. Points out the ornamented melodies and the asymmetrical rhythms played by the oud, santur, qanun, cimbalum, and

dumbek. Shows their influence on classical composers: Rimsky-Korsakov, Khatchaturian, Mozart, and Beethoven.

Discovering Your Expressive Body with Peggy Hackney *Cover art courtesy Dance Horizons Video.*

DISCOVERING YOUR EXPRESSIVE BODY WITH PEGGY HACKNEY

1981, 60 min., color, video
Distributor: Dance Horizons Video
Teacher/Dancer: Peggy Hackney

A University of Washington dance professor, who's also a certified Laban movement analyst, presents ways to become aware of vertical and diagonal connections, moving with three spatial pulls, propelling, and spiraling. The demonstration is based on the fundamentals of Irmgard Bartenieff.

DISTRICT I

1973, 12:30 min., color, video
Distributor/Producer: WGBH
Director: Fred Barzyk
Choreographer: Rudy Perez
Dance Company: Perez Dance Company

A video dance event in the Boston City Hall Plaza in which dancers flow over the landscape in colorful patterns and a marching band appears.

A DIVINE MADNESS

1979, 28 min., color, film
Distributor: Films Inc.
Producer: Oak Creek Films
Director: Leonard Aitken
Narrator: Julie Harris

Portrait of the Perry/Mansfield School of Dance founded in Steamboat Springs, Colorado, in 1910 by Portia Mansfield

Distributor: Film-maker's Coop
Director/Dancer/Editor: Amy Greenfield
Cinematographer: Hilary Harris

A woman falls, rolls, and rises out of mud. Exploring weight, tension, and texture in repetitive patterns, the collaborators probe for the essence of female sensuality. Amy Greenfield's TIDES, a similar exercise set in water rather than mud and presented in slow motion, is also available from Film-maker's Coop.

ELEMENT

1989, 8 min., color, video
Distributors/Producer/Directors: Deborah Gladstein,
Sam Kanter
Principal Dancers: Deborah Gladstein, Jennifer Lane,
Robbyn Scott
Editor: Julie Harrison

Examines the expressive force of simple gestures and stillness in the context of the body's relationship to water. The moving water of a sunlit stream creates a dynamic textural background for ever-changing configurations of abstracted images of the nude form.

THE ELEMENTS OF DANCE

Series: Arts Alive
1989, 15 min., color, video
Distributor: Ririe/Woodbury
Producer: Association of Instructional
TV/Bloomington, Indiana
Director/Writer: Shirley Ririe
Dance on Camera Festival, 1989 Gold Award

Written for teenagers to show how dance training can help develop athletic skills.

ELEVENTH ANNUAL KEIKI HULA FESTIVAL

1986, 95 min., color, video
Distributor: Media Resources
Producer: KHON-TV2, Hawaii

Highlights of ninety-eight performances in a two-day marathon in Hawaii and a children's contest of ancient and modern group and solo hula dances.

ELIOT FELD

1971, 58 min., color, video
Distributor: Christian Blackwood
Producer/Directors: Christian Blackwood, Michael Blackwood
Dancer/Choreographer: Eliot Feld
Principal Dancer: Christine Sarry
Dance Company: Eliot Feld's American Ballet Company
Composers: Gustav Mahler, Johannes Brahms
Commentator: Clive Barnes

Saga of Eliot Feld's initial struggles to form a company for an appearance at the Spoleto Festival and his American debut at the Brooklyn Academy of Music. Among the excerpts are: AT MIDNIGHT, MEADOWLARK, and INTERMEZZO.

ELLIS ISLAND

1982, 30 min., color, b&w, video, film
Distributor: Stutz Co., Databank, WGBH
Producer: Bob Rosen for WGBH

Choreographer/Director/Composer: Meredith Monk
Editor: Girish Bhargava
Prize-winner at both Atlanta and San Francisco Film Festivals

In this portrait of New York City's chief entry station for immigrants to the U.S., the camera sweeps past the debris of decaying buildings to rest on a group of turn-of-the century immigrants, whose predicament is relayed through dance and simple, telling gestures.

ELOISA

1977, 14 min., color, film
Producer/Director/Distributor: Simon Edery
Choreographer/Dancer: Eloisa Vasquel

Traditional solea, an introspective flamenco solo.

EMPEROR JONES

1972, 26 min., color, film
Distributor: Dance Film Archive
Producer: Steeg Productions
Choreographer: Jose Limon
Principal Dancers: Clay Taliaferro (Emperor Jones),
Edward Desoto (The White Man)
Dance Company: American Dance Festival's
repertory company

Choreographed in 1956, based on Eugene O'Neill's 1920 play about a Pullman porter and ex-convict who ruled a West Indian island through fear and exploitation.

ENCOUNTER

1970, 10 min., color, film
Distributor: Film-makers Coop
Producer: Dance Circle of Boston
Producer/Director/Choreographer/Dancer:
Amy Greenfield
Dancer: Rima Wolff

Struggle within one woman and between two women.

ENCOUNTER WITH THE GODS: ORISSI DANCE
WITH SANJUKTA PANIGRAHI

1989, 30 min., color, video
Distributor: Kampo Cultural Center
Producers: Kampo, Asia Society
Principal Dancer: Sanjukta Panigrahi

Performance and explanation of the Indian Orissi dance by one of the most acclaimed masters.

ENDANCE

Series: Alive from Off Center
1988, 8:30 min., color, video
Distributor: Electronic Arts Intermix
Producer/Distributor: KTCA/TV
Director/Distributors: John Sanborn & Mary Perillo
Principal Dancer: Timothy Buckley
Composer: Blue Gene Tyranny

One man's bittersweet farewell to the dance world, with a synthesis of performance, interviews, personal commentary, and comic interludes.

THE ENDURING ESSENCE: THE TECHNIQUE AND
CHOREOGRAPHY OF ISADORA DUNCAN, REMEMBERED
& RECONSTRUCTED BY GEMZE DE LAPPE

> 1990, 60 min., color, video
> Distributor: Images
> Choreographer: Isadora Duncan
> Reconstructor: Gemze De Lappe
> Producer/Director/Dancer: Sharon Arslanian
> Editor: John Gunther

A professional dancer/director/teacher recalls her early
Duncan training and describes how she has applied that
technique in her approach to dance. Includes a class at
Smith College and six dances: BALLSPIEL, CLASSICAL
DUET, WATER STUDY, BLESSED SPIRITS, THREE GRACES,
and THE MOTHER.

L'ENFANT ET LES SORTILEGES

> 1987, 51 min., color, video
> Distributor: Home Vision #ENF01
> Producer: National Video Corporation
> Director: Hans Hulscher
> Choreographer: Jiri Kylian
> Dance Company: Nederlands Dance Theatre
> Composer: Maurice Ravel
> Dance on Camera Festival, 1987 Gold Award

Based on a poem by Colette in which a boy refuses to do his home-
work and destroys his surroundings after he's punished. The ballet
begins as the objects in his room come to life seeking revenge.

ENGLISH IS A WAY OF SPEECH

> 10 min., color, film
> Distributor/Producer: Sheila Hellman
> Director: Warren Schroeder

Geared for teachers of teenagers as a guide to using the spoken
word as an inspiration for movement.

ENIGMA VARIATIONS

> 1970, 33 min., color, film
> Distributor: Dance Film Archive
> Director: James Archibald
> Choreographer: Sir Frederick Ashton
> Principal Dancers: Derek Rencher, Svetlana Beriosova,
> Stanley Holden, Anthony Dowell, Alexander Grant
> Dance Company: Royal Ballet
> Composer: Edward Elgar

This English story-ballet is a grand bow to the Edwardian
composer Edward Elgar created with colorful characters by the
director of the Royal Ballet, Sir Frederick Ashton.

ENTR'ACTE

> 1924, 18 min., b&w, film
> Distributor: Dance Film Archive
> Dance Company: Rolf De Mare's Ballets Suedois
> Director: Rene Clair
> Choreographer: Jean Borlin
> Composer: Erik Satie
> Design: Francis Picabia

Rene Clair's second film, a zany, Dada-inspired, silent

masterpiece, formed part of Jean Borlin's RELACHE,
performed by the Ballets Suedois.

ERICK HAWKINS

> 1964, 15 min., b&w, film
> Distributor/Producer: University of California at
> Los Angeles Media Center
> Dance Company: Erick Hawkins Dance Company

Erick Hawkins, a former Martha Graham dancer, and his
company perform dances from his repertory, followed by a discussion of possible interpretations of the pieces, their
significance in the modern dance movement, and the relationship of modern dance to the other performing arts.

ERIK BRUHN—ARTIST OF THE BALLET

> 1973, 21 min., color, film
> Distributor: Audience Planners, Inc.
> Producer: Danish Government Film Office
> Principal Dancers: Erik Bruhn, Carla Fracci
> Commentator: Clive Barnes

An interview with world-renowned Danish ballet dancer,
the late Erik Bruhn, onstage, in a television studio, and in
rehearsal with Italian prima ballerina Carla Fracci.

THE ERIK BRUHN GALA: WORLD BALLET COMPETITION

> 1983, 90 min., color, video
> Distributors: Home Vision #BRU01, Corinth
> Producers: RM Arts and Canadian Broadcasting Corp.
> Director: Norman Campbell
> Principal Dancers: Karen Kain, Glen Tetley,
> Natalia Makarova, Kevin McKenzie, Owen Montague,
> Bonnie Moore
> Dancers from National Ballet of Canada, Royal Ballet,
> Royal Danish Ballet, American Ballet Theatre

Gala for the first Erik Bruhn prize competition held in
Toronto, Canada with dancers from National Ballet of Canada,
Royal Ballet, Royal Danish Ballet, American Ballet Theatre in
honor of the great dancer and choreographer.

ESSENTIALS OF TAP TECHNIQUE

> 1990, 6 min., color, video
> Distributor: Electronic Arts Intermix
> Producer: The Circuit Theatre, Inc.
> Directors: Skip Blumberg, Susan Goldbetter
> Principal Dancers: Charles Cook, Brenda Bufalino,
> Kevin Ramsey

Red tap shoes open this artful short with slow motion and
amplified sound for the actual flaps, stamps, and the regular
tempos to get the rhythms. Each expert demonstrates his or
her trademark steps with inserts of the full body.

ESTAMPA FLAMENCA

> 1978, 29 min., color, video
> Distributor/Dancer/Choreographer: Maria Benitez
> Producer/Director: Dave Ellis for KNME, Albuquerque

A documentary about flamenco dancer Maria Benitez and
her Estampa Flamenca dance company in performance
and rehearsal, with insights on the influences her Native

American and Puerto Rican heritage had on her approach to Spanish dance.

ETERNAL CIRCLE

1952, 12 min., b&w, film
Distributor: Dance Film Archive
Directors: Herbert Seggelke, Harald Kreutzberg
Dancer/Choreographer: Harald Kreutzberg
Composer: Frederich Wilckens

A masked solo, choreographed in the 1930s by Harald Kreutzberg, a German dancer born in Czechoslovakia in 1902, depicting a drunk, a prostitute, a king, and finally, death.

ETHNIC DANCE AROUND THE WORLD

24 min., color, film, video
Distributor: Phoenix Films
Producer: Wayne Mitchell

Examples of dances from the Americas, Asia, Africa, Europe and Australia help us to understand why dances and music vary from one culture to the next. Depicts the religious basis of many dances, as well as dances for planting and harvesting, courtship, and entertaining royalty.

ETHNIC DANCE: ROUND TRIP TO TRINIDAD

Series: "A Time to Dance"
1960, 29 min., b&w, film, video
Distributor: Indiana University
Producer: WGBH-TV
Choreographer/Dancers: Geoffrey Holder,
Carmen de Lavallade

Explores the significance of the Caribbean dance in the context of concert dance with performances of BELE, adapted from the European minuet; YANVALLOU, part of the voodoo ritual, and BANDA, a Haitian dance of death. Performed by the multi-talented Geoffrey Holder and Carmen de Lavallade.

ETUDE IN FREE

1982, 8 min., color, video
Distributor/Producer: ARC Videodance
Directors: Celia Ipiotis, Jeff Bush
Choreographer/Dancer: Dianne McIntyre
Composer: Bobby McFerrin

Coordinating body, mind, and voice, in a style akin to singer Bobby McFerrin's, modern dancer Diane McIntyre builds a quiet, lyric solo to an explosive high and then lets it fade to black.

AN EVENING WITH ALVIN AILEY AMERICAN
DANCE THEATRE

1987, 110 min., color, video
Distributor: Home Vision
Producer: RM Assoc.
Director: Thomas Grimm
Choreographers: Alvin Ailey, Judith Jamison, Talley Beatty
Dance Company: Alvin Ailey American Dance Theatre
Composers: Alice Coltrane, Laura Nyro, Voices of
East Harlem, Gospel and Blues
Dance on Camera Festival, 1987 Honorable Mention

Performance tape of DIVINING, choreographed by Judith Jamison, former company member, and current director of the Ailey company, STACK-UP by Talley Beatty, and two by the founder Alvin Ailey, REVELATIONS, and the solo CRY.

An Evening with Alvin Ailey American Dance Theatre
Divining *performed by the company. Photo courtesy Home Vision.*

AN EVENING WITH KYLIAN AND THE NEDERLANDS
DANS THEATRE

1987, 87 min., color, video
Distributor: Home Vision #KYl01
Producer: RM Associates
Choreographer: Jiri Kylian
Directors: Hans Hulscher, Torbjorn Ehrnvall
Dance Company: Nederlands Dans Theatre
Composers: Igor Stravinsky, Toru Takemitsu,
Claude Debussy, Leos Janacek
Dance on Camera Festival, 1987 Silver Award

Program by the Dutch ballet company includes SVADEBKA (Les Noces), set to music of Igor Stravinsky; LA CATHEDRALE ENGLOUTIE, set to music of Claude Debussy; SINFONIETTA, set to music of Leos Janacek; and TORSO, set to music of Toru Takemitsu.

AN EVENING WITH THE BALLET RAMBERT

1986, 103 min., color, video
Distributor: Home Vision #RAM01
Producer: RM Arts
Director: Thomas Grimm
Choreographers: Robert North, Christopher Bruce
Dance Company: Ballet Rambert
Composers: Bill Withers, Leos Janacek
Dance on Camera Festival, 1987 Honorable Mention

A performance documentary shot in England with ballets LONELY TOWN, LONELY STREET (North/Withers), INTIMATE PAGES (Bruce/Janacek), SERGEANT EARLY'S DREAM, with choreography by Christopher Bruce set to folk songs.

AN EVENING WITH THE BOLSHOI

1987, 120 min., color, video
Distributor: Home Vision #BOl02
Producers: National Video Corporation, BBC
Director: John Vernon
Choreographers: Yuri Grigorovich, Marius Petipa, Lev Ivanov, Michel Fokine
Principal Dancers: Irek Mukhamedov, Natalia Bessmertnova
Dance Company: Bolshoi Ballet
Composers: Aram Khatchaturian, Leon Minkus, Peter Ilyich Tchaikovsky, Frederic Chopin, Dmitri Shostakovich
Dance on Camera Festival, 1987 Honorable Mention

Excerpts from eight ballets showcasing the company's young talent with excerpts from THE GOLDEN AGE (Grigorovich/Shostakovich), SPARTACUS (Grigorovich/Khatchaturian), DON QUIXOTE (Petipa/Minkus), LA BAYADERE (Petipa/Minkus), SWAN LAKE (Ivanov & Petipa/Tchaikovsky), LES SYLPHIDES (Fokine/Chopin), SPRING WATERS, and TEA FOR TWO.

AN EVENING WITH THE KIROV

1988, 129 min., color, video
Distributor/Producers: BBC, Entertainment Corp
Choreographers: Marius Petipa, Paul Taglioni, Arthur Saint Leon, Joseph Mazilier
Principal Dancer: Natalia Makarova
Dance Company: Kirov Ballet
Composers: Peter Ilyich Tchaikovsky, Leon Minkus, Adolphe Adam, Riccardo Drigo, Jacques Offenbach

For the first time since her defection, Natalia Makarova dances with the Kirov in Russia for this memorable performance of excerpts from SWAN LAKE (Petipa/Tchaikovsky), LA BAYADERE (Petipa/Minkus), LA ESMERALDA (Petipa/Drigo), DON QUIXOTE (Petipa/Minkus), LE CORSAIRE (Mazilier, Petipa, Chabukiani/Adam, Minkus, and Drigo), LA VIVANDIERE (Arthur Michel Saint-Leon), and LE PAPILLON (Taglioni/Offenbach).

AN EVENING WITH THE ROYAL BALLET

1963, 85 min., color, video
Distributor: Kultur #1182
Producer: British Home Entertainment
Choreographers: Michel Fokine, Rudolf Nureyev, Marius Petipa, Frederick Ashton
Principal Dancers: Margot Fonteyn, Rudolf Nureyev, Antoinette Sibley, David Blair
Composers: Peter Ilyich Tchaikovsky, Frederic Chopin, Adolphe Adam

Filmed live at the Royal Opera House, Covent Garden, London, LA VALSE, an excerpt from LES SYLPHIDES, pas de deux from LE CORSAIRE, Aurora's Wedding from SLEEPING BEAUTY.

EVENT FOR TELEVISION

Series: Dance In America
1977, 56 min., color, film, video
Distributor: Cunningham Dance Foundation
Producer: Emile Ardolino
Director: Merrill Brockway
Choreographer/Dancer: Merce Cunningham
Dance Company: Merce Cunningham
Composers: John Cage, David Tudor

Shows excerpts from modern dances MINUTIAE (1954), SEPTET (1953), ANTIC MEET (1958), SCRAMBLE (1967), RAINFOREST (1968), SOUNDDANCE (1974), VIDEO TRIANGLE (1976).

THE EVENT OF THE YEAR

1981, 45 min., color, film
Distributor: Troma, Inc.
Producers: Lloyd Kaufman, Michael Herz with National Dance Institute
Dance on Camera Festival, 1984 Award

Jacques D'Amboise, the former New York City Ballet principal dancer who founded the National Dance Institute (NDI), works with his students, New York City public school children, for NDI's annual performance at Madison Square Garden. Folk singer Judy Collins, choreographer George Balanchine, tap dancer Peter Gennaro, and New York City Ballet principal Patricia McBride make their guest appearances.

EVERYTHING YOU SHOULD KNOW ABOUT HAWAIIAN/TAHITIAN HULA

1990, 60 min (Tahitian), 80 min. (Hawaiian), color, video
Distributor/Dancer: Charmaine

Two videos with variations of step and arm movements, background history, explanation of language and costumes.

EX-ROMANCE

1987, 49:27 min., color, video
Distributor: WGBH-TV
Producer: Susan Dowling for WGBH New Television in association with Channel Four
Director/Editor: Charles Atlas
Choreographer/Dancer: Karole Armitage
Principal Dancers: Michael Clark, Susan Blankensop, Jean-Marie Didiere, Brenda McPherson, Louis Viana
Composers: Gene Ammons, J.S. Bach, David Allan Coe, Henry Fiol, Jeffrey Lohn, Gene Vincent

Modern dance taped in an airport terminal, rehearsal studio, and on an airplane wing, and framed with a satire of a television interview.

**Exercise with Billie: Chair Exercises to Keep
You Moving**
Cover art courtesy Dance Horizons Video.

EXERCISE WITH BILLIE: CHAIR EXERCISES TO KEEP
YOU MOVING

> 1990, 60 min., color, video
> Distributor: Dance Horizons Video
> Producer: WLRN-TV
> Principal Dancer: Billie Kirpich

An exercise program for those with movement impairment,
the elderly, and the homebound. All exercises are performed either in or with the support of a chair.

EXHIBITION

> 1985, 7:30 min., color, video
> Distributor: Antenna
> Producer: Agent Orange
> Director: Bernar Herbert
> Choreographer/Dancer: Daniele Desnoyers

A modern work shot in four different places by two
Canadian artists.

EXOTIC AND ACROBATIC DANCES

> 1900, 10 min., b&w, film
> Distributor: Dance Film Archive

Silent films from the turn of the century featuring Spanish exhibition dancing and contortionists.

THE EYE HEARS, THE EAR SEES

> 1970, 59 min., color, film
> Distributor/Producers: National Film Board of Canada, BBC
> Choreographer: Ludmilla Chiriaeff

> Principal Dancers: Margaret Mercier, Vincent Warren
> Narrators: Gavin Millar, Grant Munro

Norman McLaren explains his attraction to film and his dis-
content with conventional techniques. Includes excerpts from
his films HEN HOP and PAS DE DEUX.

EYE ON DANCE

> 1981–present, 30 min., color, video
> Distributor/Producers: Jeff Bush, Celia Ipiotis for ARC Video

The oldest weekly talk show hosted by Celia Ipiotis, now running prime time in the New York Metropolitan area on WNYC-
TV, offers a standard format of one to three guests with short
performance clips or stills. With a collection of close to 400
programs, the series includes an intensive coverage of the
issues affecting the world of dance and an introduction to the
broad spectrum of artists, producers, technicians, and
specialists in support services. The topics range from collaborations, health, partnering, and reconstructions to tricks of
surviving as an artist.

FALL RIVER LEGEND

> 1971, 10 min., color, film
> Distributor: University of Minnesota
> Producers: Camco Productions, Inc. for Group W, Westing-
> house Broadcasting in association with Griffin Productions
> Producer/Director: Bob Shanks
> Choreographer: Agnes de Mille
> Principal Dancers: Sallie Wilson, Lucia Chase, Tom Adair
> Cinematographers: Michael Waldleigh, Ted Churchill,
> Charles Levy
> Dance Company: American Ballet Theatre
> Composer: Morton Gould
> Costume Designer: Miles White

Excerpts from the 1948 ballet based on the true story of Lizzie
Borden, accused of murdering her father and stepmother with
an ax in 1892. Filmed at Sturbridge, Massachusetts.

FALLING OFF THE BACK PORCH

> Series: Educational Performance Collection
> 1983, 15 min., color, video
> Distributor/Producer: Dance Notation Bureau
> Choreographer: Clay Taliaferro
> Composer: Claude Debussy

Taped performance at Arizona State University of a dance that
acknowledges the challenge of living with inconsistencies.
Multi-media kit provides advanced-level Labanotated score by
Mary Corey, critical text, and study/performance rights.

FAN AND BUBBLE DANCE

> 1942, 9 min., b&w, film
> Distributor: Dance Film Archive
> Choreographer/Dancers: Sally Rand, Faith Bacon

Sally Rand set the reputation of strippers in America on a new
track by artfully disguising her nude, lean body with a giant fan.

FAN TECHNIQUES FOR ORIENTAL DANCE (2 videos)

> 1988–1989, 63 & 82 min. each, color, video
> Distributor/Producer/Director/Choreographer/Dancer:
> Chandra

A discussion of various types of fans with demonstrations of ways to use each type in Middle Eastern dance. In the second video, the demonstration shows how to use a fan with a veil, along with tips on dancing with two and three veils together.

FANTASIA

    1940, 120 min., color, film, video
    Distributor: Buena Vista
    Producer: Walt Disney
    Directors: Samuel Armstrong, James Algar, Bill Roberts, Paul Satterfield, Hamilton Luske, Jim Handley, Ford Beebe, T. Hee, Norman Ferguson, Wilfred Jackson
    Composers: Johann Sebastian Bach, Peter Ilyich Tchaikovsky, Paul Dukas, Igor Stravinsky, Ludwig van Beethoven, Modest Petrovitch Mussorgsky, Franz Schubert

Eight concert pieces choreographed through animation. The Sorcerer's Apprentice, among other animated characters, moves with a grace and musicality few ballerinas would dare to challenge. Also to be noted for choreographic invention within animated form: Disney's LADY AND THE TRAMP (1955), SLEEPING BEAUTY (1959), DUMBO (1941), available through Buena Vista.

FANTASY OF FEET

    Series: Magic Movements, Unit 3 Let's See Series
    1970, 8 min., color, film
    Distributors: University of Southern California, Encyclopaedia Britannica

Little feet walk, dance, run, and jump in sandals, flippers, slippers, boots, and shoe-free. Encourages children to realize how shoes and the surfaces they're designed for affect our movements.

FARRASHAH, THE VIDEO

    100 min., color, video
    Distributor: G.A.B. Productions
    Composers: Doug Adams and Light Rain, Ramal Lamarr, Jimmy Linardoes, Ray Marijanian, Mary Ellen Donald, Walter Degler

Offers a cross sampling of Middle Eastern and Moroccan dances including: Geudra, Hafla Zozak, Plaka, and other fantasies by this Georgia-based production company.

FEATHERS

    33 min., color, film
    Distributor: Dance Film Archive
    Choreographer: William Dunas

Classically oriented solos for women.

FERNANDO BUJONES IN CLASS

    1986, 31 min., color, video
    Distributor: Kultur #1142
    Producer/Director: Zeida Cecilia-Mendez
    Principal Dancer: Fernando Bujones

The ballet star executes his ballet barre and center combinations.

FERNANDO BUJONES IN COPPELIA

    1980, 110 min., color, video
    Distributor: Kultur
    Choreographer: Arthur Saint-Leon

    Principal Dancers: Fernando Bujones, Ana Maria Castanon
    Dance Company: Ballets De San Juan
    Composer: Leo Delibes

The 1870 ballet classic about the mechanical doll that comes to life.

FERNANDO BUJONES IN THE SLEEPING BEAUTY

    1982, 120 min., color, video
    Distributor: Kultur #1122
    Choreographer: Marius Petipa
    Principal Dancer: Fernando Bujones
    Dance Company: Ballet del Teatro Municipal in Santiago
    Composer: Peter Ilyich Tchaikovsky

Fernando Bujones performs the classic ballet as guest artist in Chile.

FESTIVAL IN COMMEMORATION OF THE DEAD

    1965, 14 min., color, film
    Distributor: Pennstate #EO1228
    Producer: Wissen

In a village in Mali, sacrificial goats and millet beer are brought to a festival in which dancers wearing kanaga masks appear. For a similar ceremony, see FESTIVAL IN COMMEMORATION OF THE DEAD AT NINGARI from Pennstate #EO1345.

FESTIVAL OF DANCE

    1973, 60 min., color, film
    Distributor: Dance Film Archive
    Producer/Director: Ted Steeg
    Choreographers: Doris Humphrey, Martha Graham, Charles Weidman, Jose Limon
    Composers: Hector Villa-Lobos, Lionel Nowak, Wallingford Riegger

A company performs modern dance classics at the American Dance Festival at Connecticut College with shots of auditions, rehearsals, and performance excerpts from EMPEROR JONES, FLICKERS, NEW DANCE, and WITH MY RED FIRES.

A FESTIVAL ON THE NILE

    1989, 90 min., color, video
    Distributor/Producer/Dancer: Azuri
    Principal Dancers: Amaya, Delilah, Dahlal, Margarita Tzighan

Two-day seminar and performance by Middle Eastern soloists from around the country. All proceeds from the dance video go to benefit the Leukemia Society.

FIELDS

    1987, 11 min., color, video
    Distributor: Electronic Arts Intermix
    Director: James Byrne
    Choreographer: Susan Hadley
    Composer: Bradley Sowash

Shot in plowed fields and in an urban plaza where dancers clad in suits suggest the gestures of farmers.

FIGURES

    Series: Art of Seeing
    1968, 14 min., color, film
    Distributor: PennState

Producer: ACI Productions

Creative treatment of the human figure in life, art and dance as interpreted by artists of many eras and cultures. Shows how a dancer's movements can be distorted and exaggerated through cinematic effects.

LA FILLE MAL GARDEE

1981, 98 min., color, video
Distributors: HBO #3563, Pioneer (Laserdisk)
Producer: National Video Corp.
Director: John Vernon
Choreographer: Frederick Ashton
Principal Dancers: Lesley Collier (Lise),
Michael Coleman (Colas), Leslie Edwards (Thomas)
Dance Company: Royal Ballet
Composer: Francois Joseph Herold
Set Designer: Osbert Lancaster

Instilling obedience in willful children has never been easy, whether in 1879, the premiere of this ballet by Jean Dauberval, or in 1960, the debut for Frederick Ashton's version. Ashton adds various English folk dances (maypole, Morris, sword, and Lancashire clog) to give a rustic feeling to the story about a young girl evading a planned marriage.

FILM WITH THREE DANCERS

1970, 20 min., color, film
Distributor: Film-maker's Coop
Producer/Director/Sound: Ed Emshwiller
Principal Dancers: Carolyn Carlson, Emery Hermans,
Bob Beswick

With the change of costumes, from leotards to bluejeans to nudity, the director approaches movement as stylized, natural, or abstract to present three ways of seeing.

FILMS OF DANCE BY EDISON AND DICKSON

1897–1907, 20 min., b&w, film
Distributor: Dance Film Archive
Director: Thomas Edison
Principal Dancer: Annabella Moore

A series of shorts marking the beginning of it all by the genius who invented the kinetoscope, microphone, and the record player.

FIREBIRD

1980s, 55 min., color, video
Distributor: Home Vision #FIR02
Producer: RM Arts
Director: Thomas Grimm
Choreographer: Glen Tetley
Dance Company: Royal Danish Ballet
Composer: Igor Stravinsky
RAI Prize, Prix Italia

A firebird, kept in an enchanted garden, is guarded by a severe Victorian family. With the help of her lover, the firebird liberates herself from the family's bonds. Not to be confused with the original FIREBIRD choreographed by Michel Fokine and premiered by Diaghilev's Ballets Russes in 1910, Adolph Bolm's version of 1945, or George Balanchine's of 1949.

FIRST SOLO

1982, 10 min., color, video
Distributor/Choreographer: Patrice Regnier
Director: Davidson Gigliotti
Principal Dancer: Sallie Wilson

Solo created for the dramatic ballerina.

THE FIRST STEP

1988, 60 min., color, video
Distributor/Producer: Michelle Audet for New York City
Ballet Education
Director/Editors: Roberto Romano, Len Morris
Choreographer: George Balanchine
Principal Dancers: Deborah Wingert, Marisa Cerveris, Patrick
Hinson, Russell Kaiser
Composer: Peter Ilyich Tchaikovsky

Documentary on the New York City Ballet school with an excerpt from THE NUTCRACKER.

FIRST STEPS

26 min., color, film, video
Distributor: Phoenix Films
Producer/Directors: Ted Haimes, Pamela Emil

Each fall, representatives of the Alvin Ailey Dance Center and the New York School for Circus Arts/Big Apple Circus audition public school students in search of gifted dancers and acrobats. The film follows the students through the year, as they study the arts of the trampoline, trapeze, tight rope wire, and dance.

FLAMENCO

1986, 70 min., color, video
Distributor: Films for the Humanities
Producer: Spanish Television
Director: Reni Mertens, Walter Marti
Teacher: Ciro
Principal Dancers: Pepa Guerna, Antonio El Divino

Jota, bulerias, soleares, malagena, cante jondo, intercut with sweeps of the landscape, performed by young and old for friends in the four corners of Spain.

FLAMENCO AT 5:15

1983, 30 min., color, film, video
Distributor: Direct Cinema
Producers: Cynthia Scott, Adam Symansky for National
Film Board of Canada
Director: Cynthia Scott
Teachers: Susana and Antonio Robledo
Academy Award, 1983 Best Documentary Short

Advanced students at the National Ballet School of Canada demonstrate their Spanish dance finesse under the guidance of their teachers, Susana and Antonio Robledo.

FLAMENCO GITANO

1969, 21 min., b&w, film
Distributor: Pennstate
Producer: Wissen

Spanish gypsies demonstrate five types of Andalusian dance: soleares, alegrias, tanguillos, tientos, and bulerias accompanied by guitars and palmas.

THE FLAPPER STORY

    1985, 29 min, color, film, video
    Distributor: The Cinema Guild
    Director: Lauren Lazin
    Documentary Merit Award, Academy of Picture Arts and Science; Silver Plaque, Chicago Film Festival; and Philadelphia Film Festival; CINE Golden Eagle Award

Interviews and archival film footage in this examination of the provocative "new woman" of America's roaring twenties.

FLASHDANCE

    1983, 95 min., color, film, video
    Distributor/Producer: Paramount Pictures
    Director: Adrian Lyne
    Choreographer: Jeffrey Hornaday
    Principal Dancers: Marine Jahan (Dance Double), Jennifer Beals, Michael Nouri
    Writers: Tom Hedley, Joe Eszterhas

Blue collar worker by day, erotic dancer by night, and lover whenever feasible, the heroine shocks and delights the stodgy jury when she auditions for the Pittsburgh Ballet.

FLATLAND EPISODE

    1987, 10 min., color, video
    Distributor/Producer/Choreographer/Dancer: Melanie Stewart in association with WHYY-TV
    Director: Kathryn Esher
    Principal Dancers: Mark Chatman-Royce, Debi Glennon, Renee Gomila, Donna Stewart
    Composer: Chris Unrath
    Set Designer: H.A. Phillips

In this dance created for the camera, the characters explore two-dimensional landscapes in a journey through space and time.

FLICKERS

    1972, 19 min., color, film
    Distributor: Dance Film Archive
    Producer/Director: Ted Steeg
    Choreographer: Charles Weidman
    Principal Dancer: Linda Tarnay
    Dance Company: Professional Repertory Company at Connecticut College

Spoof of the silent movies in four parts: HEARTS AFLAME, WAGES OF SIN, FLOWERS OF THE DESERT and HEARTS COURAGEOUS. Choreographed in 1941 with Doris Humphrey and Charles Weidman in the leading roles.

FLUTE OF KRISHNA

    1926, 10 min., color, film
    Distributor: Dance Film Archive
    Producer: Eastman Kodak Company
    Choreographer: Martha Graham
    Principal Dancers: Robert Ross, Evelyn Sabin, Betty Macdonald, Suzanne Vacanti
    Set/Costume Designer: Norman Edwards

    Composer: Cyril Scott

Choreographed by Martha Graham while in residence at the Eastman School of Music, which produced this silent film as part of an experiment with a two-color process.

FOLKLORICO

    1989, 29 min., color, video
    Distributor: Barr Films

Rehearsals, performances, and interviews with experts on the folk music and dance of Mexico and the Southwest of the United States.

FONTEYN AND NUREYEV/THE PERFECT PARTNERSHIP

    1985, 90 min., color, video
    Distributor: Kultur #1151
    Producer: Peter Batty
    Choreographers: Frederick Ashton, Marius Petipa, Michel Fokine, Joseph Mazilier
    Principal Dancers: Margot Fonteyn, Rudolf Nureyev, Ninette De Valois
    Composers: Sergei Prokofiev, Peter Ilyich Tchaikovsky, Adolphe Adam, Frederic Chopin
    Narrator: Robert Powell

Traces the Fonteyn/Nureyev partnership from its inception in 1962 to conclusion in 1978, with commentary, behind-the-scenes footage, and excerpts from MARGUERITE & ARMAND, ROMEO AND JULIET, LE CORSAIRE, LUCIFER, SLEEPING BEAUTY, LES SYLPHIDES.

FOOTAGE

    1976, 9:30 min., color, film
    Distributor: Film-maker's Coop
    Director: Dave Gearey
    Principal Dancer: Dana Reitz

Feet running, digging into mud and sand, playing with the air, and casting shadows.

FOOTLOOSE

    1984, 106 min., color, video
    Distributor/Producers: Rachmil and Craig Sadan for Paramount
    Director: Herbert Ross
    Choreographer: Lynn Taylor-Corbett
    Principal Dancers: Kevin Bacon, Lori Singer
    Writer: Dean Pitchford

City boy visits an uptight, small town in the Midwest and gets everyone to dance, a no-no among the majority of the people in the town who have been following the dictates of the local religious authorities.

FOR DANCERS

    1989, 17 min., color, film
    Distributor: Picture Start
    Producer/Director: Bridget Murname
    Principal Dancers: Fred Strickler, Iris Pell, Louise Burns, Susan Rose
    Composers: Megan Roberts, Benjamin Britten, sound collages by Bridget Murname

Dance on Camera Festival, 1990 Honorable Mention

Fred Strickler, a tap dancer, Louise Burns, a former Merce Cunningham dancer, and Susan Rose, a Boston-based modern dancer/choreographer perform their own choreography and a work by Bella Lewitzky.

FOR THE LOVE OF DANCE

1981, 57:46 min., color, film, video
Distributor/Producer: National Film Board of Canada
Directors: Michael McKennirey, Cynthia Scott, David Wilson, John D. Smith
Dance Companies: Les Grands Ballets Canadiens, National Ballet of Canada, Toronto Dance Theatre, Le Groupe De La Place Royale, Winnipeg Ballet, Winnipeg Contemporary Dance Company, Anna Wyman Dance Theater
Dance on Camera Festival, 1982 Award

A panorama of dance in Canada featuring seven of the country's leading dance companies.

FOR THE SPIDER WOMAN

1970s, 16 min., color, film
Distributor: Dance Film Archive
Choreographer: Jane Comfort

Silent solo repeated in various stages of pregnancy.

FORBIDDEN CITY, U.S.A.

1989, 56 min., color, film, video
Distributor: Deepfocus
Producer/Director: Arthur Dong
Principal Dancers: Tony & Wing, Mary Mammon, Dottie Sun, Jack Mei Ling
Composer: Gary Stockdale
Editor: Walt Louie

This documentary takes us back to San Francisco's Forbidden City nightclub, the Chinese Cotton Club of the '30s and '40s. Chinese American performers, who appeared regularly at the club, discuss how their careers were thwarted by racism. Clips of their performances are included.

FOUR DANCE CLASSES IN EGYPT (4 videos)

1980s, 120 min. each, color, video
Distributor/Producer/Dancer: Eva Cernik
Teachers: Raiya Hassan, Hana, Khairiya Maazin

Instructional videos on Middle Eastern dance, with the first two: classes in the Cairo cabaret style; the third, in the Reda style with a Saiidi routine; the final, a Ghawazi cane dance accompanied by rababa and darabukas.

FOUR JOURNEYS INTO MYSTIC TIME

1978, 109 min., color, film
Distributor/Director/Producer: Shirley Clarke
Producer: Spiral Productions
Cinematographer: Fuding Cheng
Choreographer/Producer: Marian Scott
Dance Company: University of California at Los Angeles Dance Company
Dance Films Festival, 1979 Honors Award

Of the four journeys, the first, MYSTERIUM, explores the dynamic union of masculine and feminine. INITIATION examines the mystery of ancient rites. In TRANCE, a dancer, through video electronics, creates the aura surrounding a soul in transition. ONE-TWO-THREE is a comic waltz.

FOUR MOVES IN SPACE: A VIDEODANCE SUITE

1980, 29 min., color, video
Distributor: ARC Video
Director: Jeff Bush
Choreographer/Dancer: Celia Ipiotis

Solos ranging from the stark A PITY to the multilayered and chroma-faceted GALAXY EBB TIDE, to CHAPPAQUIDDICK EVENING SONG, shot on the beach after the Kennedy scandal, and CRIMSON BLUE.

THE FOUR SEASONS

1983, 14 min., color, video
Distributor: Electronic Arts Intermix
Producer: Maxi Cohen
Director/Choreographer: Eva Maier
Cinematographers: Bill Marpet, Robert Hertzler, Dena Crane
Composers: Antonio Vivaldi, Paul Pratt, Tommaso Albinoni
Music: "Winter" from "The Four Seasons," "Saint Bernard Waltz," "Adagio in G Minor"

Set in a glass hothouse, pasture, sand dune, and formal room, this introspective solo suggests the seasons of life, the cycle of moods and energies, the delicate balance between light and dark.

FOUR SOLOS FOR FOUR WOMEN

1980, 28 min., color, video
Distributor: Film-maker's Coop
Producer/Director: Amy Greenfield
Cinematographer: Richard Leacock
Principal Dancers: Suzanne Gregoire, Susan Hendrickson, Sudabeh Keshmirian, Amy Greenfield
Composers: Franz Schubert, Hugo Wolf

Close-ups on four women who arch, stretch, bend with their hair unbound, their bodies wrapped in satin.

THE FOUR TEMPERAMENTS

Series: Dance in America
1977, 30 min., color, film
Distributor: Dance Films Archive
Producer: Emile Ardolino for PBS
Director: Merrill Brockway
Choreographer: George Balanchine
Principal Dancers: Bart Cook, Merrill Ashley, Daniel Duell, Peter Martins, Suzanne Farrell, Robert Weiss
Dance Company: New York City Ballet
Composer: Paul Hindemith
Dance on Camera Festival, 1981 Award

The 1946 ballet by the late Russian-born choreographer.

FRACTIONS I

1977–1978, 33 min. each, both color and b&w, film, video
Distributor/Producer: Cunningham Dance Foundation
Director: Charles Atlas
Choreographer: Merce Cunningham

Principal Dancers: Karole Armitage, Louise Burns,
Graham Conley, Ellen Cornfield, Meg Eginton, Lisa Fox,
Chris Komar, Robert Kovich
Dance Company: Merce Cunningham Dance Company
Composer: John Gibson
Set/Costume Designer: Mark Lancaster

A dance choreographed for the camera with the objective of
discovering the flexibility of our perspective. Dancers appear
both outside and within four monitors, all contained within
the frame of the fifth monitor.

FRAGMENTS: MAT/GLASS

1975, 18 min., b&w, video
Distributor: Film-maker's Coop
Producer/Director/Editor/Choreographer: Amy Greenfield
Principal Dancer: Ben Dolphin

Two-channel videotape edited from a live video dance
performance at New York City's Kitchen Center, during which two
cameramen shot a solo with live monitors surrounding the
performance area to register close-ups, pull-backs, and
image inversions.

FRAGMENTS OF VOYAGES IN AFRICA

1985, 30 min., color, video
Distributor/Producer/Director/Dancer: Henry Smith
Dance Company: Solaris Dance Theatre

Combines on-location African footage shot along the Congo River,
in tribal villages, in the rain forest, and along the rapids of the
Congo River, with dance impressions of three trips to Senegal,
Ghana, and Nigeria made by Solaris Dance Theatre in 1980–1983.

FRANK HATCHETT PRESENTS SIZZLIN' HOT JAZZ

1989, 30 min., color, video
Distributor: Taffy's
Producer/Teacher: Frank Hatchett

Warm-up exercises, isolations, progressions and routines by
the New York–based jazz teacher.

FRANK HATCHETT: INSPIRATION

1984, 60 min., color, video
Distributor: Taffy's
Producers: Ted and Diane Sorensen for Danzing
Teacher: Frank Hatchett

Shot by Arkvay Productions, this documentary catches the
excitement of a typical New York jazz class with its intense
energy and blend of talent, shapes, ages, and personalities.
Led by Frank Hatchett, a popular teacher on the dance
teachers' convention circuit. Workbook also available.

FRED ASTAIRE: LEARN TO DANCE (5 videos)

1989, 30 min. each, color, video
Distributor: Fred Astaire Performing Arts Association
Producer: Best Film & Video
Principal Dancers: Lee and Peggy Santos

Lessons for beginners with two dances taught in each video
in the styles of latin (cha cha and salsa), ballroom (fox-trot
and waltz), swing (lindy and jitterbug), and country
western (cotton-eyed Joe and polka).

FRENCH CANCAN

1954, 93 min., color, video
Distributor: Interama
Director/Writer: Jean Renoir
Principals: Jean Gabin, Dora Doll, Maria Felix

A Parisian impresario unsuccessfully tries to mount a
production, despite his bad luck streak. The high-kicking
dance with its splits and garter belt tossings provides the
centerpiece for the show.

FRENCH FOLK DANCES

1987, 45 min., color, video
Distributor/Producer: Cindy Lopez for Gessler Productions
Director/Editor: Greg Markle

A teaching kit with audio tape with instructions, booklet,
and performance tape featuring students from Colorado in
three folk dances: LE BRANLE A SIX from Brittany, accompanied by a biniou, or bagpipe, and a bombarde, an
oboe-like instrument; LA BOULANGERE from Alsace
Lorraine, which resembles our western square dance;
LA CONTRA-DANSE from Haiti.

FROM AN ISLAND SUMMER

1983–1984, 15 min., color, video
Distributor/Producer: WGBH-TV
Director: Charles Atlas
Choreographer/Dancer: Karole Armitage

Coney Island of the mind/body/spirit developed by two artists
who first worked together in Merce Cunningham's company.

FROM PURE SPRINGS

1984, 20 min., color, film
Distributor: National Council of American-Soviet
Friendship

Ukrainian folk dance.

FROM SAN FRANCISCO: DANCING ON THE EDGE

Series: Alive from Off Center
1989, 30 min., color, video
Distributor: KTCA-TV
Producer: Linda Schaller for KQED-TV and KTCA-TV
Directors: Gino Tanasescu, Tim Boxell
Choreographers/Dancers: Margaret Jenkins, Rinde Eckert,
Ellen Bromberg, Joe Goode
Dance on Camera Festival, Honorable Mention 1990

SHOEBIRDS/ATLANTIC, a new music theater piece developed
and performed by choreographers Margaret Jenkins and Rinde
Eckert; Ellen Bromberg's adaptation of her work THE BLACK
DRESS, which examines gender roles; and 29 EFFEMINATE
GESTURES, choreographer Joe Goode's examination of sexual
stereotypes.

FROM THE MINUET TO THE BIG APPLE

1940s, 7–9 min. each, b&w, film
Distributor: Ivy Films

A series of shorts of the big bands, including CAB
CALLOWAY'S JITTERBUG PARTY GYPSY REVELS, with dance
divertissements sprinkled through them.

FULL CIRCLE: THE WORK OF DORIS CHASE

1974, 10:30 min., color, film, video
Distributor: Penn State
Producer: Elizabeth Wood
Director: Doris Chase
Choreographer: Mary Staton
Composer: George Kleinsinger
Dance Company: Mary Staton Dance Ensemble

This documentary of Doris Chase, painter/sculptor/filmmaker, explains how she became interested in creating sets for choreographers and being involved in media.

FULL OF LIFE A-DANCIN'

1978, 29 min., color, film
Distributor: Phoenix Films
Producers: Robert Fiore, Richard Nevell
Director: Robert Fiore
Principal Dancer: Floyd King
Dance Company: Southern Appalachian Cloggers
American Film Festival Finalist

Features a champion clog-dancing team from the southern Appalachian mountains, accompanied by fiddles and banjos.

FUNDAMENTALS OF BALLET (3 videos)

1990, 30–50 min. each, color, video
Distributor: Magic Apple Productions
Producers: Robert L. Kahn, Elaine Loring
Directors: Howard Hill, Jeannette Cabanis
Choreographer: Douglas Davis
Teacher: Elaine Loring
Principal Dancer: Ruth Cyrk
Composers: Frederic Chopin, Ludwig van Beethoven

Directed to dance teachers, these tapes by the director of The Dancers' Workshop in Harrisburg, Pennsylvania, combines lecture, classroom, and performance to inspire an imaginative approach to dance. Her teaching technique combines body awareness games and exercises for the pre-pubescent student to preserve a sense of play and enhance self-esteem.

GAGAKU "BAIRO" IN TWO STYLES

1972, 17 min., color, film
Distributor: Pennstate #EO1990
Producers: F. Koizumi, K. Okada for Wissen

Two styles of a Japanese dance set to music of the Imperial Court and Shinto shrines with instrumental composition in 6/4 meter and a dance in 5/4 meter.

GAITE PARISIENNE

1941, 20 min., color, film
Distributor: Dance Films Association (for members only)
Producer: Warner Brothers Pictures
Director: Jean Negulesco
Choreographer/Dancer: Leonide Massine
Principal Dancers: Frederic Franklin, Igor Youskevitch, Andre Eglevsky, Casmir Kokitch, Nathalie Krassovska, Milada Miladora, Lupov Roudenko, James Starbuck
Dance Company: Ballet Russe de Monte Carlo
Composer: Jacques Offenbach
Set Designer: Comte Etienne de Beaumont

The festive, one-act ballet revolves around the exploits of a wealthy Peruvian in a Paris nightclub in the 1890s.

GAITE PARISIENNE

1944–1954, 38 min., color, film, video
Distributors: Dance Film Archive, Video Arts International #69053
Director: Victor Jessen
Choreographer: Leonide Massine
Principal Dancers: Alexandra Danilova, Frederic Franklin, Leon Danielian
Dance Company: Ballet Russe de Monte Carlo
Composer: Jacques Offenbach

A balletomane's surreptitious attempt to capture the spirited ballet on film, despite the obstacles of having his camera confiscated by dutiful ushers in the middle of performances.

GALA

1982, 90 min., color, film, video
Distributor/Producer: National Film Board of Canada
Producer/Director: John D. Smith
Directors: Cynthia Scott, Michael McKennirey
Dance Companies: Winnipeg Contemporary Dancers, National Ballet of Canada

A performance record.

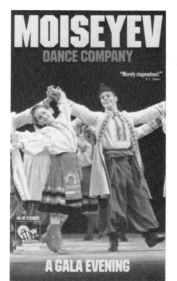

A Gala Evening with the
Moiseyev Dance Company
Cover art courtesy V.I.E.W. Video.

A GALA EVENING WITH THE MOISEYEV DANCE COMPANY

1980, 70 min., color, video
Distributor: V.I.E.W.
Producer: Soviet Film & TV
Choreographer: Igor Moiseyev
Dance Company: Moiseyev Dance Company

This virtuoso folk dance troupe, founded in 1937 in the Soviet Union, presents SUITE OF RUSSIAN FOLK DANCES, MOLDAVIAN SUITE, OLD CITY QUADRILLE, THE SOCCER MATCH, TAJIK'S DANCE OF HAPPINESS, AZERBAIJAN SHEPHERD DANCE SUITE, and UKRAINIAN GOPAK DANCE. This gala evening was held at the Congress Hall in Moscow as part of the 1980 Olympic Cultural Program.

GALINA ULANOVA

1964, 37 min., b&w, film
Distributor: Corinth
Producer: Central Documentary Film Studio, Moscow
Directors: Leonide Kristi, Maria Slavinskaya
Choreographers: Michel Fokine, Leonide Lavrovsky,
Jean Coralli, Rostislav Azkharov
Composers: Sergei Prokofiev, Adolphe Adam,
Frederic Chopin, Boris Asafiev

The life and art of the Russian ballerina Galina Ulanova, from her early days with the Kirov Ballet, to her later role as a teacher at the Bolshoi Ballet School. Includes excerpts of her performances in GISELLE (Coralli/Adam), ROMEO AND JULIET (Lavrovsky/ Prokofiev), LES SYLPHIDES (Fokine/Chopin) and THE FOUNTAIN OF BAKHCHISARAI (Zakharov/Asafiev).

GAMEEL GAMAL (OH! BEAUTIFUL DANCER)

1976, 24 min., color, film, video
Distributor: Phoenix
Producer/Director: Gordon Inkeles
Teacher: Roman Ballardine
Principal Dancers: Amina, Taia, Katarina
Cinematographer: Bill Cote

Four dances with two beginning dancers helping each other through their first nightclub performance and their encounters with the public, as well as a class in Middle Eastern dance.

GATERE-DANCE

1964, 3 min., color, film
Distributor: PennState
Producer: Wissen
Producer/Director: G. Koch

A woman's dance in Onotoa, Gilbert Islands, accompanied by a chorus. Also produced by the German film company the same year, a two-minute silent record of a dance with a Kakekekeke skirt.

GBAGBA MASK DANCE AT ASOUAKRO (2 films)

1968, 21 & 28 min., color, film
Distributor: Pennstate #EO1584-85
Producer: Wissen

Filmed during a festival in Baule, Ivory Coast, the GBAGBA is performed by a boy wearing a bird mask.

GEE, OFFICER KRUPKE

1975, 25 min., color, film, video
Distributor: PennState
Producer/Director: Edward A. Mason
Choreographer: Robert Berger after Jerome Robbins
Principal Dancers: Harvard College Students
Composer: Leonard Bernstein
American Film Festival, Blue Ribbon; Chicago
International Festival, Silver plaque

A documentary on the process of building a college production of the musical WEST SIDE STORY, from the first read-through to the opening.

GEOGRAPHY AND METABOLISM

Series: Alive from Off Center
1987, 23:30 min., color, video
Distributor: Electronic Arts Intermix
Producer: KTCA
Directors: John Sanborn, Mary Perillo
Choreographer: Molissa Fenley

Three barefoot girls dance in the great wide open of a southwest desert for the airborne cameraman who swoops about like a drunken hawk. Second half, the camera again dances with two women in a draped studio.

GERD BOHNER

20 min., color, film
Distributor: Modern Talking Picture Service #25396
Producer: German Government
Dancer: Gerd Bohner
Choreographer: Oskar Schlemmer

This portrait of Gerd Bohner, a dancer/choreographer who was considered an outsider in the German dance scene, includes scenes from Oskar Schlemmer's TRIADISCHES BALLETT.

GERMAN FOLK DANCES

1988, 42 min., color, video
Distributor/Producer: Gessler Productions
Director: Cindy Lopez

Students perform SIEBENSCHRITT from Bavaria, S TROMMT EM BABELI from Switzerland and DAS FENSTER from Germany. Teaching kit includes a costume guide and instructions to learn the dances.

GHOST DANCES

1989, 41 min., color, video
Distributor: Home Vision #GOH01
Producer: Independent Films Producers Assoc. Ltd.
Choreographer: Christopher Bruce
Dance Company: Ballet Rambert
Composer: Victor Jara, Chilean folksinger/writer

A performance video of a ballet inspired by a letter from the widow of Victor Jara, a victim of the Chilean military coup that brought Augusto Pinochet to power. The ballet evokes the gaiety and courage the South American people maintain despite oppression and murder.

GIGER, THE KINGDOM OF LIGHT

1989, 25 min., color, video
Distributor: Antenna
Producer: Scanning Pool
Director: Seigen Kyu
Dance Company: Byakko-sha
Composer: Zabadek
Dance on Camera Festival, Honorable Mention 1989

A fantasy in the style of Butoh, the dark Japanese modern dance, filmed near the sea.

GISELLE (American Ballet Theatre)

1969, 90 min., color, video, laserdisk
Distributor: Corinth
Producer: Unitel
Director: Ugo Niebling
Choreographers: David Blair after Jean Coralli and Jules Perrot
Principal Dancers: Carla Fracci, Erik Bruhn

Dance Company: American Ballet Theatre
Composer: Adolphe Adam

The romantic ballet in two acts is based on the story by Theophile Gautier on a theme by Heinrich Heine in which a country girl with a weak heart dies once she realizes her lover is not only an aristocrat but engaged. She joins the willis, a bevy of ladies who'd met a similar fate, and wanly receives her guilt-ridden, grave-visiting lover. This production is the only video in distribution starring Danish dancer Erik Bruhn and the Italian ballerina Carla Fracci. Filmed in Berlin, Germany.

GISELLE (American Ballet Theatre)

Series: Live From Lincoln Center
1976, 95 min., color, video, laserdisk
Distributor: Paramount #12702, Home Vision #GIS03
Producer/Director: John Goberman for Lincoln Center
Choreographer: Jean Coralli and Jules Perrot
Director: Robert Schwarz
Principal Dancers: Natalia Makarova, Mikhail Baryshnikov, Martine van Hamel
Dance Company: American Ballet Theatre
Composer: Adolphe Adam
Emmy Award: Outstanding Classical Program, Performing Arts

The full-length production filmed at the Metropolitan Opera House.

GISELLE (Ballet Nacional de Cuba)

1964, 90 min., b&w, film, video
Distributor: Video Arts International #69052, New Yorker (film)
Producer: Raul Canosa for the Cuban Film Institute
Director: Enrique Pineda Barnet
Choreographer/Dancer: Alicia Alonso
Principal Dancers: Azari Plisetski and Fernando Alonso
Dance Company: Ballet Nacional de Cuba
Composer: Adolphe Adam
Set Designer: Efran De Castillo
Costume Designer: Eduardo Arrocha
Dance on Camera Festival, 1979

Full-length ballet performed and choreographed by the Cuban ballerina Alicia Alonso in her prime, after the original by Jean Coralli and Jules Perrot.

GISELLE (Bolshoi Ballet)

1974, 85 min., color, video
Distributors: Kultur #1172, Corinth
Producer: Lothar Bock Associates, GMBH
Choreographer: Yuri Grigorovich
Principal Dancers: Natalia Bessmertnova, Mikhail Lavrovsky
Dance Company: Bolshoi Ballet
Composer: Adolphe Adam

The full-length classic filmed live at the Bolshoi Theatre in Moscow.

GISELLE (Bolshoi Ballet)

1990, 90 min., color, video
Distributor: Spectacor
Producer: Michio Takemora for NHK Enterprises with Simon Willock of RPTA/Primetime, Video/Film Bolshoi,

and Masaki Ishijima for Japan Arts Corp.
Director: Shuji Fujii
Choreographers: Jean Coralli, Jules Perrot, Marius Petipa, Yuri Grigorovich
Principal Dancers: Natalya Bessmertnova, Yuri Vasyuchenko, Maria Bilova
Composer: Adolphe Adam
Designer: Simon Virsaladze

Recorded live at the Bolshoi Theatre in Moscow.

GISELLE (Kirov Ballet)

1983, 115 min., color, video
Distributor: HBO #2803, Weintraub, Corinth, Pioneer (laserdisk)
Producer: Gerald Sinstadt for National Video Corporation
Director: Preben Montell
Choreographers: Jean Coralli, Jules Perrot
Principal Dancers: Galina Mezentseva, Konstantin Zaklinsky
Dance Company: Kirov Ballet
Composer: Adolphe Adam

Filmed in Leningrad.

GODUNOV: THE WORLD TO DANCE IN

1983, 60 min., color, video
Distributor: Kultur #1109
Producer/Director: Peter Rosen with Metromedia
Choreographer: Marius Petipa
Principal Dancers: Alexander Godunov, Cynthia Gregory, Maya Plisetskaya
Composer: Adolphe Adam

Alexander Godunov, a former Bolshoi dancer whose rugged face became familiar to America's movie-going public through his spot appearances in such films as WITNESS, discusses his career on a performance tour across America soon after his defection. Includes rehearsal and performance excerpts of his solo in CORSAIRE.

THE GOLDEN AGE

1987, 113 min., color, video
Distributors: Home Vision #GOl01, Pioneer (laserdisk)
Producer: Robin Scott for National Video Corporation with Gostelradio-Soviet TV and the BBC
Director: Colin Nears
Choreographer: Yuri Grigorovich
Principal Dancers: Irek Mukhamedov, Natalia Bessmertnova
Dance Company: Bolshoi Ballet
Composer: Dmitri Shostakovich
Video of the Year Award, Stereo Review, 1987

This three-act ballet, set in a nightclub popular among the bourgeoisie in the 1920's, revolves around the rivalry between a fisherman and a gang leader and their love for the same woman.

GOLDWYN FOLLIES

1938, 120 min., color, film, video
Distributor: Embassy (retail)
Producer: Samuel Goldwyn
Director: George Marshall
Choreographer: George Balanchine

Principal Dancer: Vera Zorina
Dance Company: Metropolitan Opera Ballet
Composer: George Gershwin
Writer: Ben Hecht

Hollywood musical choreographed by co-founder of
New York City Ballet George Balanchine.

GOLI MASK DANCE

1968, 31 min., color, film
Distributor: PennState #EO1554
Producer: H. Himmelheber for Wissen

Three or four pairs of masked men of Baule, Ivory Coast, try to
surpass each other by dancing to the hot rhythms of rattle
calabashes played by a men's chorus. Also available from PennState
#EO0891, a similar, but silent eight-minute film made in 1963.

GRACE, A PORTRAIT OF GRACE DECARLTON ROSS

1983, 50 min., color, film, video
Distributor: Films by Huey
Director: Huey
Choreographer/Dancer: Grace DeCarlton Ross
Principal Dancer: Coralie Romanyshyn
Composer: Mike Nobel

Chronicles the performing career and staying power of a
dancer who got her start in the circus in 1906 and continued
to draw considerable pleasure from her profession well into
her senior years spent in Portland, Maine.

THE GRAND CONCERT

1951, 102 min., color, film
Distributor: Corinth
Producer: Mosfilm, U.S.S.R.
Director: Vera Stroyeva
Choreographers: Marius Petipa, Mikhail Lavrovsky
Principal Dancers: Galina Ulanova, Olga Lepeshinskaya,
Maya Plisetskaya, Marina Semyonova, Mikhail Lavrovsky
Composers: Peter Ilyich Tchaikovsky, Sergei Prokofiev

Opera and ballet scenes with Galina Ulanova, Olga Lepeshinskaya
and others. Included are excerpts from SWAN LAKE, PRINCE
IGOR, and Lavrovsky's ROMEO AND JULIET.

THE GREAT AMERICAN BELLYDANCE

1986, 60 min., color, video
Distributor: G.A.B. Productions
Principal Dancers: Aegela, Catarina, Dhyanis, Farrashah,
Julena, Nadil, Zaira

An irreverent look at Middle Eastern dance including: CAMP
CAIRO, SLITHERY CATAROMA, THE FIRE AND ICE OF JULENA,
NADIL'S RITUAL FIRE DANCE, and SOLITARY FLOOR WORK.

GREAT PERFORMANCE IN DANCE

Series: Time to Dance
1960, 29 min., b&w, film, video
Distributor: Indiana University
Producer: Jac Venza for WGBH-TV Boston
Choreographers: Leonide Massine, Marius Petipa,
Arthur Saint-Leon, Valerie Bettis
Principal Dancers: Anna Pavlova, Argentinita, Vernon and

Irene Castle, Edith Jerell and Thomas Andrew,
Alexandra Danilova, Frederic Franklin
Composers: Peter Ilyich Tchaikovsky, Johann Strauss,
Leo Delibes
Commentators: Martha Myers, dance critic Walter Terry

Shows how one dancer may interpret choreography quite
differently from another. Alexandra Danilova and Frederic
Franklin perform a duet from Leonide Massine's LE BEAU
DANUBE and then, Edith Jerell and Thomas Andrew demon-
state an alternate version. Danilova and Franklin also perform
excerpts from Valerie Bettis' A STREETCAR NAMED DESIRE,
as well as the classics SWAN LAKE and COPPELIA. Martha
Myers and critic Walter Terry discuss the interplay of a dancer
and choreographer and the process of creating a role. Includes
film clips of ballerina Anna Pavlova, flamenco dancer Argentinita,
and ballroom team Irene and Vernon Castle.

HAA SHAGOON

29 min., color, film, video
Distributor: University of California Extension Media Center
at Berkeley
Producer/Director: Joseph Kawaky

Documents a day of Tlingit Indian ceremony held along
the Chilkoot River in Alaska. Prayers, songs, and dances
interpreted by a tribal elder.

HAIKU

1966, 28 min., b&w, film
Distributor: Dance Films Association (for members only)
Producer: Columbia University Center for
Mass Communications
Producer/Directors: Leo Hurwitz, Manfred Kirchheimer
Dance Director: Jane Dudley
Composer: Ted Dalbotten

A suite of dances based on traditional Japanese poetry,
choreographed and performed by graduate students at
Teachers College, Columbia University. The suite combines the
study of literature, theatre production, dance, and music.

HAIL THE NEW PURITAN

1986, 83 min., color, video
Distributor/Director: Charles Atlas
Distributor: Kitchen
Producer: Channel 4
Choreographer/Dancer: Michael Clark

Fantasy day-in-the-life of Michael Clark, a dancer trained at the
Royal Ballet School who then pursued his own choreography
with a punk sensibility. Shot in the streets of London, clubs,
parties, and in his apartment.

HAIR

1979, 121 min., color, video
Distributor/Producer: MGM
Director: Milos Forman
Choreographer/Dancer: Twyla Tharp
Dance Company: Twyla Tharp Dance Company
Composer: Galt MacDermot
Writer: Michael Weller

An Oklahoma farmboy travels to New York before going into the army. In Central Park, he meets a group of long-hair free spirits who subsequently help him escape from his basic training camp. Notable for the dance audience because of the choreography by modern dancer Twyla Tharp.

HANS CHRISTIAN ANDERSEN BALLET AWARDS GALA

 1988, 60 min., color, video
 Distributor: RM Arts
 Producer: Noel Fox
 Choreographers: August Bournonville, Victor Gsovsky,
 Ib Andersen, Marius Petipa
 Principal Dancers: Natalia Bessmertnova, Irek Mukhamedov,
 Trinidad Sevillano, Peter Schaufuss, Sylvie Guillem,
 Manuel Legris, Fernando Bujones, Yoko Morishita, Li Ying,
 Pang Jiabin, Cheryl Yeager, Julio Bocca
 Composers: H.S. Pauli, Leon Minkus, E. Helsted,
 H. C. Lumbye, Aram Khatchaturian, Riccardo Drigo,
 Francois Auber, Peter Ilyich Tchaikovsky, Adolphe Adam
 Editor: Christian Kronman

Leading ballet companies from around the world nominated candidates for the 1988 awards presented in Copenhagen's Royal Theatre. The twelve guest dancers performed pas de deux from SWAN LAKE, SPARTACUS, GRAND PAS CLASSIQUE, DON QUIXOTE, THE FLOWER FESTIVAL AT GENZANO, LE CORSAIRE.

Hanya: Portrait of a Dance Pioneer
Hanya Holm. Photo courtesy Dance Horizons Video.

HANYA: PORTRAIT OF A DANCE PIONEER

 1984, 55 min., color, film, video
 Distributor: Dance Horizons Video

 Producers: Marilyn Cristofori, Nancy Mason Hauser
 Directors: John Ittelson, Marilyn Cristofori,
 Nancy Mason Hauser
 Principal Dancers: Valerie Bettis, Louise Kloepper, Harold Lang
 Choreographer/Dancer: Hanya Holm
 Dance Company: Don Redlich Dance Company
 Cinematographer: Larry Schmunk
 Composer: Kenny Davis
 Narrators: Julie Andrews, Alfred Drake
 Commentators: Alwin Nikolais, Glen Tetley
 Dance on Camera Festival, 1985 Grand Prize

Portrait of Hanya Holm, a German-American choreographer who helped shape modern dance in the United States. There are clips from her early and late performances, interviews with her that reveal her belief in hard work and improvisation and with Alwin Nikolais and Glen Tetley who worked with her. Valerie Bettis dances in the Holm style, outdoors in Colorado, where Holm taught for forty years.

HARVEST DANCES

 1957, 20 min., 15 min., color, film
 Distributor: PennState #E00501, #EO552
 Producer: T. E. Laffer for Wissen

Filmed in Venezuela during the Tamunangue festivities in honor of Saint Antonio, the feast starts with a fighting game, followed by seven different dances and ends with a song to venerate Saint Antonio. In the shorter film made the same year at the time of the maize harvest, the Ayaman celebrate the great Tura together with the mestizo population around a frame of maize and sugar cane stalks.

HAVE A FLING WITH DANCE (2 videos)

 1988, 30 & 45 min. each, color, video
 Distributor: Hoctor Products
 Producer: Studio Music Corp.
 Teachers: Valene Tueller, Darryl Retter

Tap and jazz routines are broken down so that the viewer can follow, and then perform.

HAZARDOUS HOOTENANNY

 1988, 10 min., color, video
 Distributor/Producer: WGBH
 Choreographer: Charles Moulton
 Dance Company: Charles Moulton Dance Company

Boisterous twist on folk-song tradition by a former Cunningham dancer, also known in the video arena for his collaborations with videographers Skip Blumberg and John Sanborn.

HE MAKES ME FEEL LIKE DANCIN'

 1983, 51 min., color, film, video
 Distributor: Direct Cinema
 Producer: Edgar J. Scherick Associates
 Producer/Director: Emile Ardolino
 Producer: Judy Kinberg
 Dance Teacher: Jacques D'Amboise
 Hostess: Judy Collins
 Composers: Lee Norris, Martin Charnin
 Choreographers: George Balanchine and the staff of the
 National Dance Institute

Cinematographer: Scott Sorenson
Academy Award, 1983 Best Documentary Feature; 1984
Emmy Award; 1984 Christopher Award; American Film
Festival, 1985

Jacques D'Amboise, a former New York City Ballet principal dancer, auditions children to participate in his National Dance Institute. Representing a cross-section of New York City's multi-ethnic population, 1,000 children learn to dance and then perform at Madison Square Garden with guest artists Judy Collins, Kevin Kline, and other celebrities.

HELEN: QUEEN OF THE NAUTCH GIRLS

1973, 30 min., color, b&w, film
Distributor: New Yorker
Producer: Ismail Merchant for Merchant/Ivory
Director: Anthony Korner

This musical profile of India's answer to Busby Berkeley, its best-known night club performer provides insight into modern India and the Westernization of its dance. Helen is also seen in excerpts from her Bombay and Madras films.

HELEN TAMIRIS IN NEGRO SPIRITUALS

1958, 17 min., b&w, film
Distributor: Dance Films Association (for members only)
Director: Marcus Blechman
Choreographer/Dancer: Helen Tamiris
Singers: Muriel Rahn, Eugene Brice

Dance critic John Martin introduces Helen Tamiris, choreographer of many musicals including SHOWBOAT, TOUCH AND GO, and ANNIE GET YOUR GUN, revues and films. Tamiris then performs her solos: GO DOWN MOSES, SWING LOW, SWEET CHARIOT, GIT ON BOARD, CRUCIFIXION, and JOSHUA FIT THE BATTLE OF JERICO.

HELICAL WIND

1983, 10 min., color, video
Distributor/Producer/Directors: Deborah Gladstein, Sam Kanter
Choreographer/Dancer: Deborah Gladstein

A dancer twists, turns, and leaps through black space as slow-motion takes reveal the subtleties of her gestures.

HERALD'S ROUND

1982, 8 min., color, video
Distributor: ARC Video
Director: Celia Ipiotis
Choreographer/Dancer: Peter Sparling
Composer: J. S. Bach
Cinematographer: Jeff Bush

A canon made in postproduction in which a former Martha Graham soloist marks out his soul's domain and confronts his own image in a dialogue with himself.

HERE AND NOW WITH WATCHERS

1983, 5:45 min., b&w, film
Distributor: Film-maker's Coop
Director: Jonas Mekas
Principal Dancer: Erick Hawkins
Composer: Lucia Dlugoszewski

Former Martha Graham dancer who formed his own internationally touring modern dance company and Lucia Dlugoszewski, his long-time collaborating composer/musician, share a concert under the wandering eye of the camera. Commissioned originally by a magazine called Show and salvaged by the filmmaker 20 years later.

HERITAGE OF CHINESE OPERA

1978, 31 min., color, video
Distributor: Iowa State University

Illustrates the falsetto singing, symbolism in gait and gesture, acrobatics, costumes, and face painting in Chinese opera, which has a history of more than 13 centuries.

THE HIGHWAYMAN

1958, 13 min., b&w, film
Distributor: Kent State
Producer: Kurt Simon for McGraw Hill
Principal Dancers: Jerry Jackson, Maria Elna Aza
Composer: John Sentes
Narrator: John Carradine

Duet set to Alfred Noyes' poem "The Highwayman."

HIROSHIMA

1989, 10 min., color, film
Distributor: Coe Films
Producer/Choreographer/Dancer: Claire Iwatsu
Composer: Saniem Bennett
Dance on Camera Festival, Gold Award 1989

An experimental work made in reaction to the bombing of Hiroshima.

HOLLYWOOD CLOWNS

1979, 120 min., b&w, video
Distributor/Producer: MGM/UA 0688
Performers: Charlie Chaplin, Laurel and Hardy, Buster Keaton, Martin and Lewis

Compilation of the best from funniest funnymen, all of whom held their audience by their choreography as much as their scripts.

HOOLAULEA: THE TRADITIONAL DANCES OF HAWAII

1961, 20 min., color, film
Distributor: Dance Films Association (for members only)
Producer: Francis Haar for Honolulu Academy of Arts
Director: George Tahara
Principal Dancer: Iolani Luahini

Seven hulas, performed seated and standing, with explanations by the granddaughter of the dancer at the court of King Kalahaua who began her apprenticeship at the age of three.

HOPI KACHINAS

1961, 10 min., color, film
Distributor: Portland State University #10882
Producer/Director: Jack Breed for ACI Films

Documentary on the religion of the Hopi Indian tribe with particular focus on the Kachina dolls, little wooden images of dancers, made to represent supernatural spirits.

HORROR DREAM

    1972, 10 min., color, film
    Distributor: Grove Press Film
    Choreographer/Dancer: Marian Van Tuyl
    Composer: John Cage
    Producer/Director: Sidney Peterson

A dancer anxiously prepares to perform.

HOUSE OF TRES

    Series: Alive from Off Center
    1990, 16 min., color, video
    Distributor/Producer: Mindy Golberg for Epoch Films, KTCA
    Director/Choreographer: Diane Martel
    Director: Jeff Preiss
    Principal Dancer: Willi Ninja
    Dance Company: House of Chanel, House of Afrika
    Composer: Dimitri

House, hip hop, and voguing street styles fabricated and
polished by the boys of New York, who grew up break-
dancing, throwing karate kicks, and mocking the cool strut
of fashion runways.

HOW BALLET BEGAN

    Series: Ballet for All
    1975, 26 min., b&w, film
    Distributor: University of Illinois
    Director: Nicholas Ferguson
    Choreographers: August Bournonville,
    Kenneth MacMillan, Marius Petipa, Jean Coralli, Georges
    Noverre, John Weaver, Mary Skeaping
    Narrator: David Blair
    Dance Company: Ballet for All
    Composers: Leo Delibes, Peter Ilyich Tchaikovsky, Jean Lully

First in the British series of seven films presented on
Thames Television. Traces ballet from the mid-17th-century
royal European courts through the early 19th century.
Excerpts from: BALLET DE LA NUIT (1653), Jon Weaver's
LOVES OF MARS AND VENUS (1716), Noverre's PETITS
RIENS (1778), Bournonville's KONSERVATORIET (1849),
Petipa's SLEEPING BEAUTY, and MacMillan's CONCERTO.

HOW BALLET WAS SAVED

    Series: Ballet for All
    1975, 30 min., b&w, film
    Distributor: University of Illinois
    Director: Nicholas Ferguson
    Choreographer: Arthur Saint-Leon
    Principal Dancers: Janet Francis, Margaret Barbieri,
    Alison Howard, Spencer Parker and Oliver Symons
    Composer: Leo Delibes

Explores the fact that since ballet was originally performed
only by men, when women assumed roles in the 1800s, the
male dancers, with the exception of the Russians, rebelled.
Includes excerpts from the 1870 version of COPPELIA,
based on the memories of Paulette Dynalix, in which a
woman plays Franz.

HOW DO YOU FEEL, EMPEROR'S NEW CLOTHES, ROCKER

    1977, 29 min., video, film
    Distributor/Producer/Director: Doris Chase
    Principal Dancers: Kei Takei, Lloyd Ritter,
    Jonathan Hollander, Nancy Cohen
    Composer: George Kleinsinger
    Narrator: Mal Pate

The first of these three experimental pieces by the Northwestern sculptor/painter who explored video in the '60s
and '70s is an animated commercial on body movement
and self-awareness geared for children. EMPEROR'S NEW
CLOTHES presents a duet in a fable while the third, ROCKER,
a solo performed by Jonathan Hollander, demonstrates how
the Rutt/Etra synthesizer alters the image of one of Chase's
sculptures made for dance.

HOW TO MOVE BETTER

    Series: The Dance Experience
    1975, 20 min., color film, video
    Distributor: American Alliance for Health,
    Physical Education, Recreation and Dance
    Producer: Athletic Institute
    Choreographer/Dancer: Lynda Davis

Tips on how to correct alignment errors and build a positive
self-image.

HUMAN SEX

    1987, 55 min., color, video
    Distributor/Producer: Claudio M. Luca
    Director: Roberto Romano
    Choreographer: Edouard Lock
    Dance Company: Lalala Human Steps

Rock ballet/performance piece by a Canadian choreographer
who takes a slant view of the pairing of the sexes, complete
with live music, interactive digital sampling, and video.

HUMPHREY TECHNIQUE

    1936, 10 min., b&w, film
    Distributor: Dance Film Archive
    Choreographer: Doris Humphrey
    Principal Dancers: Letitia Ide, Beatrice Seckler, Edith Orcutt,
    Katherine Manning

Silent film with demonstrations of the modern technique
devised by Doris Humphrey.

HUPA INDIAN WHITE DEERSKIN DANCE

    1958, 11 min., color, film
    Distributor: University of California at Berkeley, Barr Films
    Producer: Arthur Barr Productions

A glimpse into the 10-day deerskin dance ceremony of the
Hupa Indians of Northwestern California, the most advanced
and best-known tribe of the Athabascan family. The costumes
are as elaborate as the pocketbook can bear. The dancers recite
long narratives studded with magical formulas for success
and well-being.

HUSK

    1989, 8 min., color, video
    Distributor/Director/Choreographer/Dancers: Eiko & Koma
    Dance on Camera Festival, 1989 Honorable Mention

Duet by these American Butoh-influenced artists inspired by "As dead leaves rustle across the forest floor, an indistinct figure emerges from the undergrowth. It could be the last slow heave of lost life or the tentative beginnings of a new one."

HYMN TO JERUSALEM

    1979, 21 min., color, video
    Distributor: University of Illinois #57532
    Choreographer: Jeannette Ordman
    Dance Company: Bat Dor Dance Company

A bow to the mecca by the 25-member modern dance company based in Tel Aviv, Israel.

I AM A DANCER

    1973, 90 min., color, film, video
    Distributors: Facets So 1928, HBO #1041
    Producer: Evdoros Demetriou for EMI Film Prod.
    Director: Pierre Jourdan
    Principal Dancers: Rudolf Nureyev, Margot Fonteyn, Carla Fracci, Lynn Seymour, Michael Somes, Leslie Edwards
    Choreographers: August Bournonville, Glen Tetley, Frederick Ashton, Marius Petipa
    Composers: Franz Liszt, Lovenskjold Demitriou, Peter Ilyich Tchaikovsky, Karlheinz Stockhausen
    Writer: John Percival
    Narrator: Bryan Forbes

Rudolph Nureyev, born in Ufa, USSR, prepares and then stars in sequences from the following ballets: MARGUERITE AND ARMAND, LA SYLPHIDE, THE SLEEPING BEAUTY and FIELD FIGURES.

I LIKE TO EAT MY MOUSIES RAW

    1984, 5 min., color, video
    Distributor/Director/Choreographer: John Giamberso
    Choreographer/Dancer: Paul Loper
    Dancer: Lisa Ravenholt
    Dance on Camera, Honorable Mention

Two dancers rock with a cat in an exotic setting.

ILONA VERA'S BALLET CLASS

    1988, 73 min., color, video
    Distributor: Kultur #1215
    Producer: Levine/Trowbridge
    Teacher: Ilona Vera

Explains the Vaganova method of training, which shaped such Russian greats as Mikhail Baryshnikov, Natalia Makarova, and Anna Pavlova. The instructor was born in Hungary and received her training at the Ballet Institute in Budapest.

IMAGE: A DANCER

    1974, 37 min., color, film
    Distributor: Arthur Cantor
    Dancer: Christopher Aponte

Registers the arduous life of a ballet dancer in New York City,
following from class to rehearsals, home, and performance.

IMAGE: FLESH AND VOICE

    1969, 77 min., b&w, film
    Distributors: Film-makers Coop, Canyon
    Director: Ed Emshwiller
    Principal Dancers: Carolyn Carlson, Emery Hermans
    Von Sternberg Prize for Most Original Feature Film, Mannheim Festival, 1970

"A structural interplay of sound, image and sensual tensions," as the late Ed Emshwiller describes his plotless feature.

IMAGES IN DISTRACTED TIME

    1980, 20 min., color, b&w, video
    Distributor: ARC Video
    Producer/Director: Jeff Bush
    Producer/Choreographer/Dancer: Celia Ipiotis

Five solos made specifically for the camera by the team who produce the interview program "Eye on Dance": GOOD THING GONE, FINISTERRE, MOTHERLESS CHILD IV, A PITY, TAKE ONE, and SOLO.

THE IMMORTAL SWAN

    1936, 38 min., b&w, film
    Distributor: Museum of Modern Art
    Producer: Victor Dandre
    Director: Edward Nakhimov
    Choreographers: Michel Fokine, Laurent Novikov, Anna Pavlova, Marius Petipa
    Dancers: Anna Pavlova, Pierre Vladmiroff
    Composers: Frederic Chopin, Leon Minkus, Camille Saint-Saens

In 1935, four years after the death of the great Russian ballerina Anna Pavlova, her husband and manager Victor Dandre assembled this collection of performance excerpts from INVITATION TO THE DANCE, LA NUIT, CALIFORNIA POPPY, DON QUIXOTE, COQUETERIES DE COLUMBINE, DANCE GREQUE, DRAGONFLY. Lost for some time, it is one of the few authentic documents of Pavlova with scenes of her relaxing, strolling in the garden, and talking to her pet swans. Synchronized by Vladimir Launitz and Aubrey Hutchins.

IMPACT

    1990, 12 min., color, video
    Distributor/Director/Editor: Michael Schwartz
    Producers: Character Generators with KAET and Arizona State University
    Choreographer: Elizabeth Streb
    Dance Company: Ringside Inc

Presents the hidden nature of movement as it exists in its tangible and most perceptual form, impact. Extends the boundaries of video dance by choreographing the movement in postproduction so that the bodies fill the negative space, bouncing off the four walls of the monitor frame.

IMPROVISATION

    1977, 5 min., color, video
    Distributor: Film-maker's Coop

Producer/Distributor/Director: Doris Chase
Choreographer/Dancer: Kei Takei

Modern solos choreographed for television, and altered in post-production to create a kinetic painting.

IMPROVISATION TO BANSURI FLUTE & SEASCAPES

1990, 30 min., color, video
Distributor/Choreographer/Dancer: Margaret Beals
Director/Editor: Roberto Romano
Composer/Performers: Judith Pearce, G.S. Sachdev

A record of two solos, IMPROVISATION (Beals/Sachdev) and SEASCAPES (Beals/Pearce), performed in St. Marks Church, New York.

IMPROVISATIONS TO CHOPIN

1985, 30 min., color, video
Distributor/Dancer: Margaret Beals
Composer: Frederic Chopin
Pianist: Thomas Hrynkiv

Margaret Beals improvises selected NOCTURNES, PRELUDES, and BALLADES.

IMPULSES

1974, 40 min., color, film
Distributor/Dancer: Margaret Beals
Producer: Impulses Foundation
Director/Cinematographer: Peter Powell
Cinematographer: James Signorelli
Narrator: Dance critic Walter Terry
Composer/Performers: Gwendolyn Watson (cello),
Colin Walcott (sitar)

Introduced by Walter Terry, a company of three musicians, a singer, a monologist, and a dancer interact spontaneously. Margaret Beals, a dancer dedicated to the art of improvisation, concentrates on moving from the inside, rather than from responding to the outside.

IN A JAZZ WAY: A PORTRAIT OF MURA DEHN

1986, 30 min., color, video, film
Distributor: Filmaker's Library
Producer/Director: Louise Ghertler, Pamela Katz
Principal Dancer: Mura Dehn
American Film Festival, 1986 Blue Ribbon

The late Mura Dehn, a young Russian-American who frequented the Savoy Ballroom in Harlem in the 1930s, caught the manic inspiration of the Lindy hop and be bop dancers on film, when she wasn't dancing herself. Dehn, 82 at the time of this film, recounts those halcyon days.

IN A REHEARSAL ROOM

1975, 11 min., color, film, video
Distributor: Films Inc.
Director/Cinematographer: David Hahn
Choreographer: William Carter
Principal Dancers: Cynthia Gregory, Ivan Nagy
Composer: Johann Pachelbel

A love-at-first-sight duet danced by two principals with the American Ballet Theatre to Pachelbel's CANON IN D.

IN CONCERT—PROFILE OF GUS GIORDANO
JAZZ DANCE CHICAGO

1987, 37 min., color, video
Distributor: Orion Enterprises
Choreographer: Gus Giordano
Director: Marcia Standiford
Dance Company: Gus Giordano Jazz Dance Chicago

Features THE REHEARSAL CONTINUES, HOT TAMALES, and ON THE CORNER along with discussions with the Chicago-based jazz company.

IN HEAVEN THERE IS NO BEER?

1980, 51 min., color, film
Distributor/Producer/Director: Les Blank for Flower Films
Principal Dancers: Eddie Blazonezyk's Versatones,
Dick Pillar Orchestra, Walt Solek, Jimmy Sturr, Marion Lush
Narrator/Interviewer: Chris Simon

A celebration of the dance, food, music, friendship, and religion of the polka subculture. Poles, Czechs, Germans, young and old, romp away in the eleven-day Polkabration in New London, Connecticut, a Polka mass at the International Polka Association convention in Milwaukee, a Polish wedding in Wisconsin, and a church lawn party in Buffalo.

IN PRAISE OF FOLLY

1975, 52 min., color, film
Distributor: University of Illinois
Producer: Comacico
Choreographer/Director: Roland Petit
Principal Dancer: Jean Cau
Composer: Marius Constant
Set Designers: Niki de Saint-Phalle, Martial Raysee,
Jean Tinguely

Brief ballets on the follies of violence, publicity, machinery, power, love, and drugs. Based on a 1966 stage work.

IN THE BLINK OF AN EYE . . . (AMPHIBIAN DREAMS)
IF I COULD FLY I WOULD FLY

1987, 25 min., color, video
Distributor: Electronic Arts Intermix
Producer/Director: Mary Lucier with WNET/WGBH
New Television
Principal Dancer: Elizabeth Streb
Composer: Earl Howard
Editor: Gregg Featherman

Evolution from black void to a natural world to a white void. A unique collaboration, one of three with modern dancer Elizabeth Streb, with provocative juxtapositions, close-ups, and timing.

INDEX

1972, 5 min., b&w, film
Distributor/Director/Producer/Choreographer:
Gene Friedman
Composer: Bill Dixon
Choreographer/Dancer: Judith Dunn
Dancer: Tony Holder

In this experimental film, a duet becomes a sextet through multiple exposures.

INDIA: HAUNTING PASSAGE

> Series: World Theatre Series
> 1965, 60 min., color, film
> Distributor: PennState
> Producer: Newmark Films
> Director: Robin Hardy
> Dance Company: Little Ballet Troupe Of Bombay
> Composer: Ravi Shankar

Rajashtan puppets perform RAMAYANA, classic Sanskrit epic of Rama deprived of his throne and thrown into exile with his wife Sita, who is abducted by a demon king. Whereupon, Rama allies himself with a monkey king and general who help him to free Sita and regain his kingdom. Following this performance comes a puppet-ballet, a fable by Satyajit Ray, music by Ravi Shankar, and performance by the Children's Little Theatre Unit of Calcutta, all intercut with a montage of twentieth-century India.

INDIANS OF THE PLAINS, SUN DANCE CEREMONY

> 1954, 11 min., color, film
> Distributor: Portland State University
> Producer/Director: James Larsen for Academy Films

The annual SUN DANCE includes the steps taken in the selection of the site, establishing the camp, preparing the tepees, as well as the dance ceremonies in the lodges. The concluding GRASS DANCE involves everyone present.

INDICATIONS OF DISTANCE AND DIRECTION IN THE HONEYBEE-ROUND AND WAGGLE DANCE

> 1979, 19 min., color, film
> Distributor: Cornell Cooperative
> Producer: Wissen

Analyzes the rhythm, energy expenditure, and buzzing of bees doing the round and tail-wagging dance as part of their foraging routine.

INNER RHYTHM

> 1986, 28:49 min., color, video
> Distributor: Bullfrog Films
> Producers: Rhombus Media, National Film Board of Canada
> Choreographer: Robert Desrosiers
> Director: Niv Fichman
> Composers: John Lang, Ahmed Hassan

Insights into the collaboration between two composers as they create the score for BLUE SNAKE, choreographed by Robert Desrosiers, who supplied rehearsal videos of his ballet commissioned by the National Ballet of Canada.

INSIDE EYES

> 1987, 12:03 min., color, video
> Distributor: Electronic Arts Intermix
> Choreographer/Dancer: Victoria Marks
> Director: James Byrne
> Principal Dancers: Rob O'Neil, Nancy Ohrenstein,
> Michael Nolan, Jeff Lepore, Hetty King, Barbara Canner

Modern dancers shove, hold, lift, and crash into the lens as the cameraman swoops among the bodies. Made with the assistance of the Media Arts department of Jersey City State College.

INSIDE THE HOUSE OF FLOATING PAPER

> 1984, 4:50 min., color, film
> Distributor/Producer/Director: Pooh Kaye
> Camera: Cedric Klapisch
> Composer: John Kilgore
> Black Maria Film Festival, 1984 Award

Set in the ruins of a New York City shipping wharf, a man and woman struggle to communicate within a world animated by unseen forces.

INSTRUCTIONAL BALLET TAPES DIRECTED BY DOROTHY LISTER (4 videos)

> 1985, 30 min. each, color, video
> Distributor: Hoctor Products
> Teacher: Dorothy Lister

Four tapes, graded pre-ballet and levels 1-3, designed by a performer/choreographer who ran the children's department of the Joffrey School of Ballet. Two records with notes available.

INTENSIVE COURSE IN ELEMENTARY LABANOTATION (5 videos)

> 1988, 100 min. each, color, video
> Distributor: Dance Horizons Video
> Producer: Laban Institute
> Teacher: Dr. Jill Beck

Ten basic lessons in labanotation, the system of recording dance on paper, set in a classroom with students learning symbols, asking questions and performing dance exercises. Comes with a thirty-page workbook.

INTERNATIONAL STYLE LATIN DANCING (3 videos)

> 1988, 60:39-60:44 min. each, color, video
> Distributor/Producer: Jim Forest
> Teachers: Keith Todd & Keren Alexis

Southeastern and Florida champions present the cha cha, samba, rumba, paso doble, and jive in the bronze, silver, and gold levels set by the international ballroom competitions.

INTERNATIONAL STYLE MODERN DANCING (7 videos)

> 1980s, 60-120 min. each, color, video
> Producer/Dancer/Distributor: Jim Forest
> Teachers: Maxwell and Gwynneth Bishop

Demonstration and detailed instructions by British champions who currently own the Starline Studio in Port Charlotte, Florida. Covers the bronze, silver, and gold levels of the modern syllabus for the waltz, tango, fox-trot and quickstep. Performance in tails and gown conclude each tape.

INTRODUCTION TO BALLROOM DANCING

> 1988, 60 min., color, video
> Distributor: Taffy's
> Teacher: Margot Schotz

Swing, rhumba, cha cha, waltz, fox-trot for beginners, as taught by a member of the Imperial Society of Teachers.

AN INTRODUCTION TO BELLY DANCE

> 1986, 122 min., color, video
> Distributor/Producer: Bastet Productions

Principal Dancer: Kathryn Ferguson
Houston International Film Festival, Silver Award

Shimmy variations, steps, and isolation techniques set to *beledy*, a basic rhythm in Arabic-Turkish dance, plus body waves, circles, hip sways and stretch exercises for *taxim*, a slower melodic section of the dance, and *chiftitelli*, another basic rhythm in Arabic-Turkish dance.

INTRODUCTION TO DUNCAN DANCES

1967, 15 min., color, film
Distributor: Filmmakers of Philadelphia
Producer: Calvin De Frenes Corporation
Project Director: Nadia Chilkovsky Nahumck
Associate Director: Fai Coleman
Choreographers: Isadora Duncan, Irma Duncan
(Isadora's adopted daughter)
Principal Dancers: Hortense Kooluris, Irene Abercauph,
Gwendolyn Bye, Toni Lowe, Jane Lowe, Theresa Lynch,
Sherry Sable
Consultant: Anita Zahn
Composers: Franz Schubert, Alexander Gretchaninoff,
Arcangelo Corelli, Johann Strauss
Dance Company: Students of the Philadelphia Dance Academy

Performance of Isadora Duncan dances: THREE GRACES, LULLABY, ECOSSAISE, and SCARF DANCE (Schubert); SPRINGTIME (Gretchaninoff); TANAGRA (Corelli); and WALTZ STUDIES (Strauss). Produced under the auspices of the Department of Health, Education and Welfare, the University of Pennsylvania, and the Philadelphia Dance Academy as part of the curriculum program.

INTROSPECTION

1941–1946, 6:15 min., color, film
Distributor: Film-maker's Coop
Director: Sara Kathryn Arledge
Principal Dancers: James Mitchell, John R. Baxter

Disembodied dancers float through a black space, forming a rhythmic, abstract design.

INVENTION IN DANCE

Series: A Time to Dance
1960, 29 min., b&w, film, video
Distributor: Indiana University
Producer: Jac Venza for WGBH-TV Boston
Choreographer/Composer: Alwin Nikolais
Choreographer/Dancer: Murray Louis
Choreographer: Isadora Duncan
Principal Dancers: Gladys Bailyn, Dorothy Vislocky,
Sima Boriosivana, Beverly Schmitt, Bill Frank
Dance Company: Henry Street Playhouse Dance Company

Alwin Nikolais and Martha Meyers discuss modern dance pioneers Isadora Duncan and Ruth St. Denis, the Denishawn school and its students Martha Graham, Charles Weidman, and Doris Humphrey with slides, film clips of St. Denis in RADHA, and a demonstration of the Duncan technique by Sima Boriosivana. Excerpts from Nikolais' WEB, DISCS, NOUMENON and FIXATION illustrate his innovations in electronic music, lighting, and costumes.

INVISIBLE DANCE

1981, 12 min., color, film
Distributor: Dance Film Archive
Choreographer/Dancer: David Woodberry
Composer: Laurie Spiegel
Dance Company: David Woodberry Dance Company

Dancing on the streets of New York City, oblivious to the crowds.

INVITATION TO KABUKI

33 min., color, film
Distributor: Japan Foundation
Producer: Sakura Motion Picture

An introduction to the Japanese dramatic form dating from the sixteenth century with make-up and costume sessions, the techniques behind the stylized acting and dancing, and the role of musicians in narration and accompaniment. With excerpts from several of the most popular Japanese plays: TERAKOYA, YOSHITSUNE SENBONZAKURA, and KOCHIYAMA.

INVITATION TO THE DANCE

1956, 93 min., color, film
Distributor: Films Inc.
Producer: MGM
Director/Choreographer: Gene Kelly
Principal Dancers: Carol Haney, Igor Youskevitch,
Tamara Toumanova, Diana Adams
Composers: Jacques Ibert, Ande Previn,
Nicholas Rimsky-Korsakov
Oscar, Grand Prize/West Berlin Film Festival

Gene Kelly's first effort as a solo director/choreographer with three ballets: CIRCUS, RING AROUND THE ROSY and SINBAD THE SAILOR, partially animated by the Hanna-Barbera studios.

INVITATION TO THE DANCE

1979, 17 min., color, film
Distributor: National Council for American Soviet Friendship

A documentary on a school of Georgian dance.

IOWA BLIZZARD '73

1973, 11 min., b&w, film
Distributor/Producer/Director: Elaine Summers
Director: Bill Rowley

A dance in a snow-covered field. Images of the dancers are multiplied through film laboratory superimpositions of identical footage in forward, reverse, and slow motion.

IROQUOIS SOCIAL DANCE I & II

1980, 18 min. each, color, film, video
Distributor: Green Mt. Cine
Producer/Director/Writer: Nick Manning
Teacher: Mike Mitchell

First film offers an overview of the Iroquois social dances and the second shows how to do them.

ISADORA DUNCAN: MOVEMENT FROM THE SOUL

1988, 58 min., color, film, video
Distributor: Direct Cinema
Producer: Geller/Goldfine Productions

Associate Producer: Margaretta K. Mitchell
Directors: Dayna Goldfine and Daniel Geller
Choreographer: Isadora Duncan
Principal Dancers: Madeleine Lytton, Lori Belilove
Narrator: Julie Harris
Dance Company: Oakland Ballet
Composers: Frederic Chopin, Franz Schubert,
Christoph Gluck, Johann Strauss and Alexander Scriabin
Dance on Camera Festival, Gold Award, 1990; Golden Gate
Award, San Francisco International Film Festival, 1989

A documentary based on the writings and letters of Isadora Duncan (1877–1927), the San Francisco–born dancer. A revolutionary artist who dared to defy the turn-of-the-century Victorian mores, Duncan's artistic and social milieu is depicted through archival footage, stills, and news clippings. The solo dances and duet performed include: DANCE OF THE FURIES, DANCE OF THE BLESSED SPIRITS, NARCISSUS, GYPSY MAZURKA, WATER STUDY, CLASSICAL DUET, MILITARY MARCH, MOTHER, REVOLUTIONARY, THE BLUE DANUBE.

ISADORA DUNCAN: TECHNIQUE AND CHOREOGRAPHY

1978, 29 min., color, film
Distributor/Producer/Director: Virginia Brooks
Producing Organization: Dance Films Association
Choreographer: Isadora Duncan
Principal Dancers: Gemze De Lappe, Hortense Kooluris, Julia Levien
Dance Company: Isadora Duncan Centenary Dance Company
Composers: Frederic Chopin, Franz Schubert, Alexander Scriabin

Technique class and performances of Schubert's waltzes THREE GRACES, WATER STUDY, Chopin's MAZURKA FOR TWO and POLONAISE MILITAIRE, and Scriabin's etudes THE MOTHER and THE REVOLUTIONARY.

ISADORA DUNCAN, THE BIGGEST DANCER IN THE WORLD

1966, 67 min., b&w, film
Distributor: Kit Parker Films
Producer: BBC
Director: Ken Russell
Principal Dancer: Vivien Pickles

In this feature based on the life of modern dance pioneer Isadora Duncan, the dancer is portrayed as an eccentric genius languishing over her lack of fulfillment as an artist and as a lover.

ISLAND OF THE RED PRAWNS

1978, 52 min., color, film, video
Distributor: University of California Extension Media Center

In preparation for a wedding between the children of two chieftains in the Fiji Islands, people dance ecstatically on burning coals. During the feast, dancers and singers tell the legend of sacrosanct red prawns.

IT DOESN'T WAIT

Series: Alive From Off Center
1990, 8 min., color, video
Distributor/Producers: KTCA-TV, Openhaus
Director: Mark Openhaus

Choreographer/Principal Dancer: Doug Elkins
Composers: Bob Clarida, Ken Walicki

Dancers emerge and disappear in street settings, as choreographed by an ex-breakdancer who studied ballet, modern dance, Aikido and Peking Opera traditions.

IVAN THE TERRIBLE

1977, 120 min., color, film, video
Distributors: Kultur #1205 (91 min.), Corinth Films (film)
Producer: Mosfilm Studios, U.S.S.R.
Choreographer: Yuri Grigorovich
Director: L. Ohrimenko
Principal Dancers: Yuri Vladimirov, Natalia Bessmertnova, Boris Akimov
Composer: Sergei Prokofiev
Dance Company: Bolshoi Ballet

This classic ballet, depicting the key episodes in the life of Ivan IV, the cruel sixteenth-century Russian czar, tells a story of murder and intrigue.

IVAN THE TERRIBLE

1990, 120 min., color, video
Distributor: Spectacor
Producers: Primetime Entertainment, NHK, Japan Arts Corporation, and Video/Film Bolshoi
Choreographer: Yuri Grigorovich
Principal Dancers: Irek Mukhamedov, Natalya Bessmertnova, Gedimas Taranda
Composer: Sergei Prokofiev
Dance Company: Bolshoi Ballet

Recorded live at the Bolshoi Theatre in Moscow.

JAMILA SALIMPOUR'S FORMAT (3 videos)

1979–1984, 60 min. each, color, video
Distributor/Producer/Dancers: Suhaila and Jamila Salimpour for Nine Muses

Egyptian and Arabic body locks, pivots, shimmies, isolations, body waves, ribcage circles, and taqseem produced by a mother-daughter team in California. Also offers four other instructional tapes: DRUM SOLO with an excerpt of a belly dance performed at the Chicago's World Fair in 1893, BELLEDI, CABARET (all 120 min.), and FOLKLORE (90 min.). DANCES FOR THE SULTAN (35 min.) and SUHAILA SALIMPOUR display the performance skills of this second-generation Egyptian dancer.

JAPAN: THE FROZEN MOMENT

1965, 60 min., b&w, film
Series: World Theatre
Distributor: Pennstate
Narrator: Sessue Hayakawa

A look at the dance, music, and poetry of Japan with scenes from the Noh play MATSUKAZE, Kabuki, Bugaku, and Bunraku puppet theater.

JAZZ

1985, 30 min., color, video
Distributor: Hoctor Products

Producer: Studio Music Corp.
Teacher: Scott Benson

Six jazz routines to study.

JAZZ DANCE

1980, 4 min., color, video
Distributor: Museum of Modern Art
Producer/Director: Doris Chase
Principal Dancer: Gay Delanghe
Composer: Jelly Roll Morton
Music: Uptown Lowdown Jazz Band

Dancer, transformed through synthesized images, interprets the bouncing rhythms of Jelly Roll Morton. Director Doris Chase explains, "I used an outline generator and controlled the time sequence with a slow motion disc to choreograph with the dancer."

JAZZ DANCE CLASS

1984, 63 min., color, video
Distributor: Kultur #1207
Producers: Wendell and Marge Moody for All Night Moving Pictures
Director: James F. Robinson
Choreographer/Teacher: Gus Giordano
Composer: Michael Morales

Interview, performance footage, and a jazz class with the Chicago-based teacher, Gus Giordano.

JAZZ DANCE CLASS, 1989

1989, 60 min., color, video
Distributor: Orion Enterprises
Producer: James F. Robinson
Teacher: Gus Giordano
Dance Company: Gus Giordano

Jazz dance instruction with Chicago-based teacher Gus Giordano, covering the warm-up, walks, center barre, and basic technique, with an interview and performance.

JAZZ DANCE WITH RAY LYNCH AND STUDENTS OF THE NEW YORK CITY DANCE SCHOOL, STUTTGART

1984, 57 min., color, video
Distributor: New York City Dance School
Producer: Hellthaler International, Germany
Teacher: Ray Lynch

Technique class shot in Germany.

JAZZ HOOFER: BABY LAURENCE

1981, 28 min., color, film, video
Distributor: Rhapsody Films
Producer: Bill Hancock
Director/Cinematographer: William H. Hancock
Principal Dancers: Bill "Bojangles" Robinson, John Bubbles, King Rastus Brown, Baby Laurence
Composer: Charlie Parker

Records the bebop dance style and life of one of the great old tap dancers, Baby Laurence. Performances of King Rastus Brown, Bill Robinson, John Bubbles, with unusual film clips of musicians Charlie Parker and Art Tatum, who inspired Baby Laurence.

JAZZ JAZZ JAZZ

1988, 30 min., color, video
Distributor: Hoctor Products
Producer: Studio Music Corp.
Teacher: Richard Pierlon

Jazz routines and technique for turns and jumps.

JAZZ TECHNIQUES

1980s, 30 min., color, video
Distributor: Hoctor Products
Producer: Studio Music Corp.
Choreographers/Dancers: Anita Ehrler, Frank Mastrocola

Jazz routines by Broadway performers whose credits include DANCING, THE RINK, and CHICAGO.

THE JEAN ERDMAN VIDEO ARCHIVES
Volume I: The Early Dances

1989, 52 min., color, video
Distributor: Foundation for the Open Eye
Producer/Director: Celia Ipiotis for Arc Video
Executive Producer: Nancy Allison
Directors: Jeff Bush, Maya Deren (archive footage)
Choreographer: Jean Erdman
Principal Dancers: Nancy Allison, Leslie Dillingham, Dianne Howath, Muna Tseng
Composers: Louis Horst, Lou Harrison, Otto Janowitz, John Cage, Claude Debussy

Recreation of the choreographer's work from 1942–1948, intercut with stills and narration by Jean Erdman, a featured dancer formerly with the Martha Graham Dance Company before touring the world as a soloist in the 1940s and 50s. The dances include: THE TRANSFORMATIONS OF MEDUSA, CREATURE ON A JOURNEY, PASSAGE, OPHELIA, HAMADRYAD, and DAUGHTERS OF THE LONESOME ISLE. First of a trilogy to be sold as an entity as of December 1992.

JEAN-LOUIS BARRAULT—A MAN OF THE THEATRE

1984, 58 min., color, film
Distributor: Arthur Cantor
Producer: Helen Gary Bishop
Director: Muriel Balash

A portrait of the mime-actor-director-entrepreneur Jean-Louis Barrault with scenes of his performances and interviews with colleagues, director Peter Brook and actress Jeanne Moreau.

JEAN-LOUIS BARRAULT—THE BODY SPEAKS

1984, 28 min., color, film
Distributor: Arthur Cantor
Producer: Helen Gary Bishop
Director: Muriel Balash

Excerpts from the one-man show of the French mime filmed live in Lincoln Center's Alice Tully Hall in June, 1981.

JERICO, ELDORADO, TELL

1987, 25 min., color, video
Distributor: Videographe
Producer: Bruno Jobin

Director: Francois Girard
Choreographers: Daniel Leveille, Paul-Andre Fortiers,
Jean-Pierre Perrault
Dance Company: Montreal Danse
Composer: Franz Liszt
Music: Concerto #1 In C Flat Major
Dance on Camera Festival, 1987 Gold Award

In the crossroads between dance and theatre, three modern dances
full of imagery, with imaginative sets from a Canadian team.

JESUS, SON OF MAN

1988, 72:17 min., color, video
Distributor: Coe Film Assoc.
Producer: Hungarian MTV
Choreographer/Dancer: Ivan Marko
Dance Company: National Hungarian Ballet
Composer: Franz Liszt

A dance oratorio.

LE JEUNE HOMME ET LA MORT

1951, 16 min., color, film, video
Distributor: French American Cultural Services and
Educational Aid (Facsea) #2873
Director/Choreographer: Roland Petit
Principal Dancers: Rudolf Nureyev, Zizi Jeanmaire
Composer: Johann Sebastian Bach

Inspired by playwright Jean Cocteau, this dramatic ballet is a landmark film for its sensitive camera work and acrobatic choreography. Rudolph Nureyev plays the tormented young man, originally played by Jean Babilee. Zizi Jeanmaire provides the noose.

JITTERING JITTERBUGS

1940s, 11 min., b&w, film
Distributor: Dance Film Archive

Social dances, Big Apple and jitterbug, captured in a Harlem
ballroom.

JOHN CRANKO

1970, 7 min., color, film
Distributor: Modern Talking Picture Service #25111e
Choreographer: John Cranko
Principal Dancers: Marcia Haydee, Richard Cragun
Dance Company: Stuttgart Ballet

Interviews and practice sessions with Marcia Haydee and
Richard Cragun about the late choreographer who developed the Stuttgart Ballet Company of Germany into a company of international significance.

JOHN LINDQUIST– PHOTOGRAPHER OF DANCE

1980, 28 min., color, film
Distributor/Producers: Brodsky & Treadway
Director: Robert P. Brodsky
Choreographers: Norman Walker
Cinematographer: John Lindquist
Principal Dancers: Christian Holder, Joyce Cuoco,
Youri Vamos

Portrait of the staff photographer at Jacob's Pillow Dance
Festival and his working style and philosophy. Shows

him at age 89 photographing dancers at Jacob's Pillow and
numerous photographs of Ted Shawn, Ruth St. Denis,
Alicia Alonso, and Christian Holder.

JONATHAN AND THE ROCKER

1977, 34 min., color, video
Distributor/Producer/Director: Doris Chase
Choreographer/Principal Dancer: Jonathan Hollander
Composers: William Bolcomb, Timothy Thompson,
George Kleinsinger

Modern dancer moves around video synthesized sculpture.

THE JOY OF BACH

1979, 30 and 16 min. versions, color, film, video
Distributor: Vision Video
Producing Organization: Lutheran Film Associates
Producers: Lothar Wolf, Robert E.A. Lee
Director: Paul Lammers
Principal Dancers: Teodoro Morca, Nellie Cotto,
Floyd Chisholm, Marina Otto
Choreographer: Manfred Schnelle
Composer: Johann Sebastian Bach
Dance Companies: Jacob's Pillow Dancers,
Jeff Duncan Dancers

A salute to the composer with five dances set to the Allegro
from CONCERTO FOR TWO HARPSICHORDS in C Minor,
FUGUE IN D MINOR, the Presto from CONCERTO #5 for
Harpsichord, and the Allegro from the VIOLIN CONCERTO
IN A MINOR, and AIR FROM ORCHESTRAL SUITE #3
IN D MAJOR.

THE JUDSON PROJECT TAPES 1980-82 (13 videos)

1980-1982, 2–83 min. each, b&w, video
Distributor: Kitchen
Producing Organization: Bennington College
Principal Dancers: Elaine Summers, Yvonne Rainier,
Phoebe Neville, Steve Paxton, Aileen Passloff, Jackson Maclow,
John Herbert McDowell, David Gordon, Simone Forti,
Al Carmines, Philip Corner, Lucinda Childs, Trisha Brown,
Alex Hay, Robert Rauschenberg

The founding members of the experimental modern dance
group active in New York City's Judson Church in the 1960s
discuss their work, which is illustrated with archival footage.

JUMP

1984, 15 min., color, video
Distributor: Kitchen
Producing Organization: Le Ministere de la Culture
Octet et Network
Choreographer: Philippe Decoufle
Director: Charles Atlas
Composers: Joseph Biscuit and The Residents

The cheerful, fragmented style of the director matches the
nonchalant angularity of the French choreographer whose
dancers sport whimsical costumes and headdresses by Lulu
and Bill Tornado.

JUNCTION

    1965, 12 min., color, film
    Distributor/Producer/Director: Rudolph Burckhardt
    Choreographer/Dancer: Paul Taylor
    Principal Dancers: Bettie De Jong, Carolyn Adams,
    Dan Wagoner, Daniel Grossman
    Composer: Johann Sebastian Bach
    Costume Designer: Alex Katz
    Dance Company: Paul Taylor Dance Company

A quick-paced work for the First and Fourth Suites for
Unaccompanied Cello by Johann Sebastian Bach.

JUST FOR FUN

    1980s, 30 min., color, video
    Distributor: Hoctor Products
    Producer: Studio Music Corp.
    Teacher: Mallory Graham

Jazz routines.

JUST FOR ME

    27 min., color, film, video
    Distributor: Phoenix Films
    Producer: Lauren Productions, Ltd.
    Director: Lois Tupper

Three women take time from their families and businesses to
dance and have fun.

KA

    1986, 16:40 min., color, video
    Distributor/Producer/Choreographer: Laurie Freedman
    Director: David Kedem
    Cinematographer: Nili Aslan
    Principal Dancer: Sally-Anne Friedland
    Composer: David Geyra
    Editor: Benny Kimron
    Dance on Camera Festival, 1987 Silver Award

A woman meets a desert spirit, her Ka, the Egyptian term
for the double that shadows us in life in preparation for life
after death. Shot in the Judean Desert and the Dead Sea.

KABUKI: CLASSIC THEATRE OF JAPAN

    1964, 30 min., color, film
    Distributor: Japan Foundation
    Producer: Kaga Productions

Excerpts from four plays of Kabuki, which developed 300
years ago the stylized gesture and speech of the Japanese
theatrical tradition, with the dance sequences from
MUSUME DOJOJI and KAGAMI JISHI.

KALAHARI

    1984, 7:30 min., color, video
    Distributor/Producer/Directors: Deborah Gladstein and
    Sam Kanter
    Choreographer: Deborah Gladstein
    Composer: Sam Kanter

Portions of dancers' bodies sweep across a black screen and
freeze. Slow-motion images appear and disappear, driven by
a rhythmic, pulsating soundscore.

THE KARATE RAP

    1989, 4:30 min., color, video
    Distributor: Samurai Studios
    Producer: David Seeger
    Choreographer: Michael Scott Gregory
    Principal Dancers: Charlotte D'Amboise, Jay Poindexter
    Dance on Camera Festival, 1989 Gold Award

A promotion of martial arts presented in the vein of a
music video.

KAREN KAIN: BALLERINA

    1977, 54 min., color, video
    Distributor: Master Vision
    Producers: Richard Nielsen and Pat Ferns
    Choreographers: John Cranko, Roland Petit
    Principal Dancers: Karen Kain, Frank Augustyn,
    Rudy Bryans
    Dance Company: Ballet de Marseille
    Composers: Georges Bizet, Sergei Prokofiev

Follows a National Ballet of Canada ballerina on tour in
CARMEN with a French company, the Ballet de Marseille,
directed by Roland Petit, and performing a duet from John
Cranko's ROMEO AND JULIET. Karen Kain speaks openly
about her fears and aspirations with British dance critic
Clement Crisp.

KASHIA MEN'S DANCES: SOUTHWESTERN POMO INDIANS

    Series: American Indian Series
    1963, 40 min., color, film
    Distributor: University of California Extension Media Center
    Producer: C. C. Macaulay
    Director: Clyde B. Smith

Four Pomo dances performed in elaborate headdresses and
costumes on the Kashia Reservation on the north Californian
coast in a specially made brush enclosure. The dances, a blend
of the ancient and more recently developed religion, Bole
Maru, celebrate the coming of the salmon, initiation into a
secret society or adulthood, and healing the sick.

KATHAK

    1945, 10 min., b&w, film
    Distributor: Portland State University #11580
    Producing Organization: Indian Government
    Information Services

North India's favorite classical dance performed with an
explanation of hand and finger gestures, along with facial and
body expressions.

KATHERINE DUNHAM

    1988, 15 min., color, video
    Distributor: Encyclopaedia Britannica #4775
    Producer: Turner Broadcasting

A profile of Katherine Dunham, a black matriarch of dance
with Hollywood film clips, historical materials, and footage of
Dunham's school in East St. Louis. Explores Haitian culture, a
subject of much fascination for Dunham, with a complete
performance of RITES DE PASSAGE.

KATHY'S DANCE

 1978, 28 min., color, film, video
 Distributor: Direct Cinema
 Producer: Anne Drew
 Dancer/Teacher: Kathy Posin
 American Film Festival, 1979 Blue Ribbon

Captures a modern dancer's exuberance and sense of purpose
as she teaches, choreographs, and performs.

KAZE-NO-KO

 1984, 13 min., color, video
 Distributor: Asia Society
 Director/Cinematographer: Richard Brevar
 Choreographer: Yukio Sekiva
 Dance Company: Kaze-no-ko Troupe

A Japanese troupe of dance-mime performers tells the story of
the UGLY DUCKLING using origami and Noh figures.

KEEP YOUR HEART STRONG

 1984–1986, 58 min., color, video
 Distributor: Intermedia Arts
 Producer: Deborah Wallwork for Native American TV
 Dance Company: North Dakota Indian Pow Wow
 Composer: Jim Pepper
 Dance on Camera Festival, 1987 Honorable Mention

Documentary on the native American Indian culture in its
most accessible form: the pow wow. Shows why traditional
arts are still relevant for today's Indians and how the values
they represent have helped them survive.

KELLY, GENE (11 videos)

 1944–1955, feature length, color, film, video
 Distributor/Producers: MGM
 Directors: Vincente Minnelli, Busby Berkeley,
 Charles Vidor, Gene Kelly, George Sidney, Stanley Donen
 Choreographers: Gene Kelly, Jerome Robbins,
 Agnes de Mille
 Composers: Jerome Kern, George & Ira Gershwin,
 Lerner-Loewe
 Principal Dancers: Gene Kelly, Cyd Charisse,
 Fred Astaire, Ann Miller, Rita Hayworth

A favorite for many, this dancer, singer, choreographer, actor, director may be enjoyed in his many capacities in the
following feature musicals available in retail outlets:

 AMERICAN IN PARIS (1951, with Leslie Caron)
 ANCHORS AWEIGH (1945, with Frank Sinatra)
 BRIGADOON (1954, with Cyd Charisse)
 COVER GIRL (1944, with Rita Hayworth)
 FOR ME AND MY GAL (1942, with Judy Garland)
 INVITATION TO THE DANCE (1956, see alphabetical
 listing)
 IT'S ALWAYS FAIR WEATHER (1955, with Cyd Charisse,
 Michael Kidd)

 ON THE TOWN (1949, with Ann Miller, Frank Sinatra,
 Vera Ellen)
 THE PIRATE (1947, with the Nicholas Brothers)
 SINGIN' IN THE RAIN (1952, with Debbie Reynolds,
 Donald O'Connor)
 TAKE ME OUT TO THE BALLGAME (1948, with
 Esther Williams)

KEYBOARD DANCE

 1984, 2:30 min., color, video
 Distributor/Director/Choreographer: Ye Sook Rhee
 Dancer: Pamela Lofton Alison
 Cinematographer: John Rauh
 Composer: Lyn Hammil

Hands on a keyboard with dancers as visual musical
notes and fingers.

KICKER DANCIN' TEXAS STYLE: HOW TO DO THE TOP TEN
COUNTRY & WESTERN DANCES LIKE A TEXAS COWBOY

 50 min., color, video
 Distributor: American Alliance for Health, Physical
 Education, Recreation and Dance
 Teachers: Shirley Fushing, Patrick Mcmillan

The basics of the ten popular Texan dances.

KINETIC COLOR IN DANCE

 1976, 7 min., color, film
 Distributor: Iowa State University
 Producer: R. B. Lindenmeyer

An experimental film exploring the shadows of three modern
dancers behind a translucent screen, lit from the the side
and the back.

KING KAMEHAMEHA HULA COMPETITION –
14TH ANNUAL

 1987, 110 min., color, video
 Distributor: Pacific Trade Group
 Producer: Kalama Prod.
 Writer/Producer: David Kalama
 Director: Roland Yamamoto

Highlights of the 14th competition in honor of the first king of
Hawaii with *kahiko* (ancient hula), *auana* (modern hula), and
oli (Hawaiian chanting). Shot in Hawaii.

KING KAMEHAMEHA HULA COMPETITION –
15TH ANNUAL (2 videos)

 1989, 90 min.(auana), 72 min. (kahiko), color, video
 Distributor: Pacific Trade Group
 Producer: Kalama Productions
 Director: Roland Yamamoto

Writer/Producer: David Kalama
Principal Dancer: Tangaroa Teamaru

Highlights of the 1988 competition in Hawaii in honor of the first king of Hawaii with *kahiko* (ancient hula), *auana* (modern hula) and the *oli* (Hawaiian chanting). Shot in Hawaii.

KING KONG IN A BLANKET

1978, 9 min., color, film, video
Distributor: Maine Independent Cinema Arc
Producer: Bayne Williams Film Co.
Director: Nan Ross
Principal Dancer: John Carrafa
Composer: Brad Terry
Dance on Camera Festival, 1979

Portrait of Spindleworks, a workshop for mentally retarded adults in Brunswick, Maine, selected as one of ten model sites by the National Committee/Arts for the Handicapped. John Carrafa, a longtime member of Twyla Tharp's company, shares his joy of moving with the workshop members, who also spin yarn and hook rugs.

Kirov Ballet: Classic Ballet Night
Cover art courtesy V.I.E.W. Video.

KIROV BALLET: CLASSIC BALLET NIGHT

1985, 95 min., color, video
Distributor: V.I.E.W.
Producer: Soviet Film & TV
Choreographers: Agrippina Vaganova, Marius Petipa, August Bournonville, Arthur Saint-Leon, Anton Dolin
Principal Dancers: Irina Kolpakova, Gabriela Komleva,
Tatiana Terekova, Vitali Afanaskov, Natalia Bolshkova, Vadim Gouliaev
Dance Company: Kirov Ballet
Composers: Cesare Pugni, Riccardo Drigo, E. Helsted

Program from Russia includes DIANA AND ACTHEON (Vaganova/Pugni) performed by Tatiana Terekova and Sergei Berezhoni; ESMERALDA (Petipa/Drigo) performed by Gabriela Komleva and Vitali Afanaskov; FLOWER FESTIVAL IN GENZANO (Bournonville/Helsted) performed by Natalia Bolshkova and Vadim Gouliaev; THE CANTEEN KEEPER (Saint-Leon/Pugni) performed by Alla Sizova, Boris Blankov and Kirov soloists; THE VENICE CARNIVAL (Petipa/Pugni) performed by Svetlana Efrenova and Valeri Emets; PAS DE QUATRE (Dolin/Pugni) performed by Irina Kolpakova, Gabriela Komleva, Elena Evteeva, and Galina Mezentseva.

KIROV SOLOISTS: INVITATION TO THE DANCE

1989, 54 min., color, video
Distributor: V.I.E.W. Video
Producer: Soviet Film & TV
Choreographers: Nikolai Kovmir, Roland Petit, V. Timofeev, Marius Petipa, L. Lebedev, Paul Taglioni, Agrippina Vaganova
Principal Dancers: Irina Kolpakova, Tatiana Terekova, Sergei Berezhnoi
Composers: Cesare Pugni, J. M. Jarre, Norbert Burgmuller, Hector Villa-Lobos, Jacques Offenbach

Performance and rehearsals of six ballets by the great Russian troupe: DIANE AND ACTHEON (Vaganova/Pugni), NOTRE DAME DE PARIS (Petit/Jarre), PAS DE DEUX (Timofeev/Burgmuller), CARNIVAL DE VENISE (Petipa/Pugni), BACHIANA (Lebedev/Villa-Lobos), and LE PAPILLON (Taglioni/Offenbach).

KIT'S KIDS

1980s, 30 min., color, video
Distributor: Hoctor Products
Producer: Studio Music Corp.
Teacher: Kit Andree

Jazz routines.

KOREA: PERFORMING ARTS—THE WONDERFUL WORLD OF KIM SUNG HEE

1979, 21 min., color, film
Distributor: Portland State University
Producer: Centron
Director: Harold Harvey
Cinematographer: Robert Rose
Finalist, American Film Festival

Traditional dances performed by the National Theatre of Seoul's Kim Sung Hee, who explains that unity with nature is the central theme in all Korean performing arts.

Kumu Hula: Keepers of a Culture
Dance group Halau O Kāleiho Ohie perform on the island of Kona, led by hula master Iris Nalei Napaepae-Kunewa. Photo courtesy Rhapsody Films.

KUMU HULA: KEEPERS OF A CULTURE

1989, 85 min., color, film, video
Distributor: Rhapsody Films
Producer/Directors: Robert Mugge, Vicky Holt Takamine for Cove Enterprises
Directors: Lawrence McConkey, Eric Roland
Principal Dancer: Iris Nalei Napaepae-Kunewa
Dance Company: Halau O Kaleiho Ohie

Chanting to the Goddess Pele on the Island of Kilauer to performing animal-inspired pieces, a group of Hawaiians share the history and traditions of the hula, the dance imported from Polynesia. The documentary is one of three on Hawaii that honor the advice "Au'a'la e tama e tona motu" translated to mean "Hold fast, o child, to your heritage."

THE LADY OF THE CAMELLIAS

1987, 125 min., color, video
Distributor: Kultur #1209
Producer: Polyphon with Fernseh, Hamburg
Choreographer/Director: John Neumeier
Principal Dancers: Marcia Haydee, Ivan Liska
Dance Company: Hamburg Ballet
Composer: Frederic Chopin
Set and Costume Designer: Jurgen Rose
Cinematographer: Ingo Hamer
Dance on Camera Festival, 1988 Gold Award

Inspired by the nineteeth-century French novel by Alexander Dumas, John Neumeier, the American dancer long based in Hamburg, Germany, choreographed this film of a courtesan's love for a younger man, forbidden by his father and further complicated by her tuberculosis.

LALALA HUMAN SEX DUO NO. 1

1987, 7:30 min., b&w, video
Distributor: Antenna
Producer: Agent Orange
Choreographer: Edouard Lock
Director: Bernar Herbert
Principal Dancers: Louise Lecavalier, Marc Beland
Composer: David Van Tieghem
Dance on Camera Festival, 1987 Gold Award

Punk pas de deux memorable for its wild energy, mid-air horizontal turns, its costumes, and its slow submergence. The video opens with the waves of the sea breaking against the shore. An underwater shot shows the remains of a ballroom. The images dissolve into the same ballroom emptied of its water, revealing a man and a woman who begin to dance.

LAMBACHEN AND STEINHAUSER LANDLER (2 films)

1970 & 1973, 8 and 10 min., b&w, film
Distributor: PennState #EO2003 & EO2004
Producer: Wissen

The dance from Lambach im Traunviertel, Austria, accompanied by accordion, two violins, and double bass, followed by a Bavarian polka.

LAMBETH WALK—NAZI STYLE

1942, 2 min., b&w, film
Distributor: Biograph

Satirical World War II propaganda and a takeoff on the popular ballroom dance of the 1940s.

LAMENT

1951, 16 min., b&w, film
Distributor: Dance Films Association (members only)
Producer/Director: Walter V. Strate
Choreographer: Doris Humphrey
Principal Dancers: Jose Limon, Letitia Ide, Ellen Love
Composer: Norman Lloyd
Costume Designer: Pauline Lawrence
Set Designer: Michael Czaja

Re-staged for film, this dark trio honors the death of a bullfighter as Federico Garcia Lorca's poem "Lament for Ignacio Sanchez Mejias" is recited.

LAMENT

1985, 9 min., b&w, video
Distributor: Electronic Arts Intermix
Producers: Walker Art Center, Minneapolis
Director: James Byrne
Choreographer/Dancers: Eiko & Koma
Composer: Karma Moffett

A duet performed in two adjacent puddles of water with low lighting that catches the pool reflections and sculpts the slowly twisting naked bodies.

LAMENTATION

1943, 10 min., color, film
Distributors: Dance Films Association (rental to members only), National Audio Visual Center #200HF1426
Producer: Harmon Foundation
Choreographer/Dancer: Martha Graham
Cinematographers: Mr. & Mrs. Simon Moselsio
Composer: Zoltan Kodaly

John Martin, a former dance critic of the New York Times, gives a brief history of modern dance and talks about dance as a medium of expression. Martha Graham performs excerpts from her 1930 solo, accompanied by Louis Horst on the piano. Twisting on a bench in her costume, which covers her from head to toe, Graham becomes a sculptural study of agony.

THE LANGUAGE OF DANCE

Series: A Time to Dance
1960, 29 min., b&w, film
Distributor: Indiana University
Producer: Jac Venza for WNET/13
Principal Dancers: José Limón, Pauline Koner, Lucas Hoving, Betty Jones, Robert Powell, Lola Huth
Dance Company: José Limón Company
Composer: Norman Dello Joio

Choreographer/dancer José Limón and teacher Martha Myers talk about the language of dance and movement. The film features Limón's THERE IS A TIME, a classic choreographed in 1956, inspired by the line in the Book of Ecclesiastes "To everything there is a season, and a time to every purpose under the heaven."

THE LANGUAGE OF MODERN DANCE

1958, 22 min., b&w, film
Distributor: University of Iowa
Producer/Teacher: Lila Cheville

The movements, patterns, and rhythms of modern dance, along with the advice to practice.

THE LAST DANCING ISADORABLE

1988, color, 30 min., video
Distributor/Producer: Kay Bardsley
Choreographer/Dancer: Maria-Theresa Duncan
Dancer: Clive Thompson

Focus on the life and career of the late Maria-Theresa Duncan, an adopted daughter of Isadora Duncan, portrayed through stills, paintings, and clips of her performances, including MARCH SLAV, in the 1920s and 1976.

LAURETTA: MADONNA OF THE SENIOR CITIZEN SET

1989, 20 min., color, video
Distributor/Producer/Director: Jean De Boysson
Dance on Camera Festival, 1990 Honorable Mention

Sixty-three-year-old retired factory worker talks about her second career, belly dancing, and performs in community events.

LEARN HOW TO DANCE (82 videos)

1986–1991, 60 min. each, color, video
Producer/Distributor/Director: Sherry Greene for Butterfly Video
Teacher: Kathy Blake

Series includes lessons in the fox trot, jitterbug, waltz, tango, samba, cha cha, rumba, merengue, mambo, disco hustle, charleston, polka, salsa, line dances, west coast swing, peabody, children, lambada. Also available through Butterfly Video, eleven videos with David Nicholas, make-up artist based in Boston, and a two-and-a-half-hour preview tape.

LEARNING TO DANCE IN BALI

1930s, 13 min., b&w, film
Distributor: New York University (for viewing only)
Producer/Narrator: Margaret Mead
Producer/Director: Gregory Bateson

This landmark film by two pioneers, Margaret Mead and Gregory Bateson, demonstrates the means of passing on a traditional Balinese dance through manipulation and imitation. Mead advocated that all observations should be recorded, whether by words or camera, and thereby transformed the method of social anthropological research.

LEE'S FERRY

1982, 8 min., color, film
Distributor/Choreographer/Dancer: Sally Gross
Director: Susan Brockman
Composer: Keith Jarrett
Painter: Joan Kurahara
Dance on Camera Festival, 1982 Honorable Mention

A moving landscape is realized as the images made by the dancer are combined with the forms of projected light.

THE LEGACY OF THE CHOREOGRAPHY OF ISADORA DUNCAN

1988, 45 min., color, video
Distributor: Dance Films Association (for members only)
Producer: Julia Levien with DFA
Choreographer: Isadora Duncan
Director: Penny Ward
Principal Dancers: Julia Levien, Hortense Kooluris
Dance Company: Isadora Duncan Commemorative Dance Company
Composers: Peter Ilyich Tchaikovsky, Johannes Brahms
Dance on Camera Festival, 1989 Honorable Mention

An introduction with stills to the tradition of Isadora Duncan followed by a performance of MILITARY MARCH and selected Brahms WALTZES.

LET'S DANCE SAMBA

1990, color, video
Distributor: Samba Associates
Teacher: Luci Llorens
Composer: Embrasamba

Warm up, body coordination, samba steps, with tips from Luci Llorens and percussionists of Embrasamba.

LET'S DANCE THE CHARKHUDUZONU

1971, 20 min., color, film
Distributor: National Council of American-Soviet Friendship

Uzbek folk dance.

LET'S SCUFFLE

   1942, 3 min., b&w, film
   Distributor: Dance Film Archive
   Choreographer/Dancer: Bill "Bojangles" Robinson

A vintage clip of the legendary tap dancer
Bill "Bojangles" Robinson.

LIFE IN THE DUST: FRAGMENTS OF AFRICAN VOYAGES

   1986, 28 min., color, video
   Distributor/Producer: Solaris in association with WHYY-TV,
   Congolese National Television, and Global Village
   Director/Choreographer/Dancer: Henry Smith
   Composers: Michael Sirotta, Aiyb Dieng, Philip Gilbert
   Editor: Peter Shelton

Through participation in the African/American Arts Exchange
program, Solaris visited Ghana, Senegal, and the Congo between 1980 and 1983. On the last trip to Congo-Brazzaville,
they taped a work created there entitled DZAMBA YA BILIMA
(The Sacred Forest). Interwoven among the African footage are
dance interpretations of their experience.

A LIFE IN TWO WORLDS: TAMASABURO BANDO

   1977, 20 min., color, film
   Distributor: Japan Foundation
   Producer: Broadcast Programming Center of Japan
   Principal Dancer: Tamasaburo Bando

The highly acclaimed Kabuki Onnagata, or female impersona-
tor, rehearses and performs MUSUME DOJOJI, with twenty
on-stage costume changes. Also from Japan Foundation, the
Sakura Motion Picture-made ONNAGATA: THE MAKING OF
A KABUKI, a 29-minute film on the training of student actors.

LIFTS, SPINS, AND DROPS

   1980, 7 min., b&w, film
   Distributor/Producer: See-Do Productions
   Principal Dancers: Francois Szony, Catherine Caplin

Twenty tricks and variations on adagio partnering from a team
well-known on the nightclub circuit.

LIGHT, PART 5

   1976, 22 min., color, film
   Distributor: Dance Film Archive
   Producer/Director: John Mueller
   Choreographer/Dancer: Kei Takei
   Principal Dancers: Maldwyn Pate, John De Marco

A slow, liquid trio by an Asian American acclaimed for her
hypnotic minimalism.

LIMELIGHT

   1952, 144 min., color, video
   Distributor: retail outlets
   Director/Performer: Charlie Chaplin
   Principal Dancers: Andre Eglevsky, Melissa Hayden

Music Hall performer tries to rescue a ballerina from
despair in this film featuring two of the top figures of the
ballet world along with Buster Keaton and Charlie Chaplin,
who joined forces for the first and only time.

LINDY VIDEOTAPES (4 videos)

   1988, 1:45–2:20 min. each, color, video
   Distributor/Producer/Teacher: Margaret Batiuchok
   Principal Dancers: Frank Manning, George Lloyd,
   Charlie Meade, Tom Lewis

Winner of the 1983 Harvest Moon Ball and co-founder of the
New York Swing Society, Margaret Batiuchok interviews and
dances with Frank Manning, choreographer for Whitey's Lindy
Hoppers in the 30s and 40s; George Lloyd, a Savoy dancer of
the 40s and 50s; Charlie Meade, jazz and tap dancer from
Jamaica; and Tom Lewis, a star student of hers.

THE LITTLE HUMPBACKED HORSE

   1961, 85 min., color, film, video
   Distributors: Corinth (film), Kultur #1204 (video)
   Producer: Central Documentary Film Studios
   Director: Zoya Tulubyeva
   Choreographer: Alexander Radunsky
   Principal Dancers: Maya Plisetskaya (Queen Maiden),
   Vladimir Vasiliev (Ivanushka), Alexander Radunsky (Czar)
   Dance Company: Bolshoi Ballet
   Composer: Rodion Shchedrin

This remake of a remake had its stage debut in 1864 with
choreography by the Frenchman Arthur Saint Leon. Based
on a Russian fairy tale by Yershov Ivanushka, a young man
befriends a horse with magical powers which helps him to
win the love of a woman, trick a half-witted czar, and live
happily ever after as a prince.

LIVE AND REMEMBER (WO KIKSUYE)

   1987, 28:45 min., color, video
   Distributor: Solaris
   Producer: Solaris in association with South Dakota
   Public TV
   Composer: Ironwood Singers
   Editor: Peter Shelton

Opening with footage of a Sweat Lodge Ceremony, a means
of spiritual strength, this documentary shows Lakota Indian
elders, medicine men, and dancers discussing the challenge
of keeping their native American culture alive. Shot on the
Rosebud Reservation in South Dakota, the dance footage includes performances of the EAGLE, SNEAK-UP, and HOOP
DANCE, with examples of fancy dancing.

LIVE VIDEO DANCE

   1987, 6:20 min., color, video
   Distributor: Electronic Arts Intermix
   Producer/Director: Kit Fitzgerald
   Choreographer/Dancer: Stephanie Woodard
   Composer: Peter Zummo

Electronic cloning allows a colorfully clad solo dancer to create
her own responsive environment and a mobile backdrop that
races off to the left, sinks, and disappears. The dancer pulses
in place with gentle curves of the torso and arms, seemingly
unimpressed by her visual echo.

LIVES OF PERFORMERS

   1972, 90 min., color, film, video

Distributor: First Run/Icarus Films
Producer/Director: Yvonne Rainer

A collage of performance, improvisation, and voice-over reflecting the fictional and real aspects of the life of Yvonne Rainer. This film director, choreographer, and performer was instrumental in founding the Judson Church group.

LIVING AMERICAN THEATRE DANCE

1982, 11 min., color, film, video
Distributor: Phoenix Films
Producer: A Mayqueen Production
Executive Producer: Ruth Caplin
Director/Producer: John Alper
Dancer/Choreographer: Lee Theodore
Dancer: Ann Reinking
Dance Company: American Dance Machine

The American Dance Machine, a living archive of over forty-five Broadway musical routines, rehearse a few classics under the tutelage of the late Lee Theodore, founder of the company.

LOCALE

1980, 30 min., color, film, video
Distributor/Producer: Cunningham Dance Foundation
Director: Charles Atlas
Choreographer: Merce Cunningham
Composer: Takehisa Kosugi

The camera moves with, around, and among the dancers at different speeds, its movements choreographed as precisely as those of the performers. Three cameras, Steadicam, Movieola crab dolly, and an Elemac dolly with a crane arm, provide a wide range of perspective and intensity.

LOOK! WE HAVE COME THROUGH

1978, 11 min., b&w, film
Distributor: Lightworks
Producer/Director: R. Bruce Elder

A filmmaker's attempt to parallel the intent of a choreographer through various devices of shooting and editing.

LOOKING FOR ME

1969, 29 min., b&w, film, video
Distributor: University of California Extension Media Center
Producers: Virginia Bartlett and Norris Brock for
The Shady Lane School, Pittsburgh, Pa.
Dance Therapist: Jane Adler
CINE Golden Eagle, American Psychological
Association Honoree

One of the University of California's best selling tapes about the delights of experiencing one's body and the success of therapist Janet Adler in bringing two autistic girls out of their shells.

LORD OF THE DANCE/DESTROYER OF ILLUSION

1985, 108 min., color, film, video
Distributor: First Run/Icarus Films
Producer: Richard Kohn
Principal Dancer: Trulshig Rinpoche

American Film Festival, 1987 Red Ribbon

A metaphysical travelogue to Nepal and the Mani-Rimdu festival of "awakening." The Buddhist monks dance to depict gods in battle with malevolent supernatural forces as part of a Tibetan Tantric ritual.

THE LOVERS OF TERUEL

1962, 90 min., color, film, video
Distributor: Kultur #1112
Producer: Janus
Choreographer: Milko Sparemblek
Director/Writer: Raymond Rouleau
Cinematographer: Claude Renoir
Principal Dancer: Ludmila Tcherina
Composer: Mikis Theodorakis

In a play within a play, the star of a gypsy troupe identifies with her nightly role as Duchess Isabelle of Teruel who dances nightly in public squares, waiting for the return of her lover, who is killed upon appearance by her betrothed. The parallel in her own life becomes too much, and she destroys herself.

LUIGI (3 videos)

1988, 60 min. each, color, video
Distributor: Hoctor Products
Producer: Studio Music Corp.
Choreographer/Teacher/Dancer: Luigi
Principal Dancers: Francis Roach, Ande Handler

Complete technical breakdown of the New York–based teacher's fluid style. For beginning through advanced-level students. Known for his exacting warm-up and his line of instructional records, Luigi has trained countless performers in his technique, identifiable by its grace, nuance, and lyricism.

LUMIA: THE DESIGN OF DANCE

1975, 6:30 min., color, film
Distributor: Iowa State University
Producer: R. B. Lindenmeyer

Interplay of red, green, and blue lights and shadows, with a dancer seen behind a translucent screen.

LUMINAIRE

1985, 6 min., color, video
Distributor: Kitchen
Directors: John Sanborn, Dean Winkler
Choreographer/Dancer: Charles Moulton

Patterns choreographed through postproduction with a dancer floating in an electronic web.

MA'BUGI: TRANCE OF THE TORAJA

1971, 21 min., color, film
Distributor: University of California Extension Media Center

Depicts a ritual that restores the balance of well-being for a village in the highlands of Sulawesi (Celebes), Indonesia. Taken in the Rantekasimpo village of the Makale district, known for its spectacular elaborations of this rite of renewal and invigoration.

MACBETH

    1984, 105 min., color, video
    Distributor: Kultur #1115
    Producer: Gostelradio
    Choreographer/Director: Vladimir Vasiliev
    Principal Dancers: Alexei Fadeyechev (Macbeth),
    Nina Timofeyeva (Lady Macbeth)
    Dance Company: Bolshoi Ballet
    Composers: Kirill Molchanov

William Shakespeare's tale of murder and intrigue filmed live at the Bolshoi Theatre in Moscow. Choreographer Vladimir Vasiliev focuses on the meeting of the three witches, the ambition of Lady Macbeth, the murders of King Duncan and Banquo, and the torment suffered by Macbeth and his wife after they claimed the throne.

THE MAGANA BAPTISTE SIXTH ANNUAL BELLY DANCE FESTIVAL

    1989, 90 min., color, video
    Distributor/Producer: Magana Baptiste Royal Academy
    Principal Dancers: Devi Ananda Baptiste, Horacio Cifuentes
    Composer: Nabil El Ansari

California school recital of Middle Eastern dance for teachers and dancers. Other videos on Middle Eastern dance available from Baptiste Academy: MR. AND MISS BELLY DANCE CONTEST, SAN FRANCISCO, 1988 and 1987, DR. MO GEDDAWI'S AUGUST 1988 WORKSHOP, and HORACIO CIFUENTES INSTRUCTIONAL VOLUMES I and II.

THE MAGIC FIDDLE

    1956, 16 min., color, film
    Distributor: University of Southern California
    Producer: Jan Wikbor for National Film Board of Norway
    Director: Michael Forlong
    Choreographer: Gerd Kjolass
    Composers: Sverre Bergh, Gerd Kjolass
    Dance Company: The Norwegian Ballet

Based on a Norwegian fairy tale told before the performance about a boy who befriends a beggar and receives a magic fiddle in return. Whenever the boy plays the fiddle, everyone dances wildly in response.

THE MAGIC OF THE BOLSHOI BALLET

    1987, 60 min., color, video
    Distributor: Kultur #1222
    Producer: Gostelradio
    Choreographer: Marius Petipa
    Principal Dancers: Maya Plisetskaya, Galina Ulanova,
    Vladimir Vasiliev, Natalia Bessmertnova,
    Ekaterina Maximova
    Dance Company: Bolshoi Ballet
    Composers: Peter Ilyich Tchaikovsky, Adolphe Adam,
    Sergei Prokofiev, Ludwig Minkus

A comprehensive retrospective of the past fifty years of the 200-year-old Bolshoi Ballet with rare footage of performances and classes, including scenes of SLEEPING BEAUTY, ROMEO & JULIET, DON QUIXOTE, GISELLE, and SWAN LAKE.

THE MAGIC OF THE KIROV BALLET

    1988, 60 min., color, video
    Distributor: Kultur #1216
    Producers: Gostelradio and The Entertainment Video Co.
    Choreographer: Marius Petipa
    Principal Dancers: Farouk Ruzimatov, Tatyana Terekhova,
    Olga Chenchikova
    Dance Company: Kirov Ballet
    Composers: Leon Minkus, Riccardo Drigo, Peter
    Ilyich Tchaikovsky, Alexander Glazunov

Pas de deux selections from the Kirov's classical repertoire include: Entry of the Shades and Indian Dance, Act II of LA BAYADERE, LE CORSAIRE, SLEEPING BEAUTY, the Spanish Dance in Act II of RAYMONDA, SWAN LAKE, PAQUITA, and DON QUIXOTE.

THE MAGNIFICENT BEGINNING

    Series: Magic Of Dance
    1979, 52 min., color, film, video
    Distributors: Dance Film Archive (rental), Ivy Films
    Producer: Patricia Foy for BBC
    Dancer/Choreographer: Roland Petit
    Principal Dancers: Zizi Jeanmaire, David Wall, Wendy
    Ellis, Ronald Emblem
    Choreographers: Mary Skeaping, Frederick Ashton,
    Maximilien Gardel
    Composers: Rebel, Henry Purcell, Etienne-Nicolas Mehul,
    Francois Joseph Herold
    Arranger: John Lanchbery
    Narrator: Margot Fonteyn
    Dance Companies: Royal Swedish Ballet, Royal Ballet,
    Dance Academy of Peking

This fifth program in the educational series presents Louis XIV as the champion of ballet, with a tour of the Paris Opera and the Drottningholm theater in Sweden. Royal Swedish Ballet performs three ballets of Mary Skeaping: LA CAMARGO, music by Rebel; CUPID OUT OF HIS HUMOR, music by Henry Purcell; and LA DANSOMANIA, music by Etienne-Nicolas Mehul; extracts from Frederick Ashton's LA FILLE MAL GARDEE; the bedroom scene from Roland Petit's CARMEN; and the Dance Academy of Peking's THE LITTLE MATCH GIRL.

MAKAHIKI FESTIVAL

    1987, 53 min., color, video
    Distributor: Pacific Trade Group
    Producer: Kalama Productions
    Director: Roland Yamamoto
    Principal Dancer: Waimea Falls Park
    Writer: Barry Hampe

10th annual festival in Haleiwa, Hawaii, with games and activities reminiscent of the original *makahiki* held by Hawaiians before contact with Western civilization. Solo dances in *kahiko* (ancient) and *auana* (modern) hula. The only solo competition in which men and women compete equally in Hawaii.

MAKING DANCES: SEVEN POST-MODERN CHOREOGRAPHERS

    1980, 90 min., color, video

Distributor/Producer/Director: Michael Blackwood with
Westdeutscher Rundfunk, BBC, and Sveriges Radio TV 1
Choreographer/Dancers: Trisha Brown, Lucinda Childs,
Douglas Dunn, David Gordon, Kenneth King, Meredith
Monk, Sara Rudner
Composers: Gordon Lightfoot, Meredith Monk, Peter Allen
and Adrienne Anderson, Philip Glass, John Driscoll
Interviewer/Narrator: Marcia Siegel
Cinematographer: Mead Hunt
Editor: Peter Adair

A documentary with performances and interviews with the
prime modern choreographers active in the 1970s. Perfor-
mances include ACCUMULATION WITH TALKING, PLUS
WATER MOTOR, LINE-UP, and GLACIAL DECOY,
choreographed by Trisha Brown; DANCE, by Lucinda Childs;
FOOT RULES by Douglas Dunn; AN AUDIENCE WITH THE
POPE, ONE PART OF THE MATTER by David Gordon;
WORLD RAID, WOR(L)d(T) raid by Kenneth King;
EDUCATION OF THE GIRLCHILD, DOLMAN MUSIC by
Meredith Monk; MODERN DANCES by Sara Rudner.

THE MAKING OF A BALLET
   1973, 36 min., color, film, video
   Distributor: Netherlands Consulate General
   Producer: Jan Vrijman
   Choreographer: Rudi Van Danzig
   Dance Company: Netherlands National Ballet

In this documentary on the making of a ballet, the film
shows the obsessiveness of the creative process. The ballet,
inspired by Jerzy Kosinski's THE PAINTED BIRD, centers
around a man who remains indifferent to violent attacks
and his subsequent self-destruction.

THE MAKING OF SEVERE CLEAR
   1986, 25:14 min., color, video
   Distributor/Producer: Susan Dowling for WGBH-TV
   Choreographer/Dancer: Dana Reitz
   Light/Space Artist: James Turrel

A modern dance solo.

MAKING TELEVISION DANCE
   1977, 59 min., color, b&w, film. video
   Distributor: Phoenix Films
   Producer: Twyla Tharp Dance Foundation
   Director: Don Mischer
   Principal Dancers: Twyla Tharp, Mikhail Baryshnikov
   Dance Company: Twyla Tharp Company
   Cinematographer: Joel Gold
   Dance on Camera Festival, 1978 Merit Award

Twyla Tharp explores the relationship between television
and dance and explains her rationale behind certain exercises choreographed for the camera. Features a rehearsal
with Mikhail Baryshnikov on ONCE MORE FRANK and her
COUNTRY DANCES set for five dancers.

Malambo
Photo courtesy Taller Latinoamericano.

MALAMBO
   1990, 6 min., color, video
   Distributor/Producer: Taller Latinoamericano
   Producer: Donna Light
   Director: Bernardo Palombo
   Cinematographer: Jamie Maxton-Graham
   Composers: Bernardo Palombo, Philip Glass
   Dance Company: Ballet Las Pampas

This urban folk tale uses the road as a symbol of the link
between traditional culture and modern society with parade footage taken in New York City and Peru. Las Pampas
performs the Argentinian malambo in the traditional
gaucho dress in the city streets and parks of New York.

MALAYSIAN DANCES (7 films)
   1974–1978, 10 min. each, color, film
   Distributor: Embassy of Malaysia
   Dance Company: National Cultural Troupe

A Farmers' Dance, a folk dance depicting farmers working
in the rice fields and the self-reliance of the villagers, other
folk dances are shown in two films. A five-part film of the
Asian variety show in Kuala Lumpur featuring artists from
Indonesia, Malaysia, Philippines, Singapore, and Thailand is
also available.

MAN WHO DANCES
   1968/80, 54 min., color, film, video
   Distributor: Direct Cinema
   Producer: Robert Drew
   Choreographer: George Balanchine
   Principal Dancers: Edward Villella, Patricia McBride
   EMMY Award

Edward Villella, currently artistic director of the Miami Ballet,
partners Patricia McBride in rehearsals with choreographer
George Balanchine, founder of the New York City Ballet. They

perform RUBIES, from Balanchine's JEWELS, and the pas de deux from TARANTELLA.

MANON
1982, 126 min., color, video
Distributors: HBO #3405, Pioneer (Laserdisk)
Producer: National Video Corporation
Director: Colin Nears
Choreographer: Kenneth MacMillan
Principal Dancers: Jennifer Penney (Manon), Anthony Dowell
Dance Company: Royal Ballet
Composer: Jules Massenet

The story of a love so obsessive and self-destructive that a young man of good social standing sacrifices everything to satisfy a woman of dubious morality. Based on the 1731 novel by Abbe Prevost, set to the music written for the opera composed in 1884.

MARCEAU ON MIME
1974, 22 min., color, film, video
Distributor: AIMS
Producer: Gesture Productions
Director: John Gould
Mime: Marcel Marceau

The French mime artist discusses his art.

MARCEL MARCEAU OU L' ART DU MIME
1961, 17 min., b&w, video, film
Distributor: French American Cultural Services and Educational Aid (FACSEA) #2292
Director: P. Paviot
Mime: Marcel Marceau

The French mime at home, surrounded by memorabilia of pantomime through the ages, and on stage as Bip and Don Juan.

MARCEL MARCEAU'S MIME SCHOOL
1979, 6:30 min., color, film
Distributor: Facsea
Mime: Marcel Marceau

A glimpse of the school opened by the French performer Marcel Marceau. With French or English dialogue.

MARGOT FONTEYN IN "LES SYLPHIDES"
1947, 8 min., b&w, film
Distributor: Dance Film Archive
Choreographer: Michel Fokine
Principal Dancers: Margot Fonteyn, Michael Somes
Composer: Frederic Chopin
Dance Company: Royal Ballet

An excerpt from LITTLE BALLERINA, a British feature, with a movement of LES SYLPHIDES. The performance is intercut with backstage scenes.

THE MARGOT FONTEYN STORY
1989, 90 min., color, video
Distributor: Home Vision #FON01
Producer: RM Arts
Director: Patricia Foy
Choreographers: Frederick Ashton, Marius Petipa

Principal Dancers: Frederic Ashton, Robert Helpman, Rudolf Nureyev, Anton Dolin, Ninette de Valois
Composers: Adolphe Adam, Peter Ilyich Tchaikovsky
Dance on Camera Festival, 1990 Gold Award

Ballerina Assoluta Dame Margot Fonteyn speaks from her home in Panama to tell her life story on the eve of her seventieth birthday. Her memories are intercut with interviews with mentors, partners and proteges, such as Ninette de Valois, Frederick Ashton, Robert Helpmann, and Rudolf Nureyev, plus archival footage of Fonteyn in ONDINE, SWAN LAKE, GISELLE.

THE MARRAKESH FOLK FESTIVAL AND MORE (6 videos)
1980s, 60–120 min. each, color, video
Distributor/Dancer: Morocco
Compiled by Morocco, an itinerant Middle Eastern dance teacher/performer, based in New York, on her many tours to her namesake country, Morocco and the surrounding countries. She also has a performance tape of her company MOROCCO AND THE CASBAH DANCE EXPERIENCE IN CONCERT AT RIVERSIDE CHURCH DANCE FESTIVAL (120 min.) and the NATIONAL FOLK TROUPE OF EGYPT (KAWMIYYA) (80 min.), plus
REAL GHAWAZI, DERVISH, NUBIAN, CANDELABRUM, SUDANESE, TAHTIYB & THE REDA TROUPE (60 min); STARS OF EGYPTIAN DANCE: NEGWA FOUAD, SOHEIR ZAKI, AZA SHARIF (80 min.); STARS OF EGYPTIAN DANCE: NADIA HAMDY, HANAN, EMAN WAGDI & NAHED SABRY (80 min.).

MARTHA CLARKE: LIGHT AND DARK
1981, 54 min., color, film
Distributors: Phoenix Films #21251, Ivy Films
Producer/Director: Joyce Chopra
Cinematographers: Fred Murphy, Don Lenzer
Choreographer/Dancer: Martha Clarke
Principal Dancer: Felix Blaska

Reveals the imaginative sources and working habits of Martha Clarke, the former Pilobolus member internationally celebrated for her daring approach to theater. Four dances about loneliness, being a woman, and the strangeness of performance, developed and filmed over the course of a year in her rural studio in Connecticut.

MARTHA GRAHAM, AN AMERICAN ORIGINAL IN PERFORMANCE
1958, 93 min., b&w, video
Distributor: Kultur #1177
Producer: Nathan Kroll for WQED-TV, Pittsburgh
Directors: Peter Glushanok, Alexander Hammid
Principal Dancers: Martha Graham, Miriam Cole, Yuriko Kimura, Linda Hodes, Stuart Hodes, Bertram Ross
Composers: Aaron Copland, William Schuman Peabody

A trilogy of films made in Martha Graham's middle years: A DANCER'S WORLD, NIGHT JOURNEY, and APPALACHIAN SPRING (see individual titles).

THE MARTHA GRAHAM DANCE COMPANY
Series: Dance in America

1976, 90 min., color, film
Distributors: Indiana University #RC0989, Dance
Film Archive (excerpts)
Producer: WNET/13
Director: Merrill Brockway
Choreographer: Martha Graham
Principal Dancers: Peter Sparling, Elisa Monte, Peggy Lyman,
Takako Asakawa, Janet Eilber
Dance Company: Martha Graham Dance Company
Composers: Zoltan Kodaly, Louis Horst, Aaron Copland,
Samuel Barber
Narrator: Gregory Peck
Dance on Camera Festival, 1977

Choreographer Martha Graham introduces her dances:
DIVERSION OF ANGELS (1948), LAMENTATION (1930),
FRONTIER, ADORATIONS, APPALACHIAN SPRING (1944),
and Medea's solo danced by Takako Asakawa from CAVE OF
THE HEART.

MARTHA GRAHAM: THREE CONTEMPORARY CLASSICS

1984, 85 min., color, video
Distributors: Video Arts International, Dance Horizons Video
Producers: Judy Kinberg and Jac Venza for WNET/13
Director: Thomas Grimm
Principal Dancers: Takako Asakawa, Terese Capucilli
Dance Company: Martha Graham Dance Company
Composers: Gian Carlo Menotti, Samuel Barber, Carl Nielsen

Performances of three works: ERRAND INTO THE MAZE,
ACTS OF LIGHT, CAVE OF THE HEART,   one
choreographed in 1947 on the myth of Theseus and a
woman's struggle with fear; another that premiered in 1947
set to a commissioned score by Samuel Barber; and the
third on the myth of Medea, the jilted, vengeful goddess,
which Graham choreographed in her eighties.

MARY WIGMAN

1929, 10 min., b&w, film
Distributors: Dance Film Archive, Museum of Modern Art
Choreographer/Dancer: Mary Wigman

In this silent film, the influential German dancer performs
four solos: SERAPHIC DANCE, PASTORAL, SUMMER
DANCE, and WITCHES' DANCE. At the time of the filming,
she had completed her studies with Rudolph Von Laban,
the father of Labanotation, in Switzerland and opened her
own school in Dresden.

MARY WIGMAN – MY LIFE IS DANCE

1986, 29 min., color, b&w, video
Distributor: Modern Talking Picture Service #25512
Director/Writer: Ulrich Tegeder
Choreographer/Dancer: Mary Wigman
Principal Dancers: Hanya Holm, Yvonne Georgi,
Harald Kreutzberg, Dore Hoyer, Susanna Linke

This documentary of the German dancer, made in honor of
the 100th anniversary of her birthday, shows clips of
WANDERINGS filmed in 1926, WITCH DANCE (1926),
SWINGING LANDSCAPE (1929), DEATHMARK in 1930,

FAREWELL AND THANK YOU (1942). Several of her
world-renowned students are both interviewed and caught
briefly in performance.

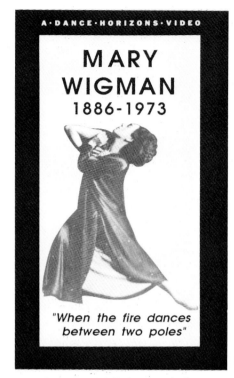

Mary Wigman: 1886-1973 "When the fire
dances between two poles"
Cover art courtesy Dance Horizons Video.

MARY WIGMAN: 1886–1973 WHEN THE FIRE DANCES
BETWEEN THE TWO POLES

1982, 41 min., b&w, film, video
Distributor: Dance Horizons Video
Producer/Directors: Allegra Fuller Synder,
Annette MacDonald
Principal Dancer: Mary Wigman
Dance on Camera Festival, Honorable Mention;
Film-Video Dance Festival

Study of the life and work of Mary Wigman (1886-1973),
Germany's foremost innovator in modern dance. Historical
footage shows her working with students, and highlights
Wigman's performances, 1923-1942 in SERAPHIC SONG,
DANCE OF SUMMER, WITCH DANCE and her last
performance in 1942, FAREWELL AND THANKSGIVING.

MASS

Series: Alive from Off Center
1990, 11:40 min., color, video
Distributor: Electronic Arts Intermix
Producer/Director: Mary Lucier
Choreographer: Elizabeth Streb
Principal Dancers: Elizabeth Streb, Paula Gifford, Henry
Beer, Jorge Collazo, Peter Larose, Christopher Batenhorst

Sound Processing: Earl Howard
Editor: Gregg Featherman

Examining force and resistance in the case of a group acting as a unified body, this third collaboration between Mary Lucier and Elizabeth Streb is a metaphor for the survival of an artist's vision in an urban environment. In a succession of brightly colored interludes shot from distorted perspectives, Streb's dancers seem to be floating, flying, pushing, or being pushed by large buildings. Available both as a three-channel installation and single video.

MASTER CLASS BY JOANNE H. RAMOS

1980s, 30 min., color, video
Distributor/Producer: JPJ Enterprises
Principal Dancer: Nicole Hlinka

Posture and placement to work out at home with two ballet barres, with narration describing each step. Led by a soloist with the New York City Ballet.

MASTERS OF TAP

1988, 61 min., color, video
Distributor: Home Vision TAP01
Producer: IFPA Ltd.
Director: George Nierenberg
Choreographer/Dancers: Charles Honi Coles, Chuck Green, and Will Gaines

A sentimental journey through the history of tap, with three masters.

MATT MATTOX

1964, 20 min., b&w, film, video
Distributor/Producer: Michael Miller for See-Do Productions
Teacher: Matt Mattox

Fifty progressions and eight jazz variations on four reels of 8mm film, shown full-length, followed by a close-up of the feet by the jazz master teacher based in France. A second film offers two other jazz classes on two reels.

MAYA DEREN: EXPERIMENTAL FILMS

1943–1959, 76 min., b&w, film, video
Distributor: Mystic Fire
Producer: Alexander Hackenschmied
Director: Maya Deren
Dancer: Talley Beatty

Enchanted by the power of movement and the challenges of space and time, Maya Deren was America's first dance filmmaker. She said, "Each film was built as a chamber and became a corridor, like a chain reaction." The collection includes MESHES OF THE AFTERNOON, AT LAND, CHOREOGRAPHY FOR THE CAMERA with an appearance by Talley Beatty, RITUAL IN TRANSFIGURED TIME, MEDITATION ON VIOLENCE, and THE VERY EYE OF NIGHT.

MEDEA

1979, 70 min., color, video
Distributor: Kultur #1114
Producer: Gostelradio
Choreographer/Writer: Georgiy Aleksidze
Director: Elgudja Zhgenti

Principal Dancers: Marina Goderdzishvili (Medea), Vladimir Julukhadze (Jason)
Composer: Revaz Gabichvadze

The one-act ballet filmed in the Soviet Union interprets the Euripides drama of lost love, revenge, and murder.

MEDITATION ON VIOLENCE

1943–1956, 12 min., b&w, film
Distributors: Grove Press Film, Mystic Fire
Producer/Director: Maya Deren

The movements and rhythms of the Wu-tang and Shao-Lin schools of Chinese boxing filmed as patterns with flute and drum accompaniment by Maya Deren, a prime mover of the avant-garde in the late 1930s and 1940s.

MEHANG SUSAH

1984, 11 min., color, video
Distributor/Producer/Director: Penny Ward
Choreographer/Dancer: Mia Borgatta

Taped outdoors among bamboo grasses, a woman blends with the environment in this gestural dance. The title may be translated as "Indeed it is difficult."

The Men Who Danced: The Story of Ted Shawn's Male Dancers, 1933–1940
Cover art courtesy Dance Horizons Video.

THE MEN WHO DANCED

1986, 30 min., color, video
Distributor: Dance Horizons Video
Producer: Ron Honsa
Choreographer: Ted Shawn
Dance Company: Ted Shawn and the members of his original troupe

Writer: Richard Philp
Dance on Camera Festival, 1986 Grand Prize

A reunion of Ted Shawn's all-male troupe includes interviews, flashback stills, and performance footage. Founded in 1933, the troupe had a daily routine of working in the fields, dancing, and building their home base and performance center, Jacob's Pillow, the setting for today's summer dance festival in the Berkshires.

MERCE BY MERCE BY PAIK

1978, 30 min., color, video
Distributor/Producer: Cunningham Dance Fdtn., Electronic Arts Intermix
Directors: Nam June Paik, Shigeko Kubota, Charles Atlas
Choreographer/Dancer: Merce Cunningham
Composers: David Held, Earl Howard
Narrator: Russell Connor

This experimental video with dance choreographed for the camera illustrates that time and movement are reversible. Includes Cunningham's BLUE STUDIO (1976) directed by Charles Atlas, later altered by Nam June Paik, who also added a sound track and MERCE AND MARCEL with excerpts from a 1964 performance of Cunningham's SEPTET in Helsinki and Russell Connor's interview with Marcel Duchamp.

MERCE CUNNINGHAM

1964, 13 min., b&w, film
Distributor: Pennstate
Principal Dancer: Merce Cunningham
Composers: John Cage, Toshi Ichiyanagi
Set Designer: Robert Rauschenberg
Dance Company: Cunningham Dance Company

STORY and ANTIC filmed in 1964 at the Theatre de l'Est Parisien and the Maison de la Culture in Bourges, France.

MERCE CUNNINGHAM

1979, 60 min., color, film, video
Distributor: Cunningham Dance Foundation
Producer: South Bank Show, London Weekend Television
Director: Geoff Dunlop
Choreographer: Merce Cunningham
Principal Dancers: Karole Armitage, Louise Burns, Ellen Cornfield, Meg Eginton, Chris Komar
Composers: John Cage, Takehisa Kosugi
Costume Designer: Mark Lancaster

Rehearsals and commentaries by Merce Cunningham, Carolyn Brown, Karole Armitage, and Chris Komar, plus excerpts from Cunningham's TRAVELOGUE, SQUAREGAME, and EXCHANGE.

MERCE CUNNINGHAM

Series: Dance in America
1978, 60 min., color, film, video
Distributor: Films Inc.
Producers: Merrill Brockway, Emile Ardolino, Judy Kinberg for WNET-TV
Dancer/Choreographer: Merce Cunningham
Dance Company: Merce Cunningham Dance Company
Composer: John Cage
Set Designer: Robert Rauschenberg

The master modern choreographer leads his company in nine dances, ranging over 20 years of works from MINUTIAE (1954) to VIDEO TRIANGLE.

MERCE CUNNINGHAM AND COMPANY

1982, 45 min., color, film, video
Distributor: Cunningham Dance Foundation
Producers: L'Institut National de L'Audiovisuel with Cunningham Dance Foundation
Director: Benoit Jacquot
Choreographer: Merce Cunningham
Dance Company: Merce Cunningham Dance Company
Composer: John Cage

Presented in English and French with English subtitles, this documentary explores Cunningham's method of choreography, his employment of random methods to determine the order of dance sequences through the use of the I CHING, his collaboration with John Cage, and his relationship with the dancers. Cunningham candidly reveals his ideas through interviews and rehearsal and performance excerpts of TRAILS, SCRAMBLE, AEON, QUARTET, SUITE FOR FIVE, ROADRUNNERS, and FRACTIONS.

MEREDITH MONK'S 16 MILLIMETER EARRINGS

1979, 24 min., color, film
Distributor/Director: Robert Withers
Choreographer/Dancer: Meredith Monk

A re-creation of a dance/theater solo first performed in 1966 by Meredith Monk, the versatile composer/dancer/filmmaker who had subsequent great success with ELLIS ISLAND and BOOK OF DAYS.

The Merry Widow
Peter Martins and Patricia McBride.
Photo courtesy Kultur.

THE MERRY WIDOW

1983, 60 min., color, video
Distributor: Kultur #1236
Producer: Chicago Educational Television
Director: Dick Carter
Choreographer: Ruth Page
Principal Dancers: Peter Martins (Prince Danilo), Patricia McBride (The Widow), Rebecca Wright, George De La Pena
Dance Company: Chicago Opera Ballet
Composer: Franz Lehar

Premiered at Chicago's Lyric Opera in 1955, this romantic ballet is set to the music of the three-act operetta written in 1905 by the Hungarian composer Franz Lehar. The plot revolves around a ball and the intricacies of various love affairs among turn-of-the century bourgeoisie.

MESQUAKIE

    1976, 10 min., color, film
    Distributor: Iowa State University

Suggests the philosophy, ritual dances, and art of these American Indians.

MEXICAN DANCES (2 films)

    1971, 17 & 18 min. each, color, film, video
    Distributor: AIMS
    Producer: Association Film Services
    Choreographer: Raoul Macias
    Teacher: Anita Cano
    Dance Company: Ballet Folklorico Estudiantil

Student production of Mexican folk dances at the Lincoln High School in Los Angeles. First film shows excerpts of the TILINGO LINGO IGUANA, LA BAMBA, LA NEGRA, and the second shows EL CARRETERO, AMOR DE MADRE, LAS ADELITAS, LOS MACHETES, ALAZANAS, JARABE TAPATICO.

MGODO WA MBANGUZI

    1973, 53 min., color, film, video
    Distributor: Pennstate
    Producer/Directors: Gei Zantziger and Andrew Tracey

Performances in a Chopi village in southern Mozambique accompanied by xylophone orchestras. Study guide also available.

MICHAEL MOSCHEN

    Series: Alive from Off Center
    1986, 20 min., color, video
    Distributor: Electronic Arts Intermix
    Producer: KTCA in association with Brooklyn
    Academy of Music
    Director/Distributor: Skip Blumberg
    Principal Dancer: Michael Moschen

Juggler/illusionist Michael Moschen demonstrates his talent for manipulating crystal balls, glowing rods, and shooting flames in three solo pieces that convey his special sense of touch.

MILDRED: THE FIRST 90 YEARS

    1989, 29 min., color, video
    Distributor: Terra Nova Films
    Producer: Melinda Prod.

A portrait of a woman 90 years old and still dancing with vibrancy and power.

MILT AND HONI (2 versions)

    1987, 41 min. and 90 min., color, video
    Distributor/Producer/Director: Louise Tiranoff
    Choreographer/Dancer: Honi Coles
    Composer/Musician: Milt Hinton

Documentary of two living legends of American jazz, bass player Milt Hinton and tap dancer Honi Coles, who have shared a friendship that has lasted over sixty years. The two black artists, who were together in Cab Calloway's band, rehearse alone and perform together. In a lunch break, they discuss everything from the mathematical principles of music to the chorus girls who played at the Apollo.

THE MIME

    1966, 29 min., b&w, film
    Distributors: Pennstate
    Director/Producers: Robert Rosen, Arthur Miller for Center
    for Mass Communication
    Mime: Tony Montanaro

The training, discipline and ingenuity of a mime currently based in Maine who performs along with presenting his personal views on mime and its effect on his private life.

LE MIME MARCEL MARCEAU

    1972, 23 min., color, video
    Distributors: Coronot/MIT #LEH021, French American
    Cultural Services and Educational Aid (FACSEA)
    Producers: Paris Match, Films Racines, Les Films Jacques
    Letienne, Or-a Films, Les Films De Valois
    Director: Daniel Camus
    Mime: Marcel Marceau

The French master mime plays Bip, the director of a theatre company, along with other characters as well as showing the study involved behind each gesture, and the nuance of expression demanded before it is perfected.

MIME TECHNIQUE – PART I

    1977, 27 min., color, film, video
    Distributor: Phoenix Films
    Producer/Director: Stewart Lippe
    Mime: Paul Gaulin

An ape, transformed into a man, takes a walk in the park, where he finds a book on mime instruction. He acts out the instructions and attempts variations.

MIMI GARRARD DANCE THEATRE

    1989, 30 min., color, video
    Distributor/Producer/Choreographer: Mimi Garrard
    Dance Company: Mimi Garrard Dance Theatre

Composite of short excerpts from several repertory works by this modern dancer known for her dramatic character studies.

MINING DANCES (4 films)

    1968, 21–25 min., color, film
    Distributor: Pennstate #EO1726, EO1727, EO1417, EO1418
    Producer: Wissen

Sotho-Ndebele, Mpondo, Setapo and Chopi dancers around the mines of the Vlakfontein near Johannesburg-Roodepoort, South Africa.

MIRACLE OF BALI: A RECITAL OF MUSIC AND DANCING

    1972, 24 and 27 min., color film
    Distributor: University of Michigan
    Producer: John Coast and David Attenborough for
    BBC/Xerox

Presents classical Balinese dance and gamelan music with the narrator describing the various forms of Balinese musical ensembles. One hundred and fifty men chant for the legendary monkey dance which dates back to the third century.

MIRROR OF GESTURE

1974, 21 min., color, film, video
Distributor: University of California Extension Media Center
Producer: Los Angeles County Museum of Art

Shots of Indian sculpture in the Los Angeles County Museum are intercut with sequences of classical Indian dance to suggest the correspondence between the two arts.

MISS JULIE

1964, 37 min., b&w, film
Distributor: Dance Film Archive
Producer/Director: Mans Reutersward for Sveriges TV 2
Choreographer: Birgit Cullberg
Dance Company: Royal Swedish Ballet
Composer: Ture Rangstrom

The 1950 classic based on August Strindberg's play of 1888 depicting a love-hate relationship between the sexes and between social classes by a Swedish choreographer, who was a pioneer in creating dances for the camera.

MIXED DOUBLE

1973, 5 min., color, film
Distributor: Audience Planners
Producer: Danish Government Film Office
Choreographer: Eske Holm
Dancers: Eske Holm, Sorella Englund
Composer: Stig Kreutzfeldt

An experimental ballet film featuring a pas de deux.

MIXUMMERDAYDREAM

1971, 11 min., color, film
Distributor: University of Illinois
Composer: Cinecentrum

An experiment in combining optical effects with ballet in which silhouettes of dancers appear, disappear, multiply, and divide, while a composer works out a musical idea at the piano. Produced in Holland.

MODERN BALLET

Series: A Time to Dance
1960, 29 min., b&w, film
Distributor: Indiana University
Producer: Jac Venza for WGBH-TV, Boston
Choreographers: Antony Tudor, Marius Petipa, Lev Ivanov
Principal Dancers: Antony Tudor, Nora Kaye, Hugh Laing, Yekaterina Geltzer, Vasily Tichomiroff
Composers: Peter Ilyich Tchaikovsky, Arnold Schonberg, Frederick Delius, William Schuman

British choreographer Antony Tudor and Martha Myers discuss the developments in the ballet world of the 1940s, the change of subject and mood and reasons for retaining the classical vocabulary. SWAN LAKE excerpt included, along with those of Tudor's PILLAR OF FIRE, UNDERTOW, ROMEO AND JULIET, DIM LUSTER, LILAC GARDEN, and GALA PERFORMANCE performed by his original cast.

MODERN DANCE: CHOREOGRAPHY AND THE SOURCE

1966, 20 min., color, film
Distributor: Kent State
Producers: Hildegard L Spreen, Margaretta Fristoe
for Bailey Films

Affirms that the source of creativity is within us and the inspiration to dance is all around us. SUMER IS ICUMEN IN, FARANDOLE, GREENSLEEVES DUET, and BOXES performed by the students of San Jose State College.

MODERN DANCE COMPOSITION

1959, 12 min., b&w, film
Distributor: Kent State
Producer: Thorne Films
Teacher: Patricia Eckert

Students at the University of Colorado analyze the elements of dance composition and develop their own dances entitled CELEBRATION and LAMENT.

MODERN DANCE: CREATIVE IMAGINATION AND CHOREOGRAPHY

1965, 17 min., color, film
Distributor: Kent State
Producers: Hildegard L Spreen, Margaretta Fristoe
for Bailey Films

Students of San Jose State College illustrate how an imaginative choreographer discovers new relationships and concepts in common subject matter by performing a children's dance, a whimsy, pantomime, and period piece.

MODERN DANCE TECHNIQUES IN SEQUENTIAL FORM

1960, 12 min., color, film
Distributor: Kent State
Producers: Hildegard L Spreen, Margaretta Fristoe
for Bailey Films

Students of San Jose State College demonstrate how natural body movements can be varied and combined to achieve dramatic results.

MODERN DANCE–THE ABC OF COMPOSITION

1964, 13 min., color, film
Distributor: Kent State
Producer: Hildegard L. Spreen, Margaretta Fristoe
for Bailey Films

Presents compositional problems of using rhythmic patterns, architectural shapes, and complementary movements.

MOIMO FESTIVAL DANCE FROM CENTRAL SUDAN

1964, 5 min., color, film
Distributor: PennState #EO1356
Producer: Wissen

Circle dance for men and women, accompanied by flutes and drums, performed at the *motyoro* feast of the Dangaleat in Chad, Africa.

MONTREAL DANSE

    1988, 26 min., b&w, color, video
    Distributor: Antenna
    Producer: Agent Orange
    Choreographers: Daniel Leveille, Jean-Pierre Perrault,
    Paul Andre Fortier
    Director: Francois Girard

Sketches of three modern choreographers active in Montreal.

MOON

    1988, 6 min., b&w, film
    Distributor: Film-maker's Coop
    Directors: Power Boothe, Catlin Cobb
    Principal Dancers: Margaret Albertson, Tina Dudek,
    Valerie Gutwirth, Nancy Sakamoto
    Composer: Brooks Williams

A dance meditation on the nature of the moon, eggs, circular saws and love, this abstract film is a surrealist wheel of fortune, according to the director.

MOON GATES I, II, III

    1952 and 1974, 6 and 5:30 min. each, color, film, video
    Distributor/Producer/Sculptor/Director: Doris Chase
    Choreographer: Mary Staton
    Dance Company: Mary Staton Dance Ensemble
    Composer: George Kleinsinger

The dancers move through and around sculptures designed by Doris Chase. Filmed at the Wadsworth Atheneum, Hartford, Connecticut. In the third version, the ensemble moves through kinetic sculptures which move when touched. Each dancer appears in a monochromatic image.

MOON GATES—THREE VERSIONS

    1974, 15:30 min., color, film
    Distributor/Producer/Sculptress/Director: Doris Chase
    Choreographer: Mary Staton
    Composer: George Kleinsinger
    Dance Company: Seattle Opera Ballet Company

A documentary on the process of the Seattle Opera Ballet Company dancing with a commissioned sculpture, seen in its purity and then transformed through a video synthesizer and transferred back to film and optically printed.

MOOR'S PAVANE (VARIATIONS ON THE THEME OF OTHELLO)

    1950, 15 min., color, film
    Distributors: Films Inc., Pennstate
    Director: Walter V. Strate
    Choreographer: Jose Limon
    Artistic Director: Doris Humphrey
    Principal Dancers: Jose Limon (Othello), Lucas Hoving,
    Betty Jones, Ruth Currier
    Composer: Henry Purcell
    Narrator: Bram Nossen

Inspired by William Shakespeare's OTHELLO, this modern dance suggests the jealousy and passion of the tragedy within the framework of a court dance.

MORNING STAR (CHOLPON)

    1961, 75 min., color, film
    Distributor: Corinth
    Producer: Lenfilm Studios, U.S.S.R.
    Director: Roman Tikhomirov
    Choreographer/Dancer: Nurden Turgelev
    Composer: Mikhail Rauchwergher
    Cinematographer: Apollinari Dudko
    Principal Dancers: Reinia Chokeyeva, Uram Sarbagishev,
    Bibisara Beishenaliyeva, S. Abdusilov
    Dance Company: Kirghizian State Opera and Ballet Theatre

A ballet based on a legend from the Tien-Shan Mountains of Kirghizia in Central Asia. Cholpon is in love with Nurdin. Their happiness is threatened by an old sorceress who turns herself into a beautiful young woman. Yet, Cholpon's love proves stronger than the sorceress' magic.

MOROCCO, BODY AND SOUL

    1987, 78 min., color, film, video
    Distributor: First Run/Icarus
    Director: Genini

Three documentary films taken in Morocco: HYMNS OF PRAISE in which participants on a pilgrimage to Moulay Idriss I's sanctuary dance into a trance; LUTES AND DELIGHTS about Abdelsadek Chekara and his orchestra, interpreters of Arab-Andalusian music; and AITA, symbolizing the climactic cry of a female troubadour performing with dancers and musicians at religious ceremonies, marriages, and circumcisions.

MOSCOW BALLET SCHOOL

    1973, 19 min., color, film
    Distributor: Corinth
    Producer: Central Documentary Film Studios

A documentary on the Moscow Academic School of Choreography with footage of classes, rehearsals and recitals.

MOSES PENDLETON PRESENTS MOSES PENDLETON

    1983, 60 min., color, video
    Distributor: Fort Worth Prod.
    Producer: Mitchell Johnson
    Director: Robert Elfstrom
    Choreographer/Dancer: Moses Pendleton
    Dance Company: Pilobolus Dance Company
    CINE Golden Eagle

Portrait of the co-founder of Pilobolus Dance Theatre, Moses Pendleton, seen on his 33rd birthday in his New England house. Pilobolus, the company known for whimsical choreography inspired by their studies as pre-med students at Dartmouth, perform VORTICELLA and SHIZEN. Pendleton performs MOMIX and BIRTHDAY DANCE OF THE DOUBLES.

MOTION

    Series: Dance As An Art Form
    1972, 32 min., color, film
    Distributor: Pro Arts
    Producer: Chimerafilm

DANCE FILM AND VIDEO GUIDE

Director: Warren Leib
Choreographer/Dancer/Narrator: Murray Louis
Composer: Alwin Nikolais

The film advocates the joy of movement: professional and amateur dancers roll down hills, fall into snow banks, and run along beaches. The versatile modern dancer improvises and performs excerpts from his dances FACITS and PERSONNAE.

MOUNTAIN VIEW

Series: Alive from Off Center
1989, 25:30 min., color, video
Distributor/Producer/Editor: Susan Dowling for WGBH New Television Workshop with KTCA-TV
Director/Writer: John Sayles
Choreographer/Writer/Editor: Marta Renzi
Composers: Mason Daring, Bruce Springsteen, Tammy Wynette, The Pogues, Marvin Gaye, Aretha Franklin

On a summer afternoon, a group of friends dance to the juke-box in a rural tavern. Shot in the country by the independent filmmaker, the video was constructed along the lines of a short story with an opening solitary walk in the high grass, a couple's arrival in a pick-up truck, and reactions of the locals hanging out at the bar.

MOURNING CELEBRATIONS FROM ETHIOPIA (2 films)

1951, 5–8 min. each, b&w, film
Distributor: Pennstate #EOO266 and EOO267
Producer: Wissen

The first silent film has excerpts from the hour-long dances in Shangama in southern Ethiopia in honor of the deceased, with a pantomime to drive away the demons. The burial concludes with the burning of the deceased's hut. In the second film, the Sala tribe express their sympathy with choral processions and dances.

MOURNING DANCES FROM CHAD (5 films)

1964–1965, 4–9 min. each, b&w, color, film
Distributor: Pennstate #EO1025, EO1360, EOO912, EO1361, EO1362
Producer: Wissen

Three African women and a man armed with a spear from the Mukulu tribe in Chad perform a mourning dance in EO1025. The following films show the darangaba, a circle dance, and the mutu dodi, stamping dances from Kenga in Barama, Chad.

MOVEMENT EXPLORATION–WHAT AM I

1968, 11 min., color, film
Distributor: Kent State
Producer: Film Associates

Children mimic birds, animals, and machines, in their exploration of movement.

MOVEMENT IN CLASSIC DANCE: THE PELVIC AREA

1980, 11 min., color, film, video
Distributor: Indiana University
Director: Phil Stockton
Choreographer/Narrator: Anna Paskevska

Principal Dancers: Jeanine Murrell, Leslie Horn, Scotty Martin
Cinematographers: Vladimir Shmikler, David Jay, William P. Orisich

Dancers demonstrate correct alignment, with slow-motion scenes and anatomical illustrations to detail the functions of the hip, leg, and abdominal muscles in controlling the pelvis.

MOVING PASTURES

1988, 20 min., color, video
Distributor/Choreographer/Dancer: Margaret Beals
Composer: G. S. Sachdev

Two solos: improvisations to Bansuri flute, and improvisations to prepared piano with composer/pianist Andre Gribou.

A MOVING PICTURE

1987, 54 min., color, film, video
Distributors: Bullfrog Films, Rhombus Media
Producer: Rhombus Media with Canadian Broadcasting Corp, Societe Radio Canada, TV Ontario with Telefilm Canada and Ontario Film Development Corporation
Director: Jurgen Lutz
Choreographer/Dancer: Ann Ditchburn
Principal Dancer: Robert Desrosiers
Dance Company: National Ballet of Canada
Composers: Kate Bush, Leonard Cohen, Laurie Anderson, Buffy Ste. Marie, Andre Gagnon, Jennifer Warnes

Laced with animation and optical wizardry, the film presents a group of dancers in and out of rehearsals in a sunny loft.

MOVING TRUE

1973, 19 min., b&w, film, video
Distributor: Creative Arts Rehabilitation Center
Director: Barry Shapiro
Dance Therapist: Anne Olin
Dancer: Chryssa

Dance therapy session with a patient, a woman suffering from deep withdrawal and insecurity.

MULTIGRAVITATIONAL AERODANCE GROUP: A DOCUMENTARY

1985, 30 min., color, video
Distributor/Producer: Multigravitational Aerodance Group
Producer: Rutgers University
Choreographer/Dancers: Barbara Salz, Kay Gainer, Donald Porteous

Rehearsals, performances, and interviews with the company, founded in 1970 by Stephanie Evanitsky, which performs on trapezes and ropes.

MUNICH COOPERS' DANCE

1963, 17 min., color, film
Distributor: Pennstate #EOO565
Producer: R. Wolfram for Wissen

Male members of the Coopers of Munich, Germany perform an historic dance in traditional costume to a brass band, followed by two hoop swingers.

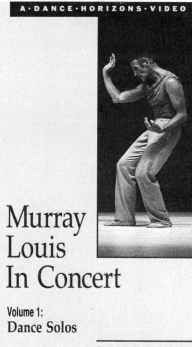

Murray Louis in Concert, Volume 1: Dance Solos
Cover art courtesy Dance Horizons Video.

MURRAY LOUIS IN CONCERT VOLUME I: DANCE SOLOS

> 1952–1988, 45 min., color, video
> Distributor: Dance Horizons Video
> Choreographer: Murray Louis
> Composer: Alwin Nikolais and others

Spans the career of the modern dancer collaborator of composer Alwin Nikolais, with solos filmed at their debut or restaged, intercut with posters, stills, and comments by the artist about the evolution of his work and his choreographic technique. DEJA VU, CHIMERA, JUNK DANCES, and ten other solos are included.

MUSIC BOX

> 1980, 30 min., color, video
> Distributor: Orion Enterprises
> Producers: Wendell and Marge Moody
> Choreographer: Gus Giordano
> Director: Jim Robinson
> Dance Company: Gus Giordano
> Composers: Sensational Nightingales
> CINE Golden Eagle Award, Silver Cindy-IFPA, Angel Award

A man trudging home from work through a dreary, icy city is surprised by gospel singing, and dancing, tuxedoed angels.

MUSIC, DANCE AND FESTIVAL AMONG THE WAIAPI INDIANS OF BRAZIL (2 videos)

> 1987–1988, 39–58 min., color, video
> Distributor: Indiana University CC3779, CC3783
> Producer: Victor Fuks

Might be any other festival from the importance these Indians of the Amazon rain forest place on their beer (caxiri) and the reinforcement of their identity and social order through participation in festivals. Also, see the WAIAPI INSTRUMENTAL MUSIC video, available from Indiana University, which shows the dance in their fish festival.

MUSIC MAKERS OF THE BLUE RIDGE

> 1965, 48 min., color, video
> Distributor: Pennstate
> Producer: WNET-TV

Singing and dancing with the hillbillies of the Blue Ridge Mountains with fiddle, banjo, cittern and guitar accompaniment. Flashes on groundhogs, moonshine stills, and mules pulling plows set the scene.

THE MYTH OF MODERN DANCE

> Series: Alive From Off Center
> 1990, 24:30 min., color, video
> Distributor: WGBH/TV
> Producer: Susan Dowling for New Television Workshop, KTCA-TV, La Sept
> Director: Charles Atlas
> Choreographer: Douglas Dunn
> Composers: Bob Dylan, Wolfgang Amadeus Mozart

Inspired in part by Douglas Dunn's solo HAOLE, this collage suggests the evolution of movement through three centuries with stock footage of dancing, old engravings, medical illustrations, World War II fighter planes, music videos, and Dunn, who appears as a muddy lump, a Renaissance dandy, a 1960s character intoxicated with his body gliding through space.

NADIA GAMAL WORKSHOP

> 1981, 90 min., b&w, video
> Distributor/Producer: John Custodio/Arabesque Magazine
> Principal Dancer: Nadia Gamal

Class with the late Egyptian celebrity Nadia Gamal who blends the Oriental dance with Beledi and Bedouin styles.

NAGRIN VIDEOTAPE LIBRARY OF DANCE
(14 films and videos)

> 1948–89, 30–120 min. each, b&w, color, film, video
> Distributor/Choreographer/Dancer: Daniel Nagrin

Fourteen videos of performances by the modern dance soloist entitled SOLOS 1948–67; FOUR FILMS: DANCE IN THE SUN, STRANGE HERO, THE DANCERS PREPARE, PATH; THE PELOPONNESIAN WAR; TWO WORKS BY THE WORK-GROUP; SPRING, '65; CHANGES; JAZZ CHANGES; RUMINATIONS '76; THE GETTING WELL CONCEPT; THE FALL, '77; JACARANDA, '79; POEMS OFF THE WALL, '81; DANCE AS ART, DANCE AS ENTERTAINMENT; plus the NAGRIN VIDEOTAPE LIBRARY SAMPLER with four selections from each of the tapes (100 min.).

NAPOLI

1986, 98 min., color, video
Distributors: Home Vision #NAP01, Pioneer (Laserdisc)
Producer: Robin Scott for National Video Corp. in association with Danmarks Radio
Director: Kirsten Ralov
Choreographer: August Bournonville
Principal Dancers: Linda Hindberg, Arne Villumsen
Dance Company: Royal Danish Ballet
Composers: Edvard Helsted, Gioacchino Rossini, Niels Gade, Holger Simon Pauli, and Lumbye

In this three-act ballet, first performed in 1842, the beloved of an Italian fisherman, Teresina, is swept overboard on a romantic cruise. Yet, despite the protests of a naiad who falls in love with her, Gennaro wins her back, providing ample cause for celebration when the couple returns to land.

NARCISSUS

1983, 22 min., color, film, video
Distributor: International Film Bureau
Producer: National Film Board of Canada
Director: Norman McLaren
Choreographer: Fernand Nault
Principal Dancers: Jean Louis Morin, Sylvain Lafortune

Modern dance duet depicting the isolation of someone infatuated with himself. In his 59th and last film, animator/experimental director Norman McLaren fed the images through an optical printer so that the two bodies merge, multiply, flicker and fade.

THE NARROW ROOM

1989, 6 min., color, video
Distributor: Antenna
Producer: Agent Orange
Director: Isabelle Hayeur
Choreographer/Dancer: Susan Marshall
Dancer: Arthur Armijo
Composers: Bill Vorn, Gaetan Gravel

Duet by a New York based modern dancer filmed by a Canadian.

NATALIA MAKAROVA: IN A CLASS OF HER OWN

1985, 60 min., color, video
Distributors: Video Arts International, Kultur
Producer: National Video Corporation
Director: Derek Bailey
Choreographer: Roland Petit
Principal Dancer: Natalia Makarova
Teacher: Irina Yakobsen

Prima Ballerina Natalia Makarova takes a private class with her Russian coach Irina Yakobsen. Makarova's voice offers information, as she goes through her daily routine on her development of roles, her insight into the differences between the romantic and classical techniques, and the Russian and Western approach to dance.

NATASHA

1985, 70 min., color, video
Distributors: Kultur #1146, Pioneer (laserdisk)
Producers: Julia Matheson and Robin Scott for National Video Corporation
Director: Derek Bailey
Choreographers: Roland Petit, Michel Fokine, Kenneth MacMillan, Frederic Ashton, Maurice Bejart, George Balanchine
Principal Dancers: Natalia Makarova, Tim Flavin, Anthony Dowell, Gary Chryst
Dance Company: Norman Maen Dancers
Composers: Georges Bizet, Camille Saint-Saens, Jules Massenet, Frederic Chopin, Johann Sebastian Bach, Sergei Prokofiev
Best Arts Program of the Year by British Television

The Russian-born ballerina Natalia Makarova (Natasha) demonstrates her versatility and rich repertory by performing excerpts from Balanchine's ON YOUR TOES, the ballets ROMEO AND JULIET (MacMillan/Prokofiev), MANON (MacMillan/ Massenet) A MONTH IN THE COUNTRY (Ashton/Chopin), CARMEN (Petit/Bizet), Roland Petit's PROUST REMEMBERED, BACH SONATA (Bejart/Bach), BEGIN THE BEGUINE (Gennaro/Porter), and solos DYING SWAN (Fokine/Saint-Saens) and LES SYLPHIDES (Fokine/Chopin).

NATIONAL FOLK FESTIVAL (3 films)

1950, 30 min. each, color, film
Distributor: National Audio Video Center

The three short films include folk dances from Germany, Philippines, New England, and Scotland (part 1); Poland, England, Croatia, Native America, Lithuania, Ukrainia, Texas and Tennessee (part 2); Israel, Russia, Czechoslovakia, and from America, our own square dances. (part 3).

NAVAJO NIGHT DANCES

1957, 11 min., color, film
Distributor: Portland State University
Producer: Walter P. Lewisohn for Coronet Films

Produced in cooperation with the National Congress of American Indians, the film presents three dances performed during a nine-day healing chant: DANCE OF THE PLUMED ARROW, FEATHER and FIRE DANCE.

NEW DANCE

1986, 24:30 min., color, video
Distributor: Electronic Arts Intermix
Director: Skip Blumberg
Choreographer/Dancers: Charles Moulton, Michael Moschen
Dance Company: Moulton's Ensemble

Three pieces, two modern and one circus arts, shot by a director known for his spare style and attention to the essential beauty within each subject: TOWARD A MINIMAL CHOREOGRAPHER (1 min.); CHARLES MOULTON'S NINE PERSON PRECISION BALL PASSING (8 min.); MICHAEL MOSCHEN: SOLOS (15:30 min.).

NEW DANCE

1972, 30 min., color, film
Distributor: Dance Film Archive

Choreographers: Doris Humphrey, Charles Weidman
Principal Dancers: Linda Tarnay, Peter Woodin
Composer: Wallingford Riegger
Dance Company: Connecticut College Repertory Company

A single, fixed-camera view of this reconstruction of the 1935 modern dance classic of affirmation performed at The American Dance Festival at Connecticut College.

NIDO TICHIUCHI: REVENGE OF THE TWO SONS

1981, 30 min., color, video
Distributor/Producer: Asia Society

A dance drama from Okinawa of two sons who disguise themselves to deceive and kill their father's murderer.

NIGHT JOURNEY

1961, 29 min., b&w, film
Distributor: Phoenix Films
Producer: Nathan Kroll
Director: Alexander Hammid
Choreographer: Martha Graham
Principal Dancers: Martha Graham (Jocasta), Bertram Ross (Oedipus), Paul Taylor (Tiresias), Mary Hinkson, Ethel Winter, Helen McGehee, Linda Hodes, Carol Payne, Betty Shaler
Composer: William Schuman
Set Designer: Isamu Noguchi
Dance Company: Martha Graham Dance Company
Berlin Film Festival, Special Award

Martha Graham's masterpiece on the question of how does a woman reconcile herself to the fact that she has unknowingly engaged in an incestuous relationship. NIGHT JOURNEY, which premiered in 1947, drew inspiration from the surrealist novel by Andre Coffrant, about a bride, a poet, a magician, and the Greek legend of Oedipus Rex.

NIGHT ON THE SEA OF GALILEE: RAEL FOLK
DANCE ENSEMBLE

1978, 60 min., color, video
Distributor: Kultur #1186
Producer: Iroex

Hebrew folkloric companies perform in a festival at Zemach on the shores of the Sea of Galilee, Israel.

NIJINSKY

1980, 125 min., color, video
Distributor/Producer: Paramount
Director: Herbert Ross
Principal Dancers: Leslie Browne, George de La Pena
Actor: Alan Bates

A feature film made on the life and times of Vaslav Nijinsky, the ill-fated Russian choreographer/dancer, with a focus on his relationship with his possessive boss/lover, Sergei Diaghilev.

NIK AND MURRAY

1986, 82 min., color, film, video
Distributor/Producer/Director: Christian Blackwood
Choreographer/Dancer: Murray Louis
Composer/Choreographer: Alwin Nikolais
Gold Plaque Award, Chicago International Film Festival

and Gold Award, Houston International Film Festival

Follows Alwin Nikolais and his collaborator of more than twenty years, Murray Louis, around the world, catching the two artists on stage, in dressing rooms, and "happenings." Includes clips of SCHOOL FOR BIRD PEOPLE performed in the streets of Aix-en-Provence, France.

NIKKOLINA

Series: Learning To Be Human
1978, 28 min., color, film, video
Distributors: University of Illinois, Learning Corp
Producer/Directors: Rebecca Yates and Glen Salzman for Cineflics
ALA Notable Children's Films

Nikkolina, a Greek-American girl, is unwilling to learn a folk dance for a family wedding, because she'd rather be skating. But later, feeling more accepting of her heritage, she incorporates the Greek costume and steps in her skating routine.

NINE VARIATIONS ON A DANCE THEME

1967, 13 min., b&w, film, video
Distributor/Director: Hilary Harris
Principal Dancer: Bettie De Jong
Composer: McNeil Robinson
Flutist: Bonnie Lichter

A dance phrase choreographed and performed by a former member of Paul Taylor's company for the camera as a means of exploring the possibilities of filming dance. The director developed nine variations in the camera viewpoint of the dance and its transformations in the editing process.

1989 LIVE PERFORMANCE OF GUS GIORDANO
JAZZ DANCE CHICAGO

1989, 56 min., color, video
Distributor: Orion Enterprises
Choreographer: Gus Giordano
Dance Company: Gus Giordano Dance Company

Performances of the Chicago-based company in CAMP MEETIN' TONIGHT, FOR YOU, CHAIN OF ROCKS, THE MAN I LOVE, BARRED and GANG HEP.

NO MAPS ON MY TAPS

1979, 58 min., color, film, video
Distributor: Direct Cinema
Producer/Director: George T. Nierenberg
Choreographer/Dancers: Sandman Sims, Chuck Green, Bunny Briggs
American Film Festival, 1979 Blue Ribbon

Insight into tap dancing with historical footage from the 1930s and portraits of three master hoofers, with a finale at Harlem's Small's Paradise, hosted by Lionel Hampton and his big band.

NOH BODY

1986, color, video
Distributor/Choreographer: Sarah Skaggs
Producer: Danspace Project at St. Mark's
Director: Mark Robeson for Character Generators
Principal Dancers: David Beadle, David Zambrano,

Paula Clements
Electric Cellist: Tom McVeety
Sound: Steven Harvey

Human motion, space, architecture, and sound magnify and diminish with fluid concentration.

NOH DRAMA

1965, 30 min., color, film & video
Distributor: Japan Foundation
Producer: Sakura Motion Picture

An explanation of Japan's 600-year-old dramatic tradition with a formal procession of musicians and chorus onto the stage. Selections from plays include the dance performances of SHOJO and TAKASAGO. Also available from Japan Foundation, three videos: INTRODUCTION TO NOH produced by Toei Video, NOH PLAY: FUNABENKEI produced by Fuji Pony, and INTRODUCTION TO NOH: NOH AND SHIMAI produced by Pony Video.

NOT FOR LOVE ALONE

Series: Educational Performance Collection
1983, 24 min., color, video
Distributor/Producer: Dance Notation Bureau
Choreographer: Buzz Miller
Composers: Alexander Scriabin, John Cage

Taped performance at Ohio State University of this modern/jazz dance in eight sections. Comes with advanced labanotated score by Jane Marriett, introductory article on labanotation, critical text for students and reconstructors, and study/performance rights.

NSAMBO DANCE FESTIVAL AT ISANGI (2 films)

1953, 11 and 17 min., b&w, film
Distributor: Pennstate #EOO280-281
Producer: E.W. Muller for Wissen

Silent films of a festival with folk and acrobatic dancers featured in Ekonda, Zaire, central Africa.

N'UM TCHAI

1957, 25 min., color, film
Distributors: Documentary Educational Resources, University of California Extension Media Center
Producer: Peabody Museum
Director: John Marshall

A documentary of an all-night "medicine dance" in the Kalahari Desert of southwest Africa during which several Bushmen go into a trance and exercise special curing powers. N'um can be translated as medicine or supernatural potency. Divided into two parts; the first offers an analysis of the dances and the second, the ceremony without narration.

N'UM TCHAI: THE CEREMONIAL DANCE OF THE !KUNG BUSHMEN

1957–58, 20 min., b&w, color, film
Distributor/Producer: Documentary Educational Resources (DER)
Producer/Director: John Marshall

The !Kung people of Africa gather for medicine dances, usually at night, and sometimes dance until dawn. Women sit on the ground, clapping and singing while men circle around them, singing and stamping rhythms. Also available from DER is THE MELON TOSSING GAME, a fifteen-minute film on the !Kung bands and their dance/trance game.

NUTCRACKER (American Ballet Theatre)

1976, 79 min., color, video
Distributor: MGM/UA #0177
Producers: Herman Krawitz for CBS, Yanna Kroyt Brandt
Director: Heinz Liesendahl
Choreographers: Mikhail Baryshnikov, Tony Charmoli, Lev Ivanov
Principal Dancers: Mikhail Baryshnikov, Gelsey Kirkland
Dance Company: American Ballet Theatre
Composer: Peter Ilyich Tchaikovsky
Emmy winner

Longest successively running dance program on television, the best-selling dance tape in the United States of the full-length ballet based on the E. T. A. Hoffman fairy tale, which premiered in St. Petersburg, Russia, in 1892. The Christmas special focuses on the little girl who dreams her new nut-cracker doll becomes an adoring prince who fights off the invasion led by the Mouse King and brings her a sampling of the dances from around the world.

THE NUTCRACKER (Bolshoi Ballet)

1978, 87 min., color, video
Distributor: Kultur #1201
Producer: Lothar Beck Associates, Gmbh
Principal Dancers: Vladimir Vasiliev, Yekaterina Maximova, Vyacheslav Gordeyev, Nadia Pavlova
Dance Company: Bolshoi Ballet

A double casting for the lead roles for the ballet filmed live at the Bolshoi Theatre in Moscow (see plot above).

THE NUTCRACKER (Bolshoi Ballet)

1984, 87 min., color, video
Distributor: Kultur
Producer: Lothar Beck Associates
Principal Dancers: Yekaterina Maximova, Vladimir Vasiliev
Dance Company: Bolshoi Ballet
Choreographer: Yuri Grigorovich
Composer: Peter Ilyich Tchaikovsky

Filmed live at the Bolshoi Theatre in Moscow (see plot above).

THE NUTCRACKER (Bolshoi Ballet)

1987, 100 min., color, video
Distributors: Corinth, Kultur #0062
Producer: Gostelradio
Choreographer/Director: Yuri Grigorovich
Principal Dancers: Yekaterina Maximova, Vladimir Vasiliev
Dance Company: Bolshoi Ballet
Composer: Peter Ilyich Tchaikovsky

Live from the Bolshoi Theatre, the Christmas favorite known as MEZHDUNARODNAYA KNIGA. Set in a small Russian town in the mid-nineteenth century, a child overcomes the tragedy of her brother breaking her new doll by falling asleep and fabricating fate as she'd like it be.

THE NUTCRACKER (Bolshoi Ballet)

    1989, 145 min., color, video
    Distributor: Spectacor
    Producers: NHK with Primetime Entertainment,
    VideoFilm/Bolshoi USSR, and Japan Arts Corporation
    Director/Choreographer: Yuri Grigorovich
    Principal Dancers: Natalya Arkhipova, Irek Mukhamedov,
    Yuri Vetrov
    Dance Company: Bolshoi Ballet
    Composer: Peter Ilyich Tchaikovsky
    Designer: Simon Virsaladze

Recorded live at the Bolshoi Theatre in Moscow with state-of-the-art technology.

THE NUTCRACKER

    1965, 60 min., color, film
    Distributor: Swank
    Producer: Warner Brothers Pictures
    Choreographers: Lev Ivanov, adapted by Kurt Jacob
    Principal Dancers: Melissa Hayden (Sugar Plum
    Fairy/Mother), Harold Kreutzberg (Herr Drosselmayer/
    Uncle Alex), Patricia McBride (Clara/Marie), Edward Villella
    (Prince), Niels Kehlet, Helga Heinrich
    Composer: Peter Ilyich Tchaikovsky
    Dance Companies: New York City Ballet,
    National Opera of Munich, Royal Danish Ballet
    Budapest Philharmonic Orchestra

A variation of the classic ballet in which Marie is given a nutcracker which is transformed into a prince by the Sugar Plum Fairy. As an insert, Niels Kehlet and Helga Heinrich perform The BLUEBIRD PAS DE DEUX from SLEEPING BEAUTY.

NUTCRACKER (Royal Ballet)

    1985, 120 min., color, video
    Distributors: HBO #3384, Pioneer (laserdisk),
    University Of Illinois #S01695
    Producer: Robin Scott for NVC in cooperation with BBC
    Choreographers: Lev Ivanov, Peter Wright
    Principal Dancers: Lesley Collier (Sugar Plum Fairy),
    Anthony Dowell (Prince), Julie Rose (Clara)
    Dance Company: Royal Ballet
    Composer: Peter Ilyich Tchaikovsky
    Editor: John Vernon

Production devised by Peter Wright, director of the Sadler's Wells Royal Ballet with the help of Tchaikovsky ballet expert Roland John Wiley to combine the original staging with modern stage effects.

NUTCRACKER

    1981, 5:30 min., color, video
    Distributor: KUTV
    Producer: Susan Lavery
    Choreographer: William H. Christensen
    Dance on Camera Festival, 1982 First Prize in TV spot

A short on William Christensen, the man who choreographed the first complete NUTCRACKER in the

United States in 1955 and established the San Francisco Ballet Company.

OBSEQUIES FOR DECEASED REGIONAL CHIEFTAINS (5 films)

    1954-1956, 4-9 min. each, color, b&w, film
    Distributor: Pennstate #EO0225, 0219, 0159, 0220, 0223
    Producer: Wissen

Five silent films made in Upper Volta, West Africa (now known as Burkina Faso), of the mask dances from Nuna and the war and harvest dances and mock combat from Kasena with much pomp and solemnity.

THE OFFICIAL DOCTRINE

    1967, 3 min., b&w, film
    Distributor/Choreographer/Director/Producer:
    Gene Friedman
    Choreographer/Dancer: Judith Dunn

A collaborative effort to match film and dance techniques.

OKLAHOMA!

    1955, 148 min., color, film, video
    Distributor: CBS Fox
    Producer: Arthur Hornblow, Jr. for Twentieth Century Fox
    Director: Fred Zinnemann
    Choreographer: Agnes de Mille
    Principal Dancers: Bambi Lynn, Gene Nelson,
    James Mitchell, Marc Platt
    Composer: Richard Rodgers
    Writers: Sonya Levien and William Ludwig

Agnes de Mille choreographed this famous Broadway musical of the Southwest, advancing the plot based on Lynn Riggs' GREEN GROW THE LILACS. The 1943 musical, adapted for cinema, honored Agnes de Mille's stage choreography, which set a new standard for musical theater.

OLD TIME DANCES

    1980s, 95 min., color, video
    Distributor: Jim Forest
    Teachers: George and Betty Montgomery

The Montgomerys of Palm Beach, known for their regular appearance at the Breakers Hotel, perform and teach the Bunny Hug, Turkey Trot, Maxixe, Castle Walk, Black Bottom, Charleston, Shag, Peabody, Polka, waltz, and two-step.

ON THE MOVE: CENTRAL BALLET OF CHINA

    1987, 60 min., color, film, video
    Distributor: Direct Cinema
    Producers: Sidney and Mary Yung Kantor, Catherine Tatge
    Director: Merrill Brockway
    Dance Company: Central Ballet of China
    Dance on Camera Festival, 1987 Gold Award

Making their American debut, the company performs at the Brooklyn Academy of Music and takes classes with Paul Taylor, Alvin Ailey, and at the School for American Ballet. The documentary registers their mixed reactions to American culture.

ONCE AGAIN

    1974, 3:45 min., color, film

Distributor: Film-maker's Coop
Choreographer: Dana Reitz
Director: Dave Gearey
Dance and Film Festival, Art Gallery of Ontario, 1977

A comical, stop-action scene of a woman expecting a telephone call, looking out the window of a stark angular room.

ONCE AT A BORDER. . .ASPECTS OF STRAVINSKY

1970s, 166 min., color, video
Distributors: Facets, Kultur #1157
Director: Tony Palmer
Choreographers: Vaslav Nijinsky, Bronislava Nijinska, George Balanchine
Dance Companies: Diaghilev Ballet Russe
Composer: Igor Stravinsky

Life and passions of the Russian composer Igor Stravinsky with archival footage of the premieres of the ballets RITE OF SPRING (1913) and LES NOCES (1923), and a brief appearance by George Balanchine, who collaborated with the composer on many ballets.

THE ONDEKO-ZA IN SADO

1973, 60 min., color, film
Distributor: Japan Foundation
Producer: Tagayasu Den

Japanese young people, who have rejected the established society, search for meaning through running and studying traditional Japanese music and dance.

THE ONE I SEE

1983, 27 min., color, video
Distributor: Dance Rep, Inc.
Director: Peter Reed
Principal Dancers: Principals from American Ballet Theatre, Joffrey Ballet, and Eliot Feld Company
Set Designer: James Ford

A tryptich: THE ONE I SEE, filmed in a deserted warehouse, and ABANDONED and SEARCHING, the latter two in Silvercup Studios. Shaped with pedestrian movements and fall and recovery rhythms. The three films are joined through an "us and them" theme, a defensive attempt to be alone with an inner strength despite an environment devoid of comforts.

ONE PAIR OF HANDS

1978, 20 min., b&w, film
Distributor: Dance Films Association (members only)
Producer: Belgian Ministry of Education
Dancer/Narrator: Juana

Demonstrates the use of hands in everyday life and at work; in pantomimic gesture used in ritual dance and in traditional gesture language. Juana, one of the first western dancers to do Hindu dances performs dance movements from China, Africa, Philippines, Saudi Arabia, Hawaii, Japan, and India with authentic music and costumes.

ONEGIN

1987, 96 min., color, video
Distributor: Home Vision #ONE01

Producer: National Video Corp.
Choreographer: John Cranko
Directors: Norman Campbell, Reid Anderson
Principal Dancers: Sabine Allemann (Tatiana), Frank Augustyn (Onegin)
Dance Company: National Ballet of Canada
Composer: Peter Ilyich Tchaikovsky
Dance on Camera Festival, 1987 Gold Award

Choreographed in 1965 for the Stuttgart Ballet by John Cranko, the dramatic ballet stems from Alexander Pushkin's 1831 tragic poem of unrequited love.

ONEIRO: IN THE SHADOW OF ISADORA

1987, 14 min. color, video
Distributor: Film-maker's Coop
Director: Silvianna Goldsmith
Choreographer: Isadora Duncan
Principal Dancer: Lori Belilove
Composer: Maurice Ravel

Five dances in the Isadora Duncan style superimposed on images of Greek temples, paintings, sculptures, and the Aegean Isles. A dream (oneiro in Greek) trip in which the self surrenders to its shadow. Shot using a Grass Valley switcher and computer-generated effects.

OP-ODYSSEY

1978, 17 min., color, video
Distributor/Producer/Director: Doris Chase
Composer: Mike Mahaffey
Choreographer: Valerie Hammer
Principal Dancer: Jonathan Hollander, Esther Chaves
Grand Prize at the Festival d'Automne in Paris

An excerpt from a multi-media piece with dance, music, kinetic sculpture, and film, based on Diane Wakowski's poetry.

OPERA

1988, 5 min., color, video
Distributor: Antenna
Producer: Agent Orange
Director: Bernar Hebert
Choreographer/Dancer: Lila Greene
Principal Dancers: Caesar Stroscio, Pierre Muller, Max Rieumal, David Baron, Denis Giuliani, Sabatino Tortora
Composers: Gaetan Fravel, Bill Vorn

A woman enters a deserted theater. Her gesture is dictated by an angel she cannot see. She dances and turns around again and again.

ORBIT

1986, 3 min., color, video
Distributor/Director/Dancer: Arturo Cubacub
Producer: Rasterdans Productions
Choreographer: Jan Heyn Cucacub
Dance on Camera Festival, 1987 Honorable Mention

Repetitive rhythm and duplicate imagery are intermingled with computer-generated video abstractions. Poetry, music, and special effects are all conceived by Arturo Cubacub.

ORFEUS & JULIE
>1970, 7 min., color, film
>Distributor: Audience Planners
>Choreographer/Dancers: Sorella Englund, Eske Holm

Abstraction of a pas de deux performed by two members of the Royal Danish Ballet.

ORIENTAL DANCE (3 videos)
>1987–1989, 60–80 min. each, color, video
>Distributor: Invision
>Producer/Editor: Elaine Trotter
>Choreographer/Dancer: Horacio Cifuentes
>Composer: Reda Darwish

Warm-ups, routines and performances by a California-based dancer and costume designer.

AN ORIGINAL BILL ROBINSON VIDEO
>1985, 60 min., color, video
>Distributor/Producer/Dancer: Julia Mayer
>Choreographer: Bill Robinson

Tap routines taught to Julia Mayer by Bill "Bojangles" Robinson followed by exercises.

AN ORIGINAL JULIA MAYER VIDEO
>1990, 120 min., color, video
>Distributor/Producer/Dancer: Julia Mayer

An instructional video on the Charleston, followed by a chair routine, two intermediate, one beginner, and three advanced tap routines for study.

ORISUN OMI (THE WELL): PROLOGUE TO THE YORUBA CYCLE
>1978–1982, 28 min., color, b&w, film, video
>Distributor: Mica
>Producer: Bayne Williams Film Company
>Director/Choreographer: Arthur Hall
>Principal Dancer: Ron Tayton
>Dance Company: Bahia State Ballet
>Composer/Narrator: Ogun Kotoko
>Editor: Bruce Williams

Filmed on location in Salvador da Bahia, Brazil, choreographer Arthur Hall directs a modern company of the Federal University in a cultural exchange sponsored by the Partners of the Americas. Layered images suggest the depth of myth contained in the dances and the African influence in South America.

OTHELLO, MOOR OF VENICE
>1964, 120 min., color, film, video (79 min.)
>Distributor: Corinth (for broadcast sales only)
>Producer: Mosfilm Studios
>Director/Choreographer/Dancer: Vakhtang Chabukiani
>Composer: Aleksei Machavariani
>Set Designer: Simon Virsaladze
>Dance Company: Georgia State Ballet Company

A classic ballet based on Shakespeare's tragedy of Othello, who was manipulated by one of his subjects to believe that his wife

had been unfaithful. Filmed at the Paliashvil Opera and Ballet Theatre in Tbilisi, Russia.

OTHER VOICES, OTHER SONGS: THE ARMENIANS
>1988, 30 min., color, video
>Distributor: Filmaker's Library
>Producer/Directors: Sari Sapir, Bernice Olenick for Sapphire Productions
>Dance Company: Sayat Nova Armenian Folk Dance Company

Archival photos recall life in the old country, while Armenian Americans strive to keep their culture alive by teaching the traditional dances and performing them at community events.

OTHER VOICES, OTHER SONGS: THE GREEKS
>1989, 30 min., color, video
>Distributor: Filmaker's Library
>Producer/Directors: Sari Sapir, Bernice Olenick for Sapphire Productions with WGBH-TV
>Dance Companies: Mandala Folk Dance Company

Shot in both Europe and America, the documentary examines the roots of Hellenic music and dance and the pivotal role of traditions in Greek life.

OUT OF CHAOS, AMOR
>1967, 14 min., b&w, film
>Distributor: Portland State University
>Producer/Director: Jean V. Cutler
>Dancer/Choreographer: Jean Erdman

Jean Erdman, a former Martha Graham soloist, teaches a class at the University of California in Los Angeles, performs a solo, AMOR.

OUT OF THE LIMELIGHT, HOME IN THE RAIN
>Series: Magic of Dance
>1979, 52 min., color, film, video
>Distributor: Dance Film Archive
>Producer: BBC and Time-Life Films
>Director: Patricia Foy
>Narrator/Dancer: Margot Fonteyn
>Principal Dancers: Rudolph Nureyev, Michael Somes
>Choreographer/Dancer: Frederick Ashton
>Composer: Edward Elgar, Franz Liszt
>Dance Company: Royal Ballet

Tour of the Royal Opera House at Covent Garden, the setting for a gala honoring Margot Fonteyn on her sixtieth birthday. Margot Fonteyn performs SALUT D'AMOUR with its choreographer Frederick Ashton, followed by Ashton's MARGUERITE AND ARMAND.

THE PAINS OF PERFORMANCE (3 films)
>Series: The Nature of Things
>1986–1989, 23:55 min., color, video
>Distributor/Producer: Canadian Broadcasting Corporation
>Host: David Suzuki

Focuses on medical treatment designed specifically to help performing artists, with visits to clinics for musicians and dancers suffering from performance ailments. Also from the same series: THE BALANCING ACT, which examines the vestibular system of the inner ear and the specific challenges of athletics, dance, flight, and space travel. Also, ROTATION, a five-minute presentation about the principle of rotation in tops, potters' wheels, dancers' pirouettes, and the earth.

PAINTED PAST OR FALLING GIRL

1988, 10 min., color, video
Distributor/Choreographer/Director/Editor:
Debra Wanner
Cameraman: John Miglietta
Cinematography: Robert Purdue
Composer: Anthony Rian Gerber

A solo woven with images of figures falling through space.

PALM PLAY

Series: Movement Style and Culture Series
1977, 30 min., color, film, video
Distributor: University of California Extension Media Center
Producer/Writer/Editor: Alan Lomax
Producers: Forrestine Paulay, Irmgard Bartenieff

Illustrates six types of palm gestures prevalent in the dances of the Far East, Indonesia, and Europe as an attempt to understand the nature of their respective societies.

PANTOMIMES

1954, 20 min., color, film, video
Distributor: French American Cultural Services and Educational Aid (FACSEA) #644
Mime: Marcel Marceau

The French mime Marcel Marceau plays dice with life, chases butterflies, tames wild beasts, and portrays life's passages: adolescence, maturity, old age.

PAPER DANCE

1988, 6 min., color, video
Distributor/Producer/Director: Abby Luby
Choreographer/Dancer: Michael Ing
Dance on Camera Festival, 1989 Honorable Mention

An experimental film in which a wall of paper seemingly partners a dancer.

PARADES AND CHANGES

1965, 40 min., b&w, film
Distributor: Canyon
Director: Anne Areborn
Dance Company: San Francisco Dancers Workshop

A product of the 1960s; dancers relate to space, trap doors, scaffolding, and a weather balloon. In act II, nude dancers tear rolls of paper.

PARAFANGO

1983–1984, 29 min., color, b&w, video
Distributor: Kitchen
Producer: Institut National de la Communication Audiovisuelle
Director: Charles Atlas
Choreographer: Karole Armitage

Principal Dancers: Michael Clark, Philippe Decoufle, Nathalie Richard, Jean Guizerox, Karole Armitage

A montage of studio rehearsals with plots and subplots revolving around the choreographer and four male partners with dramatic narrative, scenes of war, collapsing buildings, falling trees, and a bored TV-gazing cashier.

PARCELLE DE CIEL

1987, 18 min., color, video
Distributor: Electronic Arts Intermix
Producers: MCR Productions, La Sept, INA, Arcanal
Director: Robert Cahen
Choreographer: Susan Buirge
Composers: Charles Ives, Henry Purcell, Anton Webern, J. S. Bach

Slow-motion, stop-action abstraction of a barefoot group dance choreographed by an American based in southern France.

PARIS

1982, 26 min., color, video
Distributor: KTCA-TV
Directors: Mark Lowry, Kathryn Escher
Choreographer/Composers: Meredith Monk, Ping Chong

First performed in 1972 as part of the travelogue series, this dance theater piece on journeys, both imaginary and real, was shot in an abandoned grain mill in Minneapolis.

The Paris Opera Ballet:
Seven Ballets
Cover art courtesy V.I.E.W. Video.

THE PARIS OPERA BALLET: SEVEN BALLETS

1989, 66 min., color, video
Distributor: V.I.E.W. Video
Producer: 8 Productions
Choreographers: Norbert Schmucki, Marius Petipa
Principal Dancers: Patrick Dupond, Sylvie Guillem, Noella Pontois
Composers: Peter Ilyich Tchaikovsky, Edvard Grieg, Daniel Auber, Camille Saint-Saens, Jean Sibelius

Features five ballets by Norbert Schmucki: ESCAMILLO, LE

PETIT PAN, BAMBOU (extract), RIXE, and UNE FEMME, as well as Petipa's GRANDE PAS CLASSIQUE, and THE WHITE SWAN pas de deux from SWAN LAKE.

THE PARIS OPERA BALLET: SIX BALLETS

1987, 58 min., color, video
Distributor: V.I.E.W. Video
Producer: 8 Productions
Choreographers: Norbert Schmucki, Marius Petipa
Principal Dancers: Patrick Dupond, Noella Pontois
Dance Company: Paris Opera Ballet
Composers: Peter Ilyich Tchaikovský, Manuel Valera, Dmitri Shostakovich, Giacomo Meyerbeer

Five ballets by Norbert Schmucki: TCHAIKOVSKY BALLET, DELTAT, ELPHEMERA, PAILLETTES, and THE ICE SKATERS, and THE BLACK SWAN pas deux from SWAN LAKE.

PARISIAN FOLLIES

1920s, 8 min., b&w, film
Distributor: Dance Film Archive
Principal Dancer: Josephine Baker

Cabaret and nightclub acts from Paris, including the American black comedienne/dancer/singer who stunned Europe, Josephine Baker.

PARTNERING FOR THE THEATRE ARTS (2 videos)

90 min. each, color, video
Distributor: Jim Forest
Teachers: Francois Szony, Toni Ann Gardella

Two-part tape in which a world-famous adagio team perform and teach a waltz and paso doble and demonstrate in real time and slow motion many of their lifts.

PARTNERS

1980, 22:30 min., color, film, video
Distributor/Producer: Larry Schulz
Principal Dancers: Bill Davies, Sandra Cameron
Cinematographers: Dick Lombard, Alicia Weber

Bill Davies and Sandra Cameron, dance champions, practice and perform five classic ballroom dances—fox-trot, slow waltz, tango, quick step, Viennese waltz—and discuss their partnership and the future of ballroom dance.

PAS DE DEUX

1968, 14 min., b&w, film, video
Distributor: International Film Bureau
Producer: National Film Board of Canada
Director: Norman McLaren
Choreographer: Ludmilla Chiriaeff
Principal Dancers: Margaret Mercier, Vincent Warren
American Film Festival, Blue Ribbon

Two white-clad principals of Les Grands Ballets Canadiens, silhouetted by rear lighting, and multiplied through the exposure of individual frames up to eleven times.

PAS DE DEUX

1984, 81 min. color, video
Distributor: Video Arts International
Producer: Mark I. Rosenthal

Director: Ted Lin
Choreographers: Marius Petipa, Filippo Taglioni
Composers: Peter Ilyich Tchaikovsky, Leon Minkus
Principal Dancers: Patricia McBride, Wayne Eagling, Ravena Tucker, Michel Denard, Ghislaine Thesmar, Yoko Morishita

Selections from SLEEPING BEAUTY, LA SYLPHIDE, LE CORSAIRE, and DON QUIXOTE.

PAS DE QUATRE AND THE CHARIOTEER

1968, 29 min., b&w, video
Distributor: Orion Enterprises
Producer: WTTW/TV, Chicago
Director: Richard Carter
Choreographers: Jules Perrot, Anton Dolin, Dom Orejudos
Dance Company: Illinois Ballet
Composers: Cesare Pugni, Samuel Barber

PAS DE QUATRE, created by Jules Perrot in 1845 to display the talents of the four greatest ballerinas of the day, was reconstructed here by the British dancer Anton Dolin. Also included is THE CHARIOTEER, a modern ballet depicting the horses and drivers of the gods, choreographed by Dom Orejudos to the music of Samuel Barber.

PAUL TAYLOR DANCE COMPANY—AN ARTIST AND HIS WORK

1968, 32 min., color, film, video
Distributor: Pyramid, University of Michigan
Producer/Director: Paul Steeg and Harris Communications
Choreographer/Dancer: Paul Taylor
Principal Dancers: Bettie de Jong, Daniel Williams, Carolyn Adams, Dan Wagoner, Jane Kosminksy, Mollie Reinhart, Cliff Keuter, Senta Driver, John Nightingale
Dance Company: Paul Taylor Dance Company
Composers: Ludwig van Beethoven, Carlos Surinach, Franz Joseph Haydn, New Orleans jazz musicians
Narrator: Clive Barnes

One of the few films readily available on the internationally acclaimed modern dancer who began his career with Martha Graham, seen in rehearsal with excerpts from LENTO, AGATHE'S TALE, ORBS, THREE EPITAPHS, AUREOLE, and PIECE PERIOD.

PAVLOVA

1983, 81 min., color, video
Distributor: Kultur #1234
Producers: Micheline Charest, Ronald A. Winberg for Societe Radio Canada/Premiere Performance Corp
Producer/Director: Pierre Morin
Choreographers: Marius Petipa, Anna Pavlova, Ann Marie de Angelo, Hilary Cartwright, Michel Fokine
Principal Dancers: Amanda Mckerrow, Ann Marie de Angelo, Marianna Tcherkassky, Patrick Bissell, Valentino Kozlova, Frank Augustyn
Composers: Leon Minkus, Riccardo Drigo, Peter Ilyich Tchaikovksy, Leo Delibes, Fritz Kreisler, Camille Saint-Saens
Narrator: Leslie Caron

A tribute to the Russian ballerina Anna Pavlova with film clips, photography, and memorabilia drawn from her thirty-year career and choreography by the former Joffrey dancer

Ann Marie de Angelo and scenes from DON QUIXOTE, SLEEPING BEAUTY, GISELLE, and THE DYING SWAN.

PERFORMERS ON TEACHING

    1988, 28 min., color, video
    Distributor: Indiana University
    Producer: Indiana University Radio and Television Services
    Teacher: Jean Pierre Bonnefous
    Narrator: Dean Anya Royce

Three artist/teachers, a dancer, a cellist, and an actor, share their philosophies and techniques for teaching the performing arts.

THE PERSISTENT IMAGE AND VALSE FANTASTIQUE

    1969, 28 min., b&w, video
    Distributor: Orion Enterprises
    Producer: WTTW/TV, Chicago
    Directors: Richard Ellis, Christine Duboulay, Richard Carter
    Choreographers: Dom Orejudos, Hy Somers
    Dance Company: Illinois Ballet
    Composers: Sergei Prokofiev, Michael Glinka

Orejudos' THE PERSISTENT IMAGE, set in the Victorian era, revolves around an adulterous theme, a lodger copulating with the matron of the household. VALSE FANTASTIQUE, choreographed on the classical style by Hy Somers.

PETER MARTINS: A DANCER

    1979, 54 min., color, video
    Distributor: Kultur #1118
    Producers: Danmarks Radio and Film Company
    Director: Jorgen Leth
    Choreographers: George Balanchine, Peter Martins, Jerome Robbins
    Principal Dancers: Peter Martins, Suzanne Farrell, Heather Watts, Daniel Duell
    Composers: Igor Stravinsky, Peter Ilyich Tchaikovsky

The Danish-born artistic director of New York City Ballet trains, rehearses with choreographer Jerome Robbins, fusses over his costumes, and performs duets from George Balanchine's CHACONNE, AGON and TCHAIKOVSKY PAS DE DEUX, while he expresses his feelings about himself, his work and his company. Heather Watts and Daniel Duel perform Martins' CALCIUM LIGHT NIGHT.

A PHANTASY

    1952, 7:30 min., color, film
    Distributor: International Film Bureau
    Producer: National Film Board of Canada
    Director: Norman McLaren
    Composer: Maurice Blackburn

Canadian animator Norman McLaren used pastel drawings and cut-outs for a dance accompanied by saxophone and synthesizer.

PILOBOLUS AND JOAN

    1973, 58 min., color, video
    Distributor: Electronic Arts Intermix
    Producer: WNET/TV Lab

    Director: Ed Emshwiller
    Dance Company: Pilobolus Dance Company
    Actor: Joan McDermott

Reversing Franz Kafka's METAMORPHOSIS, a cockroach becomes a man, or rather four men, clumsily attached, and falls in love with Joan. Responding to her in urban streets, her apartment and a pastoral lake, the beast manages as best it can despite occasional dismemberings and momentary aerial flights. With narration and special effects.

PINA BAUSCH

    1983, 56 min., color, film
    Distributor: Kitchen
    Director: Chantal Akerman
    Choreographer/Dancer: Pina Bausch
    Dance Company: Wuppertal Tanstheater

The daily routine, rehearsals, and performances of Pina Bausch during the year NELKEN was created. The German choreographer was trained at the Juilliard School and is internationally known for her dance theater.

PLASMASIS

    1974, 14 min., color, film
    Distributor: The Cinema Guild
    Director: Melchor Casals
    Principal Dancers: Caridad Martinez, Lazaro Carreno
    Dance Company: Ballet Nacional De Cuba
    Composer: Sergio Fernandez Barroso

A modern Cuban ballet on the evolution of man.

PLISETSKAYA DANCES

    1964, 70 min., b&w, film, video
    Distributors: Corinth, Kultur #1196
    Producer: Central Documentary Film Studio
    Director: Vassili Katanyan
    Choreographers: Marius Petipa, Lev Ivanov, Agrippina Vaganova, Vakhtang Chabukiani, Alexander Gorsky, Arthur Saint-Leon, Leonid Yacobson
    Principal Dancers: Maya Plisetskaya, Yuri Zhdanov, Vladimir Vasiliev
    Dance Company: Bolshoi Ballet
    Composers: Peter Ilyich Tchaikovsky, Alexander Glazounov, Sergei Prokofiev, Leon Minkus

Presents Maya Plisetskaya, the Russian prima ballerina as a child, the development of her career and scenes of her performances in SWAN LAKE, LAURENCIA, SPARTACUS, THE LITTLE HUMPBACKED HORSE, KHOVANSCHINA, RAYMONDA, THE STONE FLOWER, ROMEO AND JULIET, WALPURGIS NIGHT, and DON QUIXOTE.

A POEM OF DANCES ALSO KNOWN AS PLISETSKAYA/CARMEN

    1973, 68 min., color, film, video
    Distributor: Corinth
    Producer: Mosfilms
    Director: Vadim Derbenev
    Choreographers: Alberto Alonso, Vladimir Vasiliev
    Principal Dancers: Maya Plisetskaya, Nikolai Fadeyechev

Dance Company: Bolshoi Ballet
Composers: Peter Ilyich Tchaikovsky, Georges Bizet,
Alexander Glazounov, Johann Sebastian Bach

The Russian ballerina Maya Plisetskaya in some of her most famous roles from CARMEN SUITE, RAYMONDA, PRELUDE,
and THE DYING SWAN.

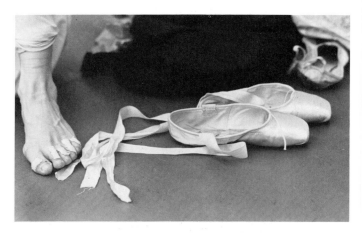

The Point Is
Photo by Sheila L. Kogan. Courtesy the photographer.

THE POINT IS
    1986, 7:10 min., color, video
    Distributor/Producer: Sheila Kogan
    Director: Yudi Bennett
    Dance Company: American Ballet Theatre

A documentary about toe shoes.

POINTE BY POINT
    1988, 45 min., color, video
    Distributor: Kultur #1235
    Producer: Ross Alley
    Teacher: Barbara Fewster

Guidelines to develop safe habits and muscular strength on pointe
presented in four sections: types of feet, preparations of the ballet
shoe, study in pointe for beginners, and, finally, placement.

POINTS IN SPACE
    1986, 55 min., color, film, video
    Distributor: Cunningham Dance Foundation
    Producers: Bob Lockyer for BBC and Cunningham
    Dance Foudation
    Directors: Elliot Caplan, Merce Cunningham
    Choreographer: Merce Cunningham
    Dance Company: Merce Cunningham Dance Company
    Composer: John Cage
    Set Designer: Bill Anatasi
    Costumes: Dove Bradshaw
    American Film Festival finalist

Rehearsals and interviews with the artists take the viewer
through the complexities of bringing new dance to television.

POLYNESIAN DANCES FROM THE ELLICE ISLANDS (4 films)
    1960, 2-8 min., b&w, film
    Distributor: Pennstate #E00415, EO00416, EOO417, EOO418
    Producer: Wissen

An improvisational solo performed to two FAKANAU narrative
songs accompanied by a drum. A FATELE, a woman's dance
accompanied by a large men's chorus. Two minutes of a SIVA
song from the Samoan Islands with a couple improvising.
Finally a group of girls sing a song of praise, VIIKI, illustrated
with arm and hand movements.

A PORTRAIT OF GISELLE
    1982, 98 min., color, film, video
    Distributors: Wombat (film), Kultur #1148 (video)
    Producer: Joseph Wishy for ABC Video Enterprises
    Choreographers: Jean Coralli, Jules Perrot
    Principal Dancers: Alicia Alonso, Yvette Chauvire,
    Carla Fracci, Alicia Markova, Olga Spessivtzeva,
    Galina Ulanova, Natalia Makarova, Patricia McBride
    Composer: Adolphe Adam
    Dance on Camera Festival, 1982 Gold Award; Academy Award

Sir Anton Dolin explains the plot of GISELLE and its performance
history, lending insights into its technical and dramatic demands.
Eight of the greatest Giselles illustrate his points with films of their
performances dating from 1932.

POW WOW
    1980, 16 min., color, film, video
    Distributor: Corinth
    Producer: Centron

Insight into Indian culture, ceremonies, and traditional dances,
including the Fire Dance and the Gourd Dance.

PRELUDE FOR SALOME
    1990, 20 min., color, video
    Distributor/Choreographer/Dancer: Sarah Skaggs
    Producer: Danspace at St. Mark's Church, New York
    Director: Character Generators
    Dancer: Donald Fleming
    Composer: Stephen Harvey

Premiere performance of a modern duet suggesting the
parallels and crossovers of religion and sexuality.

PREPARING TO DANCE
    Series: The Dance Experience
    1984, 15 min., color, film, video
    Distributor: American Alliance of Health, Physical Education,
    Recreation and Dance
    Producer: The Athletic Institute
    Choreographer: Lynda Davis

Demonstrates the components of proper training for a dancer.

PRIMITIVE MOVERS
    1983, 30 min., color, film
    Distributor/Director/Animator/Dancer: Kathy Rose
    Composer: Charles Cohen
    Costume Designer: Mary Bright

The creator dances in front of and with her animated

films, which range from the figurative to the cubistic and abstract.

THE PRINCE OF BROADWAY

    1980s, 30 min., color, video
    Distributor: Hoctor Products
    Producer: Studio Music Corp.
    Teacher: Thommie Walsh

Jazz routines by Thommie Walsh, a Broadway gypsy.

PRINCESS TAM TAM

    1935, 77 min., b&w, film, video
    Distributor: Kino International
    Director: Edmond Greville
    Principal Dancer: Josephine Baker

Singer/dancer/comedienne Josephine Baker stars as a wild, young Tunisian whom a rich Parisian author tries to civilize, but then succumbs to her charms.

PROCESSION: CONTEMPORARY DIRECTIONS IN AMERICAN DANCE

    1967, 19 min., b&w, film, video
    Distributor/Producer: University of California Extension Media Center
    Director/ Producer: Mark McCarty
    Dancer: Ann Halprin
    Dance Company: Dancer's Workshop Company

Ann Halprin explains her approach to 'total theatre' as a journey through space, adapting and responding to the light and sounds of outdoor environments. The dancers manipulate objects, costumes, and forms.

PSYCHIC SEASONS

    1981, 8:30 min., color, film
    Distributor: California Institute of the Arts
    Producer/Director: Rudi Reinbold
    Dancer: Leslie Gaumer
    Composer: Erik Satie
    Dance on Camera Festival, 1982 First Prize/ experimental category

Multi-image techniques transform backgrounds of a simple dance to be alternately realistic, stylized, or fantastic to suggest earth, air, fire, and water.

PUSS IN BOOTS

    1986, 98 min., color, video
    Distributor: Home Vision #PUS01
    Producer: Interama
    Choreographer: Roland Petit
    Principal Dancer: Patrick Dupond
    Dance Company: National Ballet of Marseille
    Composer: Peter Ilyich Tchaikovsky

Based on Charles Perrault's 1697 fairy tale of an ingenious cat who secures a fortune and a wife for his master, a penniless young miller.

PUTTIN' ON THE RITZ

    1974, 4 min., color, film
    Distributor: Kent State

    Producer: Contemporary Films
    Director: Antoinette Starkiewicz
    Composer: Irving Berlin

In this animated tribute to Fred Astaire, a tapdancing silhouette leads a chorus line through the song sung by Astaire.

QUARANTINE

    1990, 10:50 min., color, video
    Distributor/Choreographer: Melanie Stewart
    Director/Writer/Editor: Robert Palumbo
    Principal Dancer: Christopher Hawks
    Composer: Jamie Alls

A man reflects on his life and his failure to find a sexual rhythm, unaffected by societal pressures inflicted by media images. In the mode of a 1940s self-help tape, the "Voice of God" expounds on the proprieties of living well.

QUARRY

    1978, 80 min., color, film
    Distributor: Dance Film Archive
    Producing Organization: The House
    Director: Arman Nowak
    Choreographer/Composer/Dancer: Meredith Monk
    Dancers: Ping Chong, Gail Turner
    Dance Video and Film Festival, 1978 Certificate of Honor; Obie Winner

This theater piece is made up of a lullaby, march, and requiem depicting a child's half-comprehending vision of war and holocaust.

RABL

    1985, 7:40 min., color, video
    Distributor/Choreographer: Patrice Regnier
    Producer: Rush Dance Company
    Director: Ed Lachman
    Principal Dancers: Anthony Stafford, Annette White
    Composer: Carter Burwell
    Editor: Rebecca Allen

The love-hate relationship between man and computer enacted through duet and computer graphics, disembodied floating arms and legs created by the animator responsible for the effects in THE CATHERINE WHEEL.

RADHA

    1972, 19 min., color, film
    Distributor: Dance Film Archive
    Director: Dwight Godwin
    Choreographer/Dancer: Ruth St. Denis
    Dancer: Donald Saddler
    Composer: Edouard Lalo
    Narrator: Walter Terry

The modern dance pioneer Ruth St. Denis framed by a corps of men was filmed outside, at Jacob's Pillow in 1941. The cinematographer edited the footage in 1972 and inserted still photos from other performances in between sections of the dance. Dance critic Walter Terry provides a six-minute introduction.

RADL AND HATSCHO FROM JIHLAVA (2 films)

 1963, 14 min., color, film
 Distributor: Pennstate #EOO183, E00812
 Producer: Wissen

The fanfare songs and dances of Moravian farmers performed in a studio, along with the Hatscho, a dance that begins in three-quarter time, transforms into a polka rhythm and ends in a gallop.

RAG TO ROCK TO DISCO

 1980, 47 min., color, video
 Distributor: Orion Enterprises
 Director: Victor Summa
 Choreographer/Narrator: Gus Giordano

A history of jazz dance from the 1920s through the 1970s, with flashes of jazz classics culminating in the disco craze.

RAGAS FOR SWAM SATCHIDANANDA

 1974, 15 min., color, film
 Distributor/Choreographer/Dancer: Margaret Beals
 Composers: Ravi Shankar, Colin Walcott

Two dances based on yoga postures and forms, introduced by the choreographer.

RAINFOREST

 1972, 30 min., color, film
 Distributor: Pennebaker Associates
 Producer: Public Broadcasting Laboratory
 Director/Producer: D. A. Pennebaker
 Choreographer: Merce Cunningham
 Dancers: Merce Cunningham, Carolyn Brown
 Composer: David Tudor
 Set Designer: Andy Warhol
 Dance Company: Merce Cunningham Company

Performance and interview with composer John Cage and a segment of a rehearsal.

RAVEL

 1989, 105 min., color, film, video
 Distributor: Rhombus International
 Producers: Rhombus, Canadian Broadcasting Corp.,
 Societe Radio Canada, Bravo Cable Network, Danmarks Radio,
 Nederlandse Omroep Stichting, Norsk Rikskringkasting,
 Ol Yleisradio, Sveriges TV, Television Espanola, TV Ontario
 Director: Larry Weinstein
 Choreographers: Robert Desrosiers, David Earle
 Dancers: Rosemarie Arroyave, Eric Tessier-Lavigne
 Dance Company: Toronto Dance Theatre

Pianist Alicia De Larrocha plays with the Montreal Symphony Orchestra in this documentary homage to the French composer Maurice Ravel (1875-1937), with two dance sequences, home movies, stills, interviews, and the composer's unpublished letters.

RAYMONDA

 1980s, 146 min., color, video
 Distributor: Kultur #1170
 Choreographer: Marius Petipa
 Principal Dancers: Ludmilla Semenyaka, Irek Mukhamedov, Gediminas Taranda
 Dance Company: Bolshoi Ballet
 Composer: Alexander Glazunov
 Writer: Lydia Pashkova

This ballet, which premiered in 1898 in St. Petersburg, centers around a medieval tale of the kidnapping of Raymonda, a noble lady betrothed to the white knight Jean de Brienne.

RAYMONDA

 1989, 136 min., color, video
 Distributor: Spectacor
 Producers: NHK Enterprises, Video/Film Bolshoi and Japan Arts Corporation licensed by Primetime Entertainment
 Choreographers: Marius Petipa and Alexandr Gorsky, revised by Yuri Grigorovich
 Principal Dancers: Natalya Bessmertnova, Yuri Vasuchenko, Gediminas Taranda
 Composer: Alexander Glazunov
 Designer: Simon Virsaladze

Recorded live at the Bolshoi Theatre in Moscow, Russia.

RECREATIONAL DANCES FROM CENTRAL SUDAN (4 films)

 1964, 6-10 min. each, color, film
 Distributor: Pennstate #EO1366, EO1367, EO1358, EO1357
 Producer: Wissen

A couple dance, the GISESS, is accompanied by two drummers and a chorus of girls. Two circle dances, the PATIE and BIDJERUA, accompanied by five flutes, three drums, rattle, and three parna, cultic wind instruments, all of which carry the KALTUMANDASA, an energetic dance for the young. From the Dangaleat people of Chad in central Africa.

RED HOT (6 videos)

 1980s, 30-45 min. each, color, video
 Distributor: Hoctor Products
 Producer: Studio Music Corp.
 Dance Company: Faculty of Dance Caravan

Twelve to twenty jazz routines on each tape

THE RED SHOES

 1948, 135 min., color, film, video
 Distributors: Phoenix Films, Paramount,
 Home Vision #RED01
 Producer/Directors: Michael Powell and Emeric Pressburger for The Archers and J. Arthur Rank Organization
 Choreographer/Dancers: Robert Helpmann, Leonide Massine
 Principal Dancers: Moira Shearer, Ludmilla Tcherina, Allan Carter
 Composer: Brian Easdale
 Dance Company: Royal Ballet

The classic feature film based on the Hans Christian Andersen fairy tale. A young ballerina, obsessed with her art, marries a young composer equally absorbed in his. Torn between loyalties to her director and her lover, the ballerina meets a tragic ending.

REDA

1988, 90 min., color, video
Distributor: Zeina
Principal Dancers: Mahmoud Reda, Farida Fahmy

Fourteen Middle Eastern dances from the Balloon Theatre
Show in Egypt. A 120-minute dance from Mahmoud's personal
archives featuring Farida Fahmy and audiocassettes are
also available.

THE REFINER'S FIRE

1977, 6 min , color, film
Distributor: Phoenix/BFA Films
Producers: Keith Beasley, Richard Grossman,
Carl Hemenway

Squares attempt to dance with circles, suggesting our
dilemma as to whether to conform to society or not.

REFLECTIONS

Series: Magic of Dance
1979, 52 min., color, video
Distributor: Dance Film Archive
Producer/Director: Patricia Foy
Narrator/Dancer: Margot Fonteyn
Principal Dancers: Mikhail Baryshnikov, Martha Graham
Choreographers: Michel Fokine, Martha Graham
Composer: Carl Maria Von Weber

The British Prima Ballerina Margot Fonteyn comments on
the work of the pioneers of dance, from the 17th-century
commedia dell'arte to Martha Graham. Margot Fonteyn
dances with Mikhail Baryshnikov in Fokine's LE SPECTRE
DE LA ROSE, in memory of the debut performance in 1911
with Vaslav Nijinsky and Tamara Karsavina.

REFLECTIONS IN SPACE

1970, 27 min., color, film
Distributor: PennState
Principal Dancer: Edward Villella
Painters: James Wyeth, Mitchell Jamieson and Lamar Dodd
Interviewers: Archibald Macleish, William F. Buckley

Impressions of the Apollo 11 flight to the moon by visual and
performing artists set against footage of the actual mission and
scenes from the feature film 2001.

REFLECTIONS OF A DANCER: ALEXANDRA DANILOVA,
PRIMA BALLERINA ASSOLUTA

1981, 52 min., color, film, video
Distributor: Seahorse Films
Producer/Director: Anne Belle
Principal Dancers: Alexandra Danilova, Frederic Franklin
Cinematographer: Peter Aaron
Choreographers: Marius Petipa, Michel Fokine
Composers: Leon Minkus, Nicholas Tcherepnine

Alexandra Danilova, the renowned dancer who left Russia with
George Balanchine and later joined Serge Diaghilev's Ballets
Russes, coaches her students at the School of American Ballet
for a performance of LE PAVILLON D'ARMIDE (Fokine/
Tcherepnine). While setting PAQUITA (Petipa/Minkus) for the
Cincinnati Ballet Company, she demonstrates with her former
partner Frederic Franklin.

REFLECTIONS ON CHOREOGRAPHY

1973, 14 min., color, film
Distributor: University of California at Los Angeles
Media Center
Choreographer: Marion Scott

Choreographer discusses her piece entitled ABYSS, performed
by UCLA students.

THE REHEARSAL

1980, 28 min., color, video
Distributor: Orion Enterprises
Director: Richard Carter
Choreographer: Gus Giordano
Emmy, Ohio State Awards

Two dancers, who dislike one another, rehearse a pas de deux
choreographed as a celebration of love.

REHEARSAL: A ROCK BALLET

1985, 82 min., color, video
Distributor: Coe Film Assoc.
Producer: Hungarian MTV
Dance Company: Ballet Company of the Hungarian State Opera
Composer: Johann Sebastian Bach

Hungarian ballet dancers prepare for a performance of Bach's
ST. JOHN'S PASSION. They are interrupted by refugees seeking
asylum, and subsequently disrupted by their persecutors.

REINCATNATED

1984, 6 min., color, film, video
Distributor: Coe Film Assoc.
Producer/Director: Patricia Jaffe
Principal Dancer: Rita Nachtmann

A cat tries to nap, but is continually awakened by the sounds
of the household around her.

REMEMBERING THELMA

1981, 15 min., color, film, video
Distributor: Women Make Movies
Producer/Director: Kathe Sandler
Dancer/Dance Teacher: Thelma Hill
Dance Companies: Alvin Ailey Dance Theater, New York
Negro Ballet
Dance Film Festival: Gold Seal Award

Thelma Hill was one of the most sought-after modern dance
teachers in the country when she died in a tragic accident in
1977. Instrumental in the development of black dance in
America, Hill's engaging spirit is captured through footage and
stills of her days as a performer with the original Alvin Ailey
Dance Theater and the New York Negro Ballet of the 1950s.

REMY CHARLIP'S DANCES

1978, 27:46 min., color, video
Distributor: WGBH-TV
Producer: Nancy Mason
Director: David Atwood
Choreographer/Dancer: Remy Charlip
Principal Dancers: Toby Armour, Mara Colucci,
Ronald Dabney, Abelardo Gameche, Patrick Layden, Marlene

Lundvall, Claire Mallardi, Tedd Neenan

A drawing by Remy Charlip precedes each of the five dances shot in a field, an indoor track, and a studio. In GLOW WORM, modern dancer Remy Charlip speaks through sign language, and introduces a giant ruler and telephone. In ETUDE, a couple throw a beach ball replica of the world back and forth while tap dancing.

REPETITIONS

 1984, 45 min., b&w, color, video
 Distributor: Electronic Arts Intermix
 Producers: Image Video, Centre Bruxellois de L' Audiovisuel,
 Schaamte, Polygone
 Director: Marie Andre
 Choreographer/Dancer: Anne Teresa de Keersmaeker
 Dance Company: Anne Teresa de Keersmaker's company

During rehearsals in Brussels for ELENA'S ARIA (presented in the United States at the Brooklyn Academy of Music), the choreographer talks with her dancers. The close-ups, candids, and momentary shots of the world outside the studio help to convey the fragmented feeling of the creative process.

REQUIEM FOR A SLAVE

 1966, 27 min., b&w, video
 Distributor: Orion Enterprises
 Producer: WTTW-TV, Chicago
 Director: Karen Prindel
 Principal Dancers: Earnest Morgan, Rita Roles
 Composer: James Quinn
 Chicago Emmy Award

An operatic dance-drama set in a burial ground, where the wife and friends of a dead slave have gathered for graveside services. As mourners sing eulogies, the action flashes back to happier times.

RETRACING STEPS: AMERICAN DANCE
SINCE POSTMODERNISM

 1988, 88 min., color, video, film
 Distributor/Director: Michael Blackwood with
 Westdeutscher Rundfunk
 Choreographer/Dancers: Blondell Cummings, Jim Self,
 Johanna Boyce, Bill T. Jones and Arnie Zane,
 Stephen Petronio, Molissa Fenley, Diane Martel,
 Wendy Perron
 Composers: Peter Gordon, Ryuichi Sakamoto,
 David Cunningham, Giuseppe Verdi, Diane Martel, David
 Linton, David Munson, A. Leroy, Lenny Picket
 Editors: Peter Adair, Julie Sloan
 Writer/Consultant: Sally Banes
 Photographer: Mead Hunt

The eclecticism found in American dance in the 1980's. Performances include: SECOND SIGHT, ESPERANTO, SEPARATE VOICES (Fenley); FEVER SWAMP, FREEDOM OF INFORMATION PART 3, HOLZER DUETT. . . .TRUISMS, THE GIFT/NO GOD LOGIC (Jones/Zane); UNTITLED '87 and BROTHER JACKASS (Martel); #3, WALK-IN, SIMULACRUM REELS (Petronio); THE TREE ISN'T FAR FROM WHERE THE ACORN FALLS and WOMEN, WATER AND A WALTZ (Boyce); ARENA (Perron);

ALABAMA TRILOGY (Self); MOVING PICTURES, AEROBICS, and BASIC STRATEGIES (Cummings).

RHYTHM 'N RED SHOES

 1980s, 30 min., color, video
 Distributor: Hoctor Products
 Producer: Studio Music Corp.
 Choreographer/Dancer: Mallory Graham

Jazz routines.

RHYTHMETRON—WITH THE DANCE THEATRE OF
HARLEM AND ARTHUR MITCHELL

 1973, 52 min., color, film
 Distributors: PennState, University of Michigan
 Producer/Director: Milton A. Fruchtman
 Choreographer: Arthur Mitchell
 Dance Company: Dance Theatre of Harlem
 Narrator: Brock Peters
 American Film Festival, Blue Ribbon

A documentary on Arthur Mitchell, the former New York City Ballet dancer who developed the first black classical ballet company in the United States. Mitchell teaches his students in the basement of a Harlem church. Dance Theatre of Harlem company members demonstrate a ballet barre to Philadelphia school children and then perform excerpts from Mitchell's FETE NOIRE, BIOSFERA, and RHYTHMETRON.

RIGHT ON/BE FREE

 1971, 15 min., color, film
 Distributor/Producer: Filmfair Communications
 Choreographer: Alvin Ailey
 Director: Sargon Tamimi
 Principal Dancer: Judith Jamison
 Music: Voices of East Harlem
 San Francisco International Film Festival,
 1971 Best of category

Black American artists express themselves through music, poetry, painting, and dance.

RINGSIDE

 Series: Alive from Off Center
 1985, 10 min., color, video
 Producer/Distributor: KTCA
 Director: Michael Schwartz
 Choreographer: Elizabeth Streb

Modern dance shot from five vantages for a crystallization of five hundred movement components. By abolishing all movement transitions, split second, signatures of movements are retained.

RITES OF PASSING

 1981, 15 min., b&w, film, video
 Distributor/Producer/Dancer/Choreographer:
 Risa Jaroslow for High Tide Dance
 Director: Nancy Schreiber

A dance for twelve women on the sand of the Battery landfill in lower Manhattan in New York City.

RITUAL IN TRANSFIGURED TIME

1946, 16 min., b&w, film
Distributor: Biograph
Producer/Director: Maya Deren

Maya Deren, the daughter of a Russian emigre, a psychiatrist by profession, appears at first to be speaking to some invisible person as she spins wool. Three graceful, distant women dance in a circle, followed by a game between a woman and a statue made possible through re-filming.

ROAD TO THE STAMPING GROUND

1972-1987, 58 min., color, video
Distributor: Home Vision
Producers: Timothy Reed, Neil Mundy, RM Arts, and Polygon Pictures
Directors: David Muir for Australian Special Broadcasting Service, Hans Hulscher for NOS-TV
Choreographer: Jiri Kylian
Dance Company: Netherlands Dans Theatre
Composer: Carlos Chavez
Editor: Edith Muir
Dance on Camera Festival, 1987 Silver Award

In this biography of a ballet from inspiration through performance, the video opens with Czech choreographer Jiri Kylian at a gathering of 500 Aboriginal tribes on Groote Eylandt, an island off Australia. Kylian comments on the technical and spiritual aspects of the tribal dances. Ten years later, footage of Kylian's rehearsals of the dance, inspired by the event, was intercut with flashback close-ups of the Aboriginal dances.

ROAMIN' I

1980, 15 min., color, film, video
Distributor/Producer: Cunningham Dance Foundation
Director: Charles Atlas
Choreographer/Dancer: Merce Cunningham
Principal Dancers: Karole Armitage, Louise Burns, Ellen Cornfield, Meg Eginton, Susan Emery, Lisa Fox, Lise Friedman, Alan Good, Catherine Kerr, Chris Komar, Robert Kovich, Joseph Lennon, Robert Remley, Jim Self
Dance Company: Merce Cunningham Dance Company

In this documentary on the filming of LOCALE, the methods and problems encountered in filming dance are illustrated.

ROCKING ORANGE III

1975, 3:45 min., color, film
Distributor: Film-maker's Coop
Producer/Director: Doris Chase
Choreographer: Mary Staton
Dance Company: Mary Staton Dance Ensemble
Composer: George Kleinsinger

A modern group dance with Doris Chase's kinetic sculpture.

ROCKING ORANGE: THREE VERSIONS

1975, 12 min., color, film
Distributor: Film-maker's Coop
Producer/Sculptor/Director: Doris Chase
Choreographer: Mary Staton
Dance Company: Seattle Opera Ballet Company
Composer: George Kleinsinger

Of the three versions of a dance around a kinetic sculpture, the first records the dancers, the second is video-synthesized and the last is optically printed. Filmed at the Avery Court of the Wadsworth Atheneum, Hartford, Connecticut.

THE ROMANTIC BALLET

Series: Magic of Dance
1979, 52 min., color, video
Distributor: Dance Film Archive
Producer/Director: Patricia Foy for BBC and Time-Life
Choreographers: Frederick Ashton, Lev Ivanov, Michel Fokine, Roland Petit
Principal Dancers: Flemming Ryberg, Mette Honningen, Margot Fonteyn, Ivan Nagy, Yoko Morishita, Roland Petit
Dance Companies: Royal Danish Ballet, Royal Ballet
Composers: Frederic Chopin, Leo Delibes, Peter Ilyich Tchaikovsky

Discussion of choreographer/dancers Filippo Taglioni, Auguste Bournonville, and Fanny Elssler with performance excerpts from LA SYLPHIDE opening scene and Act II. The use of toe shoes through the ages is demonstrated as a lead into tales of the romantic ballerinas. Also included, the waltz from TALES OF BEATRIX POTTER, the garland waltz from SLEEPING BEAUTY and pas de deux and finale from LES SYLPHIDES. Roland Petit performs his version of COPPELIA.

ROMANTIC ERA

1980, 89 min., color, video
Distributors: Kultur #1145, NVC International
Producer: Joseph Wishy for ABC
Director: Merrill Brockway
Choreographers: Sir Anton Dolin, Jules Perrot
Principal Dancers: Alicia Alonso, Carla Fracci, Ghislaine Thesmar, Eva Evdokimova, Peter Schaufuss, Jorge Esquivel
Composers: Cesare Pugni, Burgmuller

Culminating with the famous ballet created for the four stars in 1845, four legendary ballerinas dance the LE GRAND PAS DE QUATRE, ROBERT THE DEVIL, LES PERIS, NATALIE, THE SWISS MILKMAID, and ESMERALDA.

ROMEO AND JULIET (Bolshoi Ballet)

1954, 95 min., color, film, video
Distributors: Corinth, Kultur #1202
Director: L. Arnstam
Choreographer: Leonid Lavrovsky
Principal Dancers: Galina Ulanova, Yuri Zhdanov
Composer: Sergei Prokofiev
Dance Company: Bolshoi Ballet

Filmed both onstage and outdoors, this version by a People's Artist of the USSR, Leonid Lavrovsky, stars Galina Ulanova and Yuri Zhdanov as the young lovers.

ROMEO AND JULIET (Bolshoi Ballet)

1975, 108 min., color, video
Distributors: Corinth, Kultur #1173
Producer: Lothar Bock Associates, Gmbh
Choreographers: Leonid Lavrovsky, Yuri Grigorovich
Principal Dancers: Natalia Bessmertnova, Mikhail Lavrovsky

Dance Company: Bolshoi Ballet
Composer: Sergei Prokofiev

Russians' version of the full-length ballet based on the tragedy by William Shakespeare.

ROMEO AND JULIET (Bolshoi Ballet)

    1989, 135 min., color, video
    Distributor: Spectacor
    Producers: Primetime Entertainment, NHK, Japan Arts
    Corporation, and Video/Film Bolshoi
    Choreographers: Leonid Lavrovsky, Yuri Grigorovich
    Principal Dancers: Natalia Bessmertnova,
    Irek Mukhamedov, Mikhail Sharkov
    Composer: Sergei Prokofiev

Shot live in Moscow with state-of-the-art technology.

ROMEO AND JULIET (La Scala Ballet)

    1982, 129 min., color, video
    Distributors: Corinth, Kultur #1123
    Producer: Patricia Foy for ITC, Rai, Teatro Alla Scala
    Choreographer/Director: Rudolf Nureyev
    Principal Dancers: Rudolf Nureyev (Romeo), Carla Fracci
    (Juliet), Margot Fonteyn (Lady Capulet)
    Dance Company: Ballet Company of La Scala
    Composers: Sergei Prokofiev

Rudolf Nureyev from Russia, Carla Fracci from Italy, and Margot Fonteyn from England perform Shakespeare's tragedy on the stage of Milan's Teatro alla Scala.

ROMEO AND JULIET (Royal Ballet)

    1966, 124 min., color, film, video
    Distributor: Kultur #1183
    Producer/Director: Paul Czinner for Royal
    Academy Productions
    Choreographer: Kenneth MacMillan
    Principal Dancers: Margot Fonteyn, Rudolf Nureyev
    Dance Company: Royal Ballet
    Composer: Sergei Prokofiev
    Set and Costume Designer: Nicholas Georgiadis

Margot Fonteyn and Rudolf Nureyev, who had defected only five years prior to this production, leave no doubts as to why their partnership is legendary. John Lanchbery conducts the Royal Opera House Orchestra.

ROMEO AND JULIET (Royal Ballet)

    1984, 128 min., color, video
    Distributors: Corinth, HBO #3386, Pioneer (Laserdisk)
    Producer: Robin Scott for BBC Television and NVC
    Directors: Colin Nears, Kenneth MacMillan
    Choreographer: Kenneth MacMillan
    Principal Dancers: Wayne Eagling (Romeo),
    Alessandra Ferri (Juliet)
    Dance Company: The Royal Ballet
    Composer: Sergei Prokofiev
    Set and Costume Designer: Nicholas Georgiadis

This version, which premiered in 1965, was shot live from Covent Garden just before Alessandra Ferri joined American Ballet Theatre.

RONDO

    30 min., color, film
    Distributor: Modern Talking Picture Service #25123
    Producer: West German government
    Choreographer: John Neumeier
    Dance Company: Hamburg Ballet

Performance choreographed by the American choreographer who's enjoyed a long career as a dramatic choreographer in Hamburg, Germany.

A ROOM WITH TWO VIEWS

    1988, 10 min., color, video
    Distributor/Director/Dancer: Annie Bien
    Principal Dancer: Benjamin Pierce
    Composer: Nat King Cole

Natural and theatrical environments cross as two friends try to blend dream and reality.

ROSE BLOOD

    1974, 7 min., color, film
    Distributor: Film-maker's Coop
    Producer/Director: Sharon Couzin
    Choreographer/Dancer: Carolyn Chave Kaplan
    Dance on Camera Festival, 1978 Award; Movies on a
    Shoestring, Cannes Amateur

A woman dances through images of flora, eyes, buildings, water, sunshine, sculpture as she tries to rise above her confusion, disintegration, and sorrow.

ROSELAND

    1978, color, film, video
    Distributors: New Yorker Films, Vestron (video)
    Producer/Director: Merchant Ivory
    Principal Dancer: Geraldine Page

The entangled relationships of the lonely hearts who congregate in Manhattan's dance hall, Roseland.

ROSIE RADIATOR

    1981, 8:30 min., color, film
    Distributor: Canyon
    Producer/Director: Ron Taylor
    Denver Film Festival, honorable mention, 1981

A famous San Francisco street artist, Rosie Radiator, demonstrates her unique style of tap dancing, the super shuffle. She and the Pushrods promote "Guerilla" tap dancing on the sidewalks of the city. She dances at the Bay Area Rapid Transit, in her studio, and across the Golden Gate Bridge.

ROW ROW ROW

    1930's, 7 min., b&w, film
    Distributor: Ivy Films

Animated short of the Apache, the French take-off on the Argentine tango.

The Royal Ballet
Margot Fonteyn. Photo courtesy Home Vision.

THE ROYAL BALLET

    1959, 132 min., color, film, video
    Distributor: Home Vision ROY02
    Distributor/Producers: Paramount, Paul Czinner
    Productions for J. Arthur Rank Organization
    Director/Producer: Paul Czinner
    Choreographers: Konstantin Sergeyev, Lev Ivanov,
    Marius Petipa, Lubov Tchericheva, Michel Fokine,
    Frederick Ashton, Serge Grigoriev
    Principal Dancers: Margot Fonteyn, Michael Somes,
    Antoinette Sibley
    Dance Company: Royal Ballet
    Composers: Peter Ilyich Tchaikovsky, Igor Stravinsky,
    Hans Werner Henze
    Set Designer: Nathalie Gontcharova

Forty-four cameramen captured this performance of ACT II of
SWAN LAKE, THE FIREBIRD, and Frederick Ashton's ONDINE.

THE ROYAL DANCERS AND MUSICIANS FROM
THE KINGDOM OF BHUTAN

    28 min., color, film, video
    Distributor: Asia Society

The annual festival held in the Himalayas with the dancers
preparing for and performing at the Dzong, the religious and
government center.

THE ROYAL DANISH BALLET 1902-1906

1906-1979, 14 min., color, film
Distributor: Dance Film Archive
Producers: Dance Film Archive of the University of Rochester
and Ole Brage of the Historical Archive of Danish Radio
Choreographers: August Bournonville, Poul Funk, Elizabeth Beck
Cinematographer: Peter Elfelt
Principal Dancers: Elizabeth Beck, Ellen Price, Valborg
Borchsenius, Gustav Uhlendorf, Richard Jensen, Anna Agerholm
Dance Company: Royal Danish Ballet Company and School
Composers: V.C. Holm, F. Kuhlau, Herman Von Lovenskjold,
Holger Simon Paulli, Edward Helsted, Niels W. Gade,
Giuseppe Verdi, C.C. Moller. C. W. Gluck

Nine short films mainly presenting the choreography of
Auguste Bournonville (1805-1897), filmed by the Danish Court
photographer, Peter Elfelt. The dances include: THE KING'S
VOLUNTARY CORPS ON AMAGER (1871), THE ELF-HILL
(1828), two versions of LA SYLPHIDE (1836), excerpts from
the tarantella from NAPOLI (1836), the gypsy dance from IL
TROVATORE (1856), an excerpt of the 1870 ballet FROM
SIBERIA TO MOSCOW, a ballet for four women
choreographed in 1896, restaged by Elizabeth Beck in the
1970s, set to the music for the opera ORPHEUS AND
EURIDICE.

RUMANIAN FOLK DANCES (11 films)

    1969, 3-8 min., b&w, film
    Distributor: Pennstate #EO1666, 1686, 1668, 1669, 1687,
    1688, 1671, 1672, 1673, 1651, 1689
    Producer: Wissen

Men arranged in a semi-circle dance the BRIUL, a belt dance,
and the HODOROAGA, a limping dance, accompanied by a
clarinet. Gypsy music accompanies the performance of the
FECIORASCA (lad's dance) and the BARBUNCUL, a men's
dance, and two women's circle dances, the PURTATA FETELOR
and the COCONITA, from the village of Blajel. From the village
of Vestem in the Sibiu district, couples circle in a promenade
for the HATEGANA dance, which starts out with a slow tempo
and then accelerates; the PE SUB MINA; the INVIRTITA, a
turning dance with three or four people holding each other by
the shoulders; the SALCIOARA and OBLII male dances; and
the ZALUTA and HORA MARE. Four Saxon dances performed
by eight young couples in the yard of the old parish school at
Grossau.

RUN, SISTER, RUN

    1986, 39 min., color, film, video
    Distributor: Women Make Movies
    Producer/Director: Margie Soo Hoo Lee
    Choreographer: Cleo Robinson
    Dance Company: Cleo Robinson Dance Company
    Composer: Gordon Parks

A on-stage/off-stage look at a collaboration between Denver-
based choreographer Cleo Robinson, referred to as the Alvin
Ailey of the West, and photographer/composer Gordon Parks
as they work on an urban dance based on the flight of black
activist Angela Davis.

THE RUSH DANCE COMPANY, EXCERPTS FROM "BERNARD"

1977, 10 min., b&w, video
Distributor: Rush Dance Company
Producer/Cinematographer: William Sarokin
Choreographer/Writer: Patrice Regnier
Dance Company: Rush Dance Company

A compilation of key segments from a modern dance.

RUSSIAN FOLK SONG AND DANCE

1980s, 78 min., color, video
Distributor: Kultur #1107
Dance Companies: Pyatnitsky Russian Folk Dance Ensemble, Siberian-Omsk Folk Chorus, Uzbekistan Dance Ensemble, Moldavia Folk Song and Dance Ensemble
Narrator: Tony Randall

Song, dance and instrumentalists from the Ukraine, Siberia, and northern and southwest Russia, Samarkand, Central Asia.

RUTH PAGE: AN AMERICAN ORIGINAL

1979, 60 min., color, film, video
Distributors: Coe Film Associates, Films Inc.
Producer: Nicholas Prince
Principal Dancer: Ruth Page
Director: David Hahn
Narrator: Celeste Holm

Ruth Page, the first choreographer to create an all-black and then an all-jazz ballet, and to commission the composer Aaron Copland, and who arranged Rudolf Nureyev's United States debut, reminisces about her tours with Anna Pavlova, Serge Diaghilev, teacher/choreographer Adolph Bolm, and others.

RUTH PAGE DOCUMENTARY

30 min., color, film, video
Distributor: Coe Film Assoc.
Producer: Ruth Page Foundation
Principal Dancer: Ruth Page
Narrator: Studs Terkel

An interview by Studs Turkel with the Chicago-based choreographer, Ruth Page, including sequences of some of her earliest pieces.

RUTH ST. DENIS AND TED SHAWN

Series: Wisdom Series
1958, 30 min., b&w, film
Distributor: Films Inc.
Producer: University of Minnesota
Principal Dancers: Ruth St. Denis, Ted Shawn

These two pioneers of modern dance in America discuss their lives and works at Ted Shawn's farm in the Berkshires, today's setting for Jacob's Pillow. Ruth St. Denis performs WHITE NAUTCH, and INCENSE; Ted Shawn performs his JAPANESE WARRIOR.

RUTH ST. DENIS BY BARIBAULT

1950, 24 min., color, film
Distributor: Dance Film Archive
Choreographer/Dancers: Ruth St. Denis, Ted Shawn
Cinematographer: Phillip Baribault

Five dances by Ruth St. Denis filmed in the 1940s and early 1950s: WHITE JADE, RED AND GOLD SARI, GREGORIAN CHANT, TILLERS OF THE SOIL (with Ted Shawn), and INCENSE, choreographed in 1906, which is available in a clip by itself.

S S S

1986–1989, 5 min., color, video
Distributor/Producer/Director: Henry Hills
Principal Dancers: Sally Silvers, Pooh Kaye, Mark Dendy

Filmed in the streets of New York, this fast-paced video has the look of a hooked rug, with short clips woven together.

SAEKO ICHINOHE AND COMPANY

1970s, 30 min., b&w, video
Distributor/Producer: Asia Society
Choreographer/Dancer: Saeko Ichinohe

The Japanese dancer choreographs modern dances that often reflect her cultural heritage, as shown by HINAMATSURI (The Doll's Festival) and SUN DANCE, danced to Japanese poems recited by singer Joan Baez.

SAEKO ICHINOHE DANCE: EAST AND WEST

1970s, 30 min., color, video
Distributor/Producer: Asia Society
Choreographer/Dancer: Saeko Ichinohe

A comparison of Japanese and Western dance patterns demonstrated by New York–based Saeko Ichinohe, who performs excerpts of her KITCHEN, GOZA (The Mat), and FIRE-EATING BIRD.

SAGARI DANCES FROM NEW GUINEA

1962, 10 min., color, film
Distributor: Pennstate #EOO535
Producer: E. Schlesier for Wissen

A silent film of three dances, the LAHUSA, TAHOALA, and EWAWALA from the festival cycle known as sagari on Normanby Island, held in remembrance of the dead.

SALOME

1922, 35 min., b&w, film
Distributor: Biograph
Producer: Grapevine Prod.
Director: Charles Bryant
Principal Dancers: Alla Nazimova, Mitchell Lewis
Set Designer: Mrs. Rudolph Valentino

Silent film with stylized camp: stoic slaves fanning feathers, clasping spears, sporting headdresses and shimmery tunics. Decor by Natacha Rambova (Mrs. Rudolph Valentino), after drawings by Aubrey Beardsley. Narrative scrawled on the screen before each scene inspired by the play by Oscar Wilde. Veil dance is punctuated with anguished close-ups, visions, and increasingly melodramatic music.

SALSA

1988, 96 min., color, video
Distributor: Swank
Producer: Cannon
Director: Boaz Davidson

Principal Dancer: Bobby Rosa

Rico has two passions: looking at himself in the mirror and salsa dancing. Rico also has a burning desire to be crowned King of Salsa at the upcoming Festival de San Juan in the Los Angeles Latino community.

SAMBA TO SLOW FOX

1988, 30 min., color, video
Distributor: Wombat Film & Video
Director: Maria Stratford

Filmed in Australia, this witty overview of the competitive ballroom world is unusually well shot in its close-up on details—from the sequins in the costume shot to the elderly woman admiring her figure in the mirror to the less-than glamorous shots of the dancers in their home environment.

SANKAI JUKU

Series: Alive from Off Center
1984, 30 min., color, video
Distributor: KTCA/TV
Dance Company: Sankai Juku

Japan's butoh ensemble of men performing in an abandoned London power station.

SATURDAY NIGHT FEVER

1977, 118 min., color, film, video
Distributor/Producer: Paramount
Director: John Badham
Principal Dancers: John Travolta, Julie Bovasso
Writer: Norman Wexler
Composers: Bee Gees

The blockbuster feature of the Brooklyn blue-collar boy by day/disco king by night. Sequel STAYING ALIVE, directed by Sylvester Stallone in 1983, also from Paramount, places Tony, now older and more ambitious, in Manhattan with the goal of conquering Broadway.

SCAPE-MATES

1972, 28 min., color, film
Distributor: Electronic Arts Intermix
Director: Ed Emshwiller
Principal Dancers: Sarah Shelton, Emery Hermans

Two dancers in a computer-animated environment by the late California-based pioneer.

THE SCENE CHANGES

Series: Magic of Dance
1979, 52 min., color, film, video
Distributor: Dance Film Archive
Producer/Director: Patricia Foy for BBC with Time-Life TV
Choreographers: Lev Ivanov, Marius Petipa, Roland Petit, Glen Tetley
Principal Dancers: Natalia Makarova, Michael Denard, Fred Astaire, Lynn Seymour, Rudolph Nureyev, Sammy Davis, Jr., Luigi Bonino, Galina Ulanova, Virginia Johnson, Eddie Shellman
Composers: Peter Ilyich Tchaikovsky, George Gershwin, Arnold Schoenberg
Set Designer: Rouben Ter-Artunian

Narrator: Margot Fonteyn

The first program in a six-part series, narrated by the late Margot Fonteyn, surveys the history of theatrical dance, with excerpts from the classics: SWAN LAKE, SLEEPING BEAUTY, CORSAIRE, and ROMEO AND JULIET; and contemporary works: FASCINATING RHYTHM, THE GREATEST, PIERRE LUNAIRE. Sammy Davis, Jr. demonstrates several styles of tap, and Fred Astaire and Rudolf Nureyev discuss their viewpoints.

SCENES FROM BORIS ASAFIEV'S BALLET, THE FLAMES OF PARIS

1953, 22 min., b&w, film
Distributor: University of Illinois
Choreographer: Vasily Vainonen
Dancer: Vakhtang Chabukiana
Composer: Boris Asafiev
Dance Companies: Bolshoi Ballet, Kirov State Opera Ballet Theater at Leningrad

Classic Russian ballet inspired by the French Revolution.

SCENES FROM THE BALLET OF FOUNTAIN OF BAKHCHISARAI

1953, 27 min., b&w, film
Distributor: University of Illinois
Choreographer: Rostislav Zahkarov
Principal Dancers: Galina Ulanova, Maya Plisetskaya, Pyotr Gusev, Yuri Zhdanov
Composer: Boris Asafiev
Dance Company: Bolshoi Ballet

Russian ballet inspired by a narrative poem of Alexander Sergeevich Pushkin (1799–1837).

SCENES FROM THE MUSIC OF CHARLES IVES

Series: Educational Performance Collection
1971, 23 min., color, video
Distributor/Producer: Dance Notation Bureau
Choreographer: Anna Sokolow
Composer: Charles Ives

As part of the Educational Performance Collection, the Dance Notation Bureau grades this modern dance as being on an intermediate/advanced technical level, requiring an intermediate notation reading ability. Ilene Fox notated the score, which is available along with a critical text, an introductory article on Labanotation, and the study and performance rights to the dance.

SCHOOL FOR WIVES

1974, 28 min., color, film
Distributor: Dance Film Archive
Producer: University of Wisconsin Extension Telecommunications Center WHA TV-21
Choreographer/Director: Birgit Cullberg
Principal Dancers: Mats Ek, Sighilt Pahl
Dance Company: Cullberg Ballet
Composer: Gioacchino Rossini

Moliere's comedy told with imaginative use of chromakey, choreographed by a Swedish pioneer in video dance, performed by her son, Mats Ek.

SCHOOL OF AMERICAN BALLET

1973, 43 min., b&w, film, video
Distributor/Producer/Director: Virginia Brooks
Dance Teachers: Felia Doubrovska, Alexandra Danilova,
Helene Dudin, Elise Reiman, Muriel Stuart,
Antonina Tumkovsky, Stanley Williams, Helgi Tomasson
Choreographer: George Balanchine
Principal Dancer: Fernando Bujones
Composer: Peter Ilyich Tchaikovsky

Features the school founded by George Balanchine over fifty
years ago in New York City. Helgi Tomasson, the current artistic director of the San Francisco Ballet, then a member of the
New York City Ballet, teaches a class. Balanchine works with
Madame Danilova in a rehearsal of the advanced students'
workshop. Fernando Bujones performs a variation from the
first act of SWAN LAKE.

SECOND CHORUS

1941, 83 min., b&w, film
Distributor: Dance Film Archive
Choreographer: Fred Astaire
Director: H. C. Potter
Principal Dancers: Fred Astaire, Paulette Goddard

Comedy set in a college in the swing era, with duets and solos
by Fred Astaire, who plays a musician who aspires to play with
Artie Shaw.

SECRET OF THE WATERFALL

1983, 29 min., color, video
Distributor/Producer: WGBH/TV
Producer: Susan Dowling
Director/Editor/Designer: Charles Atlas
Choreographer/Dancer: Douglas Dunn
Principal Dancers: Susan Blankensop, Diane Frank,
John McLaughlin, Deborah Riley, Grazia Della-Terza
Writers: Anne Waldman, Reed Bye

Shot in exteriors and interiors on Martha's Vineyard, a collaboration among dance, video and poetry in which the language
of words is intersected with the language of the body.

SEE-DO PRODUCTIONS: BALLROOM INSTRUCTION
(95 programs)

1958-1991, 60-90 min each, b&w, color, film, video (28
made originally on video with sound, the rest are silent
8mm film transferred to video)
Distributor/Director: Michael Miller for See-Do Productions
Principal Dancers: Stephen & Lindsey Hillier, Marcus &
Karen Hilton, Donnie Burns & Gaynor Fairweather, Richard
& Janet Gleave, Michael & Vicki Barr, Ron Montez & Liz
Curtis, Sammy Stopford & Barbara McColl,
Alan & Hazel Fletcher, John Wood & Anne Lewis,
Pierre Dulaine & Yvonne Marceau, Elizabeth Romain,
Sydney Thompson

Full range of courses and demonstrations of the foxtrot,
mambo, lindy, paso doble, waltz, cha cha, samba, merengue,
tango, rumba, peabody, hustle, disco. Exhibition tapes by
the stars of the field and records of the World Professional
Championships in Blackpool, England. Lectures and world

congresses of the National Association of Teachers of Dancing (NATD), which approved the only American style ballroom dance syllabus. Films were produced by a professional ballroom dancer who was also the photographer for
Consumer Reports for thirty years. The first to assemble instructional ballroom dance films, Michael Miller also was
the first in the United States to introduce the samba, which
he learned on his cruise ship tours for Arthur Murray to
South America. The only American allowed to tape the annual Blackpool teaching sessions for re-sale purposes.

SERAMA'S MASK

Series: World Cultures And Youth
1980, 25 min., color, film, video
Distributors: Portland State University, Coronet Films
Producer/Directors: Paul and Deepa Saltzman
Dancer: Serama

Serama, a Balinese dancer, joins his father in a masked
dance to commemorate his father's retirement, after he
carves a ceremonial mask.

SERAPHIC DIALOGUE

1969, 25 min., color, film, video
Distributor: University of Minnesota
Producer: H. Poindexter
Director: Dave Wilson
Choreographer: Martha Graham
Principal Dancers: Mary Hinkson, Bertram Ross, Patricia
Birch, Helen McGehee, Noemi Lapzeson, Phyllis Gutelius,
Takako Asakawa
Composer: Norman Dello Joio
Set Designer: Isamu Noguchi
Dance Company: Martha Graham Dance Company

Martha Graham's depiction of Joan of Arc at the moment of
her exaltation. Adapted for the camera by John Butler.

SET AND RESET, VERSION I

1985, 21:25 min., color, video
Distributor: WGBH
Producer: Susan Dowling
Director: James Byrne
Choreographer: Trisha Brown
Dance Company: Trisha Brown
Composer: Laurie Anderson
Set, Costume, and Film Design: Robert Rauschenberg

A single take with a hand-held camera of a multi-media work.

SET PIECE

1981, 9 min., color, video
Distributor: Coe Film Assoc.
Producer/Director: Duane Fulk
Dancer: Susan Watkins
Choreographer: Jeanne De Herst
Composer: Igor Stravinsky
Dance on Camera Festival, 1982 First Prize in
Experimental Category

A solo performed to Stravinsky's SERENADE IN A in a set
resembling playground equipment.

SEVEN BRIDES FOR SEVEN BROTHERS
>1954, 120 min., color, video, laserdisk
>Distributor/Producer: MGM/UA 0091
>Director: Stanley Donen
>Choreographer: Michael Kidd
>Principal Dancers: Jacques d'Amboise, Marc Platt
>Composer: Gene de Paul
>Writers: Frances Goodrich, Albert Hackett,
>Dorothy Kingsley

Oscar-winning feature loosely based on a story by Stephen Vincent Benet about six rowdy Oregon fur traders who come to town looking for wives after their eldest brother finds a mate. A landmark dance film with choreography conceived for the screen.

SEVENTH SYMPHONY
>1938, 32 min., b&w, film
>Distributor: Dance Film Archive
>Choreographer: Leonide Massine
>Principal Dancers: Alicia Markova, Igor Youskevitch,
>Frederic Franklin
>Dance Company: Ballet Russe De Monte Carlo
>Composer: Ludwig van Beethoven

Rehearsal by the original cast of the first three movements, Creation, Earth, Sky, of this four-act ballet set to a piano score synchronized by Frederic Franklin.

SHAMAN'S JOURNEY
>Series: Alive from Off Center
>1989, 8 min., color, video
>Director: Susan Rynard
>Choreographer/Dancer: Raoul Trujillo
>Composers: Gaetan Gravel, Bill Vorn

A shaman undergoes a metamorphosis while in communication with Death. Raoul Trujillo, an American Indian who performed for six years with the Nikolais Dance Theatre, choreographed this piece as a tribute to his people's folklore and rituals.

SHAPE
>Series: Dance as an Art Form
>1972, 27 min., color, film
>Distributor: Pro Arts
>Producer: Chimerafilm
>Dancer/Director/Narrator: Murray Louis
>Cinematographer: Warren Leib
>Dance Company: Murray Louis Dance Company
>Composer: Alwin Nikolais

Focuses on the sculptural dynamics of a body in motion, as demonstrated by dancers, athletes, actors, and children.

SHE STORIES
>1986, 5 min., color, video
>Distributor/Producer/Director/Choreographer:
>Debra Wanner

A cast of characters—a pillow, a sheet, pajamas, a woman—interact in "an autobiographical bedtime story." While the woman's face is cropped from view, a voice describes the plight of a female artist living in New York.

SHIRLEY TEMPLE: THE LITTLEST REBEL
>1935, 70 min., color, video
>Distributor: RKO
>Director: David Butler
>Principal Dancers: Shirley Temple, Bill "Bojangles" Robinson

Of the nineteen movies the child star made in the 1930s, this one is famous for her duet on the stairs with one of the all-time great hoofers, Bill Robinson. The story line follows Shirley's determination to save her father, a Confederate soldier, even if it requires a visit to President Lincoln.

SHOESHINE JASPER
>1930s, 9 min., color, film
>Distributor: Ivy Films
>Director: Dave and Max Fleischman

Animated short of the character Jasper beating a scarecrow at a dance contest by the animators who created Betty Boop and Popeye the sailor.

SILENCE IS THE END OF OUR SONG
>1986, 41 min., color, video
>Distributor: Facets
>Producer: RM Arts
>Director: Thomas Grimm
>Choreographer: Christopher Bruce
>Dance Company: Royal Danish Ballet
>Composer: Victor Jara

A ballet by the British choreographer dedicated to the Chilean people and their sufferings.

SILVER FEET
>1986, 51 min., color, film, video
>Distributor: Direct Cinema
>Producer: Lee Rubenstein
>Director: Kristine Samuelson
>Dance Company: San Francisco Ballet School
>National Educational Film Festival, 1986 Winner in Fine
>Arts Category

Follows the training, hopes, and fears of three teen-age girls studying dance, auditioning for the ballet school attached to the San Francisco Ballet Company.

SINGIN' IN THE RAIN
>1952, 120 min., color, video
>Distributor/Producer: MGM/UA
>Director: Stanley Donen
>Choreographer: Gene Kelly
>Principal Dancers: Gene Kelly, Debbie Reynolds,
>Donald O'Connor, Cyd Charisse
>Composer: Nacio Herb Brown
>Writer: Betty Comden and Adolph Green

Spoof of Hollywood at the dawn of the sound era with unforgettable dances in the rain, on table tops, over sofas, and on deserted sets.

SLASK
>55 min., color, video
>Distributor: Coe Film Assoc.

Producer: Michael Gelinas
Dance Company: National Folklore Ensemble of Poland

Folk dance, song, and traditional costumes of a touring troupe whose acts reflect the varied customs and regions throughout Poland.

SLEEPING BEAUTY (animated)

1959, 75 min., color, video
Distributor: Swank
Producer: Walt Disney
Director: Clyde Geronimi
Composer: Peter Ilyich Tchaikovsky

Disney's animated adaptations of Charles Perrault's tales.

SLEEPING BEAUTY (Bolshoi Ballet)

1989, 145 min., color, video
Distributors: Spectacor, University of Illinois #S03218
Producers: Primetime Entertainment with NHK, Japan Arts Corporation, and Video/Film Bolshoi
Principal Dancers: Nina Semizorova, Alexsei Fadeyechev, Nina Speranskaya
Choreographers: Marius Petipa, Yuri Grigorovich
Composer: Peter Ilyich Tchaikovsky
Dance Company: Bolshoi Ballet
Designer: Simon Virsaladze

This three-act ballet was first performed in 1890 in the Maryinsky Theatre. Based on Charles Perrault's tale of Princess Aurora put to sleep by an evil fairy, and awakened on stage by the kiss of a Prince. Recorded in Moscow.

SLEEPING BEAUTY (Kirov Ballet)

1964, 92 min., color, film, video
Distributor: Corinth
Director: Konstantin Sergeyev
Principal Dancers: Valery Panov, Natalia Makarova, Natalia Dudinskaya
Choreographer: Marius Petipa
Composer: Peter Ilyich Tchaikovsky
Dance Company: Kirov Ballet

The full-length classic filmed in Leningrad.

THE SLEEPING BEAUTY (Kirov Ballet)

1983, 147 min., color, video
Distributors: Weintraub, HBO #2810, Pioneer (laserdisk)
Producers: Svetlana Kononchuk For NVC and Gostelradio
Director: Elena Macharet
Choreographers: Ivan Vsevolozhsky, Marius Petipa
Principal Dancers: Irina Kolpakova, Sergei Berezhnoi, Lubov Kunakova
Dance Company: Kirov Ballet
Composer: Peter Ilyich Tchaikovsky
Set Designer: S. B. Virsaladze

Shot at the celebration of the Kirov's 200th anniversary in Leningrad.

SMALL DISTANCES

1987, 14 min., color, video
Distributor: Electronic Arts Intermix

Choreographer: Victoria Marks
Director: James Byrne

A synthesis of dance and camera movement in which the cameraman, who uses the camera as an extension of the body, responds to the weight and touch of the other dancers.

SNAKE DANCE TEACHER DANCE

1977-1978, 18 min., color, film, video
Distributor: Mica
Producer: Bayne Williams
Choreographer/Teacher: Arthur Hall
Editor: Bruce Williams
Dance on Camera Festival, Honorable Mention, 1978

West African dances, HAIL TO THE CHIEF, SISSONGBUKA-TAY, ROWING SONG and TCHE TCHE KULE, FETISH DANCE, CALABASH, FANZA, a drum duet, and the Dahomey SNAKE DANCE, a symbolic celebration of fertility, continuity, and longevity, as performed by the students, teachers, and administrators of the schools of Winthrop, Maine.

SNOW MOTION

40 min., color, video
Distributor: University of Illinois #S02090
Producer: Embassy
Principal Dancers: John Eaves, Suzy Chaffee
Composer: Harold Flatermeyer

Ski stunts and snow dancing from the film FIRE AND ICE, featuring a James Bond stunt man and world champion freestyle skier.

SOCIAL AND COMEDY DANCES

1900, 10 min., b&w, film
Distributor: Dance Film Archive

Brief silent films from the turn of the century showing the cakewalk and "tough" dancing.

SODANCEABIT (5 videos)

1980s, 50-100 min. each, color, video
Distributor: Hoctor Products
Producer: Sodanceabit with Extension Services, California State University, Long Beach
Teachers: Phil Martin, Betty Griffith Railey

Five dance-along sessions for social dance: EAST COAST SWING/VIENNESE WALTZ (57 min.); three combinations of patterns in swing style and two of the waltz; CHA CHA/POL-KA (50 min.), two combinations in both styles; WEST COAST SWING (76 min.), four combinations; SOCIAL DANCE AEROBICS (100 min.), a combination in east coast swing, cha cha, samba, polka, and Viennese waltz; FOLK DANCE AEROBICS (64 min.) with the Miserlou, Alunelul, Hora, Savilla Se Bela Loza and Harmonica.

SOLO

1985, 28:31 min., color, video
Distributor: Electronic Arts Intermix
Director: James Byrne
Choreographer/Dancers: Wendy Morris, Maria Cheng, Marilyn Habermas-Scher, Georgia Stephens,

Laurie Van Wieren
Composers: Victor Riley, The Suburbs, J.S. Bach,
Marilyn Habermas-Scher, Mkwaju Ensemble, Wendy Ultan

Five solos performed by Minneapolis women who designed and performed works expressly for the camera in sets ranging from the confinement of a small room to natural landscapes. With his physical approach, James Byrne captures the intimacy of each solo: THE MEMBERS OF MY PARTY; HABITAT; VISION; THIS BODY THIS PLACE, UNNAMED; BESIDE HERSELF. As an example, UNNAMED, also available alone, is a primal fantasy set in a dune. Close-ups of muddy fingers, stumbling like a creepy crawler, are intercut with aerial shots of the figure lost in the gully of an expansive terrain.

SOLOS, DUETS, AND PIZZA

1984, 38:20 min., color, video
Distributor/Producer: WGBH-TV
Directors: Geoff Dunlop, Charles Atlas, Peter Campus
Choreographer/Dancers: Bill T. Jones and Arnie Zane,
Karole Armitage, Trisha Brown

Three modern dances conceived for the camera, shot both outdoors and in studios: BILL AND ARNIE (Jones and Zane/Dunlop), ISLAND SUMMER (Armitage/Atlas), and WATERMOTOR FOR DANCER AND CAMERA, a solo (Brown/Campus).

SOMETIMES IT WORKS. SOMETIMES IT DOESN'T

1983, 63 min., color, video
Distributor: Cunningham Dance Foundation
Producer: Belgian Radio & Television
Director: Chris Dercon and Stefaan Decostere
Choreographer: Merce Cunningham
Dance Company: Merce Cunningham Dance Company
Composer: John Cage

Choreographer Merce Cunningham and composer John Cage discuss at length and in separate interviews, the influence of each on the other, as well as their collaborations. Interview scenes alternate with performance footage. Concludes with a performance of Cunningham's CHANNELS/INSERTS.

SONG AND DANCE

1984, 26 min., color, film, video
Distributor: The Media Guild
Producer: Thames Television
Composer: Benjamin Britten

Children of the Royal Ballet School dance to Benjamin Britten's songs for children, FRIDAY AFTERNOONS.

SONG OF VENEZUELA

1983, 4 min., color, video
Distributor: Kitchen
Director: M. J. Becker
Composer: Joropo

Abstraction of a belly dance shot from the side of the immobile hips.

SONGS UNWRITTEN: A TAP DANCER REMEMBERED

1988, 58 min., color, video
Distributor/Producer/Director: David Wadsworth
Principal Dancers: Leon Collins, Brenda Buffalino,
James "Buster" Brown
Dance on Camera Festival, 1989 Honorable Mention

A portrait of the late Boston tap dancer and Harvard professor Leon Collins, with sixteen jazz and classical pieces recorded in 1984 and historical perspectives from the 1930s to the present day.

SOTTO VOCE

Series: Alive From Off Center
1988, 15 min., color, video
Distributor/Producer: KTCA/TV
Producer: The Kitchen
Director: Jean Louis Le Tacon
Choreographer/Dancer: Stephen Petronio
Composer: Lenny Picket

After a brief interlude among three men, one man dances on a revolving, spotlit pedestal in this cross-cultural, experimental video involving an American modern dancer and a French director.

SOUND OF ONE

1976, 12 min., color, film
Distributor: Canyon
Dancer: Scott Bartlett
Sinking Creek Film Festival

A solo figure executes the meditative movements of T'ai Chi Ch'uan against the backgrounds of an oceanside cliff, forest, mountain, and inside a studio.

SOURCES OF DANCE

1984, 17 min., color, film, video
Distributor: American Alliance for Health, Physical
Education, Recreation, and Dance
Dance Producer: The Athletic Institute
Choreographer: Lynda Davis

Explores the origins of composition and the language of choreography.

SOVIET ARMY CHORUS, BAND, AND DANCE ENSEMBLE

1978, 70 min., color, video
Distributor: Kultur #1106
Dance Company: Soviet Army Dance Ensemble

Russian folk tunes and dances filmed on tour across the Soviet Union.

SPACE CITY

1981, 31:30 min., color, b&w, film
Distributor: Film-makers' Coop
Choreographer/Dancer: Kenneth King
Director: Robyn Brentano
Composer: William Tudor
Set Designer: Richard Brintzenhofe

The director explains, "With the poetic logic of a dream, the soloist moves from an ancient attic through the modern city, into outer space , ending in an abstract montage of futuristic architectural planes and surfaces."

SPANISH FOLK DANCES

1988, 40 min., color, video

Distributor/Producer: Gessler Productions
Director: Cindy Lopez

The HUAINO from Peru, JESUCITA EN CHICHUAHUA from Mexico, and RADO BLANQUITA from Spain performed. Audio-cassette, directions, and guide with cultural and costume notes included.

SPARTACUS (Bolshoi Ballet)

  1977, 120 min., color, film, video
  Distributors: Kultur #1198 (95 min.), Corinth Films
  Producer: Adolf Fradis for Mosfilm Studios
  Director/Screenwriter: Vadim Derbenev
  Choreographer: Yuri Grigorovich
  Principal Dancers: Vladimir Vasiliev (Spartacus),
  Natalia Bessmertnova (Phrygia, Spartacus' Lover),
  Maris Liepa
  Art Director: Simon Virsaldze
  Dance Company: Bolshoi Ballet
  Composer: Aram Khatchaturian

First-century B.C. Rome crackles with an insurrection led by the gladiator and slave Spartacus against the cruel general Crassus, who eventually defeats him.

SPARTACUS (Bolshoi Ballet)

  1984, 128 min., color, video
  Distributors: HBO #3400, Pioneer (laserdisk)
  Producer: Gerald Sinstadt for Gostelradio and National Video Corp.
  Director: Preben Montell
  Choreographer: Yuri Grigorovich
  Principal Dancers: Irek Mukhamedov,
  Natalia Bessmertnova, Mikhail Gobovich
  Dance Company: Bolshoi Ballet
  Composer: Aram Khatchaturian

Another cast for this ballet.

SPARTACUS (Bolshoi Ballet)

  1990, 120 min., color, video
  Distributor: Spectacor
  Producer: Michio Takemori of NHK with Simon Willock of RPTA/Primetime, Video/Film Bolshoi, and Masaki Ishijima for Japan Arts Corporation
  Director: Shuji Fujii
  Choreographer: Yuri Grigorovich
  Principal Dancers: Irek Mukhamedov,
  Alexsandr Vetrov, Lyudmilla Semenyaka, Maria Bilova
  Composer: Aram Khatchaturian
  Dance Company: Bolshoi Ballet

Another cast for this ballet.

SPECTER OF THE ROSE

  1946, 90 min., color, video
  Distributor: Kit Parker Films
  Producer/Distributor: Republic Pictures
  Director/Writer: Ben Hecht
  Choreographer: Tamara Geva
  Principal Dancers: Ivan Kirov, Viola Essen
  Composer: George Antheil

A feature film of the murder mystery genre involving a romance between a young ballerina and a principal dancer who slowly loses his mind.

SPRING TIME

  9:30 min., color, video
  Distributor: Coe Film Assoc.
  Producer: Thomas Howe Assoc.

The playful movements of children intercut with the controlled dance of adults.

SQUAREGAME VIDEO

  1976, 27 min., b&w, video
  Distributor/Producer: Cunningham Dance Foundation
  Director: Charles Atlas
  Choreographer: Merce Cunningham
  Dance Company: Merce Cunningham Dance Company
  Music: S. E. Wave/E. W. Song
  Composer: Takehisa Kosugi
  Costume/Set Designer: Mark Lancaster

Originally conceived for eventual adaptation to video, SQUAREGAME is a work of games involving duffel bags.

ST. FRANCIS

  1938, 39 min., b&w, film
  Distributor: Dance Film Archive
  Choreographer: Leonide Massine
  Principal Dancers: Frederick Franklin, Leonide Massine, Nina Theilade
  Dance Company: Ballet Russe de Monte Carlo
  Composer: Paul Hindemith

Record film of the ballet conjuring up the beatific visions of the saint.

STARS OF THE RUSSIAN BALLET

  1953, 80 min., b&w, film, video
  Distributors: Kultur #1199, Corinth
  Producer: Lenfilms
  Director: G. Rappaport
  Choreographers: Marius Petipa, Rostislav Zakharov, Vassily Vainonen
  Principal Dancers: Galina Ulanova, Natalia Dudinskaya, Konstantin Sergeyev, Maya Plisetskaya, Vakhtang Chabukiani, Yuri Zhdanov
  Dance Companies: Bolshoi Ballet, Kirov Opera Ballet
  Composers: Boris Asafiev, Peter Ilyich Tchaikovsky

Three ballet excerpts involving love, jealousy, and revolution from SWAN LAKE; THE FOUNTAIN OF BAKHCHISARAI, choreographed in 1934 by Rostislav Zakharov after Pushkin's poem; and THE FLAMES OF PARIS, choreographed by Vassily Vainonen in 1932 as a tribute to the French revolution of 1789. With English subtitles.

STEP BACK CINDY

  1990, 28:30 min., color, video
  Distributor/Producer: Appalshop/Headwaters TV
  Director: Anne Johnson

Interviews with traditional dancers and footage from performances in the mountains of southwest Virginia.

STEP STYLE

Series: Movement Style and Culture
1980, 30 min., color, film, video
Distributor: University of California Extension Media Center
Producer/Directors: Alan Lomax, Forrestine Paulay,
Irmgard Bartenieff

Series won CINE Golden Eagle Award, Dance Film Festival Awards Margaret Mead Film Festival Honorees, Modern Language Film Festival Award, Amerian Film Festival finalists. A cross-cultural look at how the leg and foot movements of dances relate to social structures, work habits, and sports.

STEP THIS WAY: LEARNING TO DANCE (3 videos)

50 min. each, color, video
Distributor: Instructional Videos
Principal Dancer: Cal De Pozo

The ballroom basics for the dances of the swing era, and in the Latin style.

STEPS OF LIGHT

50 min., color, video
Distributor: Coe Film Assoc.
Producer: Friends Film Prod.

Youngsters compete for entrance into the Monte Carlo Ballet School.

STICKS, LIGHT, FIRE

Series: Alive from Off Center
1986, 16 min., color, video
Distributor: Electronic Arts Intermix
Distributor/Director: Skip Blumberg
Producer: Melinda Ward for KTCA
Choreographer/Performer: Michael Moschen

The master juggler performs his feats under the direction of an artist who finds his special effects in natural accidents.

STICKS ON THE MOVE

1983, 4 min., color, film, video
Distributor/Producer/Director: Pooh Kaye, Picture Start
Producer/Director: Elisabeth Ross
Composer: John Kilgore

An experimental film made up of single shots of people chewing on, riding on, and twirling on sticks magically moving down the sidewalks of New York.

STILL LOOKING

1989, 28 min., color, film, video
Distributor: University of California Extension Media Center
Teacher: Janet Adler

Eight women strive to move closer to the self through a practice developed by Janet Adler called Authentic Movement, concerned with the relationship between moving and witnessing and one's capacity to remember and tell the truth.

STILT DANCERS OF LONG BOW VILLAGE

1980, 27 min., color, film
Distributor: Films Inc.
Producers/Directors: Richard Gordon, Carmen Hinton

Stilt dancing, banned during the Chinese Cultural Revolution, now revived, is the main feature of this record of a rural village pageant. Make-up and costume preparations included along with villagers' reminiscenses of the ban.

STILT DANCES AT KPEGBOUNI

and other films from the Dan Tribe of West Africa (11 films)

1968, 4-13 min. each, color, b&w, film
Distributor: Pennstate #EO1573, 1501, 1577, 1531, 1550, 1576, 1552, 1532, 1502, 1500, 1551
Producer: H. Himmelheber for Wissen

Mask processions, dances with poisonous snakes, a Gabun viper, imitations of slow-walking frogs, and many other dances from the Dan people of Ivory Coast, West Africa.

STOMP

1978, 3 min., b&w, video
Distributor/Dancer/Choreographer/Director: Eva Maier

An experimental video in which "a pair of mischievous feet dance up a smile," according to the creator.

THE STONE DANCES

1988, 9 min., b&w, video
Distributor/Producer/Director: Penny Ward
Choreographer/Dancer: Shelley Lee
Principal Dancers: Tim Conboy, Brenda Daniels
Composer: Mary Kelley

This video interpretation of a twenty-five minute, multi-media work explores the theme of life continuing after death. Stills of bog people are crossed with images of a dancer's face. A woman falls back repeatedly, shown in slow motion, followed by a duet, accompanied by the sounds of chanting mixed with stones dropping and reverberating.

THE STONE FLOWER

1947, 85 min., color, film
Distributor: Corinth
Director: Alexander Ptushko
Principal Dancers: Vladimir Druzhnikov,
Elena Derevschikova, Tamara Makarova
Composer: Lev Schwartz

A young stone-carver ventures into the realm of the goddess of the Copper Mountain. Once he realizes the futility of creating beautiful objects that would never be seen, he returns to his own world. A classic ballet in Russian with English subtitles.

THE STONE MEDUSA AND SPANISH SUITE

1969, 27 min., b&w, video
Distributor: Orion Dance Films
Choreographer/Directors: Richard Ellis,
Christine Duboulay
Dance Company: Illinois Ballet

Composer: Hector Villa-Lobos

THE STONE MEDUSA, inspired by the Greek myths of Pygmalion and Medusa, is set to a symphonic poem, UIRAPURA, by Hector Villa-Lobos. SPANISH SUITE is inspired by Spanish rhythms.

STOPPED IN HER TRACKS

1978, 6 min., color, film
Distributor/Dancer: Sally Gross
Editor: Susan Brockman

The choreographer crawls along a stairwell in a piece of perceptual distortion.

STORY

1964, 20 min., b&w, film, video
Distributor: Cunningham Dance Foundation
Producer: Finnish Broadcasting Company
Director: Hakki Seppala
Choreographer/Dancer: Merce Cunningham
Principal Dancers: William Davis, Viola Farber, Carolyn Brown, Deborah Hay, Barbara Lloyd, Sandra Neels, Steve Paxton, Albert Reid
Composer: Toshi Ichiyanagi
Set Designer: Robert Rauschenberg

A film of STORY performed in Helsinki's Ruotsalaisessa Teaterissa, which has a moving circular platform on the stage. The freedom granted the performers reflects what Cunningham calls his "appetite for movement. I don't see why it has to represent something," says the choreographer. "It is what it is."

THE STORY OF VERNON AND IRENE CASTLE

1939, 90 min., b&w, film, video
Distributor: Turner
Producer: George Haight for RKO
Director: H. C. Potter
Choreographer: Hermes Pan
Principal Dancers: Fred Astaire and Ginger Rogers
Writer: Richard Sherman

A film biography of the couple who triggered the popularity of ballroom dancing at the turn of the century and influenced the style of the day.

STRAVINSKY

1966, 52 min., b&w, film, video
Distributor: Carousel
Producer: CBS News
Composer: Igor Stravinsky
Principal Dancer: Maria Tallchief

The Russian composer Igor Stravinsky (1882-1971) talks about his early compositions and his creative struggles. Shows him collaborating with his longtime associate, choreographer George Balanchine, conducting RITES OF SPRING in Warsaw, and being honored by Pope Paul.

STREETCAR: A DANCE OF DESIRE

1969, 28 min., b&w, video
Distributor: Orion Enterprises

Producer: WTTW-TV Chicago
Choreographer: Gus Giordano
Director: Richard J. Carter
Composer: E. Berstein
Dance Company: Gus Giordano Dance Company

A jazz dance-drama inspired by Tennessee Williams' play focusing on the evening of Stanley's poker party. The play, which premiered in 1947 and was set in New Orleans, is the story of Blanche Dubois, the flirtatious woman whose chances for marriage are crushed by Stanley, her disapproving brother-in-law.

STRUT YOUR STUFF (2 videos)

1984, 30–45 min., color, video
Distributor: Hoctor Products
Producer: Dance Caravan
Teachers: Dance Caravan Faculty Members

Jazz routines set to such popular tunes as STEAM HEAT, SUDDEN IMPACT, IF MY FRIENDS COULD SEE ME NOW, SATURDAY NIGHT FEVER.

STUDIES IN NIGERIAN DANCE

1966, 22 min., b&w, film
Distributor: University of California at Los Angeles

Three Icough dances performed by women of Alide village, and five dances by the Iriwge men of the Jos Plateau in Nigeria, West Africa.

A STUDY IN CHOREOGRAPHY FOR THE CAMERA

1942, 4 min., b&w, film, video
Distributors: Grove Press Film, Mystic Fire Video
Producer/Director: Maya Deren
Principal Dancer: Talley Beatty

Director Maya Deren explores ways in which the camera and the resulting footage can be manipulated to create illusions or illuminations of alternative perspectives of space and time. She tries to extend motions, heighten emotions, and play with our associative minds.

STUTTGART BALLET: THE MIRACLE LIVES

1983, 60 min., color, video
Distributor: Kultur #1238
Producer/Directors: Bill Boggs and Richard Baker with Associated Productions
Choreographers: John Cranko, Uwe Scholz, Jiri Kylian, Maurice Bejart
Principal Dancers: Marcia Haydee, Richard Cragun
Composers: Domenico Scarlatti, Peter Ilyich Tchaikovsky, Johannes Brahms, Sergei Prokofiev, Jacques Offenbach, Gustav Mahler, Franz Liszt, Franz Schubert, Benjamin Britten, Francis Poulenc
Dance on Camera Festival, 1984

A tribute to choreographer John Cranko, who took over the Stuttgart Ballet company in 1961 and made it a world-class company, the film continues with the story of the company's survival after his death. Now led by Marcia Haydee, a founding member of the German company, the Stuttgart continues to thrive and perform Cranko's many ballets.

SUE'S LEG: REMEMBERING THE THIRTIES

Series: Dance in America
1976, 60 min., color, video
Distributors: PennState, Indiana University #RC0988
Producer: WNET/TV
Director: Merrill Brockway
Choreographer: Twyla Tharp
Dance Company: Twyla Tharp Dance Company
Composer: Fats Waller

Performance of Tharp's SUE'S LEG, plus a collage of movie and newsreel clips from the 1930s of dance marathons and balls as background for the choreographer's allusions. A nostalgic tribute to the spirit of another era.

SUE ZALIOK AND THE FUN DANCE KIDS

1988, 30 min., color, video
Distributor: Family Express Video
Teacher: Sue Zaliok

For very young children, an inventive teacher incorporates mime, dance, aerobics, rhythm, and basic coordination skills.

THE SUGAR PLUM FAIRY VARIATION FROM THE NUTCRACKER

1941, 2:30 min., color, film, video
Distributor/Producer: Dance Films Association (for members only)
Producer/Director: Dwight Godwin
Choreographer: Lev Ivanov
Dancer: Alicia Markova
Composer: Peter Ilyich Tchaikovsky

Outdoor performance at Jacob's Pillow in Lee, Massachusetts.

SUITE FANTAISISTE

1982, 20 min., color, video
Distributor/Producer/Directors: Celia Ipiotis and Jeff Bush for ARC Videodance
Choreographer/Dancer: Catherine Turocy
Narrator: Robert Einenkel

Eighteenth-century life seen through the dance, poetry, and the fan language of the time: A man advises his son on the subject of women, followed by the performance of the FOLLIES D'ESPAGNE and a juggling dance in the *commedia dell'arte* style.

SUMMER DANCES

1985, 25 min., color, video
Distributor: WGBH-TV
Producer: Susan Dowling
Directors: Dick Heller, Fred Baryzk, David Atwood, Charles Atlas
Choreographer/Dancers: Marta Renzi, Rudy Perez, Dan Wagoner, Douglas Dunn, Karole Armitage
Composers: Bruce Springsteen and The E Street Band, Henry Fiol, White Oak Mountain Boys

Five dances conceived for the camera shot outdoors: YOU LITTLE WILD HEART, a hymn to adolescent rebellion (1981, Renzi/Heller); DISTRICT I, a downtown frolic (1978, Perez/Baryzk); GEORGE'S HOUSE, a country pastime (1978, Wagoner/Atwood); SECRET OF THE WATERFALL, a tilted reality on Martha's Vineyard (1983, Dunn/Atlas), and FROM AN ISLAND SUMMER at Coney Island's park, ferris wheels and all (1984, Armitage/Atlas).

SUNNYSIDE OF LIFE

1985, 58 min., color, film, video
Distributor/Producer: Appalshop
Directors: Scott Faulkner, Anthony Slone, Jack Wright
Composers: Home Folks, Red Clay Ramblers, John McCutcheon, Ramona Jones, Griffin Family, and Charlie Osborne

History of the family of A. P. and Sara Carter, the country music pioneers who began recording the songs of the mountain people of southwest Virginia in 1920s, and footage of the performances in The Carter Family Fold, an old-time music hall founded in 1975 in Hiltons, Virginia.

SUPREME SWING BY JERRY CRIM (10 videos)

color, video
Distributor: Supreme Swing/Jerry Crim
Producer/Teacher: Jerry Crim

Country Western social dance for couples including the Dallas Push, Houston Whip, West Coast Swing, and St. Louis Shag.

SWAN LAKE (American Ballet Theatre)

1980, 122 min., color, video
Distributors: Paramount, Homevision #SWA05
Choreographers: Marius Petipa, Lev Ivanov
Principal Dancers: Natalia Makarova, Ivan Nagy
Composer: Peter Ilyich Tchaikovsky
Dance Company: American Ballet Theatre

In this four-act, classic ballet which premiered in 1877 at the Bolshoi Theatre, Prince Siegfried celebrates his twenty-first birthday by going hunting. Alone by a lakeside, he sees a swan turn into an enchanted princess who can be saved only by true love. He promises this, but is tricked by a magician who disguises his own daughter as the swan-maiden. In despair, Siegfried and the swan maiden leap to their death.

SWAN LAKE (Bolshoi Ballet)

1957, 81 min., color, film, video
Distributors: Corinth (film), Kultur #1197
Director: Z. Tulubyeva
Choreographers: Marius Petipa, Lev Ivanov
Principal Dancers: Maya Plisetskaya, Nicolai Fadeyechev
Composer: Peter Ilyich Tchaikovsky
Dance Company: Bolshoi Ballet

Filmed live at the Bolshoi Theatre in Moscow with one of Russia's legendary ballerinas in her prime.

SWAN LAKE (Bolshoi Ballet)

1989, 81 min., color, video
Distributor: Spectacor
Producers: Primetime Entertainment, NHK, Japan Arts Corporation, Video/Film Bolshoi
Choreographers: Marius Petipa, Lev Ivanov, Yuri Grigorovich

Principal Dancers: Alla Mikhalchenko, Yuri Vasyuchenko
Composer: Peter Ilyich Tchaikovsky

Recorded live in performance at the Bolshoi Theatre in Moscow.

SWAN LAKE (Kirov Ballet)

 1968, 82 min., color, film, video
 Distributor: Facets SO2756
 Choreographers: Marius Petipa, Lev Ivanov
 Principal Dancers: Yelena Yevteyeva, John Markovsky, Valery Panov
 Dance Company: Kirov Ballet
 Composer: Peter Ilyich Tchaikovsky

Full-length rendition of the classic.

SWAN LAKE (London Festival Ballet)

 1988, 116 min., color, video
 Distributor: Home Vision SWA06
 Producer: RM Arts
 Choreographers: Marius Petipa, Natalia Makarova
 Principal Dancers: Evelyn Hart, Peter Schaufuss
 Dance Company: London Festival Ballet
 Composer: Peter Ilyich Tchaikovsky
 Dance on Camera Festival, 1991 Best of Festival and Gold Awards in performance category

Full-length classic adapted by prima ballerina Natalia Makarova with innovative sets in an atmosphere of magic and mystery.

SWAN LAKE (Royal Ballet)

 1986, 128 min., color, video
 Distributors: HBO #3257, Pioneer (Laserdisk)
 Producer: Francis Coleman for National Video Corporation
 Director: John Michael Phillips
 Choreographers: Lev Ivanov, Marius Petipa, with additions from Rudolf Nureyev and Frederick Ashton
 Principal Dancers: Natalia Makarova, Anthony Dowell
 Dance Company: The Royal Ballet
 Composer: Peter Ilyich Tchaikovsky
 Set Designer: Leslie Hurry

Live from Covent Garden.

SWAYZE DANCING

 1988, 60 min., color, video
 Distributor: Tapeworm
 Producer: Mark Lemkin
 Principal Dancers: Patrick, Patsy, Lisa, and Bambi Swayze
 Music: "She's Like The Wind," "In The Mood," "I've Had The Time of My Life"

The star of DIRTY DANCING brings in his first teacher, his mother, along with his wife and sister as demonstrators of Latin, swing, and ballroom.

SWEAT AND TERPSICHORE

 1988, 10 min., color, video
 Distributor/Producer/Director/Editor: Laurie Freedman
 Principal Dancer: Larry Rhodes
 Composer: Sergio Cervetti
 Dance on Camera, Honorable Mention

Visual poem about dancers preparing for class.

SWEDEN: FIRE AND ICE

 1964, 54 min., b&w, film
 Distributor: University of Illinois #83099
 Producer: Newmark Films
 Choreographer: Birgit Cullberg
 Principal Dancers: Wiweka Ljung, Ture Rangstrom, Conny Borg, Catharina Ericsson
 Dance Company: Swedish Royal Ballet
 Composer: Ture Rangstrom
 Set Designer: Sven Erixson

A tour of the Drottingham Court Theatre, with readings by actor Max von Sydow and performance of MISS JULIE, based on the play by August Strindberg.

SWORD DANCE AT UBERLINGEN

 1962, 29 min., color, video
 Distributor: Pennstate #EOO536
 Producers: J. Kunzig, K. Wager for Wissen

In Southern Baden, in central Europe, a ceremony begins with breakfast, followed by a march to the divine service and then onto the town square. After the mayor has given his approval, the sword dance is performed, and followed by a maiden's dance.

SWORD TECHNIQUES (2 videos)

 1987–1988, 120 min. each, color, video
 Distributor/Producer/Choreographer/Dancer: Chandra of Damascus

Two instructional tapes, beginning and advanced, on the ways of using the sword in Middle Eastern dance.

LA SYLPHIDE (Paris Opera Ballet)

 1971, 81 min., color, video
 Distributors: Kultur #1126, Pioneer (laserdisk)
 Choreographer: Pierre Lacotte
 Principal Dancers: Michel Denard, Ghislaine Thesmar
 Dance Company: Paris Opera Ballet Company
 Composer: Jean Schneitzhoeffer
 1982 Video Review VIRA Award

Pierre Lacotte's reconstruction of Filippo Taglioni's ballet first performed in Paris in 1832, based on Adolphe Nourrit's book on sylphs, with the original costume and set designs by Eugene Lami and P. L. Ciceri. The lead, James, about to be married, chases after an airy spirit, traditionally known only to the chaste of heart, only to destroy her with a silk scarf, poisoned by a vengeful friend.

LES SYLPHIDES (Bolshoi Ballet)

 1987, 34 min., color, video
 Distributor: V.I.E.W. Video
 Producer: Soviet Film & TV
 Choreographers: Yuri Grigorovich, Michel Fokine
 Principal Dancers: Natalia Bessmertnova, Galina Kozlova, Irina Kholina, Alexandre Beogatyriov
 Dance Company: Bolshoi Ballet
 Composer: Frederic Chopin

Inspired by Isadora Duncan's visit to Russia, Michel Fokine created this one-act ballet for the Bolshoi Ballet. One of the first abstract, plotless works in the Russian repertoire, LES SYLPHIDES premiered in 1909 with Anna Pavlova and Vaslav Nijinsky in the leading roles.

LES SYLPHIDES (CHOPINIANA)

> 1952, 4:30 min., b&w, film, video
> Distributor: Corinth
> Producer: Lenfilm Studios
> Choreographer: Michel Fokine
> Principal Dancers: Galina Ulanova, Vladimir Preobrajensky
> Composer: Frederic Chopin

A pas de deux from the ballet LES SYLPHIDES.

SYLVIE GUILLEM AT WORK

> 1988, 53 min., color, video
> Distributor: Home Vision #SYL02
> Producers: RM Associates and La Sept
> Director: Andre S. Labarthe
> Choreographers: Marius Petipa, William Forsythe
> Principal Dancer: Sylvie Guillem
> Composers: Richard Strauss, Alexander Glazunov,
> Tom Willems
> Dance on Camera Festival, 1991 Gold Award

Portrait of the young phenomenon, the etoile of the Paris Opera who got her start as a gymnast, with excerpts from RAYMONDA, FOUR LAST SONGS, IN THE MIDDLE, SOMEWHAT ELEVATED.

SYVILLA: THEY DANCE TO HER DRUM

> 1979, 25 min., b&w, film
> Distributor: Women Make Movies
> Producer/Director/Narrator: Ayoka Chenzira
> Choreographer/Dancer: Syvilla Fort
> Cinematographer: Mitchell Heicklen
> Principal Dancer: Dyane Harvey

Expresses the life of Syvilla Fort, a black concert dancer who became a role model to a generation of African American dancers. Shot six months prior to her death in 1975, the film reflects the beauty of her choreography with two pieces reconstructed by Pearl Reynolds and Eugene Little and performed by Dyane Harvey, the virtuosity of her dancing, and her gifts as a teacher.

SYMPHONIE FANTASTIQUE

> 1948, 51 min., b&w, film
> Distributor: Dance Film Archive
> Choreographer: Leonide Massine
> Principal Dancers: Niels Bjorn Larsen, Stanley Williams,
> Erik Bruhn, Mona Vangsaa
> Dance Company: Royal Danish Ballet
> Composers: Hector Berlioz

A rehearsal record of the ballet based on the episodes of the life of an artist. The sound was synchronized under the direction of Niels Bjorn Larsen.

SYMPHONY IN D WORKSHOP

> 1987, 55 min., color, video
> Distributor: Home Vision SYM01

> Producer: Rm Arts
> Choreographer: Jiri Kylian
> Directors: Jack Bond, Hans Hulscher
> Dance Company: Nederlands Dans Theatre
> Composer: Franz Josef Haydn
> Dance on Camera Festival, 1987 Silver Award

Jiri Kylian rehearses one of his ballets with students of the Royal Ballet School in London, and talks about his exile from Czechoslovakia and his life as a dancer and choreographer.

SYNCOPATED MELODIES

> 1920s, 13 min., b&w, film
> Distributor: Dance Film Archive
> Principal Dancer: W. H. Berry

The high life in 1920s Britain, with glimpses of the Charleston, the ballroom craze of the day.

SYNCOPATIONS

> 1988, 50 min., color, film
> Distributor/Producer/Director/Dancer: Kathy Rose
> Composer: Charles Roth
> Costume Designer: Mary Bright

In its three-dimensional presentation, the animator-turned-filmmaker/choreographer creates a holograph effect by seeming to dance in a circle of women projected on and behind her.

TAL FARLOW

> 1981, 1:30 min., b&w, film
> Distributor: Museum of Modern Art
> Producer/Directors: Len Lye, Steven Jones
> Composer: Tal Farlow

Black scratch designs sway to a jazz guitar solo.

TALES OF BEATRIX POTTER

> 1971, 86 min., color, video
> Distributors: HBO, Home Vision BEA01
> Producers: Richard Goodwin, John Brabourne for EMI
> Director: Reginald Mills
> Choreographer: Frederick Ashton
> Cinematographer: Austin Dempster
> Principal Dancers: Wayne Sleep, Frederick Ashton,
> Alexander Grant, Lesley Collier
> Dance Company: Royal Ballet
> Composer: John Lanchbery
> Set Designer: Christine Edzard
> Masks: Rotislav Doboujinsky

Two town mice, togged up in picnic gear, hold up their tails like trailing ball-gowns in this ballet adaptation of these children's stories. Granting human traits to various dancing animal characters, mice brew tea, frogs go fishing, and pigs wear smocks.

THE TALES OF HOFFMANN

> 1952, 118 min., color, film
> Distributors: Kit Parker Films, Ivy Films
> Producer/Directors: Michael Powell, Emeric Pressburger
> for London Films
> Choreographer: Frederick Ashton

Principal Dancers: Moira Shearer, Ludmilla Tcherina,
Robert Helpmann, Leonide Massine
Set/Costume Designer: Hein Heckroth
Composer: Jacques Offenbach

Inspired by the 1881 tales, a poet recalls his three loves –
Olympia, Giulietta, and Antonia – over wine in a Nuremberg
tavern, while still contemplating his ideal woman.

TALES OF THE VIENNA WOODS

1949, 9 min., b&w, film
Distributor: University of Illinois
Dance Company: Salzburg Festival Ballet
Composer: Johann Strauss

Salzburg Festival Ballet performs waltzes played by the Vienna
Philharmonic Orchestra.

TALKING FEET

1988, 90 min., color, film, video
Distributor/Producer: Flower Films
Director: Les Blank
Principal Dancer: Mike Seeger

Solo folk dances of the Appalachian Mountains.

TALL ARCHES III

1973, 7:15 min., color, film
Distributor: Film-maker's Coop
Producer/Distributor/Director: Doris Chase
Dance Company: Mary Staton Dance Ensemble
Composer: George Kleinsinger

Three dance in and around three mobile arches of varying
sizes. Through the use of an optical printer, Chase creates over-
lapping color silhouettes.

TANGO

1987, 57 min., color, video
Distributor: V.I.E.W.
Producer: Television Suisse Romand
Director: Sandro Briner
Choreographer: Oscar Araiz
Dance Company: Geneva Grand Theatre Ballet
Composer: Atilio Stompone

Argentine choreographer Oscar Araiz's salute to his country
dance, the tango, integrating the traditional steps with ballet for
a series of vignettes played by twenty-eight dancers. The war of
the sexes, the struggles of the family, and the indulgence of the
lovelorn, the tango lyrics address them all.

TANGO

1985, 6 min., color, video
Distributor: Electronic Arts Intermix
Producer/Director: James Byrne
Choreographer: Linda Shapiro
Dance Company: New Dance Ensemble
Composer: Jacob Gade

Modern dance cut to tango rhythm, shot by a director who
moves among the dancers with the camera seemingly attached
to his body.

TANGO! A MASTER CLASS WITH THE DINZELS

1986, 47 min., color, video
Distributor: Jim Forest
Producer: Ismael Alba for American Show Brokers
Director/Producers: Juan Jose Campanella,
Juan Pablo Domenech
Principal Dancers: Gloria and Rodolfo Dinzel

The basics of the Argentinian Tango with performance at the
beginning and end by members of TANGO ARGENTINO, the
smash hit revue from Argentina, directed by Claudio Segovia
and Hector Orezzoli, which played on Broadway.

TANGO BAR

1989, color, film, video
Distributor: Warner Home Video
Composers: Carlos Gardel, Astor Piazzolla

Tryst between singers in a Buenos Aires cafe interwoven
around scenes of a couple dancing the tango with flashbacks to
the romance of another era.

TANGO TANGLES

1914, 7-9 min., b&w, film
Distributor: Ivy Films
Director: Mack Sennett
Principals: Charlie Chaplin, Ford Sterling, Fatty Arbuckle,
Chester Conklin

Dance-hall Johnny fights for the hand of the hatcheck girl
despite the interference of the bandleader in this bow to the
rage of the day, the tango.

TANGO TANGO

Series: Alive from Off Center
1989, 4:50 min., color, video
Distributors: Antenna, APA
Producer: Michel Ouellette for Agent Orange
Director: Francois Girard
Choreographer/Dancer: Lila Greene
Principal Dancers: Martha Moore, Caesar Stroscio
Composers: Bill Vorn, Gaetan Gravel

A woman meets her double, with whom she achieves a sort of
spiritual union, as an invisible angel hovers over them.

TANGOS, THE EXILE OF GARDEL

1985, 125 min., color, film
Distributor: New Yorker Films
Director: Fernando E. Solanas
Principals: Marie Laforet, Philippe Leotard,
Miguel Angel Sola, Marina Vlady
Composers: Astor Piazzola, Carlos Gardel

Argentinians bemoaning their political exile in Paris create a
tragicomedy with music and dance in many locations, with
black-and-white footage evocative of tango singer Carlos
Gardel, who died in 1935.

TANKO BUSHI: A JAPANESE FOLK DANCE

1978, 6 min., color, film
Distributor/Producer: Tempo Films

Directors: Annette Macdonald, Mary Joyce

The Japanese coal-mining dance filmed in the Bay area of California.

TAP

1980s, 30 min., color, video
Distributor: Hoctor Products
Producer: Studio Music Corp.
Teachers: Danny and Jamie Hoctor

Tap routines broken down and then danced up-to-tempo.

THE TAP DANCE KID

1979, 33- and 49-min. versions, color, film, video
Distributor: Coronet/MTI Df-lee484
Producer: Learning Council of America
Principal Dancers: Charles Honi Coles, James Pelham

An eight-year-old tap dances through life, dreaming of performing on Broadway. Encouraged and tutored by his sister and uncle, a professional dancer, but discouraged by his father, the boy finds enough drive to achieve his goal. Based on a story "Nobody's Family Is Going to Change" by Louise Fitzhugh.

TAP DANCING FOR BEGINNERS

1980s, 60 min., color, video
Distributor: Kultur #1135
Producer: Marc Weinstein
Teachers: Honi Coles, Henry Le Tang

Tap tips from Honi Coles, a master tap dancer, and Henry Le Tang, the choreographer for SOPHISTICATED LADIES and teacher of such students as Eleanor Powell.

TAPDANCIN'

1980, 58 min., color, film, video
Distributor/Producer/Director: Christian Blackwood
Principal Dancers: Bill Bojangles Robinson, Four Step Brothers, Honi Coles, Cholly Atkins, Nicholas Brothers, The Hoofers, Fred Strickler, Chuck Green, Lon Chaney, Buster Brown
Dance Companies: Jazz Tap Ensemble, The Copasetics, Third Generation Step
Chicago Int'l Dance Film Festival, Sydney Film Festival, New Directors/New Films

Documentary with performances and interviews.

TAPPERCIZE

1990, 60 min., color, video
Distributor: Tappercize Prod.
Principal Dancer: Ken Prescott
Tap rhythms combined with low-impact aerobics. Begins with a warm-up and concludes with a series of routines demonstrated by the Broadway star of such shows as 42nd STREET, PAL JOEY, GEORGE M, and ANYTHING GOES.

TARANTELLA

1970s, 3 min., color, film
Distributor: Grove Press Film

Animated photographs of feet and shoes of various ages and sizes doing the Tarantella, accompanied by shouting voices.

LOS TARANTOS

1963, 81 min., color, video
Distributor: Swank
Producer: Orion
Director: Rovira-Beleta
Principal Dancer: Carmen Amaya

Love between the children of two warring gypsy families living on the outskirts of Barcelona, dancing flamenco by the sea, in the bars, and the streets. One of the few circulating films starring one of the flamenco legends, Carmen Amaya.

A TASTE OF CARAVAN

1980s, 30 min., color, video
Distributor: Hoctor Products
Producer: Music Studio Corp.
Principal Dancers: Danny Hoctor and Dance Caravan Faculty

Routines for social and disco dance.

TCHAIKOVSKY AND THE RUSSIANS

Series: Ballet for All
1972, 27 min., b&w, film
Director: Nicholas Ferguson
Choreographers: Marius Petipa, Lev Ivanov
Principal Dancers: Doreen Wells, David Wall, Brenda Last, Alan Hooper
Dance Company: Bolshoi Ballet
Composer: Peter Ilyich Tchaikovsky
Narrator: David Blair

While discussing composer Peter Ilyich Tchaikovsky, the educational program compares two Russian classical choreographers, Marius Petipa and Lev Ivanov, with a focus on Ivanov's SWAN LAKE. Excerpts also from SLEEPING BEAUTY pas de deux and the coda of the BLUEBIRD pas de deux.

TEACH ME TO DANCE

1978, 28 min., color, film
Distributor: Films Inc. #101-9084
Producer: Vladimir Valenta
Director: Anne Wheeler
Cinematographer: David De Volpi

Two girls, one English and the other Ukrainian, are brought together because of a mutual love of dance, but their friendship is torn apart by their community's ethnic prejudices. Set in Alberta, Canada, in 1919.

TEACHING BEGINNING DANCE IMPROVISATION

1989, 120 min., color, video
Distributor/Producer/Dance Teacher: Ririe-Woodbury Co.
Director: Arthur Pembleton

Instructional video on the art of improvisation.

TEAK ROOM (AUTOBIOGRAPHY OF A DANCER)

1982, 70 min., color, video

Distributor/Dancer/Choreographer: Margaret Beals
Director: Tony Tanner
Costume Designer: Sally Ann Parsons
Composer: Gwendolyn Watson

Solo dance play in the form of an extended monologue, pantomime and dance sequences, with improvisations with the
audience in the final section. Tells how the drive to dance rose
out of her unusual childhood and created her adult lifestyle.

TEALIA

1977, 10 min., color, film, video
Distributor: Phoenix Films
Producer: Ellen Jane Kutten
Director: George Paul Csicsery, Gordon Mueller
Choreographer: John McFall
Principal Dancers: Betty Erickson, Vane Vest
Cinematographer: Ned Burgess
Dance Company: San Francisco Ballet Company
Composer: Gustav Holst
Music: The Planets
Costume Designer: Victoria Gyorfi
Dance on Camera Festival, 1978 Merit Award

Two dancers suspended in space simulate a coral-colored sea
anemone with multiple arms.

TED SHAWN AND HIS MEN DANCERS

1985, 25 min., b&w, video
Distributor: Indiana University RB1247-1249
Producer: Jacob's Pillow Dance Festival
Choreographer: Ted Shawn
Composers: Johann Sebastian Bach, Jess Meeker

Reconstructions of Ted Shawn's choreography created for his
all-male troupe 1933–1940 in three pieces: THE DOME, a
work in eight movements; KINETIC MOLPAI, expressing hu-
manity's longings in strife, love, the sacred and poetic; LABOR
SYMPHONY, a celebration of working in agriculture
and industry.

TENTACLE

1983, 10 min., b&w, video
Distributor: ARC Videodance
Directors: Jeff Bush, Celia Ipiotis
Choreographer/Dancers: Eiko & Koma

A duet conceived for close-up recording. Threads wrapping
the dancers' bodies appear to be veins binding and trapping
them in combat/symbiosis.

TEXAS STYLE POLKA DANCIN'

1988, 45 min., color, video
Distributor: Instructional Video

Lessons on the basic steps, rhythm, patterns, turns, holds, and
the lariat. Also includes instructions on the schottisch.

THAILAND DANCES (6 films)

1965, 6-16 min. each, color, b&w, film
Distributor: Pennstate
Producer: Wissen

Six dances of the Akha girls and the Akha boys of the Chieng

Rai Province, plus a solo with a sword and scabbard. Two films
were made of the dance on the New Year in Black Lahu and
Lisu from the Tak Province. Finally, an acrobatic mouth-organ
player from Miao, Tak Province, shows his talents.

THANATOPSIS

1962, 5 min., b&w, film
Distributor: Grove Press Film
Producer/Director: Ed Emshwiller
Principal Dancer: Becky Arnold

Time exposures of a dance set against the image of a face to the
accompaniment of heartbeats and rip saws.

THAT MEANS I WANT TO GO HOME

1989, 27:23 min., color, video
Distributor: Electronic Arts Intermix
Choreographer: Melanie Lien
Director: James Byrne
Dance Company: CoDanceco

Multilayered montage of a homesick dance of alienation and
loss of control.

THAT'S DANCING

1985, 120 min., color, film, video
Distributors: MGM #0613, Films Inc.
Producer/Director: Jack Haley, Jr.
Principal Dancers: Gene Kelly, Liza Minnelli, Sammy Davis, Jr.

Over fifty dancers appear in this compendium of the best of
dance in Hollywood films.

THAT'S ENTERTAINMENT (I & II)

1974–1976, 133 min., color, video, laserdisk
Distributor/Producer: MGM/UA 0007, MGM 0075, Films Inc.
Directors: Jack Haley, Jr., and Gene Kelly
Principal Dancers: Fred Astaire, Gene Kelly, Liza Minnelli,
Debbie Reynolds, Donald O'Connor

Showstoppers from over 100 musicals, comedies, and dramas
woven together with new footage of Fred Astaire and
Gene Kelly dancing together for the first time in thirty years.

THEATRE MEETS RITUAL

1976, 21:30 min., color, film
Distributor: Film-maker's Coop
Principal Dancer: Eugenia Barba
Dance Company: Odin Teatret

Fragments of BOOK OF DANCES and COME! AND THE DAY
WILL BE OURS by this European cooperative ensemble touring through Venezuela, along with dances by the Yanomami,
an Indian tribe of the Upper Orinoco, and the shaman's
interpretation of the legend about the tortoise that killed
the jaguar.

THEY ARE THEIR OWN GIFTS

1979, 52 min., color, film, video
Distributor: New Day Films
Producers: Lucille Rhodes, Margaret Murphy
Choreographer: Anna Sokolow

Portraits of Muriel Rukeyser, poet; Alice Neel, painter; and

Anna Sokolow, choreographer. Available as a trilogy or individually.

30 SECOND SPOTS

1982-1984, 30 min., color, video
Distributor: Electronic Arts Intermix
Producer/Director: Joan Logue
Principal Dancers: Bill T. Jones, Arnie Zane

Created in New York, Paris, and San Francisco, these commercials for individual artists capture the distinctive personalities with the flair of a caricaturist.

THIS IS "THE PLACE"

1970s, 35 min., color, film
Distributor: University of Illnois
Producer/Director: Peter Selby

Shows classes at the London School of Contemporary Dance and explains the pedagogical approach of the school, as modeled after Martha Graham.

3 DANCES 1964

1964, 17 min., b&w, film
Distributor/Producer/Director/Choreographer:
Gene Friedman
Dancers: Judith Dunn, Alex Hay, Debby Hay, Steve Paxton

Three modern dances: PUBLIC, photographed at the Museum of Modern Art; PARTY, photographed at Judson Church, New York City; and a solo by Judith Dunn, photographed in her studio.

THREE SOLOS

1978, 27 min., color, video
Distributor: Museum of Modern Art
Producer/Director: Doris Chase
Choreographer/Dancers: Kei Takei, Johnathan Hollander, Sara Rudner
Composers: Joan Labarbara, George Kleinsinger, Eric Eigen, Mike Mahaffey, William Bolcomb

DANCE FOUR with Kei Takei, DANCE TEN with Johnathan Hollander, and VARIATION with Sara Rudner.

THE THREE WORLDS OF BALI

Series: Odyssey
1981, 58 min., color, video
Distributor: Cornell Cooperative
Producer: PBS
Director: Ira Abrams

On the Indonesian island of Bali, dance is one means of maintaining a balance between the demons thought to dwell in the watery underworld, and the gods in the upper world. Once a century, the entire Balinese population mobilizes for the Eka Dasa Rudra ceremony to transform eleven demons into beneficent spirits (Southeast Asia Collection).

TIBETAN FOLK DANCE

1967, 4 min., color, film
Distributor: Pennstate #EO1409
Producer: Wissen

Bamboo flute and long-necked lute accompany the Kon-gZhas-mDsad-Pa'i-Riabs-Phren dance of East Tibet.

TIBETAN FOLK DANCE (4 films)

1966-1967, 4-5 min. each, color, b&w, film
Distributor: Pennstate #EO1412, 1411, 1410, 1709
Producer: Wissen

"dBusgTsan-gZhas" -"mDo-stod" - "mDo-sMad" dances accompanied by a long-necked lute; "gSer-Gyi' Khor-Lo" song and dance accompanied by bamboo flute and lute; "KhamsgSum-dBan-'Dus-gZhas-Tshig" and " gYag-' Krab-Pa" animal dance and dancing lute player.

THE TIGER AND THE BRIDE

1989, 29 min., color, film, video
Distributor/Producer/Choreographer/Dancer:
Melanie Stewart
Director: Steve Goodwin
Principal Dancers: Mark Chatman-Royce, Debi Glennon, Renee Gomila, Sean Gallagher
Composer: Michael A. Becker

Documentary of narrative choreography based on a story by Angela Carter in her collection of erotic tales.

A TIME TO DANCE

Series: A Time to Dance
1960, 29 min., b&w, film, video
Distributor: Indiana University
Producer: WGBH-TV Boston
Choreographer: Marius Petipa
Principal Dancers: Melissa Hayden, Jacques D'Amboise, Daniel Nagrin
Dance Company: Ximenez-Vargas Ballet Espagnol
Composer: Peter Ilyich Tchaikovsky

Martha Myers introduces the series with paintings, sculpture, and film clips of ethnic dance around the world. Examples given of a seventeeth-century French court dance, a pas de deux performed by New York City Ballet principals from THE NUTCRACKER, a Spanish dance by one of the leading flamenco troupes of the day and a solo satire from modern dancer Daniel Nagrin.

TO DANCE

1988, 30 min., color, video
Distributor/Producer: University of Southern Florida
Director/Teacher: Gretchen Warren

Young men enrolled as dance majors explore their motivation to be dancers, the difficulties they encounter, and their personal triumphs. Interviews interspersed with technique classes, rehearsals, and performances. Conceived by a university professor who was ballet mistress of American Ballet Theatre II.

TO DANCE FOR GOLD

1982, 98 min., color, video
Distributor: National Video Corporation Arts International
Producer: Joseph Wishy
Director: Lou Volpicelli

Recording the excitement and artistry of the Second International Ballet Competition in Jackson, Mississippi, in which 78 young dancers from 21 countries participated. Analyzes dance movements and portrays some of the dancers at the competition.

TO DANCERS

1988, 30 min., color, film, video
Distributor/Producer/Director: Bridget Murnane for BAM
Choreographer: Bella Lewitsky
Choreographer/Dancers: Susan Rose, Louise Burns, Fred Strickler
Dancer: Iris Pell
Composers: Benjamin Britten, Megan Roberts

Four solos, three modern pieces filmed on location and in a studio, and one tap piece set to the SIMPLE SYMPHONY, OP 4 by Britten, filmed in a deserted cafe.

TO MOVE IN BEAUTY: THE KABUKI TRADITION

1977, 28 min., color, film
Distributor: Japan Foundation
Producer: Broadcast Programming Center of Japan

Documents the life of a group of young apprentices at the National Theatre in Tokyo, from their daily classes in recitation, music, and dance to their first professional appearance.

TOMMY SUTTON TEACHES TAP (3 videos)

1980s, 90 min. each, color, video
Distributor/Producer/Dancer: Tommy Sutton
Principal Dancer: Stephanie Quinn

A visual aid to the three-volume manual TAP ALONG WITH TOMMY, demonstrating the basics and routines, with progressive levels of difficulty.

TONDO: A ROUND ABOUT A ROUND

1971, 10 min., color, film
Distributor: University of Michigan
Producer: King Screen Productions
Director: Skeets Mcgrew
Dance Teacher: Mary Staton
Sculptor: Doris Chase
Composer: Glen White
Dance Company: Mary Staton Dance School

Beginning and ending with children playing with circular sculpture, the film centers on the patterns formed by dancers moving around a hollow cylinder. The lighting, sound, and cinematic effects adapt to the dancers shifting against a background of brilliant colors.

TONIGHT WE SING

1953, 109 min., color, film
Distributor: Films Inc.
Director: Mitchell Leisen
Choreographers: David Lichine, Michel Fokine, Marius Petipa
Principal Dancer: Tamara Toumanova
Composers: Leon Minkus, Camille Saint-Saens

Anne Bancroft, Isaac Stern, and Roberta Peters all play a part in this feature on the life of impresario Sol Hurok, with a series of production numbers. Tamara Toumanova plays the role of the Russian balleria Anna Pavlova, as she appears in A DYING SWAN, a variation from DON QUIXOTE, a short selection from DRAGONFLY, and a dance choreographed by David Lichine.

TORCHES OF TODAIJI

40 min., color, film
Distributor: Japan Foundation
Producer: NHK Production Services
Principal Dancer: Onoe Shoroku

In the Todaiji temple in Nara and the religious festival of Shunie, which first inspired the development of Japanese performing arts, a famed Kabuki actor, Onoe Shoruoku, creates a new Kabuki dance-drama.

TORSE

1978, 55 min., color, film, video
Distributor: Cunningham Dance Foundation
Producers: New York Public Library and Museum of The Performing Arts at Lincoln Center
Director: Charles Atlas
Choreographer: Merce Cunningham
Composer: Maryanne Amacher
Costume Designer: Mark Lancaster

Two synchronous hour-long films to be projected simultaneously on adjacent screens. Provides a record of the dance and an approximation of the spectator's experience. The choreographer was inspired by the I CHING, THE BOOK OF CHANGES, and therefore any semblance of continuity was achieved unwittingly.

TORVILL AND DEAN: PATH TO PERFECTION

1984, 52 min., color, video
Distributor: University of Illinois
Choreographer/Dancers: Jayne Torvill, Christopher Dean
Composer: Maurice Ravel

Eight performances by the Olympic champion ice dancers, including BOLERO.

TOTEM

1963, 16 min., color, film
Distributors: Canyon, Film-makers Coop
Choreographer: Alwin Nikolais
Director: Ed Emswhiller
Principal Dancers: Murray Louis, Gladys Bailin
Dance Company: Alwin Nikolais Dance Company
Festival of Two Worlds, Spoleto, Italy, 1966

Through the experimental use of mirrors, cameras and dance, the collaborators present primordial mysteries in an exploration of optics, electronics and space.

TOUR EN L'AIR

1974, 49:30 min., color, film, video
Distributor: National Film Board
Producer: George Pearson for National Film Board of Canada
Producer/Director: Grant Munro
Choreographer: Asaf Messerer, David Holmes

Principal Dancers: Anna-Marie and David Holmes,
Jorge Lefebvre, Alicia Alonso, Azari Plisetski
Cinematographer: Pierre Letarte
Composer: Tommaso Albinoni
Narrator: Doulas Rain

Ballet dancers David and Anna-Marie Holmes rehearse, perform an excerpt from BALLET ADAGIO, and take classes in
Berlin, London, Lisbon, Havana, Washington and Montreal. In
East Berlin, they participate in an international dance festival
as the only Canadians. In Cuba, they share the stage with
Alicia Alonso and Azari Plisetski. In London, they entertain
friends in their apartment.

TOURNANTS

1987, 6 min., color, film, video
Distributor/Producer/Director: Bridget Murnane

A personal history of concert dance, through the animated use
of dance stills taken over the last century.

TRADITIONAL WHITSUN RITES OF THE KALUSHARS (3 films)

1969, 26-23 min., b&w, film
Distributor: Pennstate #EO1654, 1655, 1656
Producer: Wissen

Rumanian death game with a dance match between two
groups around a flagpole. Set in Priseaca, southeast Europe.

Trailblazers of Modern Dance
*"Soaring," danced by the Joyce Trisler Danscompany. Photo courtesy
Indiana University.*

TRAILBLAZERS OF MODERN DANCE

Series: Dance in America
1977, 60 min., color, film, video
Distributor: Indiana University
Producer: Merrill Brockway, Judy Kinberg for WNET/13
Director: Emile Ardolino
Choreographers: Frederick Ashton, Ted Shawn,
Ruth St. Denis, Martha Graham, Doris Humphrey,
Isadora Duncan
Principal Dancers: Annabelle Gamson, Ted Shawn,
Lynn Seymour, Helen Tamiris, Ruth St. Denis,
Doris Humphrey, Martha Graham, Vernon and Irene Castle,
Anna Pavlova, Loie Fuller
Composers: Edward MacDowell, Johannes Brahms,
Robert Shumann, Alexander Scriabin
Narrators: Michael Tolin, Rosemary Harris
Dance on Camera Festival, 1980 Award

Reviews the evolution of American modern dance from 1900
to the early 1930s with vintage clips and dances reconstructed
for television. Includes: FIVE BRAHMS WALTZES IN THE
MANNER OF ISADORA DUNCAN, choreographed by Frederick Ashton; THE MOTHER and ETUDES (Duncan-Julia Levien,
advisor/Scriabin); SOARING (St. Denis and Hum-
phrey/Schumann) reconstructed for the Joyce Trisler Dance
Company by Klarna Pinska; POLONAISE (Shawn/MacDowell)
staged by Norman Walker.

THE TRAITOR

1955, 19 min., b&w, film
Distributor: Dance Film Archive
Choreographer: Jose Limon
Principal Dancers: Lucas Hoving (Leader),
Jose Limon (Traitor)
Composer: Gunther Schuller
Music: Symphony For Brasses

A modern dance portraying the betrayal of Christ by Judas.

TRIBAL DANCES OF WEST AFRICA

1969, 28 min., color, film, video
Distributor/Producer/Director: R. A. Piper
Dance Company: Dance Ensemble at The Institute of
African Studies, University of Ghana

The sixty tribes of Ghana, West Africa, answer the call of the
talking drums with a grace distinctly their own. With their
backs curled, the barefoot dancers juggle many rhythms simultaneously, feet, hips, hands, and head responding to different
drummers.

TRIBAL EYE, NO. 3 – MAN BLONG CUSTOM

1976, 52 min., color, film
Distributor: Iowa State University
Producer: BBC
Narrator/Director: David Attenborough

Sacred ceremonies performed in the cult house in the jungle-
covered mountains of the New Hebrides and on the Solomon
Islands, where the sea spirit dances are shown.

TRIO A.

> 1978, 10 min., b&w, film
> Distributor: Dance Film Archive
> Director/Choreographer/Dancer: Yvonne Rainier

Minimalist solo, made in 1965 as a rebellion against spectacle and decoration in dance.

TRIPLE DUO

> 1989, 16 min., color, film, video
> Distributor/Producer: Rudolph Burchhardt
> Choreographer: Douglas Dunn
> Dance Company: Douglas Dunn and Company
> Composer: Elliott Carter

Shots of dancers improvising and rehearsing in a studio are intercut with those of people in the street below going about their business. We fly to Mexico as the dancers perform SKY EYE. Douglas Dunn and Grazia della Terza appear in the woods in an animal-like duo, and then walk through Queens.

TRISHA AND CARMEN

> 1987, 13 min., color, video
> Distributor: Electronic Arts Intermix
> Producer: New Television WGBH/WNET
> Director: Burt Barr
> Choreographer: Trisha Brown
> Principal Dancer: Diane Madden
> Composer: Georges Bizet

Shot in Naples, modern dance pioneer Trisha Brown, commissioned by Lina Wertmuller to choreograph the opera CARMEN, has her make-up applied. Intermittently, the scene in the dressing room is intercut with a rehearsal of a duet, and an excerpt of the performance, which integrates the Spanish persona with Brown's individuality.

TROY GAME

> 1988, 39 min., color, video
> Distributor: Home Vision #TRO03
> Producer: Independent Films Producers Assoc. Ltd.
> Director: Thomas Grimm
> Choreographer: Robert North
> Dance Company: London Contemporary Dance Theatre
> Composer: Bob Downes
> Music: Brazilian Folk Songs, "Shadow Boxing Solo"

Nine male dancers flex and pose, leap, and fight. In addition to the performance, Robert Cohan warms up the company and comments on the ballet.

TURKISH BELLYDANCE (4 videos)

> 1989, 120 min. each, color, video
> Distributor/Producer/Dancer: Eva Cernik
> Choreographer: Tulay Karaka
> Principal Dancers: Maazin Ghawai Dancers

Filmed in Istanbul's nightclubs, studios, and sulukule gypsy quarter with four dances by Tulay Karaka. Also, FOUR DANCE CLASSES by prominent dancers/teachers of Egypt in the cabaret, ghawazi, and reda styles; FOLKLORE OF EGYPT covering the festivals in upper Egypt, Maazin Ghawazi dancers (Khairiya, Rajaa).

TURKISH FOLKDANCES AT PRIZEN

> 1971, 9 min., b&w, film
> Distributor: Pennstate #EO1981
> Producers: H. Kaleshi, Sh. Pilana, H. J. Kibling for Wissen

Folk dances filmed in southern Yugoslavia.

THE TURNING POINT

> 1977, 119 min., color, film, video
> Distributor: Films Inc.
> Producer: Twentieth Century Fox
> Producer: Arthur Laurents
> Executive Producer: Nora Kaye
> Director/Producer: Herbert Ross
> Choreographers: Frederick Ashton, Jean Coralli,
> Jules Perrot, Marius Petipa
> Cinematographer: Robert Surtees
> Principal Dancers: Mikhail Baryshnikov, Leslie Browne,
> Antoinette Sibley, Clark Tippet, Martine Van Hamel,
> Starr Danias, Hideo Fukagawa, Alexandra Danilova
> Composers: Adolphe Adam, Peter Ilyich Tchaikovsky,
> Serge Prokofiev
> Costume Designer: Albert Wolsky

A young dancer on the verge of becoming a professional tries to skirt the pressures from her mother, a former dancer, and her godmother, a single, world-class ballerina just past her prime, and still woo a principal dancer, played by Mikhail Baryshnikov. Classical excerpts include: ACT II pas de deux from GISELLE; Bluebird pas de deux from SLEEPING BEAUTY; the White Swan pas de deux from SWAN LAKE; Sir Frederick Ashton's ROMEO AND JULIET.

21

> 1987, 15:45 min., color, video
> Distributor: Kitchen
> Choreographer: Bill T. Jones
> Director: Tom Bowes
> Composers: Brian Eno, Jerry Goodman, Etosha

Man reflects on the arrest of his brother, and how that fact affected him as a teenager, while in college, and in Amsterdam. He alternately sits by a window, dances in an empty studio, and poses for the camera. The intercutting of the three circumstances supports the speaker's thought pattern.

TWO BAGATELLES

> 1962, 3 min. each, color, film
> Distributor/Producer: National Film Board of Canada
> Director: Norman McLaren

Two short divertissements: ON THE LAWN, in which a male dancer waltzes to synthetic music, and a fast march IN THE BACKYARD, accompanied by an old-fashioned calliope.

TWO BY LOUIS JOHNSON

> 1970s, 5 min. color, b&w, film
> Distributor/Producer: Film-maker's Cooperative
> Director: Richard Preston
> Choreographer/Dancer: Louis Johnson

Two treatments of a work by Louis Johnson performed by a

group dancing on a rooftop. In the second, multiple exposures create a variety of stylistic effects.

TWO ECSTATIC THEMES

    1980, 13 min., color, film
    Distributor: Dance Film Archive
    Choreographer: Doris Humphrey
    Principal Dancers: Nina Watt, Carla Maxwell

Two interpretations of a solo choreographed in 1931.

TWO GIRLS DOWNTOWN IOWA

    1973, 11 min., b&w, film
    Distributor/Choreographer/Director: Elaine Summers

Slow-motion take of two girls walking, seemingly soaring, down an American main street.

TYMPANI

    1981, 29:48 min., color, video
    Distributor: Intermedia Arts
    Producer/Director: Kathryn Esher for Twin Cities Public TV
    Choreographer: Laura Dean
    Dance Company: Laura Dean Company

A geometrically patterned dance with rhythmic stamping and spinning.

TZADDIK

    1974, 30 min., color, video
    Distributor: Electronic Arts Intermix
    Producer/Director: Rick Hauser
    Producer/Distributor: WGBH (Boston) Television
    Dance Workshop
    Choreographer/Dancer: Eliot Feld
    Composer: Aaron Copland
    Dance Company: Eliot Feld Ballet

Aaron Copland's trio VITEBSK brought back memories of his own childhood and education to choreographer Eliot Feld. In deference to those days, TZADDIK celebrates the joy Hassidic Jews derive from studying and performing rituals. Shot with a 250-pound camera on a crane, mounted on a double-tilt cradle head in an environment created by using leko patterns of Hebrew characters.

UALE, THE KNOCK-KNEED DANCE
and others from Ivory Coast (8 films)

    1968, 4–25 min., color, b&w, film
    Distributor: Pennstate #EO1553,1538, 00893, 1548,
    1537, 1549, 1556
    Producer: H. Himmelheber for Wissen

The Guere tribe from the Ivory Coast, West Africa, perform THE LITTLE STOOL DANCE of the just-excised maidens, DJE, SERI, and ZAULI mask dances, dances to commemorate the end of war, others for circumcision.

THE UGLY DUCKLING

    30 min., color, film, video
    Distributor: Phoenix Films
    Director: Dan Bessie

A young man, frustrated by working in the family dry goods store, finds his own kind of people, dancers and acrobats, in a parade. He joins in, discovering his own talents.

THE ULTIMATE SWAN LAKE (Bolshoi Ballet)

    1984, 126 min., color, video
    Distributor: Kultur #1162
    Choreographer: Yuri Grigorovich
    Principal Dancers: Natalia Bessmertnova,
    Alexander Bogatyrev
    Dance Company: Bolshoi Ballet
    Composer: Peter Ilyich Tchaikovsky

Full-length classic filmed in Russia introduced by Gene Kelly, who gives a brief history of the classic ballet.

UNDERTOW

    1988, 8 min., b&w, video
    Distributor: Electronic Arts Intermix
    Director: James Byrne
    Choreographer/Dancers: Eiko & Koma

The performers appear to float through the frame, propelled by inexplicable forces in a space resembling a womb.

UNREMITTING TENDERNESS

    1977, 9 min., color, film
    Distributor: Phoenix/Bfa Films
    Producer/Director: Bruce Elder

An experimental film in which a dance sequence is broken down into its basic components, transformed in printing, and then rearranged in a variety of ways.

UNTITLED, ARMS, PART TWO: RELATIVES

    Series: Alive from Off Center
    1989, 30 min., color, video
    Distributor: Kitchen
    Producer/Distributors: KTCA-TV, Agent Orange-
    Antenna (Arms)
    Choreographers: Bill T. Jones, Susan Marshall,
    Ishmael Houston-Jones
    Directors: John Sanborn, Mary Perillo, Susan Hayeur,
    Julie Dash

In UNTITLED, Bill T. Jones creates a tribute to his late partner Arnie Zane, directed by John Sanborn and Mary Perillo. Susan Marshall adapted her work ARMS, an exploration of power relationships between men and women, directed by Isabelle Hayeur for Agent Orange. Ishmael Houston-Jones choreographed PART 2: RELATIVES, directed by Julie Dash, which addresses identity issues.

VARIATION TWO

    1978, 10:30 min., color, film
    Distributor: Museum of Modern Art
    Distributor/Producer/Director: Doris Chase for WNYC-TV
    Principal Dancer: Sara Rudner
    Composer: Joan LaBarbara
    1979 Dance and Film and Video Festival, merit award

Second alteration of a three-camera shoot of a solo by Sara Rudner, formerly of Twyla Tharp's company, using tape delay, de-beaming, colorizing, and mat key.

VARIATIONS V

   1966, 50 min., b&w, film, video
   Distributor: Cunningham Dance Foundation
   Producer: Studio Hamburg, Nordeutscher Rundfunk
   Director: Arne Arnborn
   Choreographer: Merce Cunningham
   Dance Company: Cunningham Dance Company
   Composer: John Cage
   Film Images: Stan Vanderbeek

The electronic equipment, especially designed by Bell Labora-
tories, translated the dancers' movements into sound altered or
delayed by musicians John Cage, David Tudor, and Gordon
Mumma. A montage of rehearsal footage, movie stills, and
scenes re-touched by Nam June Paik was projected on monitors during the performance. For his exit, Merce Cunningham
rides a bicycle around the space.

VEDA SEREEM'S QUALITY OF BELLY DANCING (19 videos)

   1980s, 110-120 min. each, color, video
   Distributor/Producer/Dancer: Veda Sereem

A series covering the skills for the incorporation of veils,
swords, canes, basket, and zills (finger cymbals) from this
teacher based in Germantown, Maryland.

VEIL TECHNIQUES IN ORIENTAL DANCE

   1989, 120 min., color, video
   Distributor/Narrator/Choreographer/Dancer:
   Chandra of Damascus

Demonstration of basic to advanced techniques for dancing
with veils.

THE VERY EYE OF NIGHT

   1959, 18 min., b&w, film
   Distributor: Grove Press Film
   Producer/Director: Maya Deren
   Choreographer: Antony Tudor
   Dancers: Richard Englund, Richard Sandlifer, Don
   Freisinger, Patricia Ferrier, Bud Bready, Ginaro Gomez,
   Rosemary Williams, Philip Salem
   Composer: Teiji Ito

A cine-ballet of night, filmed in the negative, creating the illusion of movement in unlimited space. The dancers resemble
sleepwalkers, advancing as if planets in the night sky.

VESPUCCILAND, THE GREAT AND THE FREE

   1989, 3 min., color, film
   Distributor: Canyon
   Producer/Choreographer: Rock Ross
   Principal Dancers: Randy Redding, Nancy Hammer
   Dance Company: Homestead Valley Dance Company
   Composer: Francis Poulenc
   Dance on Camera Festival, 1989 Silver Award

Satire on dance trends with time-lapse photography of dancers
in tunics and scarves in a backyard, going down a flight of
stairs, in and out of a tent, under an umbrella.

VIBRANT SCULPTURE FROZEN DANCE

   1987, 30 min., color, video

   Distributor/Producer/Dancer: Ritha Devi

One woman's effort to recount the legends revolving around
the Sun-God, in the style of Oudra Nrutya, performed at the
Temple of Konarka in Orissa, India.

VIDEO-DANSE JO LECHAY

   1984, 12 min., color, video
   Distributor: Videographe
   Director/Choreographer/Dancer: Jo Lechay
   Director: German Guitierrez
   Cinematographer: Serge Ladouceur
   Composers: Sayyd Abdul Al-Khabyyr, Marc Beland,
   John Cage, Martin Jenni, Rober Racine
   Dance Company: Jo Lechay Dance Company

Close-ups of this Canadian modern dance company show its
humor, vitality, and sensuality, taking the viewer from the
rehearsal to performance.

VIDEO DICTIONARY OF CLASSICAL BALLET

   1983, 270 min. (two cassettes), color, video
   Distributor: Kultur # 1100
   Director: Robert Beck
   Principal Dancers: Georgina Parkinson, Denise Jackson,
   Merrill Ashley, Kevin McKenzie
   VIRA Award Winner

Index to over 800 variations in the Russian, French and
Cecchetti styles, all numbered and explained in an accom-
panying booklet with demonstrations by principals from
American Ballet Theatre and New York City Ballet companies.

VIDEOS FLAMENCOS DE LA LUZ (6 videos)

   1984–1990, 38–60 min. each, color, video
   Distributor: Deirdre Towers
   Producer: Pilar Guzman
   Director: Antonio G. Olea
   Principal Dancers: Pilar Perez De Guzman, Manuel Badillo
   Composer/Guitarist: Miguel Rivera
   Singer: Rafael Fajardo

Comprehensive course on Flamenco with concentrated lessons in: Sevillanas, the social dance once the past time of the
Andalusians but now in discos in many parts of Europe; the
basics of the heelwork, arms, and rhythms; the rumba;
castanets; the cante or accompanying song of Flamenco; plus a
Flamenco show taped in a tablao (nightclub) in Madrid. Available in Spanish and English.

VIOLA FARBER DANCE COMPANY, 1973-74

   1974, 8 min., color, video
   Distributor/Producer/Director: Mary Lucier
   Choreographer/Dancer: Viola Farber
   Composer: Alvin Lucier

Modern dance shot in concert over one year, with interviews
interjected.

VISION DANCE

   1982, 58:30 min., color, video
   Distributor: Solaris
   Producer: Henry Smith for Solaris Lakota Project in

association with KTCA-TV and Affiliate Artists
Choreographers: Lloyd One Star, Henry Smith
Composers: Mike Sirotta and the Ironwood Singers
Dance Company: Solaris Company, Lakota Sioux
Indian Dancers
Dance on Camera Festival, 1983 First Prize; American Film
Festival, 1983 Honorable Mention; Tokyo Video Festival,
1982 Special Merit

Shot in the Badlands and Black Hills of South Dakota in collaboration with Lakota Sioux Indians drawn from the nine reservations and with modern dancer Henry Smith's company. The videotape is based on a dance theatre work, IHANBLA WAKTOGLAG WACIPI, which means to dance one's dreams, visions, or exploits.

VISUAL SHUFFLE, FRACTURED VARIATIONS

Series: Alive from Off Center
1986, 14 min., color, video
Distributor: Electronic Arts Intermix
Producer: KTCA-TV
Choreographer/Dancer: Charles Moulton
Directors: John Sanborn, Mary Perillo
Principal Dancers: Beatrice Bogorad, Jackie Goodrich,
Christopher Pilafian, Guillermo Resto
Editor: Tim Farrell

Experimental collaboration in which the choreography is as much fixed in post, as pre-production as dancers pass through environments created with the Harry paintbox, ADO, and other special effects devices.

VOICES OF SPRING

28 min., color, film
Distributor: Modern Talking Picture Service #25389
Producer: German government
Dancers: Students of Munich Ballet Academy
Documentary on young dancers in class and performance.

VOODOO CHILD

1987, 5 min., color, video
Distributor: Warner Brothers
Producer: Alan Douglas
Choreographer/Directors: Jackie and Bill Landrum
Composer: Jimi Hendrix

Fifteen years after a Jimi Hendrix concert was shot, a California team choreographed a dance to his music for the camera. The dance footage was then intercut with the concert footage of the guitarist. The guitar string was symbolically used as the link between dance and music, as close-ups of Hendrix's fingers dancing on his guitar strings switch to the dancers playing under strings long enough to cover the entire space.

VROTSOS VIDEOS (4 videos)

1986, 30-60 min. each, color, video
Distributor: Taffy's
Distributor/Producer/Teacher: Janine Vrotsos

A series of teaching videos: PRE-BALLET FOR FIVES, SIXES AND SEVENS, for young students; INTERMEDIATE BALLET CLASS, and BEGINNING/INTERMEDIATE POINTE CLASS.

Also available from Vrotsos, INTERMEDIATE JAZZ CLASS with floor stretches, barre and center.

WAKE UP CALL

1989, 8 min., color, film, video
Distributor/Producer/Director/Editor: Pooh Kaye
Animators: John Inber, Judith Rosen
Cinematographer: Richard Smith
Composer: John Kilgore
Boston Film/Video Foundation's Olive Jar

Combined live action and animation film shows a young woman struggling to face the day despite the mattress sticking to her, the breakfast table wobbling, and the dread of being followed by shadows.

WALKAROUND TIME

1973, 48 min., color, film, video
Distributor/Producer: Cunningham Dance Foundation
Director: Charles Atlas
Choreographer: Merce Cunningham
Dance Company: Merce Cunningham Dance Company
Set Designer: Jasper Johns
Composer: David Behrman

Dancers pass behind see-through vinyl inflatables in this rehearsal and performance video. The set refers to painter Marcel Duchamp in concept and detail and his concern with transparency.

WALKING DANCE FOR ANY NUMBER

1968, 7:30 min., b&w, film
Distributor: Film-maker's Coop
Director: Phil Niblock
Dancer/Editor: Elaine Summers

This experimental film focuses on a pair of legs walking down the sidewalks of a city park, making a dance within the scope of the lens, the space of the projected flat image, and the speeds of the camera.

WALLS AND WALLS

1973, 9:30 min., color, film, video
Distributor/Producer: Filmfair Communications
Director/Writer/Narrator: Ben Norman
Principal Dancers: Jerry Baden, Wendy Ziegler
Bronze Plaque, Columbus Film Festival, 1974

Two dancers suggest their own barriers while a montage of stills shows man's reliance upon physical separations. Demonstrates that attitudes or defenses deter the flow of ideas and wall others out while trapping us within.

WATCHING BALLET

1965, 35 min., b&w, film
Distributor: Association Films
Producers: New York State Council on the Arts and
Ballet Society
Choreographer: George Balanchine
Principal Dancers: Jacques D'Amboise, Allegra Kent
Composers: Paul Hindemith, Peter Ilyich Tchaikovsky,
Charles Francois Gounod, John Philip Sousa, Hersey Kay

Jacques d'Amboise, the former New York City Ballet principal and founder of the National Dance Institute, demonstrates the basic positions and steps of ballet in different styles and combinations. Excerpts from George Balanchine's NUTCRACKER, GOUNOD SYMPHONY, STARS AND STRIPES, SWAN LAKE, and THE FOUR TEMPERAMENTS.

WATER MOTOR

    1978, 9 min., b&w, film
    Distributor: Dance Film Archive
    Producer/Director: Babette Mangolte
    Dancer/Choreographer: Trisha Brown

A modern solo fades in/fades out with a quick-silver middle and then is repeated in slow motion.

WATER PIECES

    1989, 12 min., color, film, video
    Distributor/Producer/Director: Penny Ward
    Choreographer/Dancer: Sue Bernhard
    Composers: Dan Levitan, Glen Velez
    Dance on Camera Festival, Honorable Mention

The film articulates a rhythmic language of dance, memory, and sensation.

WATER PIECES No. 2

    1990, 3:50 min., color, video
    Distributor/Producer/Director: Penny Ward
    Choreographer/Dancer: Sue Bernhard
    Composer: Alvin Curran

Kaleidoscopic version of WATER PIECES involves constant movement and division, so that the body seems to fold in on itself.

WATER SPIRIT FESTIVAL

    1989, 32 min., color, video
    Distributor: MICA
    Producer: Bayne Williams Film Co.
    Director/Choreographer: Arthur Hall
    Composer: Kpe Lee
    Editor: Bruce Williams

Recreation of a Nigerian festival by 300 children from Lebanon, New Hampshire, who play everything from the council of elders to the river dragon.

WATER STUDY

    1980, 22 min., color, film
    Distributor: Dance Film Archive
    Choreographer: Doris Humphrey

The 1928 work performed by a group under the direction of Ernestine Stodelle, shown twice, once at a distance and, secondly, in close-up.

WATERPROOF

    1986, 22 min., color, video
    Distributor: Actions et Prospectives Audiovisuelles (APA)
    Producers: Arcanal/Ministere de la Culture Francaise, Astrakan, CNDC, Ex-Nihilo, Swatsch, Videogram
    Directors: Jean Louis Le Tacon, Luc Riolon

    Choreographer: Daniel Larrieu
    Dance Company: Companie Astrakan
    Composer: J. J. Palix

To be appreciated for its underwater cinematography, its playful symbolism, and abstract beauty, this widely shown video inspired confidence in French producers in the possible mass appeal of video dance.

THE WEST AFRICAN HERITAGE

    Series: Jumpstreet
    1980, 30 min., color, video
    Distributor: Portland State University #40373
    Dance Company: Wo'se Dance Theatre

Features musicians Hugh Masakela, Ahaji Bai Konte, Dembo Konte, and the Wo'se Dance Theatre from Africa.

WESTBETH

    1975, 32 min., b&w, film, video
    Distributor/Producer: Cunningham Dance Foundation
    Choreographer: Merce Cunningham
    Director: Charles Atlas
    Dance Company: Cunningham Dance Company
    Costume Designer: Mark Lancaster, from a design by Jasper Johns

Merce Cunningham's first collaboration with director Charles Atlas, this six-part collage was created with the knowledge that television changes our perception of time and space.

WEST SIDE STORY

    1961, 155 min., color, video
    Distributor/Producers: Mirisch Company, released by United Artists
    Director: Robert Wise
    Choreographer/Director: Jerome Robbins
    Composers: Leonard Bernstein, Stephen Sondheim
    Principal Dancers: Rita Moreno, Eliot Feld
    Writer: Ernest Lehman

The Academy-Award-winning Broadway musical about rival white and Puerto Rican gangs in New York coming to blows over an ill-fated love match.

WHAT DO PINA BAUSCH AND HER DANCES DO IN WUPPERTAL?

    1983, 115 min., color, video
    Distributor: Modern Talking Picture Service #25543
    Director: Klaus Wildenhahn
    Choreographer: Pina Bausch
    Dance Company: Wuppertal Dance Theatre

The crew follows the process of creating BANDONEON in Wuppertal, West Germany, over a month's time. Interjected among the rehearsal footage are interviews with a factory worker who complains of the futility and flatness of her existence. Considered one of the most influential contemporary choreographers, Pina Bausch says, in indirect response to the worker, "Everyone is looking for some kind of satisfaction which they never find." She challenges her company with daily exercises, such as expressing a symbol of freedom, or setting a trap for someone, or how you play games to subdue fear.

WHAT IS NEW

Series: Magic of Dance
1979, 52 min., color, film, video
Distributor: Dance Film Archive
Producer/Director: Patricia Foy for BBC
Narrator/Dancer: Margot Fonteyn
Principal Dancers: Mikhail Baryshnikov,
Patrick Harding-Irmes, Susanne Kirnbauer
Choreographers: Grete Wiesenthal, Robert Cohan,
Michel Fokine, Ruth St. Denis, Kurt Jooss
Dance Companies: Teatro a l'Avogaria, London
Contemporary Dance Theatre
Composers: Johann Strauss, Bob Downes, Carl Maria
Von Weber

A visit to the Parthenon in honor of Isadora Duncan's fascination with the Greeks, with a short film of Isadora dancing at a garden party; WINE WOMEN AND SONG (Wiesenthal/Strauss II); Loie Fuller's FIRE DANCE KHAMSIN (Cohan/Downes); Robert North's TROY GAME; Kurt Jooss' GREEN TABLE; Michel Fokine's LE SPECTRE DE LA ROSE; Teatro a l'Avogaria performs *commedia dell'arte*; interview with Kyra Nijinsky about her father Vaslav Nijinsky.

WHAT'S REMEMBERED

Series: Educational Performance Collection
1983, 20 min., color, video
Producer/Distributor: Dance Notation Bureau
Choreographer: Rachel Lampert
Composers: Spohr, Leclair, Jorns

Building on the theme of the tenuousness of relationships, the choreographer created romantic duets and frantic solos. Preparatory improvisational exercises are set and incorporated into the dance. Comes with an article on Labanotation, an advanced level Labanotated score by Leslie Rotman, taped performance at the University of Iowa, critical text for study as well as performance rights.

WHEN I THINK OF RUSSIA

1980, 54 min., color, video
Distributor: Mystic Fire Video
Producer/Director: Vladimir Rif
Dancer: Mikhail Baryshnikov

Six exiled Russian artists, dancer Mikhail Baryshnikov and poet Joseph Brodsky among them, discuss their feelings toward art, freedom, America and Russia, intercut with their dance, poetry, and music.

WHERE CONFUCIUS MEETS THE NEW WAVE

1987, 60 min., color, film
Distributor: Coordination Council
Producer/Director: Kim Eveleth for Kwang Hwa Mass
Communications, Taipei, Taiwan
Choreographer/Dancer: Lin Hwai-min
Dance Company: Cloud Gate Taipei Contemporary
Dance Theatre
Narrator: Geoffrey Holder

This documentary on a Taiwanese modern dance company led by Lin Hwai-min, gives a sense of the obstacles faced by Eastern artists. The artistic director, a former student of Martha Graham, respects his country's heritage and dreams of the Chinese tradition awakening to the 20th century.

WHITE NIGHTS

1985, 135 min., color, video
Distributor: Swank
Producer: Columbia Pictures
Choreographers: Twyla Tharp, Mikhail Baryshnikov,
Gregory Hines, Roland Petit
Director: Taylor Hackford
Principal Dancers: Mikhail Baryshnikov, Gregory Hines
Composers: Lionel Ritchie, Phil Collins, J. S. Bach

A Russian ballet defector lands in the Soviet Union as a result of a plane crash and find himself under the surveillance of a Vietnam vet defector, who happens to be a professional tap dancer, hired by the KGB. The film opens with an excerpt from the 1951 ballet JEUNE HOMME ET LA MORT choreographed by Roland Petit. Throughout the film, there are solos by Baryshnikov and duets with Gregory Hines.

THE WIDE WORLD OF SPORTS AND DANCE

1987, 35 min., color, video
Distributor/Director: Gus Solomons
Dance Company: Gus Solomons Dance Company

A modern dancer draws analogies between sports and dance as he directs his company in a series of exercises.

WILD FIELDS

1985, 12 min., color, video
Distributor: ARC Videodance
Producer/Directors: Celia Ipiotis and Jeff Bush
Choreographer: Pooh Kaye

Group bounds around in a studio as directed by the playful Pooh Kaye, based in New York.

WILD SWANS IN EPITAPH AND MADHONOR

1974, 30 min., b&w, film
Distributor/Choreographer/Dancer: Margaret Beals
Producer: Margaret Honeywell
Director: Peter Powell

Modern dancer Margaret Beals comments on two of her dances recorded: WILD SWANS, set to a suite of poems she recites, and MADHONOR, danced in silence.

WITH MY RED FIRES

1972, 30 min., color, film
Distributor: Dance Film Archive
Choreographer: Doris Humphrey
Dance Company: Connecticut College Repertory Company
Composer: Wallingford Riegger

The 1936 tragedy of possessive maternal love in a demagogic society, reconstructed from Labanotation by Christine Clark and performed in 1972 at the American Dance Festival.

THE WOMAN IN THE SHOE

1980s, 30 min., color, video
Distributor/Producer: Hoctor Products

Choreographers: Joan Yell, Bonnie Ratzin

Designed for teachers planning recitals for early grade school and pre-school children.

WORLD'S YOUNG BALLET

1969, 70 min., b&w, film, video
Distributors: Dance Film Archive, Kultur (video)
Producer: Tsentrnauch Film Studios, Moscow
Director: Arkadi Tsineman
Cinematographers: Anatoli Kazin, Mahmud Rafikov, Gleb Chumakov
Choreographers: Len Ivanov, Marius Petipa, August Bournonville, Vladimir Vasiliev, Maurice Bejart
Principal Dancers: Peter Schauffuss, Helgi Tomasson, Vladimir Vasiliev, Mikhail Baryshnikov, Azari Plisetsky, Loipa Araujo

The first Moscow International Ballet Competition in 1969 in which the young Soviet Mikhail Baryshnikov won the gold. Highlights of the competition include scenes from SWAN LAKE, GISELLE, FLOWER FESTIVAL AT GENZANO, WAR AND PEACE, BHAKTI, and SPARTACUS.

XIDV

1985, 5 min., color, video
Distributor/Director/Editor: Michelle Mahrer
Principal Dancers: Nina Veretennikova, Paul Saliba
Composer: Blair Greenberg

Close-ups on a blue torso slowly rolling seemingly in/by the sea. An articulate foot with bangles on the ankle gingerly makes its way. Pull back to see the beating hands of a drummer against the backdrop of fire with a final glimpse of a man in a fine costume.

XINGUANA: ABORIGINES OF SOUTH AMERICA

1971, 29 min., color, film
Distributor: Portland State University #10276

Spear dances and puberty rites of a tribe living by the Xingu River in Central Brazil.

X-RAY EYES

1985, 14:53 min., color, video
Distributor: Electronic Arts Intermix
Choreographer/Dancer: Wendy Perron
Director: James Byrne
Principal Dancers: Lisa Bush, Erica Bornstein, Mary Lyman
Composers: Arto Lindsay and The Ambitious Lovers

Playful, quirky movements of the dancers on a bare stage are mirrored by James Byrne's angled camera, quick changes of focus, and formally composed close-ups.

YAMAMBA (2 videos)

1979, 86 min. each, color, video
Distributor: University of Michigan
Producers: Karen Brazell and Monica Bethe for Cornell's East Asia Papers
Director: Roland Yamamoto
Principal Dancers: Otsuki Bunzo, Izumi Yoshio
Writer: David Kalama

Performance in full costume of the second act of YAMAMBA, a Noh play, and demonstration of the Kuse scene by a master of the Kanze School of Japan.

YOU CAN DANCE (8 videos)

1989, 30–45 min. each., color, video
Distributor/Producer: Hoctor Products
Teachers: Vicki Regan, Ron Devito

Eight lessons in the fox-trot, waltz, jitterbug, nightclub, rhumba, cha-cha, tango, and mambo as demonstrated by winners of National Ballroom Championships.

YOU CAN DO THE HULA

1986, 45 min., color, video
Distributor: Pacific Trade Group
Producer: Rainforest Publishing & Production Company
Choreographer: Debbie Oschner
Director: Patty Amaral
Teacher: Taina Passmore
Writer: Rod Anjo

Warm-up and breathing exercises for the mind and body, history of the hula, and instructions for foot and hand movements. Concludes with a performance of a hula set to LEHUA, a Hawaiian song of a lover having only the wind and stars to carry his thoughts to his beloved.

YOU LITTLE WILD HEART

1981, 28:47 min., color, video
Distributor: WGBH
Producer: Susan Dowling
Director: Dick Heller
Choreographer: Marta Renzi
Composers: Bruce Springsteen and The E Street Band

Referred to by the producer as a hymn to adolescent rebellion, the film shows sixteen kids swaggering through railroad yards as choreographed by modern dancer Marta Renzi.

ZAR AND FLOORWORK

1989, 120 min., color, video
Distributor/Producer/Choreographer/Dancer: Chandra of Damascus

A workshop on the history, rhythms, and movements associated with the Zar, a dance of exorcism and healing originating in the Middle East.

ZOU ZOU

1934, 92 min., b&w, film, video
Distributor: Kino International
Principal Dancer: Josephine Baker

The black comedian/dancer/singer Josephine Baker begins as an impoverished laundry woman, but quickly becomes the toast of Paris when in a twist of luck, she is allowed to take the place of a celebrated actress on opening night. This Cinderella story conveys Baker's comic talents and sensuality.

ZULA HULA

1937-1971, 7 min., color, film
Distributor: Ivy Films
Director/Animator: Max Fleischman
Principal Dancer: Betty Boop

In this cartoon vamp originally made in 1937 in black and white but redone in color, Crusoe survives after a plane crash by soothing the island natives with music and dance.

ZULU MEDICINE DANCES (6 films)

1965-1968, 5-17 min. each., color, film
Distributor: Pennstate #EO1087, EO1754, EO1415, EO1416, EO1702, EO1755
Producer: Wissen

Illustrates the procedures and treatments of bone tossing, skin scratching, inhaling, and divination dances used by medicine men of this South African tribe.

INDEX OF CHOREOGRAPHERS

INDEX OF COMPOSERS

INDEX OF DANCE COMPANIES

INDEX OF DANCERS

Index of Directors

SUBJECT INDEX

BALLET (continued)

DOCUMENTARY *(continued)*

EXCERPTS (ballet and modern classics shown in excerpted form
or short works shown in their entirely within a documentary are
listed first, immediately followed by the film/video title)

FILMS *(continued)*

MA'BUGI: TRANCE OF THE TORAJA
MAGIC FIDDLE
MAGNIFICENT BEGINNING
MAKING OF A BALLET
MAKING TELEVISION DANCE
MALAYSIAN DANCES (7 films)
MAN WHO DANCES
MARCEAU ON MIME
MARCEL MARCEAU OU L'ART DU MIME
MARCEL MARCEAU'S MIME SCHOOL
MARGOT FONTEYN IN LES SYLPHIDES
MARTHA CLARKE: LIGHT AND DARK
MARTHA GRAHAM DANCE COMPANY
MARY WIGMAN
MARY WIGMAN: WHEN THE FIRE DANCES BETWEEN
  THE TWO POLES
MATT MATTOX
MAYA DEREN: EXPERIMENTAL FILMS
MEDITATION ON VIOLENCE
MERCE CUNNINGHAM
MERCE CUNNINGHAM (1964)
MERCE CUNNINGHAM (1978)
MERCE CUNNINGHAM AND COMPANY
MEREDITH MONK'S '16 MILLIMETER EARRINGS'
MESQUAKIE
MEXICAN DANCES (2 films)
MGODO WA MBANGUZI
MILLER'S WIFE
MIME
MIME OF MARCEL MARCEAU
MIME TECHNIQUE – PART I
MINING DANCES (4 films)
MIRACLE OF BALI: A RECITAL OF MUSIC AND DANCING
MIRROR OF GESTURE
MISS JULIE
MIXED DOUBLE
MIXUMMERDAYDREAM
MODERN BALLET
MODERN DANCE COMPOSITION
MODERN DANCE TECHNIQUES IN SEQUENTIAL FORM
MODERN DANCE – THE ABC OF COMPOSITION
MODERN DANCE: CHOREOGRAPHY AND THE SOURCE
MODERN DANCE: CREATIVE IMAGINATION AND
  CHOREOGRAPHY
MOIMO FESTIVAL DANCE FROM CENTRAL SUDAN
MOON
MOON GATES I & II
MOON GATES III
MOON GATES – THREE VERSIONS
MOOR'S PAVANE (VARIATIONS ON THE THEME
  OF OTHELLO)
MORNING STAR (CHOLPON)
MOROCCO, BODY AND SOUL
MOSCOW BALLET SCHOOL
MOTION
MOURNING CELEBRATIONS FROM ETHIOPIA
MOURNING DANCES FROM CHAD (5 films)
MOVEMENT EXPLORATION – WHAT AM I
MOVEMENT IN CLASSIC DANCE: THE PELVIC AREA

MOVING PICTURE
MOVING TRUE
MUNICH COOPERS' DANCE
N'UM TCHAI
N/UM TCHAI: THE CEREMONIAL DANCE OF THE
  !KUNG BUSHMEN
NAGRIN VIDEOTAPE LIBRARY OF DANCE
NARCISSUS
NATIONAL FOLK FESTIVAL (3 films)
NAVAJO NIGHT DANCES
NEW DANCE – RECORD FILM
NIGHT JOURNEY
NIK AND MURRAY
NIKKOLINA
NINE VARIATIONS ON A DANCE THEME
NO MAPS ON MY TAPS
NOH DRAMA
NSAMBO DANCE FESTIVAL AT ISANGI (2 films)
NUTCRACKER
O THAT WE WERE THERE
OBSEQUIES FOR DECEASED REGIONAL CHIEFTAINS
OFFICIAL DOCTRINE
OKLAHOMA!
ON THE MOVE: CENTRAL BALLET OF CHINA
ONCE AGAIN
ONDEKO-ZA IN SADO
ORFEUS & JULIE
ORISUN OMI
OTHELLO, MOOR OF VENICE
OUT OF CHAOS, AMOR
OUT OF THE LIMELIGHT, HOME IN THE RAIN
PALM PLAY
PANTOMIMES
PANTOMIMIC INTERLUDE
PARADES AND CHANGES
PARISIAN FOLLIES
PARTNERS
PAS DE DEUX
PAUL TAYLOR DANCE COMPANY – AN ARTIST AND
  HIS WORK
PHANTASY
PINA BAUSCH
PLASMASIS
PLASTIC BODY
PLISETSKAYA DANCES
POEM OF DANCES
POINTS IN SPACE
POLYNESIAN DANCES FROM THE ELLICE ISLANDS
  (4 films)
PORTRAIT OF GISELLE
POW WOW
PREPARING TO DANCE
PRINCESS TAM TAM
PROCESSION: CONTEMPORARY DIRECTIONS IN
  AMERICAN DANCE
PROJECTIONS
PSYCHIC SEASONS
PUTTIN' ON THE RITZ
QUARRY

FILMS (continued)

THREE (3) DANCES 1964
TIBETAN FOLK DANCE (4 films)
TIGER AND THE BRIDE
TIME TO DANCE
TO MOVE IN BEAUTY: THE KABUKI TRADITION
TONDO: A ROUND ABOUT A ROUND
TONIGHT WE SING
TORCHES OF TODAIJI
TORSE
TOTEM
TOUR EN L'AIR
TOURNANTS
TRADITIONAL WHITSUN RITES OF THE KALUSHARS
  (3 films)
TRAILBLAZERS OF MODERN DANCE
TRAITOR
TRIBAL DANCES OF WEST AFRICA
TRIBAL EYE, NO. 3 – MAN BLONG CUSTOM
TRIO A
TRIPLE DUO
TURKISH FOLKDANCES AT PRIZEN
TURNING POINT
TWO BAGATELLES
TWO BY LOUIS JOHNSON
TWO ECSTATIC THEMES
TWO GIRLS DOWNTOWN IOWA
UALE, THE KNOCK-KNEED DANCE
UGLY DUCKLING
UNREMITTING TENDERNESS
VARIATION TWO
VARIATIONS V
VERY EYE OF NIGHT
VERY SPECIAL DANCE
VESPUCCILAND, THE GREAT AND THE FREE
VOICES OF SPRING
WAKE UP CALL
WALKAROUND TIME
WALKING DANCE FOR ANY NUMBER
WALLS AND WALLS
WATCHING BALLET
WATER MOTOR
WATER STUDY
WESTBETH
WHAT IS NEW
WHERE CONFUCIUS MEETS THE NEW WAVE
WILD SWANS IN EPITAPH and MADHONOR
WITH MY RED FIRES
THE WIZ
WORLD'S YOUNG BALLET
XINGUANA: ABORIGINES OF SOUTH AMERICA
ZOU ZOU
ZULA HULA
ZULU MEDICINE DANCES (6 films)

FLAMENCO See Spanish

FOLK
AFGHANISTAN DANCES (3 films)
AFRICA DANCES

ALBANIAN COUNTRY FOLKDANCES (3 films)
ALL THE BEST FROM RUSSIA
AND STILL WE DANCE
BALKAN DANCING
BALLADE
BALLET FOLKLORICO NACIONAL DE MEXICO
BAYANIHAN
BITTER MELONS
BORN FOR HARD LUCK: PEG LEG SAM JACKSON
BREAK DANCING
BREAKIN
BREAKING: STREET DANCING
BUCKDANCER
CAMBODIAN DANCES
CANADIANS CAN DANCE
CELEBRATE: A TIME TO DANCE
CHINESE FOLK ARTS
CHINESE, KOREAN AND JAPANESE DANCE
COUNTRY CORNERS
DAMBIO FESTIVAL DANCE FROM CENTRAL SUDAN
THE DANCE
DANCE AND HUMAN HISTORY
DANCES FROM DJAYA (5 films)
DANCES OF MEXICO: ANIMAL ORIGINS
DANCES OF SOUTHERN AFRICA
DANCES OF THE SILK ROAD: AN INTRODUCTION
  TO GEORGIAN DANCE
DANCES OF THE WORLD
DANZAS REGIONALES ESPANOLAS
DHANDYO
DISCOVERING AMERICAN INDIAN MUSIC
DISCOVERING RUSSIAN FOLK MUSIC
DISCOVERING THE MUSIC OF AFRICA
DISCOVERING THE MUSIC OF LATIN AMERICA
DISCOVERING THE MUSIC OF THE MIDDLE EAST
ETHNIC DANCE AROUND THE WORLD
FESTIVAL IN COMMEMORATION OF THE DEAD
FLAMENCO
FLAMENCO GITANO
FOLKLORICO
FRENCH FOLK DANCES
FROM PURE SPRINGS
FULL OF LIFE A-DANCIN'
A GALA EVENING WITH THE MOISEYEV
  DANCE COMPANY
GERMAN FOLK DANCES
HAZARDOUS HOOTENANNY
HOPI KACHINAS
IN HEAVEN THERE IS NO BEER?
INDIANS OF THE PLAINS, SUN DANCE CEREMONY
KEEP YOUR HEART STRONG
KICKER DANCIN' TEXAS STYLE: HOW TO DO THE TOP TEN
  COUNTRY & WESTERN DANCES LIKE A
  TEXAS COWBOY
KNIESPIEL (Kneeplay)
KUMU HULA: KEEPERS OF A CULTURE
LAMBACHEN AND STEINHAUSER LANDLER (2 films)
LET'S DANCE THE CHARKHUDUZONU
MALAYSIAN DANCES (7 films)

INDIAN (*continued*)
    INDIA: HAUNTING PASSAGE
    KALAKSHETRA
    KATHAK
    MIRROR OF GESTURE
    PANIGRAHI
    RAGAS FOR SWAM SATCHIDANANDA
    SUITE KINETICS
    VIBRANT SCULPTURE FROZEN DANCE

INSTRUCTIONAL
    ADRIENNE CHERIE INTERPRETS DANCES OF INDIA
    AL GILBERT PRESENTS (60 volumes)
    AMERICAN BALLROOM DANCING (6 tapes)
    ANATOMY AS A MASTER IMAGE IN TRAINING DANCERS
    ART AND TECHNIQUE OF THE BALLET
    THE ART OF BODY MOVEMENT (11 videos and films)
    IL BALLARINO
    BALLET BASICS
    BALLET CLASS (3 tapes)
    BALLET CLASSES: A CELEBRATION
    BALLROOM DANCING FOR BEGINNERS
    BASIC TAP, JACK STANLY
    BEGINNING BELLYDANCING WITH BEDIA
    BEGINNING MODERN DANCE FOR HIGH SCHOOL GIRLS
    BEING ME
    BELLY DANCE! MAGICAL MOTION
    BLACK GIRL
    THE BODY AS AN INSTRUMENT
    BONNIE BIRD DEMONSTRATES GRAHAM TECHNIQUE
    BREAK DANCING
    BROADWAY TAP
    BRYONY BRIND'S BALLET: THE FIRST STEPS
    BUILDING CHILDREN'S PERSONALITIES WITH
      CREATIVE DANCING
    BUSTER COOPER'S HOW TO TAP (6 videos)
    BUSTER COOPER WORKSHOP VIDEOS (28 videos)
    THE CAROLINA SHAG
    CHARMAINE'S HAWAIIAN/TAHITIAN VIDEO PEARLS
    CHE CHE KULE
    CHOREOGRAPHY
    THE COMPANY
    COMPLETE FLAMENCO DANCE TECHNIQUE
    COSTUMING – SKIRTS AND ACCESSORIES
    CUNNINGHAM DANCE TECHNIQUE: ELEMENTARY
      LEVEL
    CUNNINGHAM DANCE TECHNIQUE: INTERMEDIATE
      LEVEL
    DANCE BABY DANCE
    DANCE CLASS WITH SERENA
    DANCE DESIGN: MOTION
    THE DANCE EXPERIENCE (6 videos)
    THE DANCE INSTRUMENT
    DANCE ON VIDEO: AN INTRODUCTION TO
      VIDEOTAPING DANCE
    DANCE PRELUDES (4 videos)
    DANCE SPACE
    DANCE TO THE MUSIC (4 videos)
    DANCE VIDEOGRAPHY
    DANCER'S GRAMMAR
    DANCERS IN SCHOOL

DANCERS OF THE THIRD AGE
DANCIN' USA (2 videos)
DANCING THROUGH THE MAGIC EYE: PORTRAIT
  OF VIRGINIA TANNER
DEBBIE DEE TAP TECHNIQUE (4 videos)
DELILAH'S BELLY DANCE WORKSHOP (3 videos)
DISCOVERING YOUR EXPRESSIVE BODY WITH
  PEGGY HACKNEY
THE ELEMENTS OF DANCE
THE ENDURING ESSENCE: THE TECHNIQUE AND
  CHOREOGRAPHY OF ESSENTIALS OF TAP TECHNIQUE
ISADORA DUNCAN, REMEMBERED & RECONSTRUCTED
  BY GEMZE DE LAPPE
ENGLISH IS A WAY OF SPEECH
THE EVENT OF THE YEAR
EVERYTHING YOU SHOULD KNOW ABOUT
  HAWAIIAN/TAHITIAN HULA
EXERCISE WITH BILLIE
FAN TECHNIQUES FOR ORIENTAL DANCE
FERNANDO BUJONES IN CLASS
FLAMENCO AT 5:15
FOUR DANCE CLASSES IN EGYPT
FRANK HATCHET PRESENTS SIZZLIN' HOT JAZZ
FRANK HATCHETT: INSPIRATION
FRED ASTAIRE: LEARN TO DANCE (5 videos)
FRENCH FOLK DANCES
FUNDAMENTALS OF BALLET (3 videos)
GERMAN FOLK DANCES
HAVE A FLING WITH DANCE (2 videos)
HE MAKES ME FEEL LIKE DANCIN'
HOW TO MOVE BETTER
HUMPHREY TECHNIQUE
ILONA VERA'S BALLET CLASS
INSTRUCTIONAL BALLET TAPES DIRECTED BY
  DOROTHY LISTER
INTENSIVE COURSE IN ELEMENTARY LABANOTATION
  (5 videos)
INTERNATIONAL STYLE LATIN DANCING (3 videos)
INTERNATIONAL STYLE MODERN DANCING (7 videos)
INTRODUCTION TO BALLROOM DANCING
AN INTRODUCTION TO BELLY DANCE
IROQUOIS SOCIAL DANCE I & II
ISADORA DUNCAN: TECHNIQUE AND
  CHOREOGRAPHY
JAMILA SALIMPOUR'S FORMAT (3 videos)
JAZZ
JAZZ DANCE CLASS
JAZZ DANCE CLASS – 1989
JAZZ DANCE WITH RAY LYNCH
JAZZ JAZZ JAZZ
JAZZ TECHNIQUES
JUST FOR FUN
KATHAK
KICKER DANCIN' TEXAS STYLE: HOW TO DO THE TOP TEN
  COUNTRY & WESTERN DANCES LIKE A TEXAS COWBOY
KIT'S KIDS
LAMBADA: HOW TO AND MORE
THE LANGUAGE OF MODERN DANCE
LEARN HOW TO DANCE (82 videos)
LEARNING TO DANCE IN BALI

JAZZ *(continued)*
    SOPHISTICATED LADIES
    STREETCAR: A DANCE OF DESIRE
    STRUT YOUR STUFF (2 videos)
    THAT'S DANCING
    THAT'S ENTERTAINMENT
    THAT'S ENTERTAINMENT II
    VROTSOS VIDEOS (4 tapes)
    WEST SIDE STORY
    ZOU ZOU

MARTIAL ARTS
    BERIMBAU
    THE KARATE RAP
    SHAMAN'S JOURNEY
    SOUND OF ONE

MIDDLE EASTERN
    THE ANCIENT ART OF BELLY DANCING
    ARABIAN DANCE FEVER
    ARABIAN DANCES
    ARABIAN MELODIES
    BAL-ANAT
    BEGINNING BELLYDANCING WITH BEDIA
    BELLY DANCE! MAGICAL MOTION
    BELLY DANCING: IMAGES FROM VANCOUVER
    COSTUMING (5 videos)
    DANCE CLASS WITH SERENA
    DANCE DELILAH, DANCE
    DANCES OF THE SILK ROAD: AN INTRODUCTION TO
      GEORGIAN DANCE
    DANCES FROM THE CASBAH
    DELILAH'S BELLY DANCE WORKSHOP (3 Vol.)
    DISCOVERING THE MUSIC OF THE MIDDLE EAST
    FAN TECHNIQUES FOR ORIENTAL DANCE (2 tapes)
    FARRASHAH, THE VIDEO
    A FESTIVAL ON THE NILE
    FOUR DANCE CLASSES IN EGYPT
    GAMEEL GAMAL (OH! BEAUTIFUL DANCER)
    THE GREAT AMERICAN BELLYDANCE
    AN INTRODUCTION TO BELLY DANCE
    JAMILA SALIMPOUR'S FORMAT (3 videos)
    THE MAGANA BAPTISTE SIXTH ANNUAL BELLY DANCE
      FESTIVAL
    THE MARRAKESH FOLK FESTIVAL AND MORE (6 videos)
    NADIA GAMAL WORKSHOP
    ORIENTAL DANCE (3 videos)
    REDA
    SWORD TECHNIQUES (2 videos)
    TURKISH BELLYDANCE
    VEDA SEREEM'S QUALITY OF BELLY DANCING
     (19 videos)
     VEIL TECHNIQUES in ORIENTAL DANCE

MIME
    ABORIGINAL DANCE
    ART OF SILENCE SERIES
    ASIA SOCIETY COLLECTION
      KATHAKALI
      MASKED DANCE DRAMA OF BHUTAN
      P'ANSORI

    BALLET ENTERS THE WORLD STAGE
    BIP AS A SOLDIER
    BIP AT A SOCIETY PARTY
    BIP HUNTS BUTTERFLIES
    THE CAGE
    CIRCLES-CYCLES KATHAK DANCE
    THE CLOWN WITHIN
    DEAF LIKE ME
    DOLLY, LOTTE, AND MARIA
    DR. COPPELIUS (El Fantastico Mundo del Dr. Copelius)
    EDO – DANCE AND PANTOMIME
    HOLLYWOOD CLOWNS
    JEAN-LOUIS BARRAULT – A MAN OF THE THEATRE
    JEAN-LOUIS BARRAULT – THE BODY SPEAKS
    KAZE-NO-KO
    MARCEAU ON MIME
    MARCEL MARCEAU OU L'ART DU MIME
    MARCEL MARCEAU'S MIME SCHOOL
    THE MIME OF MARCEL MARCEAU
    MIME TECHNIQUE – PART I
    PANTOMIMES
    REINCATNATED
    SUITE KINETICS

MODERN
    ACCUMULATION WITH TALKING PLUS WATER MOTOR
    ACROBATS OF GOD
    THE ADDICTS
    AEROS
    AILEY DANCES
    AIR FOR THE G STRING
    AIRBORNE: MEISTER ECKHART
    AIRDANCE, LANDINGS, DAYTIME MOON
    AIRWAVES
    ALL THAT BACH: A CELEBRATION
    ALVIN AILEY: MEMORIES AND VISIONS
    AMERICAN BALLET THEATRE: A CLOSE-UP IN TIME
    AMPHIBIAN
    ANNA SOKOLOW, CHOREOGRAPHER
    ANTIGONE/RITES FOR THE DEAD
    APPALACHIAN SPRING (2 tapes)
    ASHES, MIST AND WIND BLOWN DUST
    ATTITUDES IN DANCE
    L'AURORA
    BART COOK – CHOREOGRAPHER
    THE BAUHAUS DANCES OF OSKAR SCHLEMMER –
      A RECONSTRUCTION
    BEEHIVE
    BEGINNING MODERN DANCE FOR HIGH SCHOOL GIRLS
    BLUE STUDIO: FIVE SEGMENTS
    BONE DREAM
    BREAK
    BUCKET DANCE VIDEO
    BUFFALO SOLDIER
    BULLFIGHT
    CAROLE MORISSEAU AND THE DETROIT CITY
      DANCE COMPANY
    THE CATHERINE WHEEL
    CAUGHT
    CERBERUS
    LA CHAMBRE

DIRECTORY OF DISTRIBUTORS AND RESOURCES

For feature films, check your local video store.

ACA ENTERPRISES
P.O. Box 58
Altadena, CA 91001
(213) 681-8059

ACTIONS ET PROSPECTIVES AUDIOVISUELLES (APA)
6 Rue du Jeu des Enfants
67000 Strasbourg FRANCE
88 75 03 94; FAX: 88 75 03 50
Distributes over fifty-five French dance videos

AGENCY FOR INSTRUCTIONAL TELEVISION
Box A 111 West 17th Street
Bloomington, IN 47402
(812) 339-2203

AIMS MEDIA
6901 Woodley Avenue
Van Nuys, CA 91406-4878
(800) 367-2467; FAX (818) 376-6405

AL GILBERT
STEPPING TONES RECORDS & VIDEOTAPES, LTD.
P.O. Box 35236
Los Angeles, CA 90035
(213) 737-4007

ALICIA DHANIFU PRODUCTIONS
P.O. Box 40755
Pasadena, CA 91104

AMERICAN ALLIANCE FOR HEALTH, PHYSICAL
    EDUCATION, RECREATION AND DANCE (AAHPERD)
National Dance Association (NDA)
1900 Association Drive
Reston, VA 22091
(703) 476-3400; (800) 321-0789

AMERICAN FEDERATION OF THE ARTS
41 E. 65th Street
New York, NY 10021
(212) 988-7700; FAX (212) 861-2487
Organizes travelling art, film, and video exhibitions

ANTENNA
AGENT ORANGE #104, 1178 Place Phillips
Montreal, Quebec H3B 3C8
(514) 397-1414

APPALSHOP, INC
P.O. Box 743 306 Madison
Whitesburg, KY 41858
(606) 633-5708; (800) 545-SHOP

ARABESQUE MAGAZINE/JOHN CUSTODIO
One Sherman Square, Suite 22F
New York, NY 10023
(212) 595-1677

ARC VIDEO
131 W. 24th, 5th fl
New York, NY 10011
(212) 206-6492
Celia Ipiotis & Jeff Bush

ARTHUR CANTOR, INC
Suite 400, 2112 Broadway
New York, NY 10023
(212) 496-5710; (800) 237-3801; FAX (212) 496-5718

ASIA SOCIETY
Performing Arts Department
725 Park Avenue
New York, NY 10021
(212) 288-6400
Beate Gordon

CHARLES ATLAS
319 West 14th Street
New York, NY 10014
(212) 620-5958

AUDIENCE PLANNERS, INC.
5107 Douglas Fir Road
Calabasas, CA 91302
(818) 884-3100
Free loan

219

AZURI
P.O. Box 150274
Orlando, FL 32858
(407) 299-8528

BALLET BASICS
P.O. Box 60
Arabi, LA 70032-0060
(504) 277-3293

BAM PRODUCTIONS
375 Mt. Auburn St.
Cambridge, MA 02138
(617) 547-1960
Bridget A. Murnane

MAGANA BAPTISTE
"Seacliff" Center of Yoga, Health, Belly Dance
401 32nd Ave. at Clement
San Francisco, CA 94121
(415) 387-6833

KAY BARDSLEY
6305 South Geneva Circle
Englewood, CO 80111-5437
(303) 850-0646; FAX (303) 850-5442

BARR FILMS
Centre Productions
7878 12801 Schabarum Avenue
Irwindale, CA 91706-7878
(800) 234-7879

BASTET PRODUCTIONS
P.O. Box 77029
Tucson, AZ 85703
(602) 293-8088

MARGARET BATIUCHOK
238 East 14th Street
New York, NY 10003
(212) 598-0154

MARGARET BEALS
228 West Broadway
New York, NY 10013
(212) 431-3869

BEDIA
1620 Hicks Drive
Vienna, VA 22182-2058
(703) 938-2555

BEST FILM & VIDEO PRODUCTIONS
98 Cutter Mill Road
Great Neck, NY 11021
(800) 527-2189

BIOGRAPH ENTERTAINMENT
300 Phillips Park Road
Mamaroneck, NY 10543-0190
(914) 381-2993

BLACAST ENTERTAINMENT
199-19 Linden Boulevard St
Albans, NY 11412
(718) 712-2300; FAX (718) 712-5345

BLACK FILMMAKER FOUNDATION
80 Eighth Avenue, Suite 1704
New York, NY 10011
(212) 924-1198

VIRGINIA BROOKS
460 Riverside Drive
New York, NY 10027
(212) 222-9887

CHRISTIAN BLACKWOOD PRODUCTIONS
115 Bank Street
New York, NY 10014
(212) 242-6260; FAX (212) 242-5328

JEAN DE BOYSSON
Apartment 6, 251 Elizabeth Street
New York, NY 10012
(212) 260-6011

RON BOZMAN
300 Central Park West
New York, NY 10025
(212) 874-3088

(BBC) BRITISH BROADCASTING COMPANY
80 Wood Lane
London, England
W12 0TT
011-44-81-743-8000

BRODSKY & TREADWAY
10-R Oxford Street
Somerville, MA 02143
(617) 666-3372

BUENA VISTA HOME VIDEO
500 South Buena Vista
Burbank, CA 91521
(818) 560-1000

BULLFROG FILMS
Oley, PA 19547
(215) 779-8226; (800) 543-FROG; FAX (215) 370-1978

RUDOLPH BURCKHARDT
50 West 29th Street
New York, NY 10001
(212) 679-5519

BUSTER COOPER DANCE VIDEOS
3046-A Forest Lane
Dallas, TX 75234
(214) 243-1098

BUTTERFLY VIDEO
P.O. Box 184
Antrim, NH 03440
(603) 588-2105; FAX (603) 588-3205

CAMILA CALEMANDREI
436A Guerrero
San Francisco, CA 94110
(415) 863-7809

CANADIAN BROADCASTING CORPORATION
500 Station A
Toronto, Ontario M5W 1E6
(416) 975-6384 or 3514; FAX (316) 975-3482

CANYON CINEMA COOPERATIVE
2325 Third Street, Suite 338
San Francisco, CA 94107
(415) 626-2255

CASSANDRA
3514 East 25th Street
Minneapolis, MN 55406

CBS FOX
1330 Avenue of the Americas, 5th Floor
New York, NY 10019
(212) 819-3200; (800) 800-2369

CENTRE PRODUCTIONS, INC.
Suite 207, 1800 30th Street
Boulder, CO 80301
(303) 444-1166

EVA CERNIK
419 South Sherman
Denver, CO 80209
(303) 733-9766

CHANDRA OF DAMASCUS MIDDLE EAST DANCE CENTER
1670 Jefferson Boulevard
Hagerstown, MD 21740
(301) 790-2282
Diana Kirkpatrick

CHARACTER GENERATORS
152 Mercer Street
New York, NY 10012
(212) 925-7771
Michael Schwartz

CHARMAINE
862 Pangola Drive
N. Ft. Myers, FL 33903

CHOREO RECORDS
P.O. Box 12154
Dallas, TX 75225

CINECOM INTERNATIONAL
1250 Broadway
New York, NY 10001
(212) 239-8360

CINEMA GUILD
1697 Broadway
New York, NY 10019
(212) 246-5522; FAX (212) 246-5525

CINEMATHEQUE COLLECTIONS
Div. of Media Home Entertainment
5730 Buckingham Parkway
Culver City, CA 90230
(213) 216-7900; (800) 421-4509

COE FILM ASSOCIATES
65 East 96th Street
New York, NY 10128
(212) 831-5355

CONSULATE GENERAL OF BELGIUM
50 Rockefeller Plaza
New York, NY 10020
(212) 586-5110

CONSULATE GENERAL OF INDIA
3 East 64th Street
New York, NY 10021-7097
(212) 879-7800; FAX (212) 988-6423

CONSULATE GENERAL OF THE NETHERLANDS
Netherlands Ministry of Foreign Affairs, Audio-Visual Section
P.O. Box 20061, 2500 EB The Hague, Netherlands.
1 Rockefeller Plaza
New York, NY 10020
(212) 246-1429

COORDINATION COUNCIL FOR NORTH AMERICAN AFFAIRS
159 Lexington Avenue
New York, NY 10016
(212) 725-4950
Represents the interests of the Republic of China on Taiwan

CORINTH FILMS
34 Gansevoort St.
New York, NY 10014
(212) 463-0305; (800) 221-4720

CORNELL COOPERATIVE EXTENSION
Cornell University
7-8 Research Park
Ithaca, NY 14850
(607) 255-7660, 2091

CORONET/MTI FILM AND VIDEO
Learning Corporation of America
108 Wilmot Road
Deerfield, IL 60015
(800) 621-2131; FAX (708) 940-1260

CREATIVE ARTS REHABILITATION CENTER
251 West 51st Street
New York, NY 10019
(212) 246-3113

ARTURO CUBACUB
3744 N. Hayne
Chicago, IL 60618

CUNNINGHAM DANCE FOUNDATION
463 West Street
New York, NY 10014
(212) 255-3130; FAX (212) 633-2453

DANCE FILM ARCHIVE
University of Rochester
Rochester, NY 14627
(716) 275-5236

DANCE FILMS ASSOCIATION
1133 Broadway, Suite 507
New York, NY 10010
(212) 727-0764
Susan Braun

DANCE HORIZONS VIDEO
Princeton Book Company, Publishers
P.O. Box 57 Pennington, NJ 08534-0057
(609) 737-8177; (800) 326-7149

DANCE NOTATION BUREAU
33 West 21st Street
New York, NY 10010
(212) 807-7899

DANCE REP INC.
73 Fifth Avenue
New York, NY 10003
(212) 255-3326
Peter Reed

DANCING ON AIR
6 Mount Vernon Street, Suite 199
Winchester, MA 01890
(617) 721-1362
Susan Winokur

DANISH INFORMATION OFFICE
Consulate General of Denmark
825 Park Avenue
New York, NY 10017
(212) 223-4545

DEBRA ZALKIND TALKING DANCE FOUNDATION
187 Buena Vista Drive
Ringwood, NJ 07456
(201) 839-0137

DEEPFOCUS PRODUCTIONS
4506 Palmero Drive
Los Angeles, CA 90065
(213) 254-7773

RITHA DEVI
330 E. 85th Street, Apt. #C
New York, NY 10028
(212) 988-7697

DIRECT CINEMA, LTD.
P.O. Box 69799
Los Angeles, CA 90069
(213) 652-8000; rental (800) FILMS 4-U; FAX (213) 652-2346

DOCUMENTARY EDUCATIONAL RESOURCES
101 Morse Street
Watertown, MA 02172
(617) 926-0491

DORIS CHASE/CATALYST FILMS
222 West 23rd Street
New York, NY 10011
(212) 243-3700; (206) 624-3700

EASTERN ARTS
P.O. Box 6362
Salt Lake City, UT 84106
(801) 487-9208

EASTLONG PRODUCTIONS
1225 Park Avenue
New York, NY 10128
(212) 427-2689
Patricia Lewis Jaffe

ECLIPSE PRODUCTIONS
135 St. Pauls Avenue
Staten Island, NY 10301
(718) 727-5593

SIMON EDERY
3710 Prestwick Drive
San Francisco CA 94109
(415) 509-2627

ELECTRONIC ARTS INTERMIX, INC
536 Broadway
New York, NY 10012
(212) 966-4605; FAX (212) 941-6118
Handles over 1000 international titles by more
than 120 artists

EMBASSY OF MALAYSIA
2401 Massachussetts Avenue, N.W.
Washington, DC 20008
(202) 328-2700
Films on loan free of charge.

ENCYCLOPAEDIA BRITANNICA EDUCATIONAL
   CORPORATION
310 South Michigan Avenue
Chicago, IL 60604
(312) 347-7000; (800) 621-3900 or 554-9862;
   FAX (312) 347-7903;

KIM EVELETH
194 Riverside Drive
New York, NY 10025
(212) 787-8538

FACETS MULTIMEDIA
1517 W. Fullerton Ave.
Chicago, IL 60614
(800) 331-6197; (312) 281-9075

FAMILY EXPRESS VIDEO
44925 Steeple Path
Novi, MI 48050
(313) 347-4630

FELDMAN GALLERY
31 Mercer
New York, NY 10013
(212) 226-3232

FILM AUSTRALIA
Eton Road
Lindfield, NSW 2070 Australia
02 413-8777; FAX 02 416-5672

FILMFAIR COMMUNICATIONS
10621 Magnolia Boulevard
North Hollywood, CA 91601
(818) 985-0244 (call collect)

FILM-MAKERS COOPERATIVE
175 Lexington Avenue
New York NY 10016
(212) 889-3820
Year Founded: 1962

FILMAKER'S LIBRARY
124 East 40th Street
New York, NY 10016
(212) 808-4980

FILMMAKERS OF PHILADELPHIA
725 North 24th
Philadelphia PA 19130
(215) 763-3400, 679-3388

FILMS BY HUEY
103 Montrose Avenue
Portland, ME 04103
(207) 773-1130

FILMS FOR THE HUMANITIES AND SCIENCES
P.O. Box 2053
Princeton, NJ 08543
(800) 257-5126

FILMS INCORPORATED
5547 N. Ravenswood Ave.
Chicago IL 60640-1199
(312) 878-2600, ext 42, (800) 323-4222, ext 237

FIRST RUN FEATURES
153 Waverly Place
New York, NY 10014
(212) 727-1711, (800) 876-1710

FLOWER FILMS
10341 San Pablo Avenue El
Cerrito, CA 94530
(415) 525-0942; FAX (415) 525-1204

FOLK DANCE VIDEOS INTERNATIONAL
10100 Park Cedar Drive, Suite 110
Charlotte, VA 28210
(704) 542-9437

FORT WORTH PRODUCTIONS
P.O. Box 125
Fort Worth, Texas 76101
(817) 336-0777

FRANCISCAN COMMUNICATIONS
Teleketics
1229 South Santee
Los Angeles, CA 90015-2566
(800) 421-8510, (213) 746-2916

FRED ASTAIRE PERFORMING ARTS ASSOCIATION
11945 S.W. 140 Terrace
Miami, FL 33186
(305) 252-8982

LAURIE FREEDMAN
18 LaDue Road
Hopewell Junction, NY 12533
(914) 897-3914

FRENCH AMERICAN CULTURAL SERVICES AND
   EDUCATIONAL AID (FACSEA)
972 Fifth Avenue
New York, NY 10021
(212) 439-1400, 570-4400

GENE FRIEDMAN
P.O Box 275
Wainscott, NY 11975
(516) 537-0178

G.A.B. PRODUCTIONS
P.O. Box 207
Shiloh, GA 31826

ANNABELLE GAMSON
Hillandale Road
Rye Brook, New York 10573
(914) 939-2317

GATEWAY FILMS, INC.
Box A 2030 Wentz Church Road
Landsdale, PA 19446
(215) 584-1893, (800) 523-0226

GESSLER PRODUCTIONS
55 West 13th Street
New York, NY 10011
(212) 627-1001

LOUISE GHERTLER
425 Riverside Drive, #3J
New York, NY 10025
(212) 663-4434

JOHN GIAMBERSO
599 14870 N.E. 95th St.
Redmont, WA 90852

DEBORAH GLADSTEIN & SAM KANTER
484 W.43rd Street, #16A
New York, NY 10036
(212) 684-3304, 563-2972

GOTHAM CITY FILMWORKS
Apt 6H 425 Riverside Drive
New York, NY 10025

GREEN MOUNTAIN CINE
53 Hamilton Avenue
Staten Island, NY 10301
(718) 981-0120

SALLY GROSS
463 West Street
New York, NY 10014
(212) 691-1283

GROVE PRESS FILM
841 Broadway
New York, NY 10003-4793
(212) 614-7850

GTN PRODUCTIONS
Suite 460, 230 Park Avenue
New York, NY 10169
(212) 599-3032

HILARY HARRIS
15 Raycliff Drive
Woodstock, NY 12498
(914) 246-0105

HARTLEY PRODUCTIONS
Hartley Film Foundation, Inc.
Cat Rock Road, Cos Cob Road
Cos Cob, CT 06807
(203) 869-1818

HBO VIDEO
1100 Avenue of the Americas
New York, NY 10036
(212) 512-7428

SHELIA HELLMAN
100 High Street
Lenonia, NJ 07605
(201) 947-5537

HIGH TIDE DANCE, INC
65 Greene Street
New York, NY 10012
(212) 925-5024

HENRY HILLS
303 East 8th Street
New York, NY 10003
(212) 473-0615

HOCTOR PRODUCTS
P.O. Box 38
Waldwick, NJ 07463
(201) 652-7767

HOME VISION
PMI, A Division of Films Inc.
5547 N. Ravenswood Ave.
Chicago, Illinois 60640-1199
(312) 878-2600, (800) 826-3456

IMAGES PRODUCTIONS
P.O. Box 46691
Cincinnati, OH 45246

IMAGES VIDEO PRODUCTION COMPANY
30 Crafts Avenue
Northhampton, MA 01060
(413) 585-5755

INDIANA UNIVERSITY
Audio Visual Center
Bloomington, IN 47405-5901
(812) 335-8087, (800) 552-8620

INSTITUTE FOR WISSENSCHAFTLICHEN FILMS (WISSEN)
Nonnenstieg 72
Gottingen West Germany BRD D-3400
0551-21034

INSTRUCTIONAL VIDEO
727 O Street
Lincoln, NE 68508
(800) 228-0164

INTERAMA
301 West 53rd Street, #19E
New York, NY 10019
(212) 977-4830

INTERMEDIA ARTS/MINNESOTA
425 Ontario St., S.E.
Minneapolis, MN 55414
(612) 627-4444; FAX (612) 627-4430

INTERNATIONAL FILM BUREAU, INC.
332 South Michigan Avenue
Chicago, IL 60604
(312) 427-4545, (800) 432-2241

INTERNATIONAL FILM FOUNDATION
155 West 72nd Street
New York, NY 10023
(212) 580-1111

IOWA STATE UNIVERSITY
Media Resources Center
121 Pearson Hall
Ames, IA 50011
(512) 294-1540
Rentals only

IVY FILMS
165 West 46th Street
New York, NY 10036
(212) 382-0111; FAX (212) 840-6182

JAMCAR PRODUCTIONS, LTD.
207D Rte 82, RD 2
Millbrook, NY 12545
(914) 677-3371

JAPAN FOUNDATION
142 West 57th Street
New York, NY 10019
(212) 949-6360
Rental only

JAZZ DANCE CLASS
146 Melrose Place
San Antonio, TX 78212-9990

JIM FOREST VIDEOTAPES
1200 N.E. 13th Street
Fort Lauderdale, FL 33304
(305) 764-0641

JPJ ENTERPRISES
P.O. Box 301
Jamaica, PA 18929
(215) 343-7806

KAHREEN AND KIRA
1089 NE 104th Street
Miami Shores, FL 33138

KALAMA PRODUCTIONS, INC.
1146 Fort St. Mall, Suite 203
Honolulu, HI 96813
(808) 536-5050

POOH KAYE
Eccentric Motions
99 Vandam Street
New York, NY 10013
(212) 691-9522, (617) 776-9407

KEELING RECORDS & VIDEO DIST.
190 W. 135th St.
New York, NY 10030
(212) 283-5825

KENT STATE UNIVERSITY
Audio Visual Services
Kent, OH 44242
(216) 672-3456; (800) 338-5718

KINO INTERNATIONAL
333 West 39th
New York, NY 10018
(212) 629-6880; FAX (212) 714-0871

KIT PARKER FILMS
1245 Tenth Street
Monterey CA 93940-3692
(408) 649-5573; (800) 538-5838; FAX (408) 649-8040

KITCHEN CENTER FOR VIDEO, MUSIC & DANCE
512 W. 19th Street
New York NY 10011
(212) 255-5793

SHEILA KOGAN
Kineped Productions
82 Washington Place, #1E
New York NY 10011
(212) 473-4818

HERMAN KRAWITZ
New World Records
701 7th Avenue
New York, NY 10036
(212) 302-0460

KTCA-TV
"Alive From Off Center"
172 East Fourth Street
St. Paul MN 55101
(612) 222-1717
Year Founded: 1985
Experimental series broadcast on Public Broadcasting Service

KULTUR
121 Highway 36
West Long Branch, NJ 07764
(908) 229-2342; (800) 4-KULTUR; FAX (908) 229-0066

KUTV
P.O. Box 30901
Salt Lake City, UT 84130-0901
(801) 973-3000

LA FORM DE DANSE
3575 Boulevard St. Laurent
Montreal Quebec, Canada H2X2T7

LAZIZA VIDEODANCE & LUMIA PROJECT
P.O. Box 154
New York, NY 10012-0003

LEARNING CORPORATION OF AMERICA
4640 Lankershim Boulevard, Suite 600
North Hollywood, CA 91602
(818) 769-0400

LIGHTWORKS
686 St. Clarens Avenue, Unit #10
Toronto, Ontario M6H 3X1

JAN LOCKETZ
Ayers Road
Locust Valley, NY 11560
(516) 676-3228

ABBY LUBY
214 St. John's Place
Brooklyn, NY 11217
(718) 638-0772

CLAUDIO M. LUCA
1338 Ste. Catherine Est
Montreal, Canada H2O 2H5
(514) 524-1118

MARY LUCIER
223 West 20th Street
New York, NY 10011
(212) 255-4947

LUTHERAN FILM ASSOCIATES
360 Park Avenue South
New York, NY 10010
(212) 532-6350

ELIZABETH MACKIE
1720 Spruce Street
Philadelphia, PA 19103

MAGICAL MOTION ENTERPRISES
12228 Venice Boulevard, Suite. 402
Los Angeles, CA 90066
(213) 301-4767

MAGNETIC ARTS
20 Desbrosses Street
New York, NY 10013
(212) 941-7720; FAX (212) 226-8096

BILLIE MAHONEY
Amber Manor Apartments
807-833 Ridge Drive, #1203
DeKalb, IL 60115-2054
(815) 758-4377

MICHELLE MAHRER
165 Roebling Street
Brooklyn, NY 11211
(718) 782-5644

EVA MAIER
75 Chambers Street
New York, Ny 10007
(212) 964-2054

MAINE INDEPENDENT CINEMA ARC (MICA)
P.O. Box 201
Belgrade Lakes, ME 04918
(802) 869-2276

MASS MEDIA MINISTRIES
2116 North Charles Street
Baltimore, MD 21218
(301) 727-3270

MASTERS AND MASTERWORKS PRODUCTIONS
15313 Whitfield Avenue
Pacific Palisades, CA 90272
(213) 459-8682

MASTERVISION
969 Park Avenue
New York, NY 10028
(212) 879-0448

JULIA MAYER
601-61st Avenue North
Myrtle Beach, SC 29577
(803) 449-5882

MCA HOME VIDEO
70 Universal City Plaza
Universal City, CA 91608
(818) 777-4300

JEFF MCMAHON
512 East 11th Street, #4B
New York, NY 10009
(212) 677-3214

MEDIA RESOURCES, INTERNATIONAL
P.O. Box 2816
Honolulu, Hawaii 96803
(800) 367-8047, ext 112

MERCHANT/IVORY PRODUCTIONS
250 West 57th Street
New York, NY 10019
(212) 582-8049, 582-5521

METTLER STUDIOS
Tucson Creative Dance Center
3131 North Cherry Avenue
Tucson, AZ 85719
(602) 327-7453

SYBIL MEYER
3130 College Avenue, #4
Berkeley, CA 94705
(415) 658-0636

MGM/UNITED ARTISTS HOME VIDEO
10000 Washington Boulevard
Culver City, CA 90232
(213) 280-6000

MICHAEL BLACKWOOD PRODUCTIONS
251 West 57th Street
New York, NY 10019
(212) 247-4710

MIMI GARRARD DANCE COMPANY
155 Wooster Street
New York, NY 10012
(212) 674-6868

MODERN TALKING PICTURE SERVICE, INC.
5000 Park Street North
St. Petersburg, FL 33709
(800) 243-6877; FAX (813) 546-0681
Free films courtesy of the German Consulate

FRANK MOORE
45 Crosby Street
New York, NY 10012
(212) 925-4875

MORCA FOUNDATION
1349 Franklin Street
Bellingham, WA 98225
(206) 676-1864
Teo Morca

MOROCCO
320 West 15th Street
New York, NY 10011
(212) 727-8326
Caroline Varga Dinicu

CLAUDIA MURPHEY
4000 Tunlaw Road, N.W. #809
Washington, DC 20007
(202) 338-7845

MUSEUM AT LARGE
20 West 22nd Street
New York, NY 10011
(212) 691-2977

MUSEUM OF MODERN ART
Circulating Film Library
11 West 53rd Street
New York, NY 10019
(212) 708-9530, or 9614 (study center)
Study center open by appointment only

MYSTIC FIRE VIDEO
P.O. Box 1092, Cooper Station
New York, NY 10276
(212) 677-5040; (800) 727-8433; FAX (212) 677-5056

DANIEL NAGRIN
208 East 14th Street
Tempe, AZ 85281
(602) 968-4063

NATIONAL AUDIOVISUAL CENTER
National Archives
8700 Edgeworth Drive
Capitol Heights, MD 20743-3701
(800) 638-1300

NATIONAL COUNCIL OF AMERICAN SOVIET
FRIENDSHIP, INC. SOCIETY FOR CULTURAL
RELATIONS/US/USSR
5768 West Pico, No. 203
Los Angeles, CA 90019
(213) 937-4130
Rental only

NATIONAL FILM BOARD OF CANADA
1251 Avenue of the Americas
New York, NY 10020-1173
(212) 586-5131

NATIONAL VIDEO CORPORATION ARTS INTERNATIONAL
Liberty House
222 Regent St.
London, England W1R 5DE
011-44-71 388 3833; FAX 011-44-71 383 5332

NERTY PISCOLO PANESA
236 Nelson Road
Scarsdale, NY 10583
(914) 725-2859

NEW DAY FILMS
121 West 27th St.
New York, NY 10001
(212) 645-8210

NEW YORK CITY BALLET
Education Dept.
Lincoln Center
New York, NY 10023
(212) 595-2154

NEW YORK CITY DANCE SCHOOL
Tubinger Strasser 12-16
7000 Stuttgart 1, Germany
07-11-29-32-36

NEW YORKER FILMS
16 West 61st Street
New York, NY 10023
(212) 247-6110; FAX (212) 582-4697

NINE MUSES
P.O. Box 480664
Hollywood, CA 90048
(818) 989-7728

ORION ENTERPRISES
614 Davis Street
Evanston, IL 60201
(708) 866-9443/251-4434

PACIFIC ARTS VIDEO
50 North La Cienega, Suite 210
Beverly Hills, CA 90211
(213) 657-2233

PACIFIC TRADE GROUP
94-527 Puahi
Waipahu, Hawaii 96797
(808) 671-6735

PARAMOUNT HOME VIDEO
5555 Melrose Avenue
Los Angeles, CA 90038
(213) 956-3701

PENNEBAKER ASSOCIATES, INC.
262 West 91st Street
New York, NY 10025
(212) 496-9199

PENNSYLVANIA STATE UNIVERSITY (Pennstate)
Audio Visual Services
Special Services Building
University Park, PA 16802
(814) 865-6314, (800) 826-0132

PERSPECTIVE FILMS
369 West Erie Street
Chicago, IL 60610
(312) 332-7676

PHOENIX FILMS, INC.
468 Park Avenue South
New York, NY 10016
(212) 684-5910; (800) 221-1274

PIONEER ARTISTS
2265 East 220
Long Beach, CA 90810
(213) 835-6177

RALPH PIPER
3123 D. Via Serena N.
Laguna Hills, CA 92653
(714) 586-3068

PORTLAND STATE UNIVERSITY
Continuing Education, Film & Video Library
Box 1383 1633 Southwest Park Avenue
Portland, OR 97207
(800) 547-8887, ext. 4890

PRO ARTS INTERNATIONAL
Nikolais/Louis Dance
375 West Broadway
New York, NY 10012
(212) 226 7700

PROSCENIUM ENTERTAINMENT
P.O. Box 909
Hightstown, NJ 08520
(609) 448-9129; (800) 222-6260

PYRAMID FILM & VIDEO
Box 1048
Santa Monica, CA 90406-1048
(800) 421-2304; (213) 828-7577

RAINFOREST PUBLISHING & PRODUCTION COMPANY
P.O. Box 61538
Honolulu, HI 96839-1538
(808) 988-5830
Pacific Trade Group as distributor

RCA/COLUMBIA PICTURES
3500 West Olive Avenue
Burbank, CA 91505
(818) 953-7900

PATRICE REGINER
Rush Dance Company
392 Broadway New York, NY 10019
(212) 431-7051

RHAPSODY FILMS, INC.
179 30 Charles Street
New York, NY 10014
(212) 243-0152

RHOMBUS INTERNATIONAL, INC
489 King St West, Suite 102
Toronto Canada M5V 1L3
(416) 971-7856; FAX (416) 971-9647

RIRIE-WOODBURY DANCE COMPANY
50 West 200 Street
Salt Lake City, UT 84101
(801) 328-1062

RM ARTS
250 W. 57th Street
New York NY 10019
(212) 262-3230; FAX (212) 262-5146
Beatrice Dupont

ROBERTO ROMANO
317 West 93rd Street
New York, NY 10025
(212) 662-2483

KATHY ROSE
158-14 14th Avenue
Whitestone, NY 11357
(718) 767-5937

DOUGLAS ROSENBERG
39 Ceres Street
San Francisco, CA 94124
(415) 822-1149

SAMBA ASSOCIATES
1322 Second, Suite 28
Santa Monica, CA 90401

SAMURAI STUDIOS, INC
RD #1, P.O. Box 252A
Palisades, NY 10964
(914) 359-5330

JOHN SANBORN & MARY PERILLO
125 Cedar Street
New York, NY 10013
(212) 608-3943

ROBIN SCHANZENBACH
241 Eldridge Street
New York, NY 10003
(212) 674-6004

LARRY SCHULZ
c/o Sandra Cameron Dance Center, Inc.
439 Lafayette Street
New York, NY 10003
(212) 674-0505

SEAHORSE PRODUCTIONS
12 Horatio Street
New York, NY 10013
(212) 226-0294
Anne Belle

SEARCHLIGHT FILMS
30 Berry Street
San Francisco, CA 94123
(415) 543-1254

SEE-DO PRODUCTIONS
P.O. Box 135
Croton-on-Hudson, NY 10520
(914) 271-3806

VEDA SEREEM
20130 Larkspur Court
Germantown, MD 20874
(301) 916-0177

SERENA STUDIOS
201 W. 54th Street, #2C
New York, NY 10019
(212) 247-1051

SARAH SKAGGS
22 Warren Street
New York, NY 10007
(212) 393-9302

ALLEGRA FULLER SNYDER
Department of Dance,
University of California at Los Angeles
Los Angeles, CA 90024-1608
(213) 825-3951

SOLARIS
264 West 19th Street
New York, NY 10011
(212) 741-0778; FAX (212) 242-2201
Henry Smith

RUTH SOLOMON
Dance Theatre Program
University of California
Santa Cruz, CA 95064
(408) 429-2284

GUS SOLOMONS
889 Broadway
New York, NY 10003
(212) 477-1321

SOUTHWEST DANCE ASSOCIATION
P.O. Box 50284
Tucson, AZ 85703
(602) 887-2101

SPECIAL INTEREST VIDEOS
100 Enterprise Place
Dover, DE 19901
(800) 522-0502; (818) 789-9955

SPECTACOR
Division of Connoisseur
8436 West 3rd, Suite 600
Los Angeles, CA 90048
(800) 5-BOLSHOI; (213) 653-8873

SPHINX RECORDS
P.O. Box 27241
Hollywood, CA 90027

SPRING HILL PRODUCTIONS
300 Central Park West, #12J-1
New York, NY 10024
(212) 874-3088

MELANIE STEWART
524 S. Randolph Street
Philadelphia, PA 19147
(215) 928-9277

KEITH STUART
1825 2nd Avenue, #4N
New York, NY 10128
(212) 996-4461

STUTZ CO
2600 Tenth Street
Berkeley, CA 94710
(415) 644-2200; FAX (415) 644-2230

SUE MARX FILMS, INC.
672 Woodbridge
Detroit, MI 48226
(313) 259-8505

ELAINE SUMMERS
6851 Longboat Drive South
Longboat Key, FL 34228
(813) 383-8938

SUPREME SWING/JERRY CRIM
P.O. Box 906101
Tulsa, OK 74112

TOMMY SUTTON
3180 Weslock Circle
Decatur, GA 30034
(404) 243-7196

SWANK MOTION PICTURES
2800 Market Street St.
Louis, MO 63103
(314) 543-1940; (800) 876-3344

SYRACUSE UNIVERSITY FILM RENTAL LIBRARY
1455 East Colvin Street
Syracuse, NY 13244-5150
(800) 345-6797; FAX (315) 443-9439

TAFFY'S BY MAIL
701 Beta Drive
Cleveland, OH 44143
(216) 461-3360; FAX: (216) 461-9787
Mail-order house with retail stores across the country

TALLER LATINOAMERICANO
64 East 2nd Street
New York, NY 10002
(212) 777-2250

TAPEWORM
12229 Montague Street
Arleta, CA 91331
(800) 367-8437

TAPPERCISE
1014 Mission Street
South Pasadena, CA 91030
(818) 356-9933
Ken Prescott

TELDEC CLASSICS
WEA International
Schuberstrasse 5/9,
Hamburg 76, West Germany D-2000

TEMPO FILMS
1800 Robin Whipple Way
Belmont, CA 94002
(415) 595-1359; (408) 248-6517

TENTH STREET DANCEWORKS
738 N. 5th Ave., #131
Tucson, AR 85705
(602) 792-0327

TERRA NOVA FILMS
9848 S. Winchester Ave.
Chicago, IL 60643
(312) 881-8491

LOUISE TIRANOFF
488 14th St.
Brooklyn, NY 11215
(718) 788-6403

TOM DAVENPORT FILMS
Route #1, Box 527 Pearlstone
Delaplane, VA 22025
(703) 592-3701

DEIRDE TOWERS
Apartment 14J
666 West End Avenue
New York, NY 10025
(212) 767-5772

TREMAINE DANCE CONVENTIONS
14531 Hamlin St., #104
Van Nuys, CA 91411
(818) 988-8006; FAX (818) 988-7314

TURNER HOME ENTERTAINMENT
RKO Video
5 Penn Plaza
New York, NY 10001
(212) 714-7800

UNIVERSITY OF CALIFORNIA AT LOS ANGELES (UCLA)
UCLA Media Center, Instructional Media Library
Powell Library, Room 46
Los Angeles, CA 90024
(213) 825-0755

UNIVERSITY OF CALIFORNIA EXTENSION MEDIA CENTER
AT BERKELEY
2176 Shattuck Avenue
Berkeley, CA 94704
(415) 642-0460

UNIVERSITY OF ILLINOIS
1325 South Oak Street
Champaign, IL 61820
(217) 333-1360, (800) 367-3456

UNIVERSITY OF MICHIGAN
Media Resources Center
400 Fourth Street
Ann Arbor, MI 48103-5360
(313) 764-5360; (800) 999-0424

UNIVERSITY OF MINNESOTA
Film & Video Library
Minneapolis, MN 55414
(612) 627-4270;
Rental only

UNIVERSITY OF SOUTH FLORIDA
Film and Video Library
4202 Fowler Street
Tampa, Fl 33620-6800
(813) 974-2874
Rental only

UNIVERSITY OF SOUTHERN CALIFORNIA
Film and Video Distribution Center
University Park—MC 2212
Los Angeles, CA 90089
(213) 743-2238

UZBEK DANCE SOCIETY
501 North 36th, Suite 139
Seattle, WA 98103
(206) 549-2866

VFC PRODUCTIONS
P.O. Box 813
Brookline, MA 02147

VIDEO ARTS INTERNATIONAL
P.O. Box 153, Ansonia Station
New York, NY 10023
(212) 799-7798; (800) 338-2566; FAX (212) 799-7768

VIDEOGRAPHE
4550 Garnier Street
Montreal, Quebec H2J 3S7
(514) 521-2116

VIDEO D PRODUCTIONS
29 W. 21st Street
New York, NY 10010-6807
(212) 242-3345
Dennis Diamond

VIDEO DATA BANK
School of the Art Institute
280 South Columbus
Chicago, IL 60603
(312) 443-3793

VIDEO OUT
Satellite Video Exchange Society
1102 Homer Street
Vancouver BC, Canada V6B 2X6
(604) 688-4336

VIDEOGRAPHE, INC.
4550 Garnier Street
Montreal, Quebec H2J 3S6
(514) 521-2116

V.I.E.W. VIDEO
34 E. 23rd Street
New York, NY 10010
(212) 674-5550; (800) 843-9843

VIEWFINDERS
P.O. Box 1665
Evanston, IL 60204
(708) 869-0602
Mail order company

VIRGINIA TANNER CREATIVE DANCE PROGRAM
University of Utah
1152 Annex Building
Salt Lake City, UT 84112
(801) 581-7374
Mary Ann Lee

VISIONARY DANCE PRODUCTIONS
P.O. Box 30797
Seattle, WA 98103
(206) 632-2353
Steve Flynn

VROTSOS VIDEOS
133 College Street
Wadsworth, OH 44281
(216) 334-8935

DAVID WADSWORTH
P.O. Box 28128
Philadelphia, PA 19131
(215) 878-4482

DEBRA WANNER
121 First Avenue, #2
New York, NY 10003
(212) 473-5495

PENNY WARD/VIDEO
5 Rivington Street #4
New York, NY 10002
(212) 228-1427

WARNER HOME VIDEO
4000 Warner Boulevard
Burbank, CA 91522
(818) 954-6000

WEINTRAUB
167/9 Wardour St.
London, England W1V 3TA

WGBH/NEW TELEVISION WORKSHOP
125 West Avenue
Boston, MA 02134
(617) 492-2777, ext. 4228; FAX (617) 787-0714
Susan Dowling

WHYY-TV 12
150 N. Sixth St.
Philadelphia PA 19106
(215) 351-1200
Art Ellis

WISH UPON PRODUCTIONS
2211 Broadway
New York, NY 10024
(212) 874-2806
Joe Wishy

ROBERT WITHERS
202 West 80th Street
New York, NY 10024
(212) 873-1353

WOMBAT FILM & VIDEO
250 W. 57th Street, Suite 2421
New York, NY 10019
(212) 315-2502; (800) 542-5552, FAX (212) 582-0585

WOMEN MAKE MOVIES
225 Lafayette
New York, NY 10012
(212) 925-0606

YE SOOK RHEE
24809 Sandwedge Lane
Valencia, CA 91355

DAISY YIANNAS (ZAIRA)
1215 Charles St.
Orlando, FL 32808
(407) 299-7024

ZEINA
425 First Street, #5
New Orleans, LA 70130
(504) 568-1523
Dee Birnham

RESOURCES

Check foreign and U.S. consulates for dance films and videos.

AMERICAN DANCE FESTIVAL
6097 College Station; 1697 Broadway
Durham, NC 27708; New York, NY 10019
(919) 684-6402;   (212) 586-1925
America's foremost modern dance festival, held annually with performances, workshops, symposiums. Film and video archives dating from its inception.

BILLBOARD
1 Astor Place
New York, NY 10023
(212) 764-7300
For music videos, check BILLBOARD's annual directory listing addresses and phone numbers of record companies.

CENTRE GEORGES POMPIDOU
25 Rue du Renard
75004 Paris, France

CINEMATHEQUE DE LA DANSE
29, Rue du Colisee
75008 Paris France
45-53-21-86; FAX 42-56-08-55
Collection of stills, films, and videos

CONTACT QUARTERLY
Lisa Nelson
P.O. Box 22
East Charleston, VT 05833
(802) 723-6125

DANCE COLLECTION
New York Public Library
111 Amsterdam Ave., Lincoln Center
New York, NY 10023
(212) 870-1657
JEROME ROBBINS ARCHIVE OF THE RECORDED MOVING IMAGE has over 7,000 dance films and videos.

DANCEMUSEUM
Barnhusgatan 14
S-111 23 Stockholm SWEDEN
46-8-108243
Large archive, exhibit, and research center

FUNDACION ANDALUZA DE FLAMENCO
Palacio Pemartin, Plaza de San Juan, 1
11403 Jerez SPAIN
Year Founded: 1988
Archive of stills, films and videos of flamenco artists

GOETHE HOUSE
666 Third Avenue
New York, NY 10017-4011
(212) 972-3960
Library open for private screenings

HARVARD THEATRE COLLECTION
Harvard College Library
Cambridge, MA 02138
(617) 495-2445
Jeanne T. Newlin

INTERNATIONAL TAP ASSOCIATION
Colorado Dance Festival
Box 356
Boulder, CO 80306
(303) 442-7666

JACOB'S PILLOW
P.O. Box 287
Lee, MA 01238
(413) 637-1322
Archival footage of Ted Shawn and his company

LIMON INSTITUTE
375 West Broadway
New York, NY 10013
(212) 777-3353
Archival footage of the choreographies by Jose Limon and Doris Humphrey. Viewing on the premises by appointment.

MUSEUM OF TELEVISION AND RADIO
25 West 52nd Street
New York, NY 10022
(212) 621-6600
Television programs produced from 1939 to the present available for study on the premises

METROPOLITAN MUSEUM DANCE INDEX
Metropolitan Museum of Art
81st Street and Fifth Avenue
New York, NY 10028
(212) 879-5500, ext. 3572
Constance Old is cataloguing all the images of objects, paintings, sculptures relative to dance.

PBS VIEWFINDERS
4401 Sunset Boulevard
Los Angeles CA 90027
1-900-860-9301
Provides phone service information on the distributors for feature films or programs produced by Public Broadcasting Service

STERNS PERFORMING ARTS DIRECTORY
33 West 60th Street
New York, NY 10023
(212) 245-8937
Annual, international guide to dance companies, performers, managers, festivals